W9-BMW-395

Second Edition

PSYCHOTROPIC DRUGS

FAST FACTS

Second Edition

PSYCHOTROPIC
DRUGS
FAST
FACTS

Jerrold S. Maxmen, M.D.
Nicholas G. Ward, M.D.

W. W. Norton & Company · New York · London

NOTICE
We have made every attempt to summarize accurately and concisely a multitude of references. However, the reader is reminded that times and medical knowledge change, transcription or understanding error is always possible, and crucial details are omitted whenever such a comprehensive distillation as this is attempted in limited space. We cannot, therefore, guarantee that every bit of information is absolutely accurate or complete. The reader should affirm that cited recommendations are still appropriate by reading the original articles and checking other sources including local consultants and recent literature.

DRUG DOSAGE
The authors and publisher have exerted every effort to ensure that drug selection and dosage set forth in this text are in accord with current recommendations and practice at the time of publication. However, in view of ongoing research, changes in government regulations, and the constant flow of information relating to drug therapy and drug reactions, the reader is urged to check the package insert for each drug for any change in indications and dosage and for added warnings and precautions. This is particularly important when the recommended agent is a new and/or infrequently used drug.

Printed in the United States of America

Second Edition

For information about permission to reproduce selections from this book, write to Permissions, W.W. Norton & Company, Inc., 500 Fifth Avenue, New York, NY 10110.

Library of Congress Cataloging-in-Publication Data
Maxmen, Jerrold S.
  Psychotropic drugs : fast facts / Jerrold S. Maxmen, Nicholas G. Ward. — 2nd ed.
      p.   cm.
  "A Norton professional book."
  Includes bibliographical references and index.
  ISBN 0-393-70181-6 (pbk.)
  1. Psychotropic drugs. I. Ward, Nicholas G. II. Title.
  [DNLM: 1. Psychotropic Drugs—handbooks. QV 39 M464p 1995]
RM315.M355   1995
615'.788—dc20
DNLM/DLC
for Library of Congress   95-32578 CIP

W. W. Norton & Company, Inc., 500 Fifth Avenue, New York, NY 10110
W. W. Norton & Company, Ltd., 10 Coptic Street, London WC1A 1PU

1   2   3   4   5   6   7   8   9   0

"The village doctor was a great success. His success was due to his sympathy with his patients, each of whom he treated as an individual with an idiosyncracy of his own and worthy of special and separate consideration. It was as if, instead of giving everyone mass-produced medicine, he had molded the portrait of each on his pill."

—Oliver St. John Gogarty

Introduction
to the First Edition

Wisdom arrived one afternoon. Drs. Donald F. Klein and John M. Davis' brand-new 1969 *Diagnosis and Drug Treatment of Psychiatric Disorders* came by mail. The book was splendid. Yet what electrified were pages 96 and 97, which listed the percentage of side effects of ten antipsychotics. Granted, four neuroleptics were now obsolete, and a fifth was for vomiting. Nevertheless, I was the only psychiatric resident to possess these cherished numbers.

Cherished? Well, although they were not exactly psychoanalytic theory or pharmacologic conjecture, they did reveal that chlorpromazine disturbed menstruation 16.3% of the time, thioridazine induced akathisias 8.9% of the time, and perphenazine blurred vision 17.8% of the time. When I met a patient who feared a dry mouth on neuroleptics, page 96 told me whether trifluoperazine, fluphenazine, or perphenazine caused it the least.[1]

Were these two pages number-crunching? Definitely. Were the data skewed, outmoded, or dead wrong? Occasionally. Did these figures cover vast territory? Absolutely. (Klein's second edition of the book jokes that chlorpromazine sedates 9–92% of the time.) Nonetheless, patients *do* want to know which medications cause more weight gain and which ones reduce libido; and clinicians *should* know the answers. With Klein and Davis, I finally had some informed answers.

For 16 years, Klein and Davis stuck to me. When I wrote a textbook in 1985, I wanted it stuffed with pages 96 and 97. Yet I quickly discovered that this was exasperating: Data diverged, disagreed, and didn't exist. Instead, I wrote a "normal" textbook.

[1] It's trifluoperazine at 2.3%

By the way, there was also page 229, but it was less cherished. Although affording side-effect percentages for antidepressants, it displayed *broad* numbers—imipramine gave dry mouth 10–30% of the time, tranylcypromine triggered dizziness 5–20% of the time. Broad figures were common sense, but that fluphenazine on page 96 induced hypotension precisely 0.79% of the time—that was enlightenment.

Even still, this idea of a "dictionary of details" continued. For routine clinical work, I wanted *one* place to get the *facts*. I was tired of hunting through a dozen books to unearth a mere fact: the half-life of protriptyline versus nortriptyline, the dose of amoxapine versus bupropion, or the cost of triazolam versus quazepam. What's more, new drugs kept arising; *Newsweek* announced them; so would patients. I heard too often, "I want Prozac." But aside from what pharmaceutical houses told me, or the *PDR* (written by the drug companies) told me, or even what Ted Koppel told me, I did not know whether Prozac sedated more or less than doxepin, amitriptyline, or clomipramine. I needed one source with all this information. What I wanted was not a textbook that explains everything, but a single *reference*. I wanted *Fast Facts*.

Norton obliged.

Fast Facts simply presents the facts of clinical psychopharmacology. It describes nine categories of medications: antipsychotics, anticholinergics, antidepressants, MAOIs, lithium, anticonvulsants, antianxiety agents, hypnotics, and stimulants. Every chapter details the drugs' names, forms, pharmacologies, dosages, indications, predictors, clinical applications, therapeutic levels, outcomes, alternatives, side effects (and their percentages), pregnancy and lactation data, drug/food interactions, adverse response in children, the elderly, and the sick, medication alterations of laboratory studies, withdrawal hazards, overdoses (and remedies), toxicities, suicide potentials, precautions, contraindications, nurses' information, patients' concerns, and costs. And yet, with all this information, this drug almanac still posed problems.

Fast Facts is a Book Without Verbs (BWV). (I do not consider "increase" and "decrease" to be verbs, but attitudes. Excoriate, guffaw, swoon, and sashay—these are verbs.) Good writing, "good-writing" manuals tell me, highlights good verbs. If so, a BWV could be very dull. I hope it will inform and stimulate.

A bigger dilemma was the same number problem faced by Klein and Davis. The literature bursts with scientific "facts"; numbers conflict, contradict, and confuse; they measure similar, but different, parameters; they lie. Correct numbers can be "incorrect," as when the "correct" dose can be incorrect for a particular patient. Definitions baffle. If I write that a drug generates weight gain, how much weight has to be gained? The criteria depend on the pounds increased, the period's duration, the person's size, etc. Aside from how carefully a scientist defined dizziness, how could I reconcile dissimilar "truths," as when research A found dizziness in 47 of 100 patients while researcher B uncovered it in 5 out of 1,000 patients? These problems are endless. Ultimately, I did what most authors do: I reviewed the printed material, averaged the findings, factored in personal experience, and compromised on the best clinical information. For the errors, I alone bear responsibility. Nevertheless, some people really helped. Drs. Greg Dalack, Brian Fallon, Laurence Greenhill, David Kahn, Neil Kavey, Ron Rieder, Holly Schneier, Michael Sheehy, and David Strauss made suggestions that greatly improved the book.

The enclosed data are generalizations: they do not, or could not, suit every patient under all circumstances. Patients are allergic to drugs, react atypically to the same agents, and respond paradoxically to others. Moreover, the doses, neurotransmitter actions, and other specifications must be altered to the newest scientific developments and tapered to specific patient's requirements.

Although *Fast Facts* focuses on drugs, this does not mean that only drugs are effective. Medications function best to alleviate specific *symptoms* (e.g., delusions, panic attacks). Psychotherapy, in contrast, functions best to resolves specific *issues* (e.g., marital fights); issues may accompany, cause, or result from symptoms. Psychotherapy addresses the content of symptoms (e.g., "the homeless spy on me"). Psychotherapy clarifies how medications reduce symptoms (e.g., "I understand why I'm taking this drug"). Psychotherapy puts life into perspective (e.g., "My elevator phobia is fearsome, but my wife is fantastic!"). Psychotherapy explores how to behave with a mental disorder (e.g., to tell one's husband, not one's boss, about hallucinating). If one had diabetes, a medication, insulin, would reduce blood sugar; a self-help group, a psychotherapy, would discuss the stresses of living with diabetes. Insulin and a self-help group do not conflict, but serve different, albeit complementary, purposes. The same applies for psychotropic drugs and psychotherapy. To compare the two is akin to asking whether the length *or* the width of a football field determines its size.

In short, *Psychotropic Drugs: Fast Facts* is an up-to-date reference with tables and charts for psychiatrists, psychologists, nurses, social workers, activities therapists, internists, psychotherapists, and anyone I forgot. It is *not* a beginner's manual or a "how to prescribe" book, but a comprehensive guide for experienced clinicians. Enjoy this BWV.

Jerrold S. Maxmen, M.D.
New York, January 1991

Introduction
to the Second Edition

Fast Facts continues to be a work in progress, even four years after the publication of the first edition. Fortunately this second edition was revised just following the FDA's approval of a wave of new drugs. Important changes were being incorporated even as the book was being typeset. One area, drug interactions (especially the P450 enzyme system), is expanding so quickly and complexly that a new appendix was created to keep them straight. As you read this, remember the pharmacology maxim, "All drugs have at least 2 effects: those that we know about (a short list) and those that we don't know about (a long list)."

Many people were very helpful. Donald Klein provided a 17-page letter to Jere that was passed on to me containing page-by-page critiques of the first edition. It proved to be invaluable. Gary Tucker took the initiative to be the matchmaker for me with Norton Professional Books. David Dunner, Daniel Casey, Alan Unis, Arifulla Khan, Phil Hantsen, Nelda Murri, and Karen Hansen generously provided valuable critiques and information. Leslie McEwen tirelessly typed seemingly endless revisions of chapters. She did a superb job and is even better at singing opera professionally. I am also thankful to my editor at Norton, Susan Munro, the editor's editor. She also put me in touch with Margaret Ryan, who undauntingly waded through the tables, lists, and phrases without verbs looking for flaws and potential improvements, and Christi Albouy, who got the manuscript ready for the printers.

Nicholas G. Ward, M.D.
Seattle, June 1995

Organization

Each chapter contains 16 sections—give or take a few depending on the circumstances. Here are some details:

INTRODUCTION

This section presents the general category of medications, their broad indications, the disorders they treat in this and other chapters. It's a traffic guide.

NAMES, COST, CLASSES, MANUFACTURERS, DOSE FORMS, AND COLORS

Only drugs currently sold in the United States are listed. The cost is based on the average wholesale price at the end of 1994 and best serves as a comparison with other drugs.

PHARMACOLOGY

This part sketches a medicine's basic clinical pharmacology: its absorption, distribution, metabolism, and elimination. Several terms are often employed:

- *Bioavailability* is the percentage of an oral dose that can act pharmacologically.
- *Plasma Binding* is the percentage of drug bound clinically to plasma proteins.
- *Volume of Distribution* (liters/kg) is the total body volume of distribution at the steady-state level in the plasma.
- *Half-life,* usually expressed in hours, is when 50% of the drug has been eliminated. The book's figures usually represent the

drug's major active fractions, including metabolites; the broader numbers in parentheses are ranges.

* *Excretion* is typically the percent of drug unchanged in the urine.

DOSES

Described here are the standard doses, ranges, initial dosages, therapeutic serum levels, drug amounts for different age groups, and so on.

CLINICAL INDICATIONS AND USE

This section conveys when a drug is specifically indicated. It addresses what can predict a drug's clinical potential, how to employ practically these medications, when (and how) to use different forms of the drug, what to do when problems arise, how to maintain and terminate these agents, and how to apply these drugs for other conditions.

SIDE EFFECTS

This section affords a reasonably comprehensive, but not complete, description of side effects and what to do about them. Although these agents are presented under organ categories, this does not suggest that each side effect belongs exclusively to a single system. Weight gain—prompted by brain, gut, and hormones—was placed under "Gastrointestinal." Categories are for convenience.

PERCENTAGES OF SIDE EFFECTS

This section offers the incidence of specific drug side effects. The first number is the best average we could determine from the literature, whereas the parenthesized number is the range of these side effects. We have only included ranges that we thought might clarify a side effect's frequency. For instance, if the average is 18%, but the range is 10–90%, this suggests that most of the side effects are usually closer to 10%.

For uniformity's sake, and also because most studies don't display placebo comparisons, these percentages include placebo findings. The sign "———" occurs throughout these tables and refers to the nonexistence of information and *not* to the nonexistence of the side effect. If, under vomiting, three drugs are —, —, and 5.5, this does not mean that only the third drug causes vomiting. The other two might, or might not, but there are no data to decide. If a study has demonstrated that a drug does not create a problem, the chart reads "0.0." The enclosed numbers reflect both exact percentages (e.g., 13.7%) and broad ranges (e.g., 10–30%).

The chief aim here is to compare the frequency of adverse reactions. People will have no trouble finding exceptions to these figures. If you find some, please send them along.

PREGNANCY AND LACTATION

This section summarizes these agents' adverse effects on newborns and from breast milk.

The *Milk/Plasma Ratio* underscores that milk and plasma drug concentrations are not parallel throughout breast-feeding.

The *Time of Peak Concentration in Milk* is the hours between the medication's ingestion until it peaks in the milk. It is generally safest to feed the infant at the trough of maternal plasma concentration— that is, just prior to the next dose—to minimize the baby's ingestion of the drug.

Infant Dose (μg/kilogram/day) is calculated from peak milk concentrations, unless stated otherwise. It represents the maximum likely exposure the child has to the drug.

Maternal Dose Percentage is the infant dose compared to the maternal dose controlled for weight.

Safety Rating conveys how relatively safe it is for a mother to consume a drug while breast-feeding during the first year.

DRUG-DRUG INTERACTIONS

This section indicates the major drug interactions with psychotropic agents. This list is thorough, but not complete; it stresses clinical effects and interventions, not mechanisms.

EFFECTS ON LABORATORY TESTS

This section outlines how these medications influence laboratory tests.

WITHDRAWAL

If problems emerge on withdrawal of the drug, this section depicts what happens and what to do about them.

OVERDOSE: TOXICITY, SUICIDE, AND TREATMENT

This section dispenses the opposite. It portrays clinical overdose symptoms, gives toxic and suicide blood levels, signifies how many days' suppy can be lethal, outlines drug-abuse signs and how to remedy intoxications and overdoses.

PRECAUTIONS

When should a drug *not* be taken? That's addressed here—the contraindications and dangers clinicians should exercise when prescribing these medications.

NURSES' DATA

Much of what has already been written will be of great assistance to all staff, including nurses, but this section informs staff about observing patients on medication, showing them how to handle side effects, and using the various dose forms of the drug.

PATIENT AND FAMILY NOTES

This book is written for professionals, not laymen. This section affords the key information staff should insure patients receive: whether to consume medications in relation to meals, how to deal with forgetting a dose, how to cope with immediate side effects, when to call a doctor regarding a crisis, etc.

If one member of a family is affected by a mental disorder, all members are affected. Some of these concerns, therefore, are for the entire family.

APPENDICES

Two drug identification guides, describing the major action of all drugs mentioned in the book and "translations" between generic and brand names.

A symptom checklist, to be given to patients before and during their drug-taking to see which symptoms arose before or after the drug was begun.

P450 enzyme system drug interactions

The bibliography of this book provides these data.

ABBREVIATIONS

ACA	Anticholinergic agents
Ach	Acetylcholine
AD	Antidepressant
ADR	Adverse drug reaction
bid	Twice a day
CBC	Complete blood count
d	days
D/S	Dextrose and saline
D/W	Dextrose and water
DST	Dexamethasone suppression test
ECG	Electrocardiogram
ECT	Electroconvulsive therapy
EEG	Electroencephalogram
EPS	Extrapyramidal side effects
EUCD	Emotionally unstable character disorder
g	Gram
GABA	Gamma-aminobutyric acid
GAD	Generalized anxiety disorder
h	Hours
h/o	History of
HCAs	Heterocyclic antidepressants (includes TCAs, maprotiline, and amoxapine)
hs	At sleep
IM	Intramuscular injection
IV	Intravenous injection
kg	Kilogram
LFT	Liver function tests (SGOT, SGPT, LDH, bilirubin, alkaline phosphotase)
MAOI	Monoamine-oxidase inhibitor
μg	Microgram (10^{-6} grams)
mg	Milligrams (10^{-3} grams)
NDI	Nephrogenic diabetes insipidus
ng	Nanograms (10^{-9} grams)
NIMH	National Institute of Mental Health
NMS	Neuroleptic malignant syndrome
NSAID	Nonsteroidal anti-inflammatory drug
OCD	Obsessive-compulsive disorder
PTSD	Post-traumatic stress disorder
po	Oral dose
qd	Once a day; daily
qid	Four times a day
qod	Every other day

ORGANIZATION

r/o	Rule out
SC	Subcutaneous
SGOT/AST	Aspartate aminotransferase
SGPT/ALT	Alanine aminotransferase
SSRI	Selective serotonin reuptake inhibitor
T_3	Triiodothyronine
T_4	Thyroxine
TCAs	Tricyclic antidepressants
TD	Tardive dyskinesia
tid	Three times a day
TSH	Thyroid-stimulating hormone

Contents

C
O
N
T
E
N
T
S

CONTENTS

C
O
N
T
E
N
T
S

1. Antipsychotic Agents

INTRODUCTION

This chapter discusses antipsychotics and tacrine, an antidementia agent. Antipsychotics block psychosis, whereas hypnoanxiolytics do not.

Both antipsychotics and hypnoanxiolytics can sedate, which accounts for their being named "major" and "minor" tranquilizers, respectively. To avoid confusion, this book does not use the term *tranquilizer*.

Antipsychotics, also called "neuroleptics," primarily treat schizophrenia and psychoses occurring in mania, depression, and CNS disorders.

This chapter focuses on

- Schizophrenia (pages 7–15)
- Delirium (pages 15–16)
- Autism (page 16)
- Brief psychotic disorder (pages 16–17)
- Schizotypal personality disorder (page 17)
- Delusional disorder (page 17)
- Depressive symptoms in schizophrenia (pages 17–18)
- Dementia (tacrine, a true antidementia agent, is discussed here) (pages 18–20)
- Extra pyramidal symptoms, NMS and TD (pages 30–39)

Other chapters discuss the use of neuroleptics for

- Aggression (Anticonvulsants, pages 233–235)
- Anorexia nervosa (Antidepressants, page 109)
- Anxiety (Anti-anxiety, page 267)
- Atypical psychosis (Anticonvulsants, pages 235–236)

1

- Borderline personality disorder (Lithium, page 199)
- Depression (Antidepressants, page 100)
- Hallucinogen-induced psychosis (Anticonvulsants, page 236)
- Mania (Lithium, pages 191–193).

NAMES, COST, CLASSES, MANUFACTURERS, DOSE FORMS, COLORS

Generic Names (Dollars/Dose: 100 pills in mg)[1]	Brand Names (Dollars/Dose: 100 pills in mg)[1]	Manufacturers	Dose Forms (mg)[2]	Colors
		PHENOTHIAZINES		
Aliphatics				
Chlorpromazine (7–12/100)	Thorazine (73/100)	SmithKline Beecham	t: 10/25/50/ 100/200 SR: 30/75/150/ 200/300 o: 10/30/100 p: 25 mg/ml s: 10 mg/5 ml sp: 25/100 mg/ml	t: all orange
Piperidines				
Mesoridazine	Serentil (78/50)	Boehringer Ingelheim	t: 10/25/50/ 100 o: 25 mg/ml p: 25 mg/ml	t: all red
Thioridazine	Mellaril (14–24/100)	Sandoz (54/100)	t: 10/15/25/ 50/100/150/200 o: 30/100 mg/ml	t: chartreuse/ pink/tan/white green/yellow/ pink o: straw yel- lows/light yellow
	Mellaril-S (94/100)	Sandoz	su: 25/100 mg/5 ml	
Piperazines				
Fluphenazine (42–84/5)	Permitil (123/5)	Schering	t: 2.5/5/10 o: 5 mg/ml	t: light orange/ purple-pink/ light red
	Prolixin (140/5)	Apothecon	t: 1/2.5/5/10 e: 0.5 mg/ml o: 5 mg/ml p: 2.5 mg/ml	t: pink/yellow/ green/red
Fluphenazine decanoate (16/25)	Prolixin Decanoate (20–25)	Apothecon	p: 25 mg/ml	——
Fluphenazine enanthate	Prolixin Enanthate (97/25)	Apothecon	p: 25 mg/ml	——

Generic Names (Dollars/Dose: 100 pills in mg)[1]	Brand Names (Dollars/Dose: 100 pills in mg)[1]	Manufacturers	Dose Forms (mg)[2]	Colors
Perphenazine	Trilafon (60–78/8)	Schering (94/8)	t: 2/4/8/16 o: 3.2 mg/ml p: 5 mg/ml	t: all gray
Trifluoperazine (40/5)	Stelazine (102/5)	SmithKline Beecham	t: 1/2/5/10 o: 10 mg/ml p: 2 mg/ml	t: all blue
BUTYROPHENONES				
Haloperidol (22–36/2)	Haldol (81/2)	McNeil	t: 0.5/1/2/5/ 10/20 o: 2 mg/ml p: 5 mg/ml	t: white/yellow/ pink/green/ aqua/ salmon
Haloperidol decanoate	Haldol Decanoate (256/100)	McNeil	p: 50/100 mg/ml	——
THIOXANTHENES				
Thiothixene (25–35/5)	Navane (77/5)	Roerig	c: 1/2/5/10/20 o: 5 mg/ml p: 2/5 mg/ml	c: orange-yel- low/blue-yel- low/orange- white/blue- white/dark blue-light blue
DIPHENYLBUTYLPIPERDINES				
Pimozide	Orap (133/4)	Lemmon/Gate	t: 2 mg	t: white
DIBENZAZEPINE				
Loxapine (74–132/25)	Loxitane (154/25)	Lederle	c: 5/10/25/50	t: dark green/ yellow- green/light green-dark green/blue- dark green
	Loxitane-C (227/25 [120 doses])	Lederle	o: 25 mg/ml	——
	Loxitane-IM (93/25 [20 doses])	Lederle	p: 50 mg/ml	——
DIHYDROINDOLONE				
Molindone	Moban (111/25)	Lemmon/Gate	t: 5/10/25/50/ 100 o: 20 mg/ml	t: orange/laven- der/light green/blue/tan o: cherry
DIBENZODIAZEPINE				
Clozapine	Clozaril (342/100)	Sandoz[3]	t: 25/100	t: all yellow

Generic Names (Dollars/Dose: 100 pills in mg)[1]	Brand Names (Dollars/Dose: 100 pills in mg)[1]	Manufacturers	Dose Forms (mg)[2]	Colors
	BENZISOXAZOLE			
Risperidone	Risperdal (315/2)	Janssen/ SmithKline Beecham	t: 1/2/3/4	t: white/orange yellow/green

[1] 1994 average wholesale price for 100 pills at this dose (e.g., 78/50 means 100 pills 50 mg cost $78). If depot form, cost is of single dose.

[2] c = capsules; e = elixir; o = oral concentrate; p = parenteral concentrate; s = syrup; sp = suppository; SR = sustained release spansules; su = suspension; t = tablets.

[3] Must prescribe clozapine through Sandoz; cost listed does not include monitoring system cost.

PHARMACOLOGY

Antipsychotics are dopamine antagonists; they also elevate prolactin and are antiemetics. All neuroleptics (except clozapine and risperidone) are probably equally effective for psychosis and differ mainly in side effects.

Risperidone and clozapine are more effective for negative symptoms and can be effective in psychosis not responsive to other neuroleptics. Clozapine differs from other neuroleptics because it apparently does not cause dystonia reactions, tardive dyskinesia, or increase prolactin levels. Risperidone differs from other neuroleptics because (at usual therapeutic doses, under 6 mg qd) it apparently does not

- Cause extrapyramidal symptoms (EPS) and perhaps has much lower TD risk (see Chapter 2 for further details).
- When switching a responder from clozapine to risperidone, do it very gradually or relapse risk is increased.
  √ Unknown how much overlap between clozapine responder patients and risperidone responder patients.

The antidopaminergic antiemetics—metoclopramide (Reglan), thiethylperazine (Torecan), and promethazine (Phenergan) are neuroleptics and have all the side effects of neuroleptics, including EPS and TD.

- Triflupromazine (Vesprin) and prochlorperazine (Compazine) are the only 2 with an antipsychotic indication.
  √ Not generally used or recommended for this indication.
- Promazine (Sparine) is a very low-potency neuroleptic that is not recommended because of probable decreased efficacy.

Most patients respond to 300–500 mg chlorpromazine equivalents. Higher doses are seldom needed and may be less effective.

Most neuroleptic metabolites are inactive, but a few retain antipsychotic actions (e.g., mesoridazine's 7-hydroxychlorpromazine).

Oral form

- Antipsychotics' peak concentrations usually occur around 2–4 h.
  √ Pimozide peaks at 6–8 h, with range from 4–12 h.
- Neuroleptics are highly lipophilic.
- They accumulate in the brain, which typically permits once-a-day doses for psychosis.
  √ Aside from antipsychotic actions, oral neuroleptics have side effects, which can arise quickly (e.g., dry mouth in 30 minutes) or slowly (e.g., 2 years in tardive dyskinesia).
- Avoid prescribing 2 neuroleptics concurrently.

IM (not depot) form

- Peak concentrations occur 15–30 minutes after injection.
- Expect 3–4 fold greater potency in IM over po doses.

The different neuroleptic groups have different side-effect profiles (see Side Effects, pages 20–41).

Pharmacology of Neuroleptics

Generic Names	Bioavailability (%)	Plasma Binding (%)	Half-Life (hours)	Excretion (%)*
Chlorpromazine	32 ± 19	95–98	30 ± 7	25 ± 15 R / 70–80 F
Clozapine	50–60	95	8 ± 4 / 12 (4–66)	50 R / 30 F
Fluphenazine	?	80–90	14.7–15.3 (16–24)	R/F
Haloperidol	70 ± 18	91 ± 1.4	17.9 ± 6.6	40 R
Loxapine	?	90	3.4 (1–19)	61.6 R / 22.6 F
Mesoridazine	?	70	24–84	R/F
Molindone	?	98	1.5 (4–12)	R/F
Perphenazine	low	high	9.5 (8–21)	R/F
Pimozide	>50	99	55	38–45 R
Thioridazine	30	70–99	16 (7–42)	?
Thiothixene	?	?	34	?
Trifluoperazine	?	>80	9.3	R/F
Risperidone	70	90	20	70 R / 15 F

* B = bile; F = fecal; R = renal; ? = unavailable or inconsistent.

DOSES

General Neuroleptic Doses

Generic Names	Chlorpromazine Equivalent Doses (100 mg)	Acute Doses (mg/day)	Ranges (mg/day)	P.R.N. (mg/po)	P.R.N. (mg/IM)
Chlorpromazine	100	200–1600	25–2000	25–100	25–50
Clozapine	75	150–500	75–700	N/A	N/A
Fluphenazine	2	2.5–20	1–60	0.5–10	1–5
Haloperidol	2	2–40	1–100	0.5–5	2–5
Loxapine	15	60–100	30–250	10–60	12.5–50
Mesoridazine	50	75–300	30–400	10–100	25
Molindone	20	50–100	15–25	5–75	N/A
Perphenazine	10	16–32	4–64	4–8	5–10
Pimozide	0.5	10–12	1–20	N/A	1–3
Risperidone*	1	2–8	1–16	N/A	N/A
Thioridazine	100	200–600	40–800	20–200	N/A
Thiothixene	0.5	6–30	6–60	2–20	2–4
Trifluoperazine	5	6–50	2–80	5–10	1–2

* Doses over 6 mg yield less improvement and more side effects than 6 mg.

Specific Neuroleptic Doses

Generic Names	First Oral Dose (mg)	First Day Total Dose (mg/day)	Therapeutic Plasma Levels (ng/ml)
Chlorpromazine	50–100	300–400	30–100
Clozapine	25	50	141–204*
Fluphenazine	1–2	2.5–10	0.2–3
Fluphenazine decanoate	12.5	12.5	0.15–2.7
Haloperidol	1–5	3–20	3–12
Loxapine	10–25	20–50	—
Mesoridazine	50	150	—
Molindone	10–25	50–75	—
Perphenazine	4–8	16–32	0.8–12.0
Pimozide	1–2	2	—
Risperidone	0.5–1	1–2	—
Thioridazine	50–100	150–300	1–1.5
Thiothixene	5	4–13	2–20*
Trifluoperazine	2–5	4–20	1–2.3

* Women statistically higher than men.

Age-Related Doses

Generic Names	Childhood		Geriatric Dose Range (mg/day)
	Weight (mg/kg/day)	Dose Range (mg/day)*	
Chlorpromazine	3–6	45–430 (196)	25–200
Clozapine	——	——	100–400
Fluphenazine	0.05–0.1	4.9–50 (10)	2–10
Haloperidol	0.05	1–4.5	1–6**
Loxapine	0.5–1	25–60	——
Mesoridazine	?	(153–174)	75–200
Molindone	0.5–1	25–50	50–150
Perphenazine	0.05–0.1	4–24	4–48
Pimozide†	——	——	10–50
Thioridazine	2–5	160–500 (282)	25–200
Thiothixene	0.5–1	2–24 (16)	2–15
Trifluoperazine	0.5	6–10 (0.5–15)	2–15
Risperidone	——	——	0.5–4

* Mean in parentheses.
** 0.3–0.5 mg/kg often enough.
† Not officially recommended for psychiatric disorder; is used for Tourette's.

CLINICAL INDICATIONS AND USE

Neuroleptics generally relieve schizophrenia's "positive" symptoms (e.g., hallucinations) better than its "negative" symptoms (e.g., blunted affect).

*Target Symptoms For Antipsychotic Agents**

Anorexia	Agitation	Assaultive behavior
Blunted affect	Bizarre thinking	Catatonic behavior
Confusion	Delusional thinking	Disorientation
Hallucinations	Insomnia	Manic symptoms
Paranoid thinking	Psychomotor agitation	Social withdrawal
	Thought withdrawal	

* Applicable only if they are a result of a psychotic process.

Initiating Therapy

Start with large enough dose to squelch symptoms, but low enough to minimize side effects. The equivalent of 300–600 mg chlorpromazine is a reasonable target dose for a majority of patients, then wait two weeks. Exceeding a patient's own antipsychotic threshold doesn't speed recovery. Generally less sedating, more potent neuroleptics are preferred because they have fewer side effects during the maintenance phase than the highly sedating ones (e.g., chlorpromazine or thioridazine).

- The use of neuroleptic threshold (NT) is sometimes used.
  - √ Not expected to work with risperidone or clozapine.
  - √ May work best with high-potency neuroleptics.
    - □ Low-potency neuroleptics with intrinsic anticholinergic effects may mask threshold EPS.
- Rather than guessing the right dose, the use of neuroleptic threshold (NT) is sometimes recommended.
  - √ The neuroleptic threshold is defined as a slight increase in cogwheel rigidity after starting the neuroleptic.
    - □ This can be tested by flexing and extending the patient's arms at the elbow and the wrist.
    - □ If patient is unable to relax the tested arm, have patient perform and concentrate on rapid, alternating movements with the other arm.
  - √ Others have argued that the fine motor signs of micrographia or decreased arm swing while walking are more sensitive indicators of threshold.
- To establish baseline rigidity
  - √ The patient should be evaluated for 1–3 days before medications are started.
  - √ Initially haloperidol 2 mg qd (or its equivalent) is given, and if no increase in rigidity occurs, this is increased by 2 mg every other day.
  - √ If rigidity is equivocal, wait 1 or 2 days to see if it increases, and if not, increase by one more 2 mg dose.
- Effective antipsychotic dosing in the 3–5 mg range of haloperidol can often be achieved.
- This approach may be particularly helpful in certain problematic populations, including
  - √ Adolescents
  - √ Geriatrics (use 0.5 or 1 mg equivalents of haloperidol)
  - √ Patients who have never been on neuroleptics before.

Good and Bad Predictors of Antipsychotic Treatment for Schizophrenia

Good Outcome	Poor Outcome
Later age of onset	Earlier age of onset
Short duration of illness	Long duration of illness
Acute onset	Slow onset
Good premorbid functioning and social competence	Poor premorbid functioning and social competence
Anxiety, tension, or other affective symptoms	Emotional blunting
Highly systematized and focused delusions with clear symbolism	Unsystematized and unfocused delusions

Good and Bad Predictors of Antipsychotic Treatment for Schizophrenia (Cont.)

Good Outcome	Poor Outcome
Confusion and disorientation	Clear sensorium
Precipitating factors	No precipitating factors
Married	Single
Family h/o affective disorder	No family h/o affective disorder
Family without h/o schizophrenia	Family with h/o schizophrenia

Since the efficacy among antipsychotics is roughly equivalent, choosing the "right" antipsychotic can be elusive. Best to

- Select an agent that has previously helped the patient, but if none exists:
  - √ If the first dose seems to be tolerated by the patient, continue it.
  - √ If not (e.g., patient is dangerously woozy), try a much lower dose or consider another neuroleptic.
- If patient is not agitated, give a less sedative antipsychotic (e.g., fluphenazine, trifluoperazine) in a single dose 30 minutes before bedtime.
- Bedtime doses lessen the experience of side effects, since some may arise only during sleep.
- If the patient requires sedation or is agitated
  - √ Choose a more sedating neuroleptic (e.g., perphenazine or loxapine).
  - √ Rapidly increase to target antipsychotic dosage.
  - √ Take advantage of sedating effects by using tid or qid doses.
  - √ Make sure patient is getting medication: Give IM neuroleptic (e.g., haloperidol 5 mg) if rapid effect is needed, or give liquid form and observe patient taking it.
  - √ If at target dose, to avoid unnecessary further risks of EPS, add benzodiazepines (e.g., lorazepam 1–2 mg/po or IM, diazepam 5 mg IM). Beware of disinhibition at low and intermediate benzodiazepine doses.
- Special precautions with clozapine
  - √ Do not rapidly increase clozapine; increases seizure risk.
  - √ For clozapine start at 12.5 mg qd or bid and increase by 25–50 mg qd every 2 days.
  - √ Monitor clozapine for sedation and hypotension and beware of rare (1:3,000) respiratory or cardiac arrest.
- In cases of severe refractory psychotic agitation, droperidol 2.5–15 mg (1–6 ml) can be considered.
  - √ 0.15–0.25 mg/kg can be started in physically healthy adults (< 65 y.o.).
  - √ Duration of action usually under 5 h but can be as high as 12 h.

√ Shows rapid onset (3–10 minutes) and peak action (20–30) minutes).

√ Can be very sedating/tranquilizing.

  □ Low risk of prolonged oversedation.

√ Occasionally doses up to 50 mg required.

√ Less hypotensive than low-potency sedating phenothiazines.

√ Increases EPS risk of other drugs.

Choosing a Neuroleptic

Problem	Choice
High dystonia risk (under 30-y.o. male; under 25-y.o. female)	Midpotency neuroleptic or risperidone; if high potency chosen, place on ACA for 14 days.
Geriatric (high anticholinergic, orthostatic, sedation) risks, cognitive impairment, or delirium	High potency (e.g., haloperidol) or risperidone
Predominant or severe negative symptoms	Risperidone or clozapine
Treatment resistant	Risperidone or Clozapine (see Augmentations on pages 11–12)
TD or Parkinson's disease	Clozapine (possibly risperidone); first consider reducing L-dopa, which may be causing or exacerbating psychosis.
Seizure risk	High-potency neuroleptic (possibly molindone)
Obesity	Molindone; advise patient to lose weight. Avoid low-potency neuroleptics.
Cardiac arrhythmia	High potency (possibly medium potency). Avoid pimozide, thioridazine, and clozapine.
Extreme unresponsive agitation	Droperidol prn as adjunctive agent
Minimal compliance with medications	Haloperidol or prolixin decanoate, rarely pimozide orally

Treatment Resistance

What happens if patient does not improve sufficiently?

• Psychotic symptoms may vanish in days, but many require 2–12 weeks (or more) to disappear.

• If all symptoms remain unchanged after initial 2 weeks, consider:

  √ Is patient taking the medication?

    □ If patient does not have a common side effect (e.g., dry mouth), he probably is *not* ingesting the medication.

    □ To be certain, obtain a therapeutic plasma level by drawing blood 12 h after an oral dose.

    □ Too high levels may interfere with antipsychotic effect.

    □ Too low levels suggest noncompliance or unusual metabolism of drug.

  √ Liquid medication is more readily swallowed than pills, which are graciously "cheeked."

- If patient is taking the pills, but without a good response, then:
  - √ Re-examine diagnosis and make sure there are clear target symptoms.
    - □ Raise (or lower) the dose of the same neuroleptic.
    - □ Try an IM form.
    - □ Switch to depot medication (see below). (This may particularly help the fast metabolizer whose liver eliminates most oral medication.)
    - □ If on high doses (e.g., 50 mg/qd haloperidol), gradual reduction to 50–60% of this dose may help more than 50%.
- If there is inadequate response after 3–4 weeks on neuroleptic, consider measuring prolactin level.
  - √ On haloperidol, 16–30 ng/ml prolactin may be optimal range.
    - □ Adjust dose up or down if outside this range.
- If prominent negative symptoms remain, consider risperidone or clozapine.
  - √ Effects of clozapine usually seen within 12 weeks.
  - √ If patient is on high-potency neuroleptic with partial response, clozapine can be added safely.
    - □ At 100 mg/day of clozapine, tapering of conventional neuroleptic can be started as dose of clozapine is increased.
- If negative symptoms are worse, consider neuroleptic akinesia and lower dose and/or add anticholinergic agent.
- If prominent positive symptoms remain, consider a different class of neuroleptic.
- If patient is treatment-resistant to 2 or more typical neuroleptics, consider risperidone or clozapine.
- If partial response observed, consider augmentations.

Augmentations

- Benzodiazepines can improve positive and negative symptoms.
  - √ 50% response rate
  - √ 2–3 mg qd alprazolam typical dose.
- Clonazepam may diminish schizophrenia, although findings are unclear.
  - √ For instance, 31% improvement in 4 studies;
  - √ Decreased paranoid thinking and hallucinations when combined with neuroleptic;
  - √ Helped 4 patients with atypical psychosis who were unresponsive to neuroleptics.
  - √ Dose:
    - □ Start at 0.5 mg bid-tid.
    - □ Increase 0.5–1.0 mg every 3 days until stabilization occurs.
    - □ Dose may reach 3 mg/day.

- Adding lithium can help "good prognosis" schizophrenics as well as schizoaffectives with bipolar moods.
- Anticonvulsants may help
  - If "atypical" features, seizure-like, organic symptoms (e.g., olfactory, tactile, or kinesthetic hallucinations);
  - With prominent negative symptoms (e.g., affective flattening);
  - If bipolar symptoms observed.
- Bromocriptine 2.5 mg/qd (case reports positive in treatment-resistant psychosis).
- Trazodone 100–300 mg (mixed results; used for negative symptoms).
- Famotidine (Pepcid), a potent lipophylic histamine-2 blocker, 20 mg bid (improved negative symptoms in small [N = 12] open trial).
- Glycine, a potentiator of NMDA neurotransmission, started at 2 gm/qd, with maximum dose 0.4 g/kg (~ 30 gm qd), significantly decreased negative symptoms in 8-week placebo-controlled trial of 14 chronic schizophrenic patients already on neuroleptics.
- Anticholinergic agents may worsen positive symptoms and improve negative symptoms. In patients with mostly negative symptoms, might be adjunct.
- Pimozide 4–20 mg qd may have more effect on refractory negative symptoms.
- Selegiline 5 mg po bid taken for 1 month in an open trial significantly reduced negative symptoms with no effect on positive symptoms.
- Antidepressants may help negative symptoms/depression.
  - √ Risk exacerbation of psychosis, positive symptoms.
- Propranolol in doses > 800 mg qd
  - √ May function as anticonvulsant at this dose.

Maintenance

After the initial schizophrenic break

- qd dosing for most patients; divided dosing only if side-effect problem (e.g., orthostatic hypotension).
  - √ Risperidone is recommended in bid dosing, but if there is no hypotension, it can be given qd.
- From 6–9 months after discharge (or point of maximum improvement), start to taper the dose to 20–50% of the highest dose.
  - √ If symptoms recur, increase dose.
- If patient will be under high stress (e.g., new job), do not alter medication until stressor has past.

- Some studies suggest that serum prolactin predicts relapse risk.
  - √ In fluphenazine decanoate study
    - □ ≥ 16 ng/ml level was protective.
    - □ ≤ 6 ng/ml level was high relapse risk.
- In patients who unilaterally stop medication, a 15%/month relapse rate can be expected.

Depot neuroleptics, which are IM antipsychotics lasting 2–4 weeks, are employed for maintenance therapy, particularly for patients with poor or inconsistent compliance.

- They are preferable treatment for a majority of chronic psychoses.
- Their advantages are:
  - √ Patient does not have to remember to take pills every day;
  - √ Certainty that drug is in the patient;
  - √ Less staff work;
  - √ Lower relapse rates than with oral meds.
- Their disadvantages are:
  - √ Once injected, they are injected, and patient must deal with any adverse consequences, such as an EPS.
- Be aware of the following precautions.
  - √ Do not start any treatment with depot neuroleptics.
  - √ Suddenly switching from oral to depot forms can radically alter serum level.
    - □ For instance, 4 weeks of fluphenazine 10 mg/day po was stopped, replaced by fluphenazine decanoate 12.5 mg IM; 2 weeks later the serum level dropped from 0.51 ng/ml to 0.08 ng/ml and symptoms appeared.
    - □ Because of long half-lives for depot neuroleptics, it takes 1–3 months to reach steady state using depot alone.
    - □ Oral neuroleptics can reach steady state in 3–7 days.
- Safety factors
  - √ *Gradually* shift from oral to depot forms, and
  - √ Test dose.
- Method
  - √ No depot form is clearly better than another in controlling psychosis.
    - □ Fluphenazine enanthate has signifcantly higher side effects, especially EPS, and is not recommended.
  - √ First, stabilize the patient on a dose of oral fluphenazine or haloperidol; ensure adequate blood level and side-effect tolerance.
  - √ To detect rare sensitivity to vehicle (sesame oil) or side effects, inject 6.25 mg (by insulin syringe for accurate measurement) of fluphenazine decanoate (or any depot form).

√ Dose schedules include
  □ Fluphenazine decanoate (FD) and fluphenazine enanthate (see tables below and on page 6).
  □ Haloperidol decanoate (HD) dose should equal 10–20 times the daily dose of haloperidol orally. The initial dose is usually 20 times oral dose and the maintenance dose is closer to 10 times the oral dose.
√ Maintain stable blood level.
  □ Continue po medication.
  □ Gradually taper oral medication as depot levels increase.
  □ Example schedule: Give full po dose on first day of IM; decrease po dose 20% of original dose each day; add more po medication if clinically indicated; po medication may accompany IM for 1 or 2 months until proper IM dose is determined.
• After being stabilized on fluphenazine decanoate 25 mg, many patients continue to do well with much lower doses (as low as 5–10 mg).
• Depot neuroleptics have not been approved for children under 12.

Approximate Equivalents of Oral and Depot Fluphenazine

	PO	IM*
Low dose	1–8 mg	6.25–12.5
Medium dose	8–20 mg	12.5–37.5
High dose	20–40 mg	37.5–100

* One study suggested 12.5 mg decanoate = 10 mg po.

*The Use of Depot Neuroleptics**

	Fluphenazine Decanoate	Fluphenazine Enanthate**	Haloperidol Decanoate
Usual dose (mg)	25 (6.25–100)	25–75 (12.5–100)	50–100 (50–300)
Usual frequency of injections (weeks)	3 (2–6)	2 (1–3)	4 (2–5)
Antipsychotic action begins (days)	1–3	1–3	6–7
Peak plasma level (days)	1–2	2–4	3–9
Protein binding	80	80	92
Half-life (days)	6.8–9.6 (one injection) 14.3 (many doses)	3.5–4 (one injection)	21 (one injection) 12 (many doses)
Maximum dose recorded	400 mg/week	1250 mg/week	1200 mg/injection

* Ranges in parentheses.
** Not generally recommended because of high EPS risk (> 40%) compared to decanoates.

Pimozide as an alternative to depot neuroleptics in low-compliance patients:

- Frequently patients refuse depot neuroleptics because they do not want IM.
  √ Check with patient to see if it is the site of administration and not IM that is reason for refusal.
  √ Some patients resist buttocks IM but tolerate thigh or shoulder.
- If patient refuses IM medication and is part of a program that cannot monitor daily oral meds but can oversee 3–5 doses a week, then consider pimozide.
  √ Pimozide's 55-h half-life allows dosing every 2–3 days.
  √ However, this use of pimozide has not been extensively evaluated.

Indications for long-term antipsychotic therapy:

- After 2 schizophrenic episodes, probably need neuroleptics for years (if not for life), always weighing the risks of psychosis against those of tardive dyskinesia and other side effects. Consider clozapine or risperidone.
- Maintenance antipsychotic therapy over 2 years is superior to placebo. Averts schizophrenic relapses in 40–70% of patients.

Delirium

A delirium is a clouding of consciousness, disorientation, and loss of recent memory.

- It usually lasts no more than several days.
  √ Patients either improve or die.
- Ensure that medications are not causing the delirium.
  √ Anticholinergic toxicity is the most common medication cause.
    □ In addition to many psychotropic medications, many routine nonpsychiatric medications have significant anticholinergic activity (see pages 61 and 69, Chapter 2).
  √ Sedative medications are the next most common cause (e.g., benzodiazepines, opiates, meprobamate), sedating (and anticholinergic) antidepressants, and neuroleptics.
  √ Other medications associated with delirium include
    □ Amantadine
    □ Aspirin
    □ Cimetidine
    □ Hydrochlorthiazide
    □ Insulin

□ Methyldopa
□ Propranolol
□ Reserpine

To manage combative, disorganized, or confused behavior, haloperidol is useful.

* Haloperidol affords limited anticholinergic and hypotensive effects.
* Avoid toxicity by avoiding standing regular orders.
* Haloperidol 1–5 mg po or IM:
  √ Wait 1 h and
  √ Titrate repeat doses q 2–8 h.
* Delirious patients rarely need > 10 mg of haloperidol.
  √ 2–4 mg/day typically suffices.
* Avoid adding ACAs, since
  √ Increased anticholinergic actions can worsen delirium, and
  √ Only 20% of delirious patients develop dystonia.

Benzodiazepines are an alternative to antipsychotic agents.

* Example: lorazepam 1–2 mg po or 2–4 mg IM.
  √ May risk increased confusion secondary to sedative effects.

Carbamazepine with buspirone reported effective in early posttraumatic delirium.

* Combine controlled-release carbamazepine 400 mg qd with buspirone 10 mg tid.
  √ Quieting effect noted in 12 h.
  √ Well tolerated.
  √ No comparison made with carbamazepine alone.

Brief Psychotic Disorder

* Often lower doses (2–5 mg haloperidol) are effective.
* Improvement frequently seen in days, not weeks.
  √ May be a result of high spontaneous remission rate.
* Benzodiazepines for sleep and agitation may be valuable if psychosis with marked stressors.
* Lithium or anticonvulsant may be helpful for patients with bipolar II history or strong family h/o disorder.
* Antidepressants should be considered in patients who have h/o major depression.

Autism/Pervasive Development Disorder

Serotonergic antidepressants (SSRIs) and chlomipramine have decreased autistic symptoms in open trials.

- May best help decrease repetitive behaviors and
- Increase interaction with others.

Haloperidol (0.5–4.0 mg/day) may decrease uncooperative behavior, emotional lability, and irritability.

- Avoid sedating antipsychotics.
- Carefully monitor target symptoms to be treated.

Fenfluramine (Pondimin), a serotonin depleting agent, when used chronically has not performed as well as initial case reports suggested.

- May decrease hyperactivity but not other autistic symptoms.
- Many side effects (e.g., insomnia, weight loss, decreased learning) lead to drop-outs.

Schizotypal Personality Disorder

Ideas of reference, odd communication, social isolation, and transient psychosis respond to neuroleptics.

- Haloperidol 2–6 mg often effective range.
- Positive results often seen in 2 weeks.
- Higher drop-out rate from side effects (as much as 50%) seen when compared to schizophrenic patients.

Delusional Disorder

Many case reports but no controlled studies suggest that pimozide is effective for

- Somatic type
  √ Case reports suggest that some somatic types may have severe body dysmorphic disorders and should be treated with OCD medications, the serotonergic antidepressants.
- Jealous type

Antipsychotic trials are recommended for erotomanic, grandiose, and persecutory types.

- Low (< 30%) response rate usually reported.

Depressive Symptoms in Schizophrenia

Depressive mood, insomnia, and poor concentration are frequently the earliest prodromal symptoms before a psychotic relapse.

- These often occur before hallucinations, delusions, or thought disorder appear.
- Symptoms may have regularly preceded prior psychotic episodes.

- A temporary increase in antipsychotic medication, along with benzodiazepines for sleep and agitation, may prevent the full relapse.
- Depressive symptoms, including anhedonia, low energy, and poor concentration, may occur 3–4 weeks after treatment and may be symptoms of akinesia.
  - √ If akinesia is diagnosed, reduction of antipsychotic dose may relieve this depression-like syndrome.
- If a true major depression occurs, antidepressants should be considered (see Antidepressants).
- Sometimes depressive symptoms are grief reactions that are not amenable to medications. Clues to this include
  - √ Symptoms occur after psychosis is nearly or completely gone, and
  - √ Content of depressive thoughts is completely centered on what has been lost or not accomplished because of the psychotic illness.

Dementia

A dementia is the loss of intellectual abilities, especially judgment, memory, abstract thinking, control over impulses, and language.

- Unlike in delirium, in dementia there is no clouding of consciousness.
- Dementias are often long-term and permanent.

Tacrine (Cognex)

Reversible cholinesterase inhibitors can help in Alzheimers dementia. Tacrine (Cognex by Parke-Davis) is first approved drug.

- Cholinergic system deteriorates in Alzheimers dementia.
- Tacrine inhibits breakdown of endogenously released acetylcholine.
- In theory tacrine should be less effective as dementia progresses.
  - √ Less endogenous acetylecholine available.

Tacrine modestly helps mild to moderate dementia in those who can tolerate it.

- On average, tacrine appears to reverse 6 months of dementia's progression.
- Significant effects can be seen in 6 weeks.
- Tacrine's effects are dose-related, with significant effects first seen at 40 mg a day (10 mg qid).
  - √ More improvement noticed in 80–160 mg range.
- Initially, responders improve compared to baseline.

- By 6 months patients on tacrine are back to original baseline.
  - √ By 6 months placebo group is significantly worse than original baseline.
- Improvement of dementia seen first by caregiver and then on MD rating scales.
- 51% of those who stayed on tacrine 12 weeks had a 4-point (considered modestly clinically significant) improvement on Alzheimers Disease Assessment Scale.

Pharmacology of tacrine includes:

- 2–4 h half-life.
  - √ Needs qid dosing.
- 55% protein bound
- Bioavailability reduced 30–40% by food in stomach.
- Blood levels up to 50% higher in women.
  - √ May partially be due to weight.
- Metabolized by P450 1A2 enzyme (see Appendix p. 391).
  - √ Drugs that inhibit or induce this system may change tacrine levels.
  - √ Fluvoxamine and cimetidine inhibit this system and increase tacrine levels.
  - √ Theophyline, phenacetin, acetaminophen, carbamazepine, and caffeine metabolized by 1A2 and compete with tacrine.
    - ◻ Uncertain effects on level.
  - √ Smoking, barbiturates, carbamazepine, rifampin, amino-glutethimide, primidone, phenytoin, and ritabutin all induce 1A2 and could lower tacrine levels.
  - √ Anticholinergic agents can reverse tacrine's effects.
  - √ Cholinergic agents risk increased toxicity with tacrine.

Dosing of tacrine

- Start at 10 mg qid and continue 6 weeks if tolerated.
- Every 6 weeks increase each dose by 10 mg qid (40 mg total qd).
- If tolerated, go to 160 mg/day.

Most common side effects, that are greater than placebo, are flu-like without fever.

- Gastrointestinal (nausea, diarrhea, dyspepsia, anorexia)
- Myalgia

Most serious side effect, and most common reason for drop-outs, is elevation of transaminase, especially ALT/SGPT (alanine aminotransferase), but also AST/SGPT (aspartate aminotransferase).

- About 50% of patients (43% men, 54% women) have ALT > upper limit of normal (ULN).

√ Median time to > ULN is 6 weeks.

√ In 95% of patients who have > 3X ULN, this value was reached by 18 weeks.

- Need to monitor ALT weekly for 6 weeks after each dose increase.

  √ Then if stable, q 3 months ALT levels.

- If ALT > 3 to ≥ 5 X ULN, return to 40 mg.
- If ALT ≥ 5 X, stop tacrine.

Patients with too high ALT can be rechallenged later.

- With rechallenges of 40 mg, only 33% will develop elevated ALT.

Ancillary Agents for Dementia*

Antipsychotic agents may reduce agitation and confusion in dementia, although they are not a first choice for these symptoms.

- Haloperidol 0.5–2 mg po or IM q 4–6 h

  √ Bedtime dosing might help regulate sleep cycle.

  √ Low-potency neuroleptics (e.g., chlorpromazine) risk further cognitive impairment, hypotension, and possible seizure.

  √ Avoid adding an ACA, since it may augment toxicity.

  √ For agitation with psychosis, 1–3 mg daily dose is usually optimal.

Short-acting hypnoanxiolytics (lorazepam 0.5 mg po) have less drug accumulation and therefore induce less confusion than do longer-acting hypnoanxiolytics (chlordiazepoxide).

Trazodone in daily total doses between 25 and 500 mg, and buspirone in daily total doses between 10 and 60 mg, can decrease agitation and aggression without decreasing cognitive performance. (For further discussion of agents that treat agitation and aggression, see pages 233–236.)

SIDE EFFECTS

The 3 phenothiazine groups have different side-effect profiles.

- Aliphatic—chlorpramazine (Thorazine) causes more hypotension, sedation, dermatitis, and convulsions, but less EPS.
- Piperidines—thioridazine (Mellaril) and mesoridazine (Serentil) cause more ECG effects, retinal toxicity, and ejaculatory problems, but least EPS.

  √ Mesoridazine has serotonin blocking features that in theory (so far unresearched) could protect it from EPS and perhaps TD.

- Piperazines—perphenazine (Trilafon), fluphenazine (Prolixin), and trifluoperazine (Stelazine) cause more EPS but less sedation, hypotension, and lens opacities.

Comparison of Antipsychotic Side Effects

	Sedation	Anticholinergic Effects	Orthostatic Hypotension	Extrapyramidal Symptoms
Chlorpromazine	+ + + +	+ + +	+ + + +	+ +
Chlorprothixene	+ + +	+ + + +	+ + +	+ +
Clozapine*	+ + + +	+ + + +	+ + + +	+ /0
Fluphenazine	+	+	+	+ + + +
Haloperidol	+	+	+	+ + + +
Loxapine	+ +	+ +	+ + +	+ + +
Mesoridazine	+ + +	+ + + +	+ + +	+
Molindone	+ +	+ +	+	+ + +
Perphenazine	+ +	+ +	+ +	+ + +
Pimozide	+ + +	+ + +	+ +	+ + + +
Risperidone*	+	+	+ +	+ /0
Thioridazine	+ + +	+ + + +	+ + + +	+
Thiothixene	+	+	+	+ + + +
Trifluoperazine	+	+	+	+ + +

+ + + + = most; + = least; * Dystonia not seen with risperidone or clozapine.

Anticholinergic Effects

Most anticholinergic symptoms decrease in 1–4 weeks but don't completely remit. Anticholinergic actions affect many systems and produce a variety of symptoms:

- Hypotension
- Dry mouth
- Constipation
- Paralytic ileus
- Urinary hesitancy or retention
- Blurred near vision
- Dry eyes
- Narrow-angle glaucoma
- Photophobia
- Nasal congestion
- Confusion and decreased memory.

(These anticholinergic effects are discussed with their respective organ systems.) Bethanechol 10–50 mg po tid or qid can reverse peripheral but not central effects. Duration of action is 2–8 h.

Cardiovascular Effects

Orthostatic hypotension

See table (page 21) for drug rankings.

- Dizziness, lightheadedness, weakness, fainting, and syncope on standing up. Worse at times of peak blood levels.
- Management
  - √ Hypotension is more frequent with low salt intake, low fluid intake, antihypertensive agents, hypothyroidism, or stimulant withdrawal.
    - □ Correct these first.
    - □ Use least hypotensive antipsychotic drugs in these high-risk patients.
  - √ Suggest that patient stand up slowly over 15–60 seconds.
  - √ If more severe hypotension, lower head and elevate legs.
  - √ Use support hose. Since middle of the night is highest risk time, patient needs to wear hose day and night.
  - √ Use divided doses to avoid peak blood levels.
  - √ If medically serious, employ volume expanders and, if necessary,
    - □ Alpha-adrenergic pressor agents, such as metaraminol, phenylephrine, or norepinephrine.
    - □ *Do not use epinephrine or isoproteronol.*
  - √ Fludrocortisone 0.1—0.2 mg/daily.
    - □ Check electrolytes and BP regularly.

Tachycardia

- More often seen as isolated symptom without hypotension in young adults.
  - √ Stronger heart adequately compensates for BP drop.

Non-specific ECG changes and arrythymia

- Especially with thioridazine, clozapine, and pimozide.
  - √ Usually quinidine-like effects (prolonged QT and PR interval and wave).
- *Torsade de Pointes* seen with high-dose IV haloperidol that usually begins with OT interval lengthening.

Gastrointestinal Effects

Dry mouth

- Management
  - √ Sugar-free gum and sugarless candy to reduce dental cavities, thrush, and weight gain

√ Cool drinks (minimal sugar, e.g., Gatoraid, or drinks with sugar substitutes)
√ Biotène—sugar-free cool mints
√ Ice chips
√ Frequent tooth brushing
√ Wash mouth with
  □ Pilocarpine 1% solution, or
  □ Gradually dissolve (cholinergic) bethanechol 5–10 mg tablets.

Excessive salivation

- Seen most often with clozapine (32%).

Anorexia, nausea, vomiting, dyspepsia
Diarrhea (occasionally)
Constipation

- Management
  √ Increase bulk (e.g., bran, salads) and fluids (water, milk).
  √ Improve diet (e.g., prunes).
  √ Add stool softener (e.g., docusate), fiber (e.g., psyllium), or
  √ Bethanecol 10–50 mg tid-qid.

Paralytic ileus
Allergic obstructive hepatitis

- This cholestatic jaundice is much less common now than when chlorpromazine (and its impurities) was introduced.
- Occurred in < 0.1% of patients in first month of treatment.
- Rarely leads to hepatic necrosis or permanent damage.
- Reversible if drug stopped.
- Routine LFT do not predict.
- Lower risk with higher-potency neuroleptics.

Weight gain

- Due to increased appetite or decreased activity.
- More common with clozapine, chlorpromazine, chlorprothixene, thioridazine, and mesoridazine.
  √ Most common with clozapine.
    □ About 70% gain an average of 14–17 lbs in 4–6 months.

Weight loss

- Molindone can, and loxapine may, lower weight.
  √ Molindone average weight loss at 100 mg dose is 4.8 lbs in 2 months.

Renal Effects

Urinary hesitancy or *retention*

- Urinary retention increases urinary tract infections, which require periodic urinalyses and cultures.
  √ Occurs equally often in males and females.
- Management
  √ Bethanechol 10–25 mg tid-qid or 5–10 mg qd until symptom abates.
  √ May prescribe IM/SC bethanechol 5–10 mg for more serious cases.

Endocrine and Sexual Effects

Increased blood prolactin can occur with all neuroleptics except clozapine. Elevated prolactin may produce

- *Breast enlargement* and *tenderness, in women and men (gynecomastia)*
- *Galactorrhea* (rare)
- *Diminished libido*
  √ Changed quality of orgasm for men and women
  √ Diminished ability to reach orgasm
- *Amenorrhea, menstrual irregularities, delayed ovulation*
- Increased *breast cancer growth*
  √ Approximately 1/3 of breast cancers have increased growth rate with increased prolactin.
  √ In patients with these tumors, clozapine may be safer.

Management

- Bromocriptine, which inhibits prolactin secretion, exists as 2.5 mg tablets or as 5 mg capsules.
  √ Start at 1.25–2.5 mg/day.
  √ Add 2.5 mg every 3–7 days as tolerated,
  √ Until optimal dose of 5–7.5 mg/day is reached, or
  √ The therapeutic range of 2.5–15 mg/day is satisfied.
- Bromocriptine occasionally worsens psychoses.
  √ Amantadine sometimes can substitute.

Diminished sexuality

- Reported in 25% of patients taking neuroleptics.
- Affects 60% of patients on thioridazine.
- Management
  √ Cyproheptadine 2–8 mg po prn or tid
  √ Yohimbine 2.7–8.1 mg prn or tid

Retrograde ejaculation/erectile dysfunction

- May be physically painful.
- Occurs with patients on all neuroleptics, but especially common with thioridazine (other neuroleptics in parentheses). Also
  - √ 44% had difficulties achieving an erection (19%).
  - √ 35% had troubles maintaining an erection (11%).
  - √ 49% had "changes" in erections (0%).

Priapism

- Occurs most often with alpha$_2$ adrenergic blockade (e.g., low-potency antipsychotics).

Hypoglycemia, hyperglycemia, glycosuria, high or prolonged glucose tolerance tests

Hematologic Effects

Agranulocytosis (Schultz syndrome)

- Agranulocytosis is a granulocyte count (polys 4 bands) < 500/mm^3.
- Occurs suddenly, often within hours, usually in the first month of treatment, but can erupt any time during the initial 12 weeks of therapy.
- Arises in < 0.02% of patients on neuroleptics.
- Results most frequently with clozapine (1.3% over 1 year) and chlorpromazine (0.7%).
  - √ Extremely rare with high-potency neuroleptics.
- Statistically, more frequent in white females over 40 y.o.
- Major signs are
  - √ Acute sore throat
  - √ High fever
  - √ Mouth sores and ulcers
- Also possible are
  - √ Upset stomach
  - √ Weakness, lethargy, malaise
  - √ Lymphadenopathy
  - √ Asthma
  - √ Skin ulcerations
  - √ Laryngeal, angioneurotic, or peripheral edema
  - √ Anaphylactic reactions
- Management
  - √ Do not start any patient on low-potency neuroleptic if WBC is < 3000–3500/mm^3.

√ With onset of sore throat and fever, *stop* all non-life sustaining drugs (e.g., neuroleptics).
√ Routine or frequent CBCs do not help, except with clozapine.
• Mortality high if drug not ceased and treatment initiated.

Clozapine-induced agranulocytosis—special considerations:

• High risk groups include
  √ Women twice as often as men
  √ Lower baseline WBC counts
  √ Over 40 y.o. but may be < 21 y.o.
  √ Ashkenazi Jews with specific HLA haplotype
• Cumulative incidence over time of 73 patients who developed agranulocytosis
  √ 2 months—31%
  √ 3 months—84%
  √ 6 months—96%

Agranulocytosis prodrome (time from first WBC drop to agranulocytosis):

• Mean—28 days
• 28% dropped abruptly in 8 days or less.

May be 2 types of neutropenia.

• 500–1500/m^2 neutrophils ↓
  √ Probably 2° to destruction in blood or spleen
  √ Recovery usually asymptomatic in 3–7 days after clozapine dcd.
• < 500/m^3 neutrophils
  √ Neutrophil precursor production stopped.
  √ Recovery in 14–22 days (mean = 16 days)
    □ Risks neutropenic sepsis.
    □ Count may initially fall further after clozapine dcd.

Treatment of agranulocytosis

• Hematopoietic growth factors (e.g., granulocyte colony stimulating factor and granulocyte-macrophage colony stimulating factor) given 48 h after onset.
  √ Both accelerate recovery in mean of 8 days.

Starting clozapine contraindicated if

• WBC < 3500/m^3 or neutrophils < 1500/m^3
• These limitations include those with benign neutropenia, cancer chemotherapy, or HIV infection.

Clozapine WBC monitoring

- Weekly while on drug and for 4 weeks after dc.
- Patient must report any sign of infection (e.g., lethargy, weakness, fever, sore throat).
- Sandoz controls protocol (e.g., when to increase monitoring and when to stop medication).

Leukopenia

- WBC from 2000–3500/mm^3
- Usually gradual and without symptoms, and
- More common than agranulocytosis,
   √ Usually transient

Management

- Symptoms may be similar to agranulocytosis
- If no symptoms and not severe, wait and repeat labs.
- If more severe, reduce or stop antipsychotic.

Eyes, Ears, Nose, and Throat Effects

Blurred vision

- Difficulty for vision close up, not far away
- Management
   √ Pilocarpine 1% eye drops or
   √ Bethanechol 5–30 mg po effective for 2–8 h.
   √ Eye glasses can be used temporarily, but they need frequent changing.

Photophobia

- Pupils dilated by anticholinergic effects.

Pigmentation

- Long-term neuroleptic use, especially chlorpromazine, places granular deposits chiefly in the back of the cornea and the front of the lens.
   √ Star-shaped opacities in front of the lens indicate a more advanced case.
- Pigmentation probably is dose-dependent.
- Vision usually unimpaired.
   √ Eye pigmentation often co-exists with neuroleptic-induced skin pigmentation or photosensitivity reactions.
- Eye pigmentation does not require slit-lamp examination,
   √ But if shining a light into the eye displays an opaque pupil, patient should consult ophthalmologist.

Pigmentary retinopathy

- Caused almost always by chronic use of > 800 mg/day of thioridazine.
- Reduced visual acuity and blindness.
- Management
  - √ Stop thioridazine.
  - √ Symptoms may disappear, if caught early.
  - √ *Never* prescribe > 800 mg/day of thioridazine for more than a few days.

Dry eyes

- This anticholinergic disturbance particularly bothers the elderly or those wearing contact lenses.
- Management
  - √ Artificial tears
    - □ Employ cautiously with soft contact lenses or
    - □ Apply patient's usual wetting solution or comfort drops.
  - √ Bethanachol 5–30 mg po.

Narrow-angle glaucoma

- Highly anticholinergic neuroleptics can trigger narrow-angle glaucoma.
- A h/o eye or facial pain, blurred vision, or halos circling outside lights suggest acute narrow-angle glaucoma.
  - √ When shining a penlight across the eye's anterior chamber, if the entire eye does not illuminate, suspect narrow-angle glaucoma.

Nasal congestion, dry throat

Dry bronchial secretions and *strained breathing* aggravate patients with respiratory ailments.

Skin, Allergies, and Temperature Effects

Photosensitivity

- Chlorpromazine, and other neuroleptics, foster severe sunburn after 30–60 minutes of direct sunlight.
- Management
  - √ Cautious exposure to the sun and
  - √ Apply sun screens with high UV^{β} blocking.

Skin rashes

- Seborrheic dermatitis highly associated with Parkinsonian signs.
  - √ As high as 60% in this group.
  - √ Treat with appropriate soaps, lotions, and shampoos.

- Check nature and distribution R/O contact dermatitis.
  - √ If only on neck or wrists, probably need new soap.
- Stop neuroleptic if not contact dermatitis.

Hypothermia more common than *hyperthermia.*

Management

- Warn patients in advance so they can protect themselves.
- Proper heated (or cooled) environment.
- Avoid overexercising or working in hot places.
- Fluids, etc.

Decreased sweating

- May cause a secondary, and sometimes fatal, hyperthermia.
- Be careful with patients who
  - √ Work in hot weather,
  - √ Take neuroleptics with high-anticholinergic effects,
  - √ Drink excessive alcohol, or
  - √ Suffer from CNS disease.

Central Nervous System Effects

See table (page 21) for drug EPS rankings.

- Low serum iron has been reported as common in patients with akathisia, dystonic reactions, and neuroleptic malignant syndrome.
  - √ Anecdotal evidence suggests measuring this (serum ferritin) and correcting with supplemental iron, if needed.
    - □ May improve EPS.
- Atypical neuroleptics
  - √ Clozapine infrequently causes EPS and perhaps never TD.
  - √ Risperidone causes EPS in doses over 6 mg.
  - √ Risperidone cause EPS at lower doses in high-risk patients, including
    - □ Geriatric patients
    - □ Parkinson's patients
    - □ Adolescent patients
    - □ Bipolar patients on lithium
    - □ Patients on SSRIs.
  - √ Dyskinesia has been observed following risperidone withdrawal.

A
N
T
I
P
S
Y
C
H
O
T
I
C

A
G
E
N
T
S

Types of Extrapyramidal Symptoms

Type	Onset	Risk Groups	Clinical Course
Dystonia*	8 h–5 days	Young males (under 30 y.o.) and females (under 25 y.o.)	Acute, spasmodic, painful; usually remits spontaneously in 10 days; can be prevented with ACA.
Parkinsonism	5 h–30 days	12–45% of patients; elderly, particularly women	Occurs throughout treatment.
Akathisia*	2 h–60 days	20–50% of patients, 35–50 y.o., women and men	Persists during treatment; propranolol and amantadine may be more effective than ACA.
Neuroleptic malignant syndrome (NMS)*	Weeks	0.5–1% of patients; 80% are under 40; affects 2X men as women; high-potency neuroleptics	Mortality rate is 20–30%; symptoms typically persist 5–10 days on oral forms and 20–30 days after depot injections.
"Rabbit" syndrome	Months— years	4% of patients untreated with ACAs	Usually reversible with ACAs.
Tardive dyskinesia (TD)	Months— years	20–30% of patients with range of 0.5–60%; women, the elderly, and patients with mood or CNS disorders.	Treat best with prevention; 50% irreversible; vitamin E 400 mg tid or qid may help. ACAs usually hurt.
Tardive dystonia	Months— years (avg. 2–5 yrs)	< 2% of patients; men, younger 40 y.o.	May start with blephanospasm; seldom remits; may partially respond to ACAs.

* Risk is substantially increased by rapid dosage increase of neuroleptic.

Dystonia

- Acute contractions of tongue, face, neck, and back.
  - √ Patient may describe stiff tongue as a "thick" tongue.
- Spasms of tongue, jaw, and neck are the first to erupt, typically in a few hours or days.
- Other dystonic symptoms include
  - √ *Opisthotonos*, a tetanic tightening of the entire body with head, back, and belly up
  - √ *Oculogyric crisis* with eyes locked upward
  - √ *Laryngospasm* with respiratory difficulties
  - √ *Torticollis*—a twisting of cervical muscles with an unnatural head position.
- When less severe, patient has some voluntary control, as with normal eye blinking.
  - √ Voluntary control does not mean patient faking.

- More common with manics (26%) than with schizophrenics (6%).
- So common (>70%) with high-potency neuroleptics in males under 30 and females under 25 that prophylactic treatment with anticholinergic advised for 10 days if high-potency agent started.
- Generally self-limited duration 10–14 days.

Parkinsonism (a.k.a. pseudoparkinsonism)

- Symptoms include:
  - √ Decreased arm swing
    - □ Often the first sign and easiest to detect.
  - √ Stiffness, stooped posture
  - √ Masklike faces
  - √ Bradykinesia
  - √ Shuffling, festinating gait (with small steps)
  - √ Cogwheel rigidity
  - √ Drooling, seborrhea
  - √ Tremor
  - √ Coarse pill-rolling of thumb and fingers at rest
  - √ Micrographia
- In elderly, check for signs of Parkinsonism *before* treatment.
  - √ Shuffling gait, stooped posture, bradykinesia, increased extremity tone, and decreased facial mobility are not rare baseline signs in this population.
- Parkinsonism contributes to passive inactivity, which can be misdiagnosed as catatonia; withdrawn, negative symptom, schizophrenia; or depression.
- Case reports suggest that pyridoxine 50 mg bid may help drug-induced Parkinsonism.
- Treat by
  - √ Lowering dose, or
  - √ Switching to lower-risk EPS drug, or
  - √ Adding anticholinergic agent, or
  - √ Adding amantadine.

Akinesia

Symptoms include
  - √ Paucity of spontaneous gestures or voluntary useful movements.
  - √ Apathy
  - √ Rigid posture
  - √ Diminished, or total lack of, conversation
  - √ Arm swing decreased
  - √ Walk with a shorter stride

- May or may not be associated with Parkinsonism.
  - √ Sedation 12 h after last dose suggests akinesia.
  - √ Absence of leg crossing also indicates akinesia.
- First approach to akinesia is to lower neuroleptic dose,
  - √ Then add ACAs, if needed.

Akathisia

- The least obvious, but the most prevalent EPS, is akathisia.
- The most common side effect that causes patients to stop neuroleptics.
- Symptoms include
  - √ Motor, inner-driven restlessness
  - √ The "jitters," fidgety," or "inner itch"
  - √ Tapping feet incessantly, "restless legs"
  - √ Rocking forward and backward in chair
  - √ Shifting weight from side to side when standing
  - √ Standing and sitting
- May present as a muscular discomfort in an agitated, frightened, dysphoric, pacing, hand-wringing, and weeping individual.
- Patients might not notice, or be bothered by, their regular, rhythmic leg-jiggling.
- Differs from restless legs syndrome (RLS). Frequent features of RLS, rarely seen in akathisia, include
  - √ Restlessness restricted to legs
  - √ Unpleasant sensory symptoms in calves
  - √ Myoclonic jerks
  - √ Insomnia
  - √ Worse, or only occurs, in evenings
  - √ Worse on lying, relief with walking
  - √ Responds best to benzodiazepines, L-dopa, and bromocriptine.
- Akathisia can be misdiagnosed as anxiety or psychotic agitation.
  - √ Important to know patient's presentation before medication is started.
  - √ If diagnosis is unclear, ask patient if restlessness is a "muscle" feeling or a "head" feeling; the muscle feeling often experienced in the limbs suggests akathisia; the head feeling, anxiety.
  - √ Myoclonic jerks sometimes accompany akathisia.
  - √ May only be a subjective state with no observable behaviors.
- Treat with propranolol, amantadine, or benzodiazepine (see Chapter 2).
  - √ Anticholinergic agents may be less effective.

Neuroleptic malignant syndrome (NMS)

- Uncommon, yet hardly rare, disorder; potentially fatal, unless recognized and treated early.
- NMS affects 1% of patients treated with antipsychotics.
- Typically erupts in 24–72 h.
- Deaths, which usually result in 3–30 days, occur in 11–18% of NMS patients.
    - √ Estimated that 1,000–4,000 NMS fatalities happen in America every year.

DSM-IV Research Criteria for NMS*

A. The development of severe muscle rigidity and elevated temperature associated with the use of neuroleptic medication.

B. Two or more of the items labeled (B) below. NMS symptoms are not accounted for, or due to, another substance, general medical condition, or mental disorder.

- NMS displays
    - √ Severe parkinsonism with
        - □ Muscle (akinesiac) rigidity, catatonic appearance (A)
        - □ Tremors (B), dyskinesias
        - □ Akinesias, "lead-pipe" muscle tone
        - □ Flexor-extensor posturing
        - □ Festinating gait.
    - √ Hyperpyrexia (101° F→ 107° F) (A)
    - √ Altered consciousness, which may present first, can be
        - □ Alert look
        - □ Dazed mutism (B)
        - □ Agitated, confused, or comatose (B)
        - □ Obtunded (B), incontinent (B), or
    - √ Autonomic dysfunction with
        - □ Tachycardia (> 130 beats/minute) (B)
        - □ Increased BP (> 20 points diastolic) or labile (B)
        - □ Profuse sweating (B), more salivation
        - □ Tachypnea (> 25 respirations/minute)
        - □ Pallor, or
        - □ Dysphagia (B).
    - √ Severe abnormalities on laboratory tests
        - □ Evidence of severe muscle damage with high creatine phosphokinase (CPK 347 → 4286 U/ml) or myoglobinuria (B)
        - □ Renal decline or failure

---

* (A)—in criteria A *DSM-IV*.
  (B)—criteria B *DSM-IV*.

ANTIPSYCHOTIC AGENTS

▫ Raised WBCs (15,000–30,000/mm^3) (B), and/or
▫ Often elevated LFTs.

Hyperthermia in NMS differs from other drug-induced hyperthermic syndromes. Each of the following has hyperthermia but with different symptoms than NMS hyperthermia.

Anticholinergic syndrome

* Dry skin
* Pupil dilation
* Hyperreflexia
* Muscle relaxation

Metabolic hyperthermia from drugs (e.g., lidocaine, meperidine, NSAID toxicity) or metabolism (e.g., hyperthyroidism)

* No muscle effects

Autonomic hyperreflexia from CNS stimulants (e.g., amphetamine)

* Hyperreflexia

NMS more common with

* Patients under 20 and over 60 y.o. have higher mortality rates from NMS.
* Patients with CNS syndromes, mental retardation, and drug addiction have greater fatality rates from NMS.
* High neuroleptic doses, another reason to generally avoid them.
* Rapid neuroleptization
  √ Another reason not to use this approach.
* Depot antipsychotic agents generate more NMS, but the same number of deaths from NMS.
* Higher- rather than lower-potency antipsychotics, although greater use of high-potency drugs, may inflate the frequency.
  √ If NMS with low-potency drug, generally higher fatality.
  √ One-third of NMS patients develop it again if placed on any antipsychotic.
* Lithium.
  √ Risk factor may be mood disorder.
* Low serum iron.
  √ Cause vs. effect of NMS not resolved.
* High ambient temperatures.
  √ More often in summer.
* Dehydration.
* Taking 2 or more neuroleptics.

Fatalities from NMS in percentage of patients who developed NMS on a specific antipsychotic are

- Trifluoperazine (43%)
- Chlorpromazine (40%)
- Thiothixene (40%)
- Fluphenazine (depot) (33.3%)
- Fluphenazine (8.3%)
- Haloperidol (5.5%)
- Thioridazine (0.0%)

Supportive measures must be instituted immediately.

- Stop neuroleptics and anticholinergic agents.
- Maintain hydration by oral or IV routes.
- Correct electrolyte abnormalities.
- Use antipyretic agents.
- Cool body to reduce fever.
- Diagnose and treat pneumonia or pulmonary emboli.
- If patient has survived and requires antipsychotic agents, they may be re-introduced cautiously.
- No drug treatment has been proven to be more effective than intensive supportive measures.
- One study compared supportive care with supportive care plus dantrolene alone, bromocriptine alone, or dantrolene/bromocriptine combined.
  - √ All treatments showed improvement within 2–4 days after neuroleptic was stopped.
  - √ Duration of NMS with supportive treatment was 5–14 days.
  - √ Duration of NMS with drug treatments was longer, averaging 14 days.
    - □ 20% lasted 4 weeks or more.
    - □ 30% of bromocriptine-treated patients had recurrence of NMS signs when bromocriptine reduced.
- For patients not markedly better after a few days of intensive supportive treatment, consider drug treatments, including
  - √ Bromocriptine
    - □ Rigidity quickly disappears.
    - □ Temperature, BP instability, and creatine kinase levels normalize after a few days.
    - □ Safest drug treatment for NMS.
  - √ Dantrolene
    - □ Lowers hyperthermia and creatine kinase, while increasing muscle relaxation, often in hours.
    - □ Initial dose may be 2–3 mg/kg/day.
    - □ Hepatic toxicity occurs with doses > 10 mg/kg/day.
- ACAs do not help.

Neuroleptic rechallenge after prior NMS

- High (> 80%) success rates reported.
- Best chances of success (no NMS) with
  - √ 2 or more week wait after the last clinical sign of NMS.
  - √ Start with low doses and very gradual dose increases.
    - ▫ Low-potency antipsychotics may be safer, but this is unproven.
  - √ Keep patient well-hydrated.
  - √ Keep room temperatures cool.
  - √ Monitor temperature and other vital signs frequently.
  - √ Check WBC and CPK regularly.

Drugs Used to Treat NMS

Generic Name	Dose
Anticholinergic agents	——
Bromocriptine	7.5–60 mg/day po
Dantrolene	0.8–10 mg/kg/IV; 50 mg qd-qid po
Levodopa	100 mg bid po
Carbidopa-levodopa	25 mg tid-200 qid po
Amantadine	100 mg bid po
Lorazepam	1.5–2 mg IV, then po

"Rabbit syndrome" (a.k.a., perioral tremor)

- Arises late during neuroleptic treatment.
- Consists of rapid lip (typically a 5 Hz tremor) and buccal masticatory movements that mimic a rabbit.
- Unlike TD, continues during sleep.
- Responds well to ACAs.

Tardive dyskinesia (TD)

- Consists of involuntary face, trunk, and limb movements.
- Arises after 6–36 months of treatment.
- May also appear when antipsychotic is lowered or stopped.
  - √ Symptoms emerge in weeks or months.
  - √ Rarely occurs before 3 months.
  - √ Often seen while still on full antipsychotic dose.
  - √ Severity often reaches a plateau after 3–6 years and may not worsen further.
- Drug-induced rate may be lower than suspected because spontaneous dyskinesias occur in 15% of chronic untreated schizophrenics.
  - √ Risk factors for spontaneous dyskinesia include

- Prominent negative symptoms, deficit form of schizophrenia
- Lower premorbid IQ
- Hebephrenic subtype (46% prevalence)
- Drug-induced frequency varies enormously between studies.
  - ✓ Probably closest to 15% (over spontaneous dyskinesia rate) in patients treated with antipsychotics for over 2 years.
  - ✓ Most cases mild.
  - ✓ 2–5% of patients get severe symptoms.
  - ✓ Once TD syndrome manifests, it doesn't usually progress.
  - ✓ Dyskinesia of some type affects 1–5% of nonschizophrenics *never* exposed to neuroleptics.
    - Particularly the elderly.
  - ✓ Dyskinesia affects 15% of untreated chronic schizophrenics.
- Initially appears milder in people consuming larger neuroleptic doses, which mask TD.
- Risk factors include
  - ✓ Longer use and higher dose equivalents of neuroleptics.
  - ✓ Being female over 40 y.o.
  - ✓ Being male under 30 y.o.
  - ✓ Mood disorder
    - May be 2° to intermittent neuroleptic use.
  - ✓ African genetics
  - ✓ Brain impairment.
  - ✓ Diabetes (2 × higher).
  - ✓ Prior EPS symptoms.
    - However, TD can occur when EPS has never occurred.
- TD presents with 3 major types of symptoms
  - ✓ *Facial-lingual-oral involuntary hyperkinesis* (most common type)
    - Frowning, blinking, smiling, grimacing, puckering, pouting, blowing, smacking, licking, chewing, clenching, mouth opening, rolling and protruding ("fly catcher's") tongue, and spastic facial distortions.
  - ✓ *Limb choreoathetoid movements*
    - Choreic movements that are rapid, purposeless, irregular, and spontaneous.
    - Athetoid movements that are slow, irregular, complex, and serpentine.
    - Tremors that are repetitive, regular, and rhythmic.
    - Lateral knee movements.
    - Foot tapping, squirming, inversion, and eversion.
  - ✓ *Trunk movements*
    - Movements of neck, shoulders, dramatic hip jerks.
    - Rocking, twisting, squirming, pelvic gyrations, and thrusts.
- Alternatively, patients may experience

- √ Tardive akathisia (with persistent restless feelings),
- √ Tardive dystonia (with recurrent muscle contractions of neck and shoulders),
  - □ Bipolars have 2-fold higher risk.
- √ Tardive tics.
- TD patients may
  - √ Grunt,
  - √ Suppress symptoms temporarily by intense voluntary effort and concentration,
  - √ Exacerbate symptoms under stress, or
  - √ Have symptoms disappear while asleep.
- All neuroleptics can cause TD, except perhaps clozapine.
  - √ Risperidone theoretically has lower TD risk.
    - □ Withdrawal dyskinesia seen.
  - √ Other drugs may generate TD, such as
    - □ Amoxapine, an antidepressant;
    - □ Dopamine-blocking antiemetic, e.g., prochlorperazine (Compazine), metoclopramide (Reglan), promethazine (Phenergan), trimethobenzamide (Tigan), thiethylperazine (Torecan), triflupromazine (Vesprin).
- Make sure "TD" does not stem from ill-fitting dentures!
- Prevention best treats TD.
  - √ Regularly monitor patients on antipsychotics with a standardized TD assessment scale, such as the Abnormal Involuntary Movement Scale (AIMS).
  - √ Neuroleptics should not be used longer than 6 continuous months in nonschizophrenic patients who do not have chronic psychotic symptoms or high risk of relapse.
  - √ Assess long-treated patients at least every 6 months to see if neuroleptics can be reduced or stopped.
  - √ May vary over time from remission to exacerbation and back to remission.
  - √ If antipsychotic discontinued and TD emerges, allow at least 3–7 months for symptoms to disappear or lessen on their own.
    - □ Spontaneous remission rate in 6 months about 50%.
    - □ After 6 months spontaneous remission rate for 10 yrs about 2.5–5% a year.
    - □ After 18 months, abnormal movements diminish by mean of 50%.
  - √ ACAs and amantadine do not usually alleviate TD and often aggravate it.
  - √ Neuroleptics can temporarily mask TD, but symptoms eventually re-emerge, frequently worse.
  - √ Lacking convincing evidence, drugs that might inhibit TD include:

- Vitamin E 1200–1600 mg qd, strongest evidence of efficacy compared to placebo, particularly in cases with TD under 5 yrs. Not curative; symptoms return 12 weeks after Vitamin E stopped.
- Amantadine (100 mg bid-tid)
- Baclofen (5–20 mg tid)
- Benzodiazepines (e.g., diazepam, clonazepam)
- Bromocriptine 2.5 mg/day helped in placebo-controlled trial, perhaps by preferentially stimulating autoreceptors.
- Buspirone (45–120 mg/day)
- Calcium channel-blockers (Verapamil 160–320 mg qd, Diltiazem 120–240 mg qd)
- Carbamazepine (100–800 mg/day)
- Choline (2–8 grams/day)
- Clonidine (0.3–0.7 mg/day)
- Lecithin (10–40 grams/day)
- Levodopa (100–2000 mg/day)
- Lithium (300 mg tid-qid)
- Reserpine (1–6 mg/day)
- Valproic acid (1000–1500 mg/day)

Seizures

- Uncommon,
- Flair up by raising (especially abruptly) or lowering antipsychotics, and
- More common with clozapine.
  - √ Dose related:
    - 1–2% with < 300 mg qd
    - 3–4% with 300–500 mg qd
    - 5% with 600–900 mg qd.
  - √ In patients on > 300 mg clozapine, 65% have abnormal EEGs.
  - √ Increased risk with large single doses;
    - Lower risk with tid or qid dosing.
  - √ Increased risk with high plasma levels.
    - Obtain plasma levels in high seizure-risk patients.
- Less common with molindone and fluphenazine.
- Seizures common in epileptics, although epileptics can usually tolerate neuroleptics without seizures.

Sedation

See table (page 21) for drug sedation rankings.

- Sedation declines during first 2 weeks of therapy.
- Management
  - √ Prescribe full dose at bedtime.

√ Diminish daytime doses.

√ Switch to less sedating neuroleptic.

Tardive dystonia

- Tardive dystonia consists of sustained or repetitious contractions of one or more muscle groups.
  - √ Like tardive dyskinesia, occurs after prolonged neuroleptic exposure.
    - □ Appears while on medication or after withdrawal.
- Differs from tardive dyskinesia:
  - √ Occurs more often in men.
  - √ Occurs after a relatively short history of exposure.
    - □ Average < 2.5 years
  - √ Often causes significant disability.
  - √ Rarely remits.
  - √ May partially respond to anticholinergic agents.
  - √ May first present with blepharospasm.

Confusion, delirium, disturbed concentration, disorientation, memory impairment

- This toxicity occurs more often in high doses of low-potency antipsychotics, in patients already on a drug with anticholinergic effects (see Chapter 2, pages 61, 69), and in the elderly.
- To ensure that it is an *anticholinergic toxicity*, should see
  - √ Dilated pupils
  - √ Hot, dry skin
  - √ Dry mucous membranes
  - √ Tachycardia
  - √ Absent bowel sounds
- Memory impairment alone can occur without other signs of toxicity.
- Can be a medical emergency.
- Management
  - √ Stop all neuroleptic and antiparkinsonian agents.
  - √ If medical emergency, IM/IV physostigmine can diagnose and treat this toxicity.
  - √ Physostigmine's (cholinergic) risks include
    - □ Increased salivation, sweating, bradycardia, abdominal cramps, desire to urinate or defecate, seizures;
    - □ Transient sinus arrest in cardiac patients;
    - □ Bronchospasm in asthmatics.
  - √ Before and after injecting physostigmine, obtain BP and pulse rate.
  - √ Give 1–2 mg IM/IV physostigmine no faster than 1 mg/minute.

√ Anticholinergic delirium clears in 15–20 minutes after injection.

  □ Physostigmine's effect lasts 30–60 minutes.

  □ If patient does not improve with 1 mg of physostigmine, may repeat 1 mg dose in 30–40 minutes.

  □ May inject up to 4 mg IV of physostigmine in one day.

√ Switch to less anticholinergic neuroleptic and/or, if an ACA, switch to amantadine.

√ If patient is agitated during anticholinergic delirium, may use lorazepam to calm, since it is shorter-acting benzodiazepine without significant anticholinergic activity.

Side Effects from Depot Neuroleptics

Side Effects	Fluphenazine Decanoate (FD)	Fluphenazine Enanthate (FE)	Haloperidol Decanoate (HD)
Anticholinergic	Occasional	More anticholinergic than FD	Occasional
Cardiovascular	Hypotension occasionally; some hypertension reported	Hypotension and no severe hypertension reported at start of therapy	Occasional hypotension
Weight gain	11% of patients had a 10% weight increase; 4 times more patients gain weight than on oral fluphenazine	Similar to FD	Weight loss and weight gain noted
Endocrine effects	Menstrual disturbances, galactorrhea, amenorrhea	Same as FD	Same as FD
Eye changes	17% (11/63) of patients after 5 years displayed lens and/or corneal opacities	None reported	None reported
Skin and local reactions	One case of induration at high doses; skin reactions arise	No indurations reported; skin reactions occur	Inflammation at injection site; "tracks" observed
EPS	EPS frequent, FD > HD; 25% have dystonias; NMS more common than with po forms	EPS more frequent (30–50%) than with FD, but 11.7% have dystonias; more NMS than po forms	EPS common, but equal to po form; TD in HD > FD; more NMS than with po form
CNS	Drowsiness and insomnia	Same as FD	Same as FD
Mood	May increase depression in vulnerable patients	Same as FD	No data
Laboratory changes	One case of jaundice; ECG changes noted	No account of jaundice; some ECG changes	Within normal variation

PERCENTAGES OF SIDE EFFECTS

Part I

Side Effects	Chlorpro- mazine	Clozapine	Fluphen- azine	Haloperidol
CARDIOVASCULAR EFFECTS				
Hypotension	6	9 (0.55–13)	0.79	1
Hypertension	0.0	3.5	—	1
Dizziness, light- headedness	10 (6–14)	19 (1.7–22)	7	14 (10–30)
Fainting, syncope	3	6 (0.62–7)	—	2
Tachycardia	11 (10–30)	22	2 (5.3–25)	1
ECG abnormalities	20	1.0 (0.17–1)	2	< 2
Cardiac arrhythmias	6	—	—	< 2
Sweating	9	7.3		15
GASTROINTESTINAL EFFECTS				
Dry mouth and throat	23 (10–30)	6.6	8	13 (10–30)
Anorexia, lower appetite	2 (0.5–0.29)	0.6	—	0.0
Nausea, vomiting	6	4.4 (1.1–11)	4.3	6
Diarrhea	1.1	1.1	1.1	—
Constipation	13	14 (1.9–16)	9.6	6
Jaundice	0.64	1	0.0	< 2
Salivation	11	32	—	16
Weight gain	13.3 (0–30)	67 1	16.0	3
Edema	2.8	(0.73–3)	0.0	—
RENAL EFFECTS				
Urinary hesitancy or retention	3	2	1.3	1.5
Enuresis	—	1	—	—
ENDOCRINE AND SEXUAL EFFECTS				
Menstrual changes	16.3	—	4.4	—
Breast swelling	1.1	—	2.2	—
Lactation	0.72	—	3.3	—
Inhibited ejaculation	6	1	2	< 2
Disturbed sexual function	—	0.19	—	—

Side Effects	Chlorpro- mazine	Clozapine	Fluphen- azine	Haloperidol
HEMATOLOGIC EFFECTS				
Agranulocytosis	0.67 (0.32–1.1)	0.9 (0.004–3.0)	—	—
Leukopenia	3 (1–10)	2.7 (0.63–3.0)	1	—
EYES, EARS, NOSE, AND THROAT EFFECTS				
Blurred vision	14.4	5	4.3	6.8
Lenticular pigmen- tation	6	—	< 2	< 2
Pigmentary retin- opathy	6	0.0	< 2	0.0
Nasal stuffiness	2.5	1	9.2	15
SKIN, ALLERGIES, AND TEMPERATURE				
Allergies	6.6	0.1	2.6	0.0
Photosensitivity	6	—	< 2	< 2
Rashes	4	1.5	< 2	1.2
Abnormal skin pigment	15	—	< 2	< 2
Fever, hyperthermia	1	5.3 (1–13)	—	1
CENTRAL NERVOUS SYSTEM SYSTEM EFFECTS				
Dystonia	3	0.0	5 (2.5–8)	30 (16–65)
Parkinsonism	12.5	6	15.4	> 30
Akinesia	10	4 (0.36–5.0)	—	16
Akathisia	8.4 (6–12.1)	3.5	21.6	29
NMS	0.6	—	0.5	0.9
Weakness	1	1	—	1
Rigidity	6	3	—	30
Seizures	1 (0.5–1.5)	2.3 (0.36–5)	0.0	1
Headache	8	5.9 (0.86–7)	—	6
Slurred speech	1	1	—	0.0
Tremor	12	7	—	25
Drowsiness, fatigue	39.8 (23.4–50)	39 (9–44)	16.2 (13–19.5)	21.8 (2–39)
Confusion, disori- entation	6.8 (5–6.8)	2.4 (0.74–4)	—	4
Insomnia	22	3 (0.19–6)	—	36
Restlessness, agitation (motoric)	8	5	—	24
Anxiety, nervousness (mental)	10	2	—	24
Excitement	0.5	2	—	12
Depression	13.9	1	—	—

Part II

Side Effect	Loxapine	Mesori-dazine	Molin-done	Perphen-azine	Pimozide
CARDIOVASCULAR AND RESPIRATORY					
Hypotension	20	8.4 (1–11.7)	6	4	7
Dizziness	20	8 (1–10.2)	20	12	12 (0–30)
Tachycardia	20	1.8	< 2	—	6
ECG abnormalities	< 2	20	< 2	—	6
Cardiac arrhythmias	—	—	—	—	< 2
GASTROINTESTINAL EFFECTS					
Dry mouth and throat	20 (10–30)	13.7	20 (7.4–30)	18.8	22.5
Anorexia, lower appetite	—	—	—	4.2	—
Increased appetite	—	—	—	—	5
Nausea, vomiting	—	2.3	—	0.9	0.0
Taste changes	—	—	—	—	5
Diarrhea	—	—	—	—	5
Constipation	—	10 (1–20)	—	4.2	20
Jaundice	< 2	< 1	< 2	0.0	—
Thirst	—	—	—	—	5
Weight gain	2	20	< 2	5.9	4
Edema	—	—	—	0.8	—
RENAL EFFECTS					
Urinary hesitancy or retention	15	5	15	—	15
ENDOCRINE AND SEXUAL EFFECTS					
Menstrual changes	—	5	—	—	0.0
Breast swelling	—	5	—	—	0.0
Lactation	—	—	—	0.9	15
Inhibited ejaculation	6	—	—	—	—
Disturbed sexual function	—	5.5	—	—	15
HEMATOLOGIC EFFECTS					
Agranulocytosis	—	—	—	0.0	—
Leukopenia	< 2	—	—	—	—
EYES, EARS, NOSE, AND THROAT EFFECTS					
Lenticular pigmentation	< 2	—	—	—	< 2
Increased light sensitivity	—	—	—	—	5
Blurred vision	15	8.9 (2.8–20)	15	17.8	20
Nasal stuffiness	20	20	20	18	20

Side Effect	Loxapine	Mesori-dazine	Molin-done	Perphen-azine	Pimozide
SKIN, ALLERGIES, AND TEMPERATURE					
Allergies	—	—	—	0.8	—
Photosensitivity	< 2	—	—	—	< 2
Rashes	6	5.5	6	—	6
Itch	—	0.9	—	—	—
CENTRAL NERVOUS SYSTEM EFFECTS					
Dystonia	14 (8–30)	3.4 (1.7–5)	> 30	4.2 (2.8–5.6)	16.3 (10–30)
Parkinsonism	23	5.5	> 30	21.1	16.3
Akinesia	—	—		—	26.3
Akathisia	24 (17–30)	0.8	> 30	27.3	19.9 (7.3–40)
NMS	—	—	—	0.5	—
Weakness	—	9.5	—	—	—
Muscle cramps	—	—	—	—	15
Rigidity	—	1.4	—	—	10
Seizures	1.8	—	< 2	0.7	6
Headache	—	—	—	—	5
Slurred speech	—	1.4	—	—	10
Tremors	—	4	—	—	—
Drowsiness, fatigue	24 (16–30)	15.7 (6–25)	> 30	16.3	36.3 (10–70)
Insomnia	—	—	—	—	10
Agitaton, restlessness (motoric)	—	1.5	—	—	5
Depression	—	—	—	6.2	10

Part III

Side Effects	Risperidone	Thioridazine	Thiothixene	Trifluoperazine
CARDIOVASCULAR EFFECTS				
Hypotension	16	> 30	11.2	2.4 (0.8–4)
Dizziness	42.3	23.3	18 (21.2–35)	28.1
Tachycardia	3	6	6	—
ECG abnormalities	2.1	15	< 2	6
Cardiac arrhythmias	< 1	15	< 2	—
GASTROINTESTINAL EFFECTS				
Dry mouth and throat	>1	28.1	12	2.3
Anorexia, lower appetite	>1	0.0	—	27.7 (12.3–43)

Side Effects	Risperidone	Thioridazine	Thiothixene	Trifluoperazine
Nausea, vomiting	6	9.3	—	2.4
Diarrhea	> 1	3.3	—	1.1
Constipation	7	16.8	—	1.1
Jaundice	—	< 2	< 2	0.0
Weight gain	18	15	20	5.6
Edema	< 1	2.3	—	1.4
RENAL EFFECTS				
Urinary hesitancy or retention	< 0.1	22 (5.5–30)	12	0.6
ENDOCRINE AND SEXUAL EFFECTS				
Menstrual changes	> 1	3.3	—	4.4
Breast swelling	< 1	0.6	—	—
Lactation	< 1	3.1	—	—
Inhibited ejaculation	< 1	37 (10–44)	< 2	—
Disturbed sexual function	> 1	—	—	3.4
HEMATOLOGIC EFFECTS				
Agranulocytosis	0.0	0.0	—	—
Leukopenia	< 1	—	< 2	—
EYES, EARS, NOSE, AND THROAT EFFECTS				
Lenticular pigmentation	0.0	0.0	6	—
Blurred vision	2	18.1	5	4
Nasal stuffiness	10	20	20	3
SKIN, ALLERGIES, AND TEMPERATURE				
Allergies	< 0.1	3.2	—	4.2
Photosensitivity	> 1	6	< 2	6
Rashes	2	15	20	14
Abnormal skin pigment	> 1	6	< 2	< 2
CENTRAL NERVOUS SYSTEM EFFECTS				
Dystonia	0.0	0.7	14.2 (8.3–30)	5.1 (3–8.2)
Parkinsonism	*	11.8	30	35.9 (23.7–48)
Akathisia	*	8.9	> 30	15.9 (4.8–27)
NMS	*	< 0.1	0.6	0.7
Weakness	—	—	—	40
Seizures	0.3	1.2	6	1.3
Drowsiness, fatigue	3	28.6 (21–36.2)	19.5 (10–30)	24.5 (3–61)
Confusion, disorientation	< 1	5.2	—	—
Insomnia	26	0.0	—	4.3

* EPS risks not available separately. Total EPS risk 16% (not significantly different than placebo) at 6 mg qd, 20% at 10 mg, 31% at 16 mg, and 13% with placebo. Most of these were Parkinson-type side effects.

PREGNANCY AND LACTATION

Teratogenicity (1st trimester)	• No proven risk of increased anomalies.
	• Low-potency phenothiazines may increase malformations during weeks 4–10.
Direct Effect on Newborn (3rd trimester)	• EPS (may last 6 months), excessive crying, hyperreflexia, hypertonicity, vasomotor instability can occur.
	• Neonatal jaundice.
	• Up to 18% of patients on chlorpromazine have had a marked fall in BP during last 10 days of pregnancy; this can harm mother and newborn.
	• Although chlorpromazine is usually safe during pregnancy, other neuroleptics are preferred.
Lactation	• Present in milk or no available reports.

*Drug Dosage in Mother's Milk**

Generic Names	Milk/ Plasma Ratio	Time of Peak Concentration in Milk (hours)	Infant Dose (μg/kg/day)	Maternal Dose (%)	Safety Rating*
Chlorpromazine	?	2	44	0.2	A**
Chlorprothixene	?	4–4.5	4.7	0.14	A**
Haloperidol	?	?	0.75–3.2	0.15–2	B**

* Significant levels of clozapine have been reported in breast milk, e.g., 60–110 ng/ml. Breast-feeding not advised for clozapine.

** A: Safe throughout infancy, but unsafe for infants suspected of a glucose-6-dehydrogenase deficiency; B: Reasonably unsafe before 34 weeks, but safe after 34 weeks.

DRUG-DRUG INTERACTIONS

Drugs (X) Interact with:	Anti-psychotics (A)	Comments
Acetaminophen	X ↓	May overuse acetaminophen.
*Alcohol	X ↑ A ↑	CNS depression; haloperidol increases alcohol.
Alpha-methyldopa	X ↑	Increases hypotension and confusion.
Alprazolam	A ↑	Increases sedation, haloperidol and fluphenazine levels.
Aluminum hydroxide	A ↓	Give aluminum hydroxide at least one hour before, or 2 h after, antipsychotic agents. (*See also* calcium carbonate.)
Amphetamines (*see* dextroamphetamine)		
Anesthetics (general)	X ↑	CNS depression, hypotension.
*Anticholinergics	X ↑ A ↓ ?	Added anticholinergic effect. Consider amantadine. May decrease antipsychotic effect.
Anticonvulsants	X ↓ ?	Carbamazepine level unchanged. Clozapine could interfere with anticonvulsant.
Antihistamines	X ↑ A ↑	CNS depression. Added anticholinergic effect.
Antihypertensives	X ↑	Increased hypotension, particularly with low-potency neuroleptics.
Bromocriptine	X ↓ A ↓	All neuroleptics except clozapine can reduce effectiveness for reducing prolactin. Increased psychosis.
Caffeine	A ↓	Increased psychosis in high doses, 600–1000 mg.
Calcium carbonate	——	No effect, unlike aluminum and magnesium hydroxides.
Clonidine	X ↑	Hypotension.
*Dextroamphetamine	X ↓ A ↓	Chlorpromazine treats dextroamphetamine overdose, but amphetamines should never treat neuroleptic overdose. Each interferes with the other's effects.
Dichloralphenazone	A ↓	Hastens neuroleptic metabolism.
Digoxin	X ↑ A ↑	Each may increase unbound fraction of the other.
Diuretics (thiazides)	X ↑	Increased orthostatic hypotension, hypotension, risk of shock.
†Epinephrine	X ↓	Hypotensive, phenothiazine-treated patients might do better on levarterenol or phenylephrine.
Estrogen	A ↑	May increase phenothiazine level.
Fluoxetine (*see* SSRIs)		
Griseofulvin	A ↓	Speeds neuroleptic metabolism.
*Guanethidine	X ↓	Hypotensive action inhibited by phenothiazines, haloperidol, and possibly thioxanthines.
Hypnoanxiolytics	X ↑ A ↑	CNS depression.
*Isoproterenol	X ↓	Marked hypotension.
*Levodopa	X ↓	Antagonizes effects of dopamine agonists. Try clozapine or possibly risperidene.

Drugs (X) Interact with:	Anti-psychotics (A)	Comments
*Lithium	X↑ A?	May cause EPS; extremely rare. Acute neurotoxicity at normal serum levels, especially with haloperidol or thioridazine. Chronic combination a smaller problem. Lithium and chlorpromazine may *lower* levels in both. Increases molindone levels.
Magnesium hydroxide	A↓	Give magnesium hydroxide at least one hour before, or 2 h after, antipsychotic agents. (*See also* calcium carbonate.)
MAOIs	X↓ A?	Hypotension may result. MAOIs may trigger EPS.
Methyldopa	X↑	Hypotension, rarely delirium.
Methylphenidate (*see* dextroamphetamine)		
Nicotine	A↓	Decreased blood levels.
Norepinephrine	X↓	Hypotension.
*Opiates	X↑ A↑	CNS depression.
*Orphenadrine	X↓ A↓	Lowers neuroleptic levels; with CPZ may cause hypoglycemia; increases anticholinergic effects.
Paroxetine (*see* SSRIs)		
Phenylbutazone	X↑ A↑	More drowsiness.
Phenytoin	X? A↓?	Toxicity may occur. Obtain phenytoin level and adjust; can reduce clozapine and other levels.
*Propranolol	X↑ A↑	Hypotension, toxicity, and seizures. Monitor serum levels; decrease dose.
Quinidine	X↑ A↑	Increased quinidine-like effects with dysrhythmias, especially phenothiazines. Increases risperidone levels.
Rifampin	A↓	Speeds neuroleptic metabolism.
SSRIs (fluoxetine, fluvoxamine, paroxetine, sertraline)	A↑	May increase EPS and plasma levels. Fluvoxamine least likely to increase antipsychotic levels. Haloperidol, perphenazine, thioridazine most likely to be increased.
Stimulants (*see* dextroamphetamine)		
Succinylcholine	X↑	May have prolonged paralysis.
*TCAs	X↑ A↑	Possible toxicity or hypotension; TCAs may diminish EPS. TCA levels increased by phenothiazine and haloperidol.
Trazodone	X↑ A↑	Additive hypotensive effects.
Tobacco (*see* nicotine)		
Valproic acid	A↑	Potentially increases levels; reported with risperidone and clozapine.
Warfarin	X↑ A↑	Increased bleeding time by increasing warfarin. May increase unbound antipsychotic.

Drugs (X) Interact with:	Chlor-promazine (C)	Comments
Antimalarial agents (amodiaquine, chloroquine, pyrimethamine, sulfadoxine)	C↑	Chlorpromazine 2–4 times higher levels.

Drugs (X) Interact with:	Chlor-promazine (C)	Comments
Anorectic agents	X ↓	Inhibits anorectic effect.
Antidiabetics	X ↑ ↓	Loss of glucose control possible; change neuroleptics.
*Barbiturates	X ↑ C ↓	CNS depression acute; antipsychotic effects lowered.
Captopril	X ↑	Hypotension.
Cimetidine	C ↓	Avoid cimetidine; try ranitidine or nizatidine.
Enalapril	X ↑	Hypotension.
Insulin (see anti-diabetics)		
Meperidine	X ↑ C ↓	Hypotension, lethargy, CNS depression; switch one drug.
*Phenmetrazine (see anorectic agents)		
Sulfonylureas	X ↑	Change neuroleptic.
Valproic acid	X ↑ C ↑	Toxicity; switch to haloperidol.

Drugs (X) Interact with:	Clozapine (C)	Comments
*Carbamazepine	X ↑ C ↑	Increases agranulocytosis risk.
Cimetidine	C ↑	Increases clozapine levels; consider ranitidine as alternative.
Diltiazem	C ↑	Increases clozapine levels.
Fluvoxamine	C ↑	Increases clozapine levels.
*Hypnoanxiolytic benzodiazepines	H ↑ C ↑	Increased risk of respiratory arrest.
†Phenytoin	C ↑	Increases agranulocytosis risk.
Risperidone (see risperidone below)		
Verapamil	C ↑	Increases clozapine levels.

Drugs (X) Interact with:	Halo-peridol** (H)	Comments
*Carbamazepine	H ↓	Psychosis; 50% lower serum level.
Indomethacin	H ↑	Drowsiness, tiredness, and confusion; change one agent.
Buspirone	H ↑	About 26% increase in haloperidol level.

Drugs (X) Interact with:	Loxapine (L)	Comments
Lorazepam	X ↑	Rare respiratory depression, stupor, and hypotension. Switch one drug. No other benzodiazepine apparently interacts with loxapine.

Drugs (X) Interact with:	Thiorida-zine** (T)	Comments
*Phenylpropanol-amine	X ↑	One sudden death. Name common over-the-counter drugs with PPA (e.g., Dexatrim, Allerest, Dimetapp) for patients to avoid; causal effect not proven.

Drugs (X) Interact with:	Risper- idone**	Comments
Carbamazepine	R ↓	Decreased level with chronic carbamazepine.
Clozapine	R ↑	Increased level with chronic clozapine.
SSRIs	R ↑ ?	Probable increase in risperidone levels.
P4502D6 metabo- lized drugs** Haloperidol Thioridazine Perphenazine Dextromethor- phan Bufaralol Propranolol Tricyclic anti- depressants Timolol	X ↑	Increased levels possible.

* Moderately important; † Extremely important; ↑ Increases; ↓ Decreases; O = No effect; ? Unsure or increases and decreases.
** See 2D6 table in appendix.

A
N
T
I
P
S
Y
C
H
O
T
I
C
A
G
E
N
T
S

EFFECTS ON LABORATORY TESTS†

Generic Names	Blood/Serum Tests	Results*	Urine Tests	Results*
Chlorpromazine	LFT	↑	VMA	↓
	Glucose	↑ ↓	Urobilinogen	↑
Clozapine	WBC	↓	?	
	LFT	↑		
Fluphenazine	LFT	↑	VMA	↓
	Cephaline flocculation	↑	Urobilinogen	↑
Haloperidol	Only prolactin		None	
Loxapine	LFT	↑	None	
Molindone	LFT	↑	?	
	Eosinophils	↑		
	Leukocytes	↓		
	Fatty acids	↑		
Perphenazine	Glucose, PBI	↑ ↑	Pregnancy tests	False ↑ ↓
Risperidone	Only prolactin	↑		
Thioridazine	None		Pregnancy tests	False ↑ ↓
Thiothixene	LFT	↑	None	
	Uric acid	↓		
Trifluoperazine	LFT	↑	VMA	↓
	Glucose	↑ ↓	Urobilinogen	↑

* ↑ Increases; ↓ Decreases; ↑ ↓ Increases and decreases; ? Undetermined or unclear.
** LFT = liver function tests refer to AST/SGOT, ALT/SGPT, alkaline phosphotase, bilirubin, and LDH.
† All except clozapine can elevate prolactin.

WITHDRAWAL

Neuroleptics do not cause

- Dependence
- Tolerance
- Addiction
- Withdrawal (unless high dose suddenly stopped)

Suddenly stopping high antipsychotic doses may produce

- Gastritis, nausea, vomiting, diarrhea
- Headaches
- Insomnia and nightmares

Less often, the sudden stopping generates

- Sweating
- Rhinorrhea
- Increased appetite
- Giddiness
- Dizziness
- Warmth or cold sensations
- Tremors
- Tachycardia

These symptoms

- Begin 2–4 (up to 7) days after discontinuing antipsychotics.
  - √ Symptoms worse when patients are on antipsychotics *and* ACAs or TCAs and both are stopped.
- Can persist 2 weeks.
- Can cease by more gradually withdrawing neuroleptics over 1–2 weeks.

Maintain ACAs a week after terminating antipsychotics to prevent EPS; this allows for full clearing of antipsychotic. When long-term neuroleptics are rapidly stopped or quickly lowered, a long-term TD can appear, as discussed above. But also, a *short-term withdrawal dyskinesia* (probably caused by dopaminergic rebound) can arise occasionally if antipsychotics are quickly halted.

- Withdrawal dyskinesia resembles a long-term tardive dyskinesia with abnormal movements of the neck, face, and mouth.
- Antiparkinsonian drugs do not relieve it.
- Withdrawal dyskinesia stops with
  - √ Re-establishing maintenance neuroleptic dose and
  - √ Reducing neuroleptics more gradually (1–3 months).

OVERDOSE: TOXICITY, SUICIDE, AND TREATMENT

Even if consumed all at once, antipsychotics are relatively nonlethal drugs.

- A 30–60 day supply of antipsychotics can be fatal.
  √ This amount is 10 times less dangerous than TCAs or MAOIs.
- Neuroleptics can still create serious problems.

Suicide more common with less potent antipsychotics (e.g., chlorpromazine).

- The therapeutic index—the ratio of the lethal to the effective— ranges from
  √ 25–200 for low-potency phenothiazines, to
  √ > 1000 for high-potency piperazines and haloperidol.

More serious symptoms emerge when antipsychotics are consumed with another drug, particularly one that increases or exaggerates antipsychotic CNS effects. In one series of studies,

- A chlorpromazine overdose induced coma in 4%, whereas
- A chlorpromazine and TCA overdose taken together produced coma in 13%.

The general management of neuroleptic overdoses includes:

- Stop all neuroleptics and ACAs.
  √ Be alert for dystonias.
- Hospitalize, if needed.
- Obtain ECG, temperature, vital signs, and if needed, an airway.
- Arousal may not occur for 48 h.
- Observe patient for 8–12 h after ingestion.
- Ascertain other drugs ingested during past 2–10 days.
- Speak soon with family or friends who might afford life-saving information.
- Begin gastric lavage as soon as possible.
  √ Before initiating gastric lavage, employ cuffed endotracheal intubation to prevent aspiration and pulmonary complications.
    □ Stop convulsions before passing stomach tube.
- Avoid emetic because an acute dystonic reaction of the head or neck could cause aspiration.
- Lavage best if overdose transpired within 4 h, yet it can remove drugs consumed 24–36 h earlier.
- *After* lavage, supply activated charcoal (40–50 g in adults, 20–25 g in children) by mouth or through lavage tube to prevent further absorption.
- Loss of consciousness can be reversed with stimulants.

√ Use amphetamine, dextroamphetamine, or caffeine with sodium benzoate.

√ Avoid stimulants that can cause convulsions, e.g., picrotoxin or pentylene tetrazol.

* If slow-release pills ingested, follow with a saline cathartic to speed evacuation.

Most overdoses accentuate side effects, and so their treatment is akin to treating side effects. These treatments include:

* For hypotension, dizziness
  √ May appear in 2–3 days.
  √ May evolve into shock, coma, cardiovascular insufficiency, myocardial infarction, and arrhythmias.
  √ First treatment is fluids.
  √ Second treatment is sympathomimetics, such as levarterenol (norepinephrine), metaraminol, phenylephrine.
  √ *Do not use epinephrine*; may result in lower blood pressure.
* For severe urinary retention
  √ Catherterize patient, if no recent voiding.
  √ Hemodialysis is relatively useless because of low drug concentrations.
  √ Hematuria, which arises later, often occurs with chlorprothixene and loxapine.
* For seizures
  √ Common in children.
  √ Manage with standard interventions.
    □ IV diazepam is first choice.
    □ Avoid barbiturates; they risk respiratory depression.
    □ Avoid pentylenetrazol, picrotoxin, and bemegride.

Toxicity and Suicide Data

Generic Name	Toxicity Doses Average (Highest) (g)	Mortality Doses Average (Lowest) (g)
Chlorpromazine	25.0 (30.0)	(1.250)
Chlorprothixene	(8.0)	—
Clozapine	(4.0)	2.50
Fluphenazine	—	—
Haloperidol	—	—
Loxapine	—	1.5–3
Mesoridazine	—	—
Molindone	—	—
Perphenazine	—	—
Pimozide	—	—
Thioridazine	20.0 (2.0)	5–10

Toxicity and Suicide Data (Cont.)

Generic Name	Toxicity Doses Average (Highest) (g)	Mortality Doses Average (Lowest) (g)
Thiothixene	20.0	(0.736)
Trifluoperazine	—	—

PRECAUTIONS

Hypotension occurs most with parenteral use and high doses, and especially > 50 mg of IM chlorpromazine.

Use antipsychotics cautiously with

- Narrow-angle glaucoma
- Prostatic hypertrophy
- CNS depressive agents
- Breast cancer
- Bone marrow depression, blood dyscrasias
- Parkinson's disease
- Neuroleptic hypersensitivity
- Extreme hypotension or hypertension
- Acutely ill children (e.g., chickenpox, measles, Reye's syndrome, gastroenteritis, dehydration)
  - √ Increased EPS, particularly dystonias and akathisias
  - √ Increased hepatotoxicity risk
- Elderly who have
  - √ Hepatic disease
  - √ Cardiovascular illness (especially low potency)
  - √ Chronic respiratory disease
  - √ Hypoglycemic conditions
  - √ Seizures (especially low potency)

Avoid pimozide in patients with

- Tics other than Tourette's disorder,
- Medications stimulating tics (e.g., methylphenidate, dextroamphetamine), or
- Prolonged QT interval.

Sudden death has occurred with patients on neuroleptics.

- Sudden death has also occurred in seemingly healthy adults for no obvious reason.
  - √ Ventricular fibrillation, aspiration from food or vomit, and grand mal seizures may be culpable.

NURSES' DATA

Discuss with the patient the reasons and myths for taking medications.

Oral medication

- Take with milk, orange juice, or semi-solid food to reduce bitter taste.
  - √ Haloperidol is a tasteless and colorless elixir, unlike chlorpromazine and thioridazine.
- Protect oral liquids from the light.
- Discard markedly discolored solutions (slight yellowing does not alter potency).

Injections

- Do not hold drug in syringe for > 15 minutes, as plastic may absorb drug.
- Administer IM injections very slowly.
- To thwart contact dermatitis, keep antipsychotic solution off patient's skin and clothing.
- Give IM injections into upper outer quadrant of buttocks, deltoid, or thigh.
  - √ Deltoid speeds absorption because of faster blood perfusion.
  - √ Tell patient injection may sting.
  - √ Massage slowly after injection to prevent formation of sterile abscesses.
  - √ Alternate sites.
- Watch for orthostatic hypotension, especially with parenteral administration.
  - √ Show patients how to stand when dizzy (see page 22).

Depot injections

- Use dry needle (at least 21 gauge).
- Give deep IM injection into a large muscle using Z-track method.
- Rotate sites and specify in charting.
- Can inject SC.
- Do not let drug remain in syringe for more than 15 minutes.
- Do not massage injection sites.

PATIENT AND FAMILY NOTES

Patients and family should notify doctor if

- Patient has a sore throat during first several months of treatment.
- NMS appears.
- Patient is having general or dental surgery.

Tell patients and families:

- Antipsychotics treat psychotic symptoms, including hallucinations, delusions, confused thinking, paranoia, and oversensitivity of stimuli.
  √ Many patients who deny that their symptoms are psychotic will try antipsychotic medication to treat insomnia, poor concentration, over-worrying (paranoia), and/or short temper.
- Particularly if on high- or mid-potency antipsychotic, patients may have
  √ Anticholinergic side effects (e.g., dry mouth, constipation, blurred vision, fuzzy thinking),
  √ Sedation that should wear off and can help with sleep and anxiety,
  √ Low blood pressure with dizziness when standing up.
- The 3 main forms of EPS are
  √ Dystonia, a sudden and often sustained pull of any muscle group;
  √ Akathisia, a feeling of physical (not necessarily mental) restlessness; and
  √ Parkinsonism, involves stiff muscles, slowed movements, tremor, and drooling.
- TD not necessarily discussed during acute treatment phase while patient actively psychotic.
  √ TD won't occur in that phase and there is no assurance that drug will be taken chronically.
- Discuss TD, especially *before* 3 months of neuroleptic treatment.
  √ Best to do it when patient and physician are beginning a chronic course of treatment.
- When starting neuroleptics, carefully drive cars, work around machines, and cross streets.

Patients initially should check "reflexes" to ensure their "timing" is okay.

- May drink alcohol with antipsychotics, but "one drink often feels like 2 drinks."
- Avoid overexposure to sun; use sunscreens.
- Do not keep medication at bedside to avoid accidental ingestion.
  √ Keep safely away from children.
- If forget a dose, patient can take up to 3–4 h late, but
  √ If more than 3–4 h late, wait for next scheduled dose.
  √ Do not double the dose unless this has already been tried successfully.
- Do not suddenly stop medication.
  √ Even if there is no immediate return of symptoms, there is a very high risk of relapse in the weeks and months after medication has been stopped.

2. Extrapyramidal Drugs

INTRODUCTION

Neuroleptic-induced extrapyramidal side effects (EPS) are diminished by anticholinergic agents (ACAs) includes most antihistamines, β-blockers (BB), benzodiazepines (BZ), and dopaminergic agonists (DA).

Some extrapyramidal drugs (EPD) (e.g., benztropine) are prescribed almost exclusively for EPS, while others (e.g., propranolol) are given for both nonEPS and EPS. One ACA, ethopropazine (Parsidol), a phenothiazine derivation, will not be discussed. It is mainly used in Parkinson's disease and is less effective than other ACAs for drug-induced EPS.

EPS fall into 4 major categories described on pages 29–32, 36, 63:

- Dystonia
- Pseudoparkinsonism (including akinesia)
- Akathisia
- Rabbit syndrome

Other EPS not treated with ACAs are discussed in the antipsychotic chapter and include

- Neuroleptic malignant syndrome (NMS) (pages 33–36).
- Tardive dyskinesia (TD) (pages 36–39).

NAMES, COST, MANUFACTURERS, DOSE FORMS, COLORS

Generic Names (Dollars/Dose: 100 pills in mg)*	Brand Names (Dollars/Dose: 100 pills in mg)*	Manufacturers	Dose Forms (mg)**	Colors
Amantadine (30–36/100)	Symmetrel (85/100)	Du Pont	c: 100 s: 50 mg/5 ml	c: red
Benztropine (5–11/1)	Cogentin (24/1)	Merck Sharp & Dohme	t: 0.5/1/2 p: 1 mg/ml	t: all white
Biperiden	Akineton (24/2)	Knoll	t: 2 p: 5 mg/ml	t: white
Bromocriptine	Parlodel (143/2.5)	Sandoz	t: 2.5 c: 5	t: white c: caramel-white
Diazepam (2–21)	Valium (57/5)	Roche	t: 2/5/10 p: 5 mg/ml	t: white/yellow/blue
Diphenhydramine† (3–8/25)	Benadryl (21/25)	Parke-Davis	c: 25/50 p: 10/50 mg/ml	c: all pink-white
Lorazepam (5–49/2)	Ativan (102/2)	Wyeth-Ayerst	t: 0.5/1/2	t: all white
Procyclidine	Kemadrin (40/5)	Burroughs Wellcome	t: 5	t: white
Propranolol (4–16/20)	Inderal (39/20)	Wyeth-Ayerst	t: 10/20/40/80 p: 1 mg/ml	t: orange/blue/green/pink/yellow
Trihexyphenidyl (6–26/5)	Artane (15/5)	Lederle	t: 2/5 SR: 5 mg e: 2 mg/5 ml	t: all white SR: blue

* 1994 average wholesale price for 100 pills at this dose (e.g., 78/50 means 100 pills 50 mg cost $78).
** c = capsules; e = elixir; p = parenteral; s = syrup; SR = sustained release sequels; t = tablets.
† Can be purchased over the counter only in 25 mg.

PHARMACOLOGY

Theoretical Mechanisms for EPS

The basal ganglia, which mediate involuntary movements, have a critical ratio of

$$\frac{Dopamine}{Acetylcholine}$$

When neuroleptics block these dopamine receptors, they lower this ratio and generate EPS.

By reducing acetycholine, ACAs help to restore this balance. By releasing dopamine in the basal ganglia system, amantadine also helps restore this balance.

For akathisia there may be a critical ratio of

$$\frac{Dopamine}{\text{Norepinephrine}}$$

By reducing norepinephrine, β-blockers may restore this balance. For EPS there may also be a critical ratio of

$$\frac{Dopamine}{\text{Serotonin}}$$

By reducing serotonin, as clozapine and risperidone do, balance may be restored. By increasing or augmenting serotonin, as selective serotonin reuptake inhibitors (e.g., fluoxetine, etc.) and perhaps lithium do, increased EPS risk may occur.

Pharmacology of Anticholinergic Drugs and Amantadine

	Time to Peak Concentration (hrs)*	Half-Life (hrs)*	Oral Bioavailability** (%)
Amantadine	1–6	16	60–95
Benztropine	—	12–24	—
Biperiden	1–1.5	18–24	29
Procyclidine	1–2	12	52–97
Trihexyphenidyl	1.2	6–10	100

* Higher numbers generally in elderly.
** Lower numbers generally in elderly.

DOSES

Generic Names	Oral Doses (mg)	IM/IV Doses (mg)	Major Chemical Group
Amantadine	100 bid-tid*	—	Dopaminergic agonist
Benztropine	1–3 bid	1–2	ACA
Biperiden	2 tid-qid	2	ACA
Diazepam	5 tid	5–10	Benzodiazepine
Diphenhydramine	25–50 tid-qid	25–50	Antihistamine and ACA
Lorazepam	1–2 tid	—	Benzodiazepine
Procyclidine	2.5–5 tid	—	ACA
Propranolol	10–20 tid; up to 40 qid	—	β-blocker
Trihexyphenidyl**	2–5 tid	—	ACA

* Amantadine can often be given 200 mg qd instead of 100 mg bid. In geriatrics, 100 mg qd is usually enough.
** Start with trihexyphenidyl tablets or elixir; only later transfer to sustained-released sequels (capsules). Use sequels as a single dose after breakfast or one dose q12 h. For akathisia, give trihexyphenidyl 6–10 mg qd; other EPS, provide 2–6 mg qd.

EXTRAPYRAMIDAL DRUGS

CLINICAL INDICATIONS AND USE

*Influence on Extrapyramidal Symptom**

Generic Names	Akathisia	Akinesia	Dystonia	Rabbit	Rigidity	Tremor
Amantadine	3	3	2	2	3	2
Benztropine	2	2	3	3	3	3
Biperiden	1	2	3	3	3	3
Diazepam	2	0	1-2	1	1-2	0-1
Diphenhydramine	2	1	2–3	3	1	2
Lorazepam	2	0	1-2	1	1-2	0-1
Procyclidine	1	2	3	3	3	3
Propranolol	3	0	0	1	0	1-2
Trihexyphenidyl	2	2	3	3	3	3

* 0 = no effect; 1 = some effect (20% response); 2 = moderate effect (20–40% response); 3 = good effect (> 40% response).

ACAs' effects depend on the symptom. Therefore, when should one use ACAs or other EPDs?

- The *pro* arguments include:
  √ EPS are uncomfortable.
  √ EPS can induce patients to stop taking neuroleptics.
  √ High-potency neuroleptics often bring on EPS.
  √ ACAs especially help patients under 45.
  √ ACAs clearly relieve some EPS (a.k.a. dystonia, akinesia, pseudoparkinsonism).

- The *con* arguments include:
  √ Low-potency neuroleptics less frequently produce EPS.
  √ Patients without EPS initially can receive EPDs if EPS arise later.
  √ ACAs yield side effects, which may compound neuroleptic side effects (e.g., dry mouth, confusion).
  √ ACAs are not very effective for other EPS (e.g., akathisias).
  √ Avoid ACAs in children under 3.

- In general, prophylactic ACAs are indicated for patients who are
  √ Males under 30 y.o. and females under 25 y.o. starting high-potency neuroleptics (e.g., haloperidol) (dystonia rate without ACA over 70%.) or have
  √ Dystonia (or have h/o dystonia).

- When depot antipsychotics peak after 2–14 days, patient may need ACAs.

- Whether to use them in other circumstances depends on the seriousness of symptoms and the preferences of patients.

Starting Oral Doses of Antiparkinsonian Drugs

Symptom	Medication
Dystonia	Diphenhydramine 25–50 mg IV/IM as first choice; often provides complete relief in minutes and reduces patient anxiety. Hydroxyzine alternative Benztropine 1–2 mg IV/IM is the second choice, and always works quickly. If patient does not respond to the above, question the diagnosis. Prevent future dystonias with any ACA.
Akathisia	Propranolol or other lipophilic β-blocker (e.g., metoprolol, pindolol, or nadolol, but not atenolol) are first choices if akathisia is an isolated symptom. Amantadine or benzodiazepines (lorazepam or diazepam) are second choices. ACAs are third choices. If other EPS also occur, which are better treated with ACA, use ACA first. Clonidine (0.15–2 mg/qd) also reported to help. If patient has not improved, double check the diagnosis. May help in chronic or "tardive" akathisia.
Parkinsonism	Reduce neuroleptics to lowest effective dose. Try any ACA. Prescribe amantadine if troublesome anticholinergic symptoms already exist. Consider amantadine in geriatrics and to preserve new memory acquisition in any age group.
Rabbit syndrome	Responds well to any ACA.

General Considerations of EPDs

- β-blockers, clonidine, and benzodiazepines (e.g., clonazepam 1 mg q A.M.) mostly limited for use in akathisia and perhaps tremor.
  - √ Clonidine's effect may be secondary to sedation and not a specific effect.
  - √ β-blockers are first choice for akathisia alone.
- Amantadine is well-tolerated, broadly effective (including on akathisia), does not effect memory, protects from type A influenza, is expensive, and occasionally may worsen psychosis.
- Anticholinergics are broadly effective (except on akathisia), have highest side effects, including on memory, and probably don't cause psychosis unless in toxic range.
- Buspirone 5–10 mg tid may help akathisia.
  - √ Only a few case reports but no controlled studies.

Speed of Response

- Only dystonia routinely responds in minutes to hours.
- Other symptoms (including akathisia) may take 3–10 days to respond significantly, although responses after 1–2 doses are not rare.

- Do not keep increasing daily dose just because effect is not yet visible.
- Pick a target dose and stay with it for 3–4 days.

ACA Dosage Adjustment

- Benztropine drug levels can vary 100-fold with comparable dosing.
  - √ Both under- and over-dosing is common.
  - √ This may also be true of other ACAs.
- Some patients can become toxic at very low doses.
- Poor correlation between ACA dosage and control of EPS.
- High correlation between ACA blood levels (greater than 7 pmol of atropine equivalents) and control of EPS.
- 25% of patients on normal doses of ACA (usually 4 mg/qd benztropine) have very low blood levels.
  - √ In these patients, most responded when dose was increased to 6–12 mg/day
  - √ If this is done, carefully monitor patient for ACA effects (e.g., dry mouth, constipation, memory impairments).
- Dry mouth often early sign of clinically significant ACA activity.
  - √ If patient has poor control of EPS and no dry mouth, might try increasing ACA dose.
  - √ If patient has good control of EPS but with severe ACA symptoms, try lowering ACA dose.
- Once a day dosing is often possible with long half-life ACAs (i.e., benztropine, biperiden).
  - √ This should be tried only after optimal dose for patient has been established.

After 1–6 months of long-term maintenance on antipsychotic therapy, ACAs often can be withdrawn.

- About 15% of patients will re-experience clear neurological side effects, whereas about 30% will feel "better"—less anxious, depressed, sleepy—on continued ACAs.
- Because antipsychotics have longer half-lives than ACAs, prescribe ACAs for several days *after* stopping neuroleptics.

SIDE EFFECTS

Side effects of ACAs and amantadine are listed below. β-blocker and clonidine side effects are listed in Chapter 7, Antianxiety Agents (pages 288–290).

In order of frequency, the most common (> 3%) side effects of

- ACAs
  - √ Memory impairment (see page x for age effect of memory impairment)
  - √ Dry mouth, nose, and throat
  - √ Blurred vision
  - √ Light sensitivity
  - √ Urinary hesitancy
  - √ Constipation
  - √ Appetite loss/nausea
  - √ Listlessness
  - √ Excitement
- Amantadine
  - √ Blurred vision
  - √ Dry mouth
  - √ Urinary hesitancy
  - √ Nausea
  - √ Insomnia

Amantadine's side-effect frequencies are only slightly more than placebo. In experimental trials in healthy volunteers, ACAs interfered with learning new material in adults of all ages and caused ratings of fatigue-inertia, tension-anxiety, and depression-dejection. Amantadine had none of these effects.

The side effects of diazepam, lorazepam, and propranolol are listed in Chapter 7 (see pages 287–290).

Since the side effects of ACAs are anticholinergic, deal with them by

- First, eliminate or reduce the ACA.
- Second, change to a less anticholinergic antipsychotic (see page 21).
- Third, substitute the non-anticholinergic amantadine for the ACA.

Cardiovascular Effects

Palpitations, tachycardia
Dizziness

Gastrointestinal Effects

Dry mouth

- Management (see pages 22–23).

Nausea, vomiting

- Reduce ACA.

E
X
T
R
A
P
Y
R
A
M
I
D
A
L

D
R
U
G
S

Constipation

- Management (see page 23).

Paralytic ileus

Renal Effects

Urinary hesitancy or retention (see page 24).

Endocrine and Sexual Effects

Amantadine may reduce galactorrhea provoked by neuroleptic-induced increased prolactin.

Eyes, Ears, Nose, and Throat Effects

Blurred vision (see page 27).
Photophobia

- From dilated pupils

Dry eyes (see page 28).
Narrow-angle glaucoma

- ACAs can trigger narrow-angle glaucoma.
- If patient has anything like a h/o glaucoma, test before giving ACAs, TCAs, or neuroleptics (see page 28).
- If narrow-angle glaucoma becomes a problem, stop all ACAs and neuroleptics.

Nasal congestion, dry throat
Dry bronchial secretions and *strained breathing* aggravate patients with respiratory ailments.

Skin, Allergies, and Temperature

Diminshed sweating (see page 29)
Skin flushing
Rashes

- Stop ACA.

Fever

- Apply ice bags.

Central Nervous System Effects

Confusion, delirium, disturbed concentration, disorientation (see pages 40–41, 121).
Restlessness, tremors, ataxia

Weakness, lethargy
Numb fingers, inability to move particular muscles, slurred speech, incoherence

- More common in the elderly and in high doses.

Stimulation, nervous excitement, insomnia, depression

- All may be more common with trihexyphenidyl (*see* Precautions).

Psychosis

- This occurs especially with amantadine (0.5% psychosis, 3% hallucinations). Rate for ACA may be same, but good data not available. Before changing a neuroleptic in a "treatment resistant" psychotic patient, first try the patient off of amantadine.

PERCENTAGES OF SIDE EFFECTS

Side Effects	Anticholinergics	Amantadine	Diphenhydramine
CARDIOVASCULAR EFFECTS			
Dizziness	< 1	2	20
Hypotension	< 0.1	1	—
Tachycardia	< 0.1	1	< 1
Congestive heart failure	—	< 1	—
GASTROINTESTINAL EFFECTS			
Dry mouth	33	9	20
Anorexia	4.7	0.7	5.5
Nausea	15	7.5	20
Vomiting	3	1.4 (0.1–1)	—
Constipation	15	1.4	—
Sore mouth	< 1	—	—
Edema	—	3	—
RENAL EFFECTS			
Urinary hesitancy	15	3	—
Painful or difficult urination	—	—	5.5
HEMATOLOGIC EFFECTS			
Easy bruising	—	—	< 1
EYES, EARS, NOSE, AND THROAT EFFECTS*			
Blurred vision	26	10	—
Light sensitivity	20	—	—

EXTRAPYRAMIDAL DRUGS

Side Effects	Anticholinergics	Amantadine	Diphenhydramine
Narrow-angle glaucoma	< 1	——	——
Visual disturbance	——	0.5	5.5
Oculogyric episode	——	< 0.1	——
Less tolerance for contact lenses	——	——	5.5
Dry nose and throat	20	——	20
Sore throat	——	——	< 1
Dyspnea	——	0.5	——
SKIN, ALLERGIES, AND TEMPERATURE			
Rash	1.4	0.5	——
Eczematoid dermatitis	——	< 0.1	——
Fever	——	——	< 1
Decreased sweating	2.0	< 0.1	3.0
CENTRAL NERVOUS SYSTEM EFFECTS			
Confusion	2	0.7	——
Drowsiness	2.8	2.0	20
Muscle cramps	< 1	——	——
Numbness	< 1	——	——
Weakness in limbs	2.7	1.4	< 1
Fatigue	——	0.5	19
Headache	0.0	2	——
Ataxia	——	3	——
Seizures	——	< 0.1	——
Slurred speech	——	0.5	——
Insomnia	0.0	3.1	——
Nightmares	——	——	< 1
Anxiety	4	2	——
Agitation	2.0	0.0	< 1
Irritability	——	3	——
Hallucinations	——	3	——
Depression	< 1	0.7	——
Psychosis	——	0.5	——

* —— No report

PREGNANCY AND LACTATION

Teratogenicity (1st trimester)
- No apparent fetal risk from trihexyphenidyl.
- No reports on biperiden.

- A few cases of amantadine-induced cardiovascular anomalies may exist, but relationship to drug unknown.

Direct Effect on Newborn (3rd trimester)
- A few cases of paralytic ileus with mother on chlorpromazine and benztropine.

Lactation
- No data.

- Amantadine secreted in milk.

DRUG-DRUG INTERACTIONS

Drugs with significant anticholinergic effects all interact with each other, causing increased anticholinergic effects (toxicity and/or better control of EPS).

- Psychiatric drugs (e.g., low-potency tricyclic antidepressants)
- Nonpsychiatric medical drugs that are commonly prescribed
- Antihistamines

Anticholinergic Drugs

Commonly Prescribed Medications	Nonpsychiatric Anticholinergic Agents	Antihistamines
Codeine	Anisotropine (Valpin)	Brompheniramine (Dimetane)
Coumadin	Atropine	Chlorpheniramine (Chlor-Trimeton)
Digoxin	Belladonna alkaloids	Clemastine (Tavist)
Dipyridamole	Clidinium (Quarzan)	Cyproheptadine (Periactin)
Disopyramide	Dicyclomine (Bentyl)	Dexchlorpheniramine (Polaramine)
Isosorbide	Ethopropazine (Parsidol)	Diphenhydramine (Benadryl)
Meperidine	Glycopyrrolate (Robinul)	Hydroxyzine (Atarax, Vistraril)
Nifedipine	Hexocyclium (Tral)	Methdilazine (Tacaryl)
Prednisone	Homatropine	Promethazine (Phenergan)
Procainamide	Hyoscyamine	Trimeprazine (Temaril)
Quinidine	Ipratropium	Triprolidine (Actidil)
Ranitidine	Isopropamide (Darbid)	
	Mepenzolate (Cantil)	
	Methantheline (Banthine)	
	Methscopolamine (Pamine)	
	Orphenadrine (Disipal)	
	Oxyphencyclimine (Daricon)	
	Propantheline (Pro-Banthine)	
	Scopolamine	
	Tridihexethyl (Pathilon)	

Drugs (X) Interact with:	Anticholinergics (A)**	Comments
Acetaminophen	X ↓	May increase acetaminophen use.
Amantadine	X ↑ A ↑	Increased amantadine and ACA effects.
* Antihistamines	X ↑ A ↓	Increased anticholinergic effects.
* Antipsychotics	X ↓ A ↑	ACAs may slow antipsychotic actions. ACAs enhance anticholinergic effects of antipsychotics, particularly low-potency phenothiazines.
Atenolol	X ↑	May increase atenolol's concentration.
* Cocaine	A ↓	Decreased anticholinergic effects.
Digoxin	X ↑	Increases level, more slowly dissolved digoxin tablet.
Levodopa (L-dopa)	X ↓	May reduce L-dopa's availability; when ACAs stopped, L-dopa's toxicity may erupt.
* Methotrimeparazine	A ↓	Combination may increase EPS.
MAOIs	A ↑	May increase anticholinergic effects.
Nitrofurantoin	X ↑	ACA may increase nitrofurantoin effects.
Primidone	X ↑	Excessive sedation.
Procainamide	X ↑	Increased procainamide effect.
Propranolol	X ↓	ACAs can block β-blocker's bradycardia.
* TCAs	A ↑ X ↑	May diminish EPS; increased risk of anticholinergic toxicity.
Tacrine	X ↓ A ↓	Interfere with each other's effects.

Drugs (X) Interact with:	Amantadine (A)	Comments
Alcohol	X ↑	Increased alcohol effect; possible fainting.
Anticholinergics	X ↑ A ↑	Increased amantadine and ACA effects.
Anti-emetics	X ↓	Possible decreased efficacy.
Antipsychotics	X ↓	May interfere with antipsychotic effect.
* Cocaine	X ↑	Major overstimulation.
* Sympathomimetics	X ↑	Increased stimulation and agitation.
Trimethoprim, sulfamethoxazole (Bactrim, Septa)	X ↑ A ↑	May increase each other's levels. CNS toxicity possible.
Quinidine†	A ↑	Modest increase in amantadine levels.
Quinine†	A ↑	Modest increase in amantadine levels.
Triamterene (in Dyazide)†	A ↑	Modest increase in amantadine levels.

* Moderately important reaction; ↑ Increases; ↓ Decreases.
** See also preceding lists of other drugs with anticholinergic effects.
† Decreases renal clearance of amantadine.

EFFECTS ON LABORATORY TESTS

Generic Names	Blood/Serum Tests	Results*	Urine Tests	Results*
Amantadine	WBC Leukocytes	↓↓	?	
Benztropine	None		None	
Biperiden	?		?	
Diphenhydramine	WBC, RBC, platelets	↓↓ ↓	?	
Procyclidine	?		?	
Trihexyphenidyl	None		None	

* ↑ Increases; ↓ Decreases; ? = Undetermined.

WITHDRAWAL

ACAs do not cause

- Dependence (but abuse is possible)
- Tolerance
  - √ Some tolerance with amantadine occurs after 8 weeks.
- Addiction
- Withdrawal, unless done abruptly

ACA Withdrawal

Yet, even more than with antipsychotic agents, abruptly stopping ACAs can induce, in 2–4 (up to 7) days, a flu-like syndrome without a fever.

- Nausea, vomiting, diarrhea
- Hypersalivation
- Headaches
- Insomnia
- Nightmares

Less often develop

- Rhinorrhea
- Increased appetite
- Giddiness
- Dizziness
- Tremors
- Warm or cold sensations

These symptoms

- May persist 2 weeks,
- Are not life-threatening,
- Can diminish substantially by more gradually tapering off neuroleptics and ACAs.
- This approach also decreases risk of rebound EPS.

Amantadine Withdrawal

Stopping amantadine abruptly can result in rebound EPS with "parkinsonian crisis" in patients with Parkinson's disease and a severe worsening of neuroleptic-induced EPS.

OVERDOSE: TOXICITY, SUICIDE, AND TREATMENT

As overdoses, ACAs' side effects escalate.

Treatments as listed above.

For general managment of overdoses, see pages 53–54.

If overdosage (OD) is with ACA or amantadine alone, unlike with antipsychotics, emetics are okay. Physostigmine 1–2 mg IV q 1–2 h may decrease CNS toxicity for both ACA and amantadine.

For amantadine OD, acidifying the urine may speed elimination; specifically watch out for hyperactivity, convulsions, arrhythmias, and hypotension.

PRECAUTIONS

Be alert to growing reports of ACA abuse.

- Arises in 0–17.5% of patients taking ACAs.
- Occurs with all ACAs.
- Most common with trihexyphenidyl, due far less to alleviating EPS, and far more to side effects of
  √ Energizing
  √ Inducing euphoria
  √ Sedating
  √ Enhancing socializing
  √ Affording psychedelic and psychotogenic experiences

ACAs contraindicated in patients with

- Urinary retention, prostatic hypertrophy
- Paralytic ileus, bowel obstruction, megacolon
- Hyperthermia, heat stroke
- Congestive heart failure

- Narrow-angle (i.e., acute angle-closure) glaucoma
- Hypersensitivity to ACAs
- Dry bronchial secretions (especially in the elderly)
- Delirium and dementia
- Cardiac patients with hypertension

Use ACAs with extreme caution in patients with

- Cardiac arrhythmias
- Hypotension
- Liver or kidney disorders
- Geriatric conditions
- Peripheral edema

NURSES' DATA

EPS are tough. These tips might help.

- Teach patients to explain to others about EPS, especially TD.
  - √ Have patients role-play explanations; it is good practice for real life and ensures that patients have accurate information.
- Patients should wear loose, lightweight clothing, with garments closing in front and fastening with velcro instead of with buttons or zippers.
  - √ If one side of the body is stiffer, recommend that patient put on or remove clothes from the other side first.
  - √ Shoes—slip-on or those that fasten with elastic laces or velcro—are preferable to standard laced or zipped shoes.
    - □ Long-handled shoe horn might assist.
    - □ Avoid high-heeled shoes or other styles that make walking difficult.
- Prevent bathing accidents.
  - √ Recommend use of no-slip rubber mat.
  - √ Recommend insertion of grab-bars.
  - √ Recommend removal of glass tub or shower doors.
  - √ Recommend installation of a shower chair.
  - √ Recommend soap attached to a rope and placed conveniently in bath or shower.
- Walking can be complicated and too fast, especially when people walk on the balls of their feet and with raised heels.
  - √ To discourage shuffling, teach patients the following routines.
    - □ Stop their usual walking.
    - □ Place their feet at least 8 inches apart.
    - □ Correct their posture.
    - □ Take a large step.
    - □ Bring their foot higher in a "marching fashion."

EXTRAPYRAMIDAL DRUGS

- Because patients may fall on turns, show them how to walk (not pivot or swing) into turns.
- For patients with problems getting out of bed at night because of stiffness or rigidity,
  - √ First lie (and then sit) on the side of the bed.
  - √ Slowly drop one leg over the edge while pushing down with elbow on the bed with the opposite hand.

Dentures can rub and ulcerate gums as well as provoke mouth movements that imitate TD.

Apply elastic stockings to reduce swelling from orthostatic hypotension.

Make referrals for physical, occupational, or speech therapy as TD or other EPS problems arise.

PATIENT AND FAMILY NOTES

General Information

If blurred vision occurs or alertness is lowered, do not drive or work in situations needing close-up focusing or quick reflexes.

For dry mouth, avoid calorie-laden beverages and candy; they foster caries and weight gain. Increase sugar-free fluid intake and try sugar-free candy.

To avoid accidental ingestion, do not keep medication at bedside; keep safely away from children.

To prevent or relieve constipation, increase bulk-forming foods, water (2500–3000 ml/day), and exercise. Stool softeners are okay, but laxatives should be avoided if possible.

ACA Information

Most common side effects of ACAs are dry mouth, and throat, blurred vision, light sensitivity, urinary hesitancy, constipation, and less memory.

Take ACAs with meals to reduce dry mouth and gastric irritation.

Although one may consume alcohol on ACAs, "one drink often feels like 2 drinks" and confusion is much more likely.

Use extra caution in hot weather. Heat stroke more likely.

May take oral dose up to 2 h late.

- If dose is more than 2 h late, skip it; do not double the dose.

- Benztropine's and biperiden's relatively long action may allow for a single bedtime dose.

Do not stop ACAs or amantadine until a week after antipsychotic agents have been stopped.

Amantadine Information

Most common side effects are blurred vision, dry mouth, urinary hesitancy, nausea, and insomnia. Most people don't get these side effects.

Take it once a day (up to 200 mg), but if side effects become a problem, divide the dosage into a twice-a-day regimen. Sometimes taking on a full stomach reduces nausea.

May consume alcohol on amantadine.

EXTRAPYRAMIDAL DRUGS

3. Antidepressants

INTRODUCTION

Antidepressants (ADs) are of 4 types:

- Multicyclic, often called heterocyclic, antidepressants (HCAs)
  - √ All of these except maprotiline and amoxapine have 3 rings and are called *tricyclic* antidepressants (TCAs).
  - √ The abbreviation TCA will be used if data is only available for TCAs but not for the larger group of HCAs (which include tetracyclics, maprotiline, amoxapine).
- Selective serotonin reuptake inhibitors (SSRIs)
- Atypical (bupropion, nefazodone trazodone, venlafaxine)
- Monoamine-oxidase inhibitors (MAOIs)

This chapter discusses HCAs, SSRIs, and atypicals; the next chapter, MAOIs.

This chapter focuses on

- Major depression (pages 84–96, 106–107)
- Treatment-resistant depression (pages 96–102)
- Electroconvulsive therapy and medications (pages 102–106)
- Seasonal Affective Disorder (mood disorder with seasonal pattern) (pages 107–108)
- Bereavement (page 108)
- Chronic physical pain disorders (pages 108–109)
- Premature ejaculation (page 109)
- Anorexia nervosa (page 109)
- Bulimia (pages 109–110)
- Premenstrual syndrome (premenstrual dysphoric disorder) (page 110)
- Pseudodementia (page 110)
- Pseudobulbar affect (page 110)

- Adult physical disorders (pages 111–112)
  √ Cardiac conduction problems
  √ Cataplexy
  √ Congestive heart failure
  √ Constipation (chronic)
  √ Diarrhea (chronic)
  √ Epilepsy
  √ Impotence (organic)
  √ Irritable bowel syndrome
  √ Migraine
  √ Narrow-angle glaucoma
  √ Neurogenic bladder
  √ Parkinson's disease
  √ Peptic ulcer
  √ Sleep apnea
  √ Tardive dyskinesia
- Childhood stage-4 sleep disorders (pages 112–113)
  √ Enuresis
  √ Night terrors
  √ Sleepwalking

As detailed elsewhere, ADs treat

- Agoraphobia (Anti-anxiety, page 295)
- Attention-deficit hyperactivity disorder (Stimulants, pages 355–359)
- Atypical depression (MAOIs, page 153)
- Borderline personality disorder (Lithium, page 199)
- Dysthymic disorder (MAOIs, page 153)
- Hypochondriasis (Anti-anxiety, page 281)
- Narcolepsy (Stimulants, page 361)
- Obsessive-compulsive disorder (Anti-anxiety, page 278)
- Panic disorders (Anti-anxiety, page 271)
- Schizoaffective disorders (Lithium, page 198)
- Social phobia (Anti-anxiety, page 276)
- Treatment-resistant depression (Stimulants, pages 360–361)

NAMES, COST, CLASSES, MANUFACTURERS, DOSE FORMS, COLORS

Generic Names (Dollars/Dose: 100 pills in mg)*	Brand Names (Dollars/Dose: 100 pills in mg)*	Manufac-turers	Dose Forms (mg)	Colors
		HETEROCYCLICS		
Tertiary				
Amitriptyline 6–16/100	Elavil 110/100	Stuart	t: 10/25/50/ 75/100/150 p: 10 mg/ml	t: blue/yellow beige/orange mauve/blue
	Endep 96/100	Roche	t: 10/25/50/ 75/100/150	t: orange/or-ange/orange/ yellow/peach/ salmon
Clomipramine	Anafranil 141/75	CIBA/Basel	c: 25/50/75	c: ivory-melon-yellow/ivory-aqua-blue/ ivory-yellow
Doxepin 16–45/100	Sinequan 107/100	Roerig	c: 10/25/50/ 75/100/150 o: 10 mg/ml	c: red-pink/blue-pink/peach-off white/pale pink-light pink/ blue-white/ blue
Imipramine 4–9/50	Tofranil 72/50	Geigy	t: 10/25/50 p: 25 mg/2 ml	t: triangular coral/round biconvex coral/round biconvex coral
	Janimine 9/50	Abbott	t: 10/25/50	t: orange/yel-low/peach
Imipramine pamoate	Tofranil-PM (sustained release) 72/50	Geigy	c: 75/100/ 125/150	c: coral/dark yellow-coral/ light yellow-coral/coral
Trimipramine 63–79/100	Surmontil 34/100	Wyeth-Ayerst	c: 25/50/ 100	c: blue-yellow/ blue-orange/ blue-white
Secondary				
Desipramine 32–110/100	Norpramin 180/100	Marion Merrell Dow	t: 10/25/50/ 75/100/150	t: blue/yellow/ green/orange/ peach/white
Nortriptyline 125–150/50	Pamelor 166/50	Sandoz	c: 10/25/50/ 75 o: 10 mg/5 ml	c: orange-white/ orange-white/ white/orange
	Aventyl 166/50	Lilly	c: 10/25	c: cream-gold
Protriptyline	Vivactil 68/10	Merck, Sharp & Dohme	t: 5/10	t: orange/yellow

Generic Names (Dollars/Dose: 100 pills in mg)*	Brand Names (Dollars/Dose: 100 pills in mg)*	Manufac- turers	Dose Forms (mg)	Colors
		TETRACYCLIC		
Amoxapine 43–189/100	Asendin 196/100	Lederle	t: 25/50/ 100/150	t: white/orange/ blue/peach
Maprotiline 45–62/75	Ludiomil 87/75	CIBA	t: 25/50/75	t: oval orange/ round or- ange/oval white
		SELECTIVE SEROTONIN REUPTAKE INHIBITORS		
Fluoxetine	Prozac 208/20	Dista/Lilly	c: 10/20 o: 4 mg/ml	c: green-gray off-white
Fluvoxamine	Luvox	Solvay	t: 50/100	t: yellow/beige
Paroxetine	Paxil 179/20	Smith Kline Beecham	t: 20/30	t: pink/blue
Sertraline	Zoloft 194/50 200/100	Roerig/ Pfizer	t: 50/100	t: light blue/ light yellow
		ATYPICALS		
Bupropion	Wellbutrin 72/100	Burroughs Wellcome	t: 75/100	t: yellow-gold/ red
Nefazodone	Serzone 83/all doses	Bristol Myers Squibb	t: 100/150/200/ 250	t: white/peach/ light yellow/ white
Trazodone 20–48/100 63–89/150 (dividose)	Desyrel 100/150	Apothecon (Bristol Meyers Squibb)	t: 50/100/ 150/300	t: orange/white/ orange/yellow
Venlafaxine	Effexor 105/100	Wyeth- Ayerst	t: 25/37.5/ 50/75/100	t: all peach

PHARMACOLOGY

TCAs are divided into tertiary and secondary amines.

- Tertiary TCAs have 2 CH_3 groups on a side chain, whereas secondary TCAs have one CH_3 on a side chain.
- Tertiary TCAs are more potent blockers of serotonin reuptake, whereas secondary TCAs are more potent blockers of norepinephrine reuptake.
- Tertiary TCAs tend to be more anticholinergic, antihistaminic, and anti-alpha adrenergic than secondary TCAs.

Sedative effects of TCAs are attributed to antihistaminic (H_1 receptor) actions and somewhat anticholinergic actions.

ANTIDEPRESSANTS

Receptor:	Histaminic-1	Dopaminergic	Cholinergic (Muscarinic)	α₁-Adrenergic	α₂-Adrenergic	Norepinephrine	Serotonin
Potential results from blockade:	• Sedation • Weight gain • Hypotension	• EPS • Prolactin elevation	• Blurred vision • Dry mouth • Memory loss	• Postural hypotension • Dizziness • Tachycardia	• Block clonidine's antihypertensive effects	• Sweating • Anxiety	• Diarrhea • Nausea
Generic Names	H_1	DA	ACH	α_1	α_2	NE	5HT
Amitriptyline	3	1	4	4	3	2	2
Amoxapine	2	2	1	3	2	3	+/-
Bupropion	+/-	+/-	0	+/-	0	+/-	0
Clomipramine	3	1	3	4	2	2	3
Desipramine	1	1	2	2	1	4	+/-
Doxepin	4	1	3	4	3	2	1
Fluoxetine	+/-	0	+/-	+/-	0	1	3
Fluvoxamine	0	0	0	+/-	0	1	4
Imipramine	2	1	3	3	2	2	2
Maprotiline	3	1	1	3	1	3	0
Nefazodone	+/-	0	1	2	0	1	2
Nortriptyline	2	1	2	3	2	3	+/-
Paroxetine	0	0	2	+/-	0	+/-	4
Protriptyline	2	1	4	2	1	4	+/-
Sertraline	0	3**	+/-	1	0	1	4
Trazodone	1	1	0	4	4	+/-	1
Trimipramine	4	2	3	4	4	1	0
Venlafaxine	0	+/-	0	0	0	1	2/3

* 4 = most potent; +/- = weak effect; 0 = no effect.
** This primarily represents presynaptic uptake blockade rather than postsynaptic blockade.

Antidepressants are completely absorbed from the gastrointestinal tract and largely metabolized by first-pass metabolism.

- These highly lipophilic compounds are concentrated in the heart and brain.

Peak concentrations are reached at 2–8 h, but may extend to 10–12 h. Trazodone peaks in ½–2 h.

Pharmacology of Antidepressants

Generic Names	Bio-availability (%)	Plasma-Bound (%)	Half-Life (hours)* Mean	Half-Life (hours)* Range	Excretion† (%)
Amitriptyline	48 ± 11	94.8–0.8	21	6–44	98 R
Amoxapine	——	90	8	8–30	69 R / 18 F
Bupropion	——	>80	9.8	3.9–24	87 R / 10 F
Clomipramine	——	97	32	19–77	51–60 R / 24–32 F
Desipramine	33–51	87 ± 3	22	12–36	70 R
Doxepin	27 ± 10	90	17	8–68	98 R
Fluoxetine	——	94 ± 1	60	48–216	60 R / 30 F
Fluvoxamine	53	80	15.6	——	90 + R
Imipramine	50	93 ± 1.5	25	15–34	98 R / 2 B/F
Maprotiline	——	88	40	27–58	60 R / 30 F
Nefazodone	20	> 99**	4	3–6	55R
Nortriptyline	51 ± 5	92 ± 2	32	18–93	67 R / 10 F
Paroxetine	100	94 ± 1	26	——	64 R / 36 F
Protripyline	——	92	78	55–127	50 R / ? F
Sertraline	——	98	26	15–95	45 R / 45 F
Trazodone	——	93 ± 2	5	3–9	70–75 R / 20–25 F
Trimipramine	——	95	10	9–30	80 R / 10 F
Venlafaxine	92	30 ± 2	5 ± 1	4–24	87 R

* Half-lives of parent compound; active metabolites have different half-lives and are reflected in range.
** Despite high % binding, it is loosely bound and has not yet been shown to displace other drugs to any clinically significant degree.
† B = bile; F = fecal; R = renal; ? = unavailable or inconsistent.

Children and adolescents:

- TCAs function differently in children and adolescents.
  - √ Children have less fat/muscle ratio and
  - √ Decreased volume distribution.

√ Children and adolescents have faster metabolism resulting in shorter half-lives,
√ Quicker absorption, and
√ Lower protein binding.
- Therefore, some children and adolescents are
  √ Likely to have higher, faster peak levels and sooner, lower, trough levels.
  √ Not as protected from large doses as adults.
- Ineffectiveness and toxicity of TCAs may stem from the increased fluctuation of serum TCAs in children and adolescents; more frequent doses (e.g., bid rather than qd) provide more stable therapy.

DOSES

General Doses

Generic Names	Equivalent Doses (mg)	Usual Therapeutic Doses (mg/day)	Extreme Doses* (mg/day)	Geriatric Doses** (mg/day)
Amitriptyline	100	100–300	25–450	25–100
Amoxapine	100	200–400	50–600	100–150
Bupropion	150	225–450	100–450	75–150
Clomipramine	100	125–300	25–500	50–150
Desipramine	150	150–300	25–400	20–100
Doxepin	150	150–300	25–350	30–150
Fluoxetine	20	20–40	20–80	5–40
Fluvoxamine	100	100–300	50–400	50–200
Imipramine	150	150–300	25–450	30–100
Maprotiline	75	150–225	25–225	50–75
Nefazodone	150	300–600	100–600	200–600
Nortriptyline	50	75–150	20–200	10–75
Paroxetine	20	20–40	10–50	10–40
Protripyline	20	30–60	10–80	10–30
Sertraline	50	50–150	25–200	25–150
Trazodone	150	200–600	50–600	50–200
Trimipramine	100	150–300	25–350	25–150
Venlafaxine	100	75–225	25–350	25–225

* The low doses are used for children and sometimes geriatric.
** These doses apply to 50–70% of geriatric patients; 30–50% still require usual adult doses.

Specific Antidepressant Doses

Generic Names	Starting Dose (mg/day)	Days to Reach Steady State Levels	Therapeutic Plasma Levels[1] (ng/ml)	Active Metabolite	Reliability of Plasma Level
Amitriptyline	25–75	4–10	> 95–160*	Nortriptyline	Maybe
Amoxapine	50–150	2–7	150–500*	8-hydroxyamoxapine	No

Specific Antidepressant Doses (Cont.)

Generic Names	Starting Dose (mg/day)	Days to Reach Steady State Levels	Therapeutic Plasma Levels[1] (ng/ml)	Active Metabolite	Reliability of Plasma Level
Bupropion	200–225	4–15	10–29**		Maybe
Clomipramine	75–225	7–14	72–300*	Desmethylclomipramine	No
Desipramine	25–75	2–11	>115	——	Maybe
Doxepin	25–75	2–8	100–200	Desmethyldoxepin	Maybe
Fluoxetine	20	21–35	72–300*	Norfluoxetine	No
Fluvoxamine	100	3–8	——		
Imipramine	25–75	2–5	> 175–350*	Desipramine	Yes
Maprotiline	25–75	6–10	200–300	Desmethylmaprotiline	No
Nefazodone	100	4	——	Hydroxynefazodone	No
Nortriptyline†	20–40	4–19	50–150		Yes
Paroxetine	20	5–10	——		No
Protripyline	10–20	10	100–240		No
Sertraline	50	4–21	——	Desmethylsertaline***	No
Trazodone	50–100	7–14	650–1600	Oxotriazolo-pyridin-propionic acid	Maybe
Trimipramine	25–75	2–6	200–300		No
Venlafaxine	50–75	3	100–500	O-desmethylvenlafaxine	No

* Parent compound plus active metabolite.
† Only TCA with a definite therapeutic window.
1 With drugs that have no plasma level reliability, these numbers represent population norms.
** Therapeutic window possible.
*** Serotonin syndrome not seen with MAOI/desmethylsertraline together; significant clinical activity questionable.

CLINICAL INDICATIONS AND USE

General Information

Antidepressants typically require 10–14 days on a therapeutic dose to start working. Their full effect may take 6 weeks.

Two major mistakes in prescribing TCAs are inadequate dose and time.

One major mistake in prescribing SSRIs is inadequate time.

Some symptoms on TCAs may improve before 10–14 days.

- Insomnia abates after 3–4 days, secondary to side effects.
- Appetite returns after 5–7 days, secondary to side effects.

Different symptoms on SSRIs improve before 10–14 days.

- Energy better in 4–7 days.
- Mood, concentration, and interest begin to improve in 7–10 days.

Symptoms of TCAs or SSRIs that improve before 10–14 days include:

- Diurnal mood variation (worse in A.M., better in P.M.) recedes around 8 days.
- Libido revives in 9–10 days.
- Anhedonia, hopelessness, and helplessness fade after 10–14 days.
- Dysthymia, excessive guilt, and suicidal thoughts dwindle by 12–16 days.

Antidepressants have equal efficacy for major depressions with or without major stressors.

- However, if the major stressor is continuing when antidepressant treatment first begins, then the antidepressant will be less effective.
- When the stressor resolves, the antidepressant returns to its usual level of efficacy.

For a "typical" depression all antidepressants have equal efficacy if the patient can tolerate a full therapeutic dose.

Relative predictors of a *good* AD response are

- Insidious onset
- Anorexia
- Middle or late insomnia
- Psychomotor retardation
- Emotional withdrawal
- Anhedonia
- Past success with ADs
- Guilt

Relative predictors of a *poor* TCA response are

- "Atypical" symptoms (hypersomnia, hyperphagia, rejection sensitivity, profound anergy)
  √ Just one of these symptoms lowers response to under 50%.
- Hypochondriasis (under 50% response)
- Childhood depression
  √ No proven effectiveness over placebo
  √ Same may be true for SSRIs
    □ 1 open study found fluoxetine effective in adolescents who had failed on TCAs.
- Anxiety, agitation, panic attacks with depression

MAOIs and probably SSRIs and bupropion do not lose effectiveness with atypical symptoms, hypochondriasis.

- Average drop-out rate for SSRIs, bupropion, nefazodone, and venlafaxine is only 15%, secondary to few side effects.
- Usually starting dose for SSRI is the therapeutic dose.

- Very low lethality in OD.
- Strongly consider SSRI as first treatment.

Severe Inpatient, Melancholic, or Geriatric Depression

- TCAs and venlafaxine may be more effective than SSRIs for geriatric melancholic depression and, perhaps, for nongeriatric melancholic depression.
- In 3 studies, TCAs performed better than fluoxetine.
- In 1 study, paroxetine not as good as amitriptyline at 4 weeks of treatment, but equal at 6 weeks.
- In other studies in patients with Hamilton's depression scores over 25, SSRIs and TCAs had same outcome.
- Published data comparing SSRIs with TCAs not available for very severe Hamilton scores $\geq$ 30.
- Venlafaxine's effects on serotonin and norepinephrine are very similar to the TCA clomipramine.
  - √ Venlafaxine probably has TCAs' advantage in this severely depressed population.
    - □ One study suggests superiority over SSRIs.

Mild to Mild-Moderate Depression (Hamilton $\leq$ 15)

- Placebo and antidepressants have same outcome.
- Psychotherapy and counseling have same outcome as antidepressants.
- Several studies suggest that nonsuppressors on the dexamethasone suppression test respond poorly to psychotherapy alone.

A trial of antidepressants not recommended initially in mild depression if patient will accept a supportive or psychotherapeutic approach.

Bipolar Depression: Mania Induction Risk

In known bipolar patients

- TCAs induce mania in 10–15% of patients.
- Paroxetine and sertraline (and probably other SSRIs) induce mania less often (2–3%) than TCAs.
- Bupropion has been reported anecdotally to have low mania rates.
- Nefazodone induces mania in 1.5%.

Delusional Depression

Antidepressants benefit about 65–80% of patients with nondelusional, unipolar depressions, but help a mere one-third of delusional depressions. Neuroleptics alone help 40–50% of delusional depressions; neuroleptics with AD help 65–70%; ECT helps 75–85%.

The dexamethasone suppression test might have limited usefulness in helping treatment plans.

- When a healthy person receives dexamethasone, blood cortisol is usually suppressed for over 24 h.
  - ✓ However, many depressed patients will have an abnormal "escape" in which their cortisol does not remain suppressed that long.
- An abnormal (escape) response predicts
  - ✓ Failure in psychotherapy.
  - ✓ High risk of relapse if ADs are withdrawn.
- An abnormal response does not adequately help
  - ✓ Make a diagnosis of depression.
  - ✓ Predict response to antidepressants.
- DST protocol
  - ✓ On day 1, give 1 mg dexamethasone po at 11 P.M.
  - ✓ On day 2, draw venous blood for a cortisol assay at 4 P.M. and 11 P.M.
  - ✓ DST is positive if either value is equal to, or above, 5 μg/dl.
    - □ The greater the value, the greater the certainty of an abnormal response.

Comparison of Antidepressants

There are significant differences between the classes of antidepressants. Venlafaxine's therapeutic profile (effects on NE + 5HT) resembles that of TCAs, particularly clomipramine but low side-effect profile resembles SSRIs. The atypicals and SSRIs are better tolerated and less toxic.

Side Effects and Compliance

Drop-outs due to side effects from premarketing clinical research studies:

Drop-Out Rate (4–6 Weeks)

Highly sedating TCAs	> 30%
Low sedation TCAs and trazodone	> 25%
Paroxetine	21%
Venlafaxine	19%
Nefazodone	16%
Fluoxetine	15%
Sertraline	15%
Bupropion	10%

Drop-outs due to side effects during the maintenance stage of treatment are also higher with TCAs.

Adequacy of Dosing

- Only 1/3 of family practitioners' patients on HCAs have a therapeutic dose or plasma level.
- For imipramine, desipramine, or doxepin, therapeutic dose is about 3–3.5 mg/kg (e.g., 200–225 mg for 70 kg person).
- With SSRIs, the first dose is usually a therapeutic dose.

Suicide Risk

- HCAs have a very high suicide risk.
  - √ Often a 2-week supply is lethal.
  - √ SSRIs and all atypical antidepressants have a very low lethality risk.
  - √ Usually a 2–3 month supply is not lethal.
  - √ Deaths strictly from an SSRI in U.S. are under 10.

Expense

Generic HCAs cost less. There are no generic forms for SSRIs, bupropion, venlafaxine, or nefazodone, but many for HCAs. Cost in 1995 for a one-month supply was usually over $60 for the non-HCAs and usually under $30 for generic HCAs.

- Cutting SSRI costs
  - √ Sertraline 100 mg costs nearly the same as 50 mg.
    - □ Prescribing sertraline at 100 mg and dividing the scored tablet in half can make it nearly as affordable as many TCAs.
  - √ Paroxetine has a free medication program for low-income patients.

Recommendation

If a particular antidepressant previously (without significant side effects) aided the patient or a close blood relative, use it with the patient.

Selecting an Antidepressant

SSRIs (and if no sezure risks, buproprion) are recommended as first choices in all depressions except severe inpatient or melancholic depression and mild outpatient depressions.

- SSRIs and bupropion have low lethality and side effects and higher compliance and chance of getting a therapeutic level.
- The total cost of the drug is usually significantly less than the total costs of inadequately treated depression or treatments with multiple side effects.

A panel of international experts on the pharmacologic treatment of depression, convened at the NIMH, unanimously made the above recommendations. As more experience develops with venlafaxine and nefazodone, these too might also be considered a first choice.

Side effects as clinical considerations:

- SSRIs are far more alike than different.
- SSRI differences include
  - √ Fluoxetine has slightly higher agitation (in mild form) and slightly lower somnolence rate.
  - √ Paroxetine has slightly higher somnolence (23%) in mild form, antianxiety and constipation (13%), and slightly lower diarrhea (11%) rate.
    - ▫ Paroxetine is only SSRI with significant anticholinergic effects.
  - √ Fluvoxamine has higher rate for nausea (40%), and insomnia (21%).
  - √ Sertraline tends to be "neutral" or average, having no side effect particularly more or less than average SSRIs.
  - √ Fluoxetine has a much longer half-life (> 7 days) than other SSRIs (25 h).

Choosing an Antidepressant

Antidepressants can be chosen for a potentially positive side effect, e.g., activation or sedation to treat a particular symptom. This choice should be made with caution.

- This choice should be made only if side effect would still be an advantage 4 weeks later.
- If the symptom to be treated is a symptom of depression, then any successful antidepressant trial will improve it.
- May be better to begin temporary treatment for a symptom that can be terminated later.
  - √ Hypnotic for sleep
  - √ Antianxiety agent for anxiety and agitation
- Using an adjunctive agent for sleep and anxiety is especially preferred over using sedating TCAs that have many other significant side effects (orthostatic BP, anticholinergic).

Comorbid conditions or depression subtypes may help determine best choice. (See depression subtypes, pages 85–87).

Pros and Cons of Specific Antidepressants

Choosing TCAs

Desipramine and nortriptyline are lowest in side effects on average and are first choices if TCA is used.

- Anticholinergic: desipramine < nortriptyline.

- Orthostatic hypertension: nortriptyline < desipramine.
- Sedation: desipramine < nortriptyline.

Choosing non-TCAs (only characteristics that differentiate these drugs listed)

Fluvoxamine is an SSRI, but because of high nausea and other side effects, is not generally recommended for depression.

Fluoxetine

- Pros
  - √ Long half-life
    - ▫ Missed doses less of a problem.
  - √ Activating
    - ▫ Patient experiences more energy quickly.
  - √ Decreased appetite
    - ▫ May help hyperphagic or overweight patient.
  - √ Somnolence and lethargy very uncommon.
- Cons
  - √ Long half-life
    - ▫ High levels could build up in geriatric and liver-impaired patients.
  - √ Agitation
    - ▫ May cause immediate worsening of depression.
  - √ Decreased appetite
    - ▫ May be a problem in 25% of low-weight geriatric patients.
  - √ Potent inhibitor of II D6 enzyme
    - ▫ Regularly increases TCAs, and other drugs metabolized by this pathway, by 200+%.

Sertraline

- Pros
  - √ Generally low in side effects
  - √ Low in nervousness
  - √ Lowest in anorexia
  - √ Half-life 26 h
    - ▫ Not likely to build up excessively.
    - ▫ Main metabolite N desmethylsertraline, 62–104 h half-life, significantly less active.
  - √ Weaker inhibitor of II D6 enzyme system
    - ▫ At 50 mg dose expect ~ 30% increase of TCA.
  - √ Low mania induction in bipolars (< 3%).
- Cons
  - √ Maximum absorption requires full stomach.
    - ▫ 25% higher levels this way.
  - √ Slightly higher dry mouth than other SSRIs.

√ Can cause somnolence.

√ Does not significantly inhibit its own metabolism.

▫ Very high blood levels for OCD may be hard to get.

Paroxetine

- Pros
  - √ Somnolence more common
    - ▫ May assist insomnia and anxiety.
  - √ Half-life 26 h
    - ▫ Not likely to build up excessively at initial dose.
    - ▫ No active metabolite.
  - √ Diarrhea less common
  - √ Low mania induction in bipolars (~ 2.2%).
- Cons
  - √ Somnolence more common
    - ▫ May interfere with functioning.
  - √ Anticholinergic effects more common
    - ▫ Constipation definitely more common
    - ▫ Other anticholinergic effects (e.g., decreased memory could be risk in geriatric patients).
  - √ Significantly inhibits II D6 enzyme.

Venlafaxine

- Pros
  - √ Affects NE and 5HT systems in similar way as TCAs but with fewer side effects.
  - √ Has minimal drug interaction risk.
    - ▫ 30% protein bound
    - ▫ Minimal effect on P 450 enzyme
  - √ Short half-life and 87% renal excretion avoids build-up in geriatric patients.
  - √ Effective in severe geriatric and inpatient melancholic depression.
    - ▫ First choice for this indication
  - √ Geriatric dosing is similar to nongeriatric.
  - √ Low sexual side effects under 300 mg dosing
- Cons
  - √ Increased diastolic (10–15 mHg ↑) blood pressure risk
    - ▫ Ranges from 3% (75 mg) to 13% (375 mg)
    - ▫ Tolerance does not usually develop.
  - √ Nausea risk 26% more than placebo
    - ▫ Dose-related, and tolerance develops in most over 2–6 weeks.
  - √ Requires bid dosing.
  - √ Final dose quite variable.
  - √ Somnolence, dry mouth, and dizziness can be problematic.

Bupropion

- Pros
  - √ Low overall side effects make it lowest in drop-outs (10%).
  - √ Unique (but unknown) mechanism of action makes it high choice in treatment-resistant depression.
  - √ Low mania induction.
  - √ Short half-life avoids build-up in geriatric and medically compromised patients.
  - √ Low sexual side effects
    - □ Case reports suggest sexual increase in some.
- Cons
  - √ Seizure risk significantly higher in "at risk" individuals.
    - □ Bulimics, head injury, seizure history
  - √ In low-risk patients, seizure risk slightly higher than with other antidepressants (~ 0.36%).
    - □ To avoid peak plasma levels, divided dosing required.
    - □ Need to build up dose gradually.
  - √ Requires bid or tid dosing secondary to short half-life and seizure risk.
  - √ May have therapeutic window, with high levels not therapeutic.
    - □ Makes adequate dosing trickier.

Nefazodone

- Pros
  - √ Almost no anxiety, nervousness, or insomnia side effects
  - √ Almost no sexual side effects
  - √ Low mania induction
  - √ Low risk of excessive build-up in geriatrics or medically compromised.
    - □ Relatively short half-life
    - □ Okay in renal and liver diseases
- Cons
  - √ Requires bid dosing.
  - √ Modest somnolence, dry mouth, nausea risk, dizziness
    - □ ~ 10–12% more than placebo
  - √ Bradycardia risk ~ 1.5% more than placebo
  - √ Potent III A_4 inhibitor
    - □ Increases triazolobenzodiazepines levels (alprazolam, triazolam, estazolam).
    - □ Increases certain H_2 blockers (terfenadine, asternizole).

With depression *and* preexisting

- Panic disorder, avoid trazodone and bupropion because they are relatively ineffective for panic.

- Bipolar disorder, avoid TCAs, consider lower mania risk, such as paroxetine or bupropion.
- Obsessive-compulsive disorder, pick a serotonergic antidepressant or clomipramine.
- Physical disorders, see chronic pain disorder (page 108) and other physical disorders (pages 111–112).
  √ If patient has longstanding symptom (e.g., constipation, diarrhea), choose antidepressant that does not risk worsening it.

When starting SSRIs, begin at 20 mg for fluoxetine and paroxetine, 50 mg for sertraline, and wait 3–6 weeks for response before increasing dose.

- Sertraline and paroxetine are not predictably activating or sedating. Patient may try test dose in middle of day to find out.
- Sertraline has increased (25%) absorption on a full stomach.

When starting TCA (e.g., desipramine), begin at 25 mg on day one and increase around 25 mg/day to reach a therapeutic dose by days 6–10.

- Because of low side effects, nortriptyline and desipramine are recommended as first choice TCAs.
- Maprotiline, because of seizure risk, and amoxapine, because of EPS and potential TD, are not generally recommended at all.
- Body size has some effect on target dose.
  √ Doxepin, desipramine, and imipramine often need 3.0–3.5 mg/kg.
  √ Amitriptyline needs 2.5–3.0 mg/kg (see table).
- If patient has no improvement after one week, escalate by 25 mg/day until reaching high side of usual therapeutic dose.
- If patient is not better by 6th week, obtain plasma level from a trusted laboratory.
- If plasma level suggests changing the dose, do so by 25–50 mg q 2–3 days.

Prescribe antidepressants in the following ways:

- Except for the new atypicals, dispense in a single, easy-to-remember (usually bedtime) dose to minimize side effects experienced during the day.
- Fluoxetine, desipramine, and protriptyline are often activating and need A.M. dosing.
  √ Sertraline and paroxetine can be activating, but not typically.
- Bupropion requires divided doses to reduce seizure risk.
  √ To reduce seizure risk with bupropion, give at least 3 doses per day; increase total daily dose no faster than 75–100 mg every 3 days, and do not exceed 450 mg/qd.

- To reduce seizure risk with maprotiline, do not exceed 225 mg/qd.
- Venlafaxine and nefazodone have a short half-life and require multiple dosing.
- Trazadone also has a short half-life and may perform better with multiple dosing.
  - √ If given in daytime, take on a full stomach to increase absorption and decrease peak side-effect level.

Explain most common side effects to patient.

- For tertiary TCA (amitriptyline, doxepin, imipramine), sedation, dry mouth, urinary hesitancy, constipation, and lightheadedness on standing up are common.
- For secondary TCA, all of the above can occur, but most patients do not get any one of these side effects.
  - √ With desipramine and protriptyline, activation is more common than sedation and therefore an A.M. trial might be considered first.
- For SSRIs, nausea, diarrhea, overactivation, insomnia, dizziness, dry mouth, tremor, and drowsiness are most common.
  - √ 5% drop-out on fluoxetine because of insomnia and/or overactivation/agitation.

In treating depressed children:

- ADs not proven to be better than placebo.
- SSRI safest option.
- If TCA, use desipramine, nortriptyline, or imipramine.
  - √ Imipramine only one officially approved by FDA for use with children.
  - √ Start at doses of 1 mg/kg/day.
- Get baseline 12-lead EKG.
  - √ In ≤ 10 y.o. incomplete right intraventicular conduction defect is normal, and if without other cardiac disease, benign.
  - √ Sinus tachycardia (> 100 6 pm) is common in younger children.
  - √ Escalate q4d by 1 mg/kg/day to a maximum of 3 mg/kg/day.
- At target dose, get repeat EKG at maximum plasma level, preferably 2–4 h after ingestion of medicine.
  - √ PR interval should be < 0.2 sec.
  - √ QRS duration < 0.12 sec.
  - √ Qtc ≤ 0.45 sec.
  - √ Avoid > 250 ng/ml imipramine plus desipramine level.
    - ▫ Risks delayed cardiac conduction, HR ↑, BP ↑
    - ▫ HR > 130 should be evaluated further.
  - √ Increase dose further if needed,

- Using plasma level and not mg/kg as guide.
- Up to 5 mg/kg may be possible.

- Because of anticholinergic effects of TCA, there is increased risk of dental cavities.
  - √ Children on long-term TCA need increased frequency of dental evaluation.
- Sudden death in 5–14 y.o. may be 8 per million on desipramine compared to baseline rate of 4 per million.
  - √ Desipramine may have higher lethality risk in overdose.

Delusional, depressed patients respond poorly to antidepressants, when sole treatment.

- Under 33% of delusional, depressed patients improve with TCA alone.
- TCAs can trigger psychoses, suicide attempts, and hospitalization.
- Treat delusional-depressed patients with
  - √ ECT—1st choice if patient is suicidal or extremely impaired.
    - 80–85% effective
  - √ TCAs with neuroleptics—1st choice if patient safe and can wait 4–6 weeks.
    - Can have > 70% response if maintained on this combination.
    - TCA can then be continued to prevent relapse.
  - √ Neuroleptic alone—2nd choice; 40–50% response for full effect.
  - √ Antidepressant alone—3rd choice.
- Combining antidepressants and antipsychotics:
  - √ Amoxapine, a dopaminergic blocker, may diminish the need for a neuroleptic, but locks in a neuroleptic effect during maintenance phase.
  - √ Amitriptyline with perphenazine found slightly superior to amoxapine, but latter had fewer EPS.
  - √ Avoid low-potency neuroleptics (e.g., chlorpromazine) because they aggravate the high anticholinergic action of TCAs.

In treating the depressed elderly

- AD efficacy is 70%.
- SSRIs, bupropion, venlafaxine, nefazodone, or secondary amine TCAs (e.g., nortriptyline, desipramine) most tolerated by the elderly.
- Initiate about one half (or less) the starting dose in adults, but for people weighing < 70 kg, 10 mg/day of nortriptyline might suffice.
- If TCA used, get baseline EKG.

- Increase dose slowly until
  - ✓ Clinical response noted,
  - ✓ Sufficient plasma levels attained, or
  - ✓ Intolerable side effects arise.
- Tertiary amines tend to show twice the plasma levels of younger patients on the same dose.
- Venlafaxine dosing about 25% less in geriatric than in younger patients.
- Nefazodone initiate at 50 mg in geriatrics, but go to same final dose (300–600 mg) as in younger patients.

Treatment-Resistant Patients

Before changing treatment, assess:

- Is diagnosis accurate?
  - ✓ Is there a hidden psychosis?
- Is dosing adequate?
- Is the patient on other drugs that could cause or exacerbate the depression?
  - ✓ Common ones are
    - □ β-blockers
    - □ High-dose benzodiazepines (≥ 3 mg alprazolam)
    - □ Corticosteroids
- Are there untreated illnesses (e.g., hypothyroidism, Cushing's) causing or exacerbating depression?

Plasma Levels

Most patients do *not* need AD *plasma levels.*

- Therapeutic plasma levels for many antidepressants are based on average blood levels sent to the labs (i.e., population norms) and not based on efficacy.

Plasma levels are useful for patients who

- Have not responded to adequate 4–6 week trials of nortriptyline, desipramine, imipramine, or amitriptyline.
- Are at high risk from age or medical illness, are at very high risk at high plasma levels, and thus benefit from low doses.
- Are prone to overdose.
- Display medication noncompliance.
- Require documentation of TCA plasma levels for future treatment.
  - ✓ Example: Patients attain therapeutic plasma level on small TCA doses (e.g., imipramine 50 mg/day).

- Have a potential for unexpected raised or lowered TCA levels because of drug interactions (e.g., SSRI also being used).

Measured plasma levels may be of

- The drug only (e.g., desipramine) or
- The drug and its chief metabolites (e.g., imipramine → imipramine + desipramine).

There may be a 30-fold difference in TCA levels after a single fixed dose.

- Slow metabolizers (e.g., elderly) are at higher risk for toxicity.
- Fast metabolizers may have trouble reaching adequate levels.

The menstrual cycle may affect AD blood levels.

- Desipramine and trazodone case reports suggest
  √ Plasma level 5 days before menses can be 50% lower than 7 days after cessation of menses.

Patients have 1 of 2 types of plasma-level response curves.

- *Linear*
  √ A direct, straight-line (linear) relationship exists between plasma level and clinical response. A specific plasma level yields a favorable response.
  √ An example is imipramine (with metabolite desipramine), which collectively must equal 200–250 ng/ml to be maximally effective.
  √ If the patient's plasma level is low, raise the dose. If very high with significant side effects, lower the dose to avoid toxicity.
- *Curvilinear*
  √ A curvilinear response appears as a ∩ curve.
  √ This curve shows an unfavorable response on the 2 vertical axes, but a therapeutic action on the horizontal plane.
  √ Nortriptyline may have a curvilinear response, also known as a "therapeutic window," which is 50–150 ng/ml.
    □ Nonresponding nortriptyline patients with plasma levels of above 150 ng/ml often improve by *lowering* the dose into the therapeutic window. A few do better with raising the dose.
  √ Bupropion may also have a therapeutic window.
    □ Some studies suggest 300 mg dose is better than 400–450 mg.
  √ Some patients on fluoxetine (total half-life over 3 weeks) may respond quickly in 5–14 days and then lose this effect at 3–4 weeks.
    □ Case reports suggest that lowering dose might return response because 3-week level was too high.

To obtain plasma levels

- Wait until ADs have reached a steady-state level, which is usually 5–7 days.
- Draw blood 10–14 h after last dose.
- Make sure tube is free of the contaminant tris-butoxyethyl.
  √ Can use Venoject vacutainer or glass syringes.
  √ Do not use rubber stoppers.
  √ Promptly centrifuge.

Increasing Dose or Augmentation

If patient shows partial response, higher doses should be tried if tolerated.

If patient is partially responsive at 3 to 4 weeks

- Raising fluoxetine dose increases responsiveness at 6 weeks.

If patient has no or minimal response at 3–4 weeks, T_3 or lithium augmentation (see pages 99–100, 194) may increase responsiveness by 6 weeks.

- Probably better than dose increase if
  √ Reasonable dose has been used with certain TCAs.
  √ Therapeutic plasma levels were achieved.

If patient has had aggressive dosing and adequate plasma levels and is definitely not responsive at 6 weeks

- Change to a different drug or
- Add an augmentation.
- The comparative outcomes of these 2 alternatives have not been researched.

Changing Antidepressants

- If patient could not get an adequate trial on one class of AD drug because of side effects, a trial of another drug in the same class may not have the same side effects and might work.
  √ About 70% of patients who could not tolerate fluoxetine tolerated sertraline.
- If patient had an adequate trial but drug was ineffective
  √ Moving to another drug in the same class (e.g., fluoxetine to paroxetine or fluoxetine to fluvoxamine) may be effective, or
  √ Change to a drug in a different class with a different mechanism of action.
- The distinctly different classes of antidepressant treatments, based on similarity of neurotransmitters affected (trazodone does not easily fit in), include:
  √ TCAs and venlafaxine: serotonin and norepinephrine

- √ SSRIs: primarily serotonin
  - □ Trazodone and nefazodone have mixed serotonergic effects (both inhibiting and increasing).
- √ Bupropion: unique and unknown mechanism of action
  - □ Dopamine?
- √ MAOIs: norepinephrine, serotonin, dopamine, phenylalanine
- √ ECT: most neurotransmitters
- Most AD treatments eventually down-regulate beta-adrenergic receptors.
- When switching from SSRI, if
  - √ Typical depression, consider venlafaxine or TCA trial.
  - √ Atypical depression, consider bupropion or MAOI.
  - √ If severely impaired or suicidal, consider ECT.
- MAOIs often effective alone when other meds have failed.
  - √ Do *not* add a TCA to ongoing MAOI! (See pages 155–157.)
  - √ May start MAOI and TCA together, both in low doses initially; or
  - √ Safer to add MAOI to amitriptyline, doxepin, or trimipramine.
  - √ Avoid adding MAOI to imipramine, desipramine, venlafaxine, bupropion, or SSRIs.
  - √ Before starting MAOI, must stop fluoxetine 5–6 weeks and sertraline and paroxetine for 2 weeks.

Augmentations: Lithium, T_3, TCA/SSRI, and Neuroleptics

Lithium augmentation or triiodothyronine (T_3) is preferred for these patients. Some will need to stay on augmentation, while others can stop in one month without relapse.

- In one study, about 30% of lithium-augmented patients (300 mg tid) improved markedly; 25% improved partially.
  - √ Most patients recovered in 19–24 days; 3.6%, in 2 days.
  - √ Clinical response did not correlate with serum lithium levels (usual levels = 0.5–0.7 mEq/l).
  - √ Melancholic patients reacted better than nonmelancholic patients.
- Another approach is to *add* T_3 (but in euthyroid patients, not thyroxine, T_4) to the AD.
  - √ Triiodothyronine (T_3) 50 μg/day lifts mood after 3 to 21 days in about 50–55% of patients in controlled and uncontrolled reports. 25 μg/day has had several negative trials.
    - □ Benefits euthyroid patients. Not usually enough to suppress normal thyroid function or cause hypermetabolic state, but can suppress TSH.
  - √ Thyroxine (150 μgm), when started with AD in euthyroid patients, blocked antidepressant effect.

    □ Average outcome on this combination was worse than placebo.

    √ Patients with subclinical hypothyroidism or with hypothyroidism treated with T_4 may benefit from increasing T_4.

       □ Many patients already being treated with T_4 are determined to be "euthyroid" but are at the low end of the normal range.

       □ Correcting T_4 to the high end of the normal range may make depression less treatment-resistant.

       □ T_3 in these hypothyroid patients also reported to help.

       □ May help females more than males.

TCA and SSRI can augment each other.

- If failed on either, cautiously add other.
  √ Response often < 1 week.
- Paroxetine and fluoxetine can increase TCA plasma levels several times; sertraline, less so (average 30%).
- If TCA failed, reduce dose to about 10–25% of final dose and add paroxetine or fluoxetine; reduce by 50% when adding sertraline. Because the amount of plasma level change is unpredictable, best to check level after 3–5 days and/or carefully monitor side effects.
- If SSRI failed, add 10–25 mg of TCA and very slowly increase, if needed.
- Neuroleptic (e.g., trifluoperazine 2–6 mg/day, perphenazine 4–8 mg/day) in delusional or severely agitated.
- Some patients who are "softly" delusional (e.g., nihilistic or over-valued negative ideas) may respond to added neuroleptic.
- Use briefly to avoid tardive dyskinesia.

Stimulants (see also pages 360–361)

Stimulants are better than placebo in treatment-resistant depression, geriatric depression, and medically-induced depressions.

- Hidden comorbidity of stimulant responsive syndromes (e.g., sleep apnea, ADHD) might account for some of the response in these groups.
- Usual doses
  √ Methylphenidate 10–40 mg/day
  √ Dextroamphetamine 5–30 mg/day
  √ Pemoline 37.5–75 mg/day
- A predominantly dysphoric response to dextroamphetamine has been reported in
  √ Postmenopausal women, but not in men or premenopausal women.
  √ Patients with borderline personality disorder.
  √ Patients with atypical depression.

Sleep Deprivation

- By itself, a single night of sleep deprivation has transient positive effects in 50% of patients.
- With antidepressant or lithium, positive effect is usually maintained.
- All-night, or just second half of night, deprivation equally effective, but any nap until next night can cancel effect.
  - √ REM deprivation may be the mechanism.
- If single night positive, can add booster nights every 3–6 days.

Less Proven Approaches to Treatment-Resistant Depression

- Carbamazepine (300–1200 mg qd) may relieve unipolar depression.
  - √ Valproic acid not shown to be effective.
  - √ Both carbamazepine and valproic acid may augment antidepressant.
- Other reported positive augmentations include:
  - √ Buspirone (40–60 mg: > 60% response in case series).
    - □ Buspirone reported to be effective alone in 45–90 mg qd dose range.
  - √ Dopamine agonists (bromocriptine, pergolide, amantadine)
  - √ Estrogen in pre- and postmenopausal women
    - □ R/o breast and endometrial carcinoma.
    - □ Gradually increase dose from 1.25 mg conjugated estrogen qd to 3.75–4.375 mg qd during the first 21 days of menstrual cycle.
    - □ Then progesterone 5 mg qd for 5 days to permit menstruation and reduce endometrial CA risk.
    - □ Supplement with pyridoxine 25–50 mg bid and prenatal vitamins to prevent estrogen-induced reductions.
  - √ 5,000–10,000 LUX light from 6–7 A.M. daily for 2 weeks
    - □ 7 of 10 substantially improved.
    - □ Patients did not have SAD but had winter worsening of depression.
  - √ Phenylalanine 500–2000 mg given in A.M. in single or divided dose.
    - □ Expect responder to have stimulant effect with risk of small BP rise and insomnia.
    - □ Research outcomes mixed; favors highly treatment-resistant women but not patients newly starting on ADs.
  - √ Pindolol 2.5 mg tid added to SSRI, MAOI
    - □ When started with AD, speeds time to response (< 1 week).
    - □ When added in treatment resistance, facilitates response.
  - √ Captopril (50–100 mg qd) alone or with other ADs
    - □ Can induce mania.

- Definite ineffective treatments for depression when compared with placebo include
  - ✓ Tyrosine 900 mg/kg/day
  - ✓ Baclofen
  - ✓ Reserpine

Electroconvulsive Therapy (ECT) and Medications

- Most effective treatment for depression
  - ✓ 75–85% efficacy
    - ▫ Does best with melancholic and psychotic depressions.
    - ▫ Atypical depressions respond less well.
  - ✓ Also effective in stopping mania with only 2–3 treatments.

ECT concerns

- Need adequate seizure length to be effective but avoid status epilepticus.
  - ✓ > 20–30 sec duration desirable.
  - ✓ Motor seizure > 120 sec or EEG seizure > 180 sec undesirable.
    - ▫ Treat with IV benzodiazepine.
- Minimize cardiovascular risk during ECT.
  - ✓ Death from ECT ~ 2 in 100,000 individual treatments
    - ▫ Hypertension, tachycardia pose M.I. and stroke risk.
    - ▫ Post-seizure bradycardia, asystole, arrhythmias pose further cardiac risk.
- Minimize motor component of seizure.
- Minimize post-ECT confusion.

To get adequate seizure length, minimize use of drugs that decrease seizure activity.

- Anticonvulsants
- Benzodiazepines
- Barbiturate anesthesia
- Propofol
- Lidocaine and related antiarrhythmics (e.g., procainamide)
  - ✓ Also can enhance succinylcholine's neuromuscular blockade.
- Dextromethorphan
- High doses of propranolol and perhaps other β-blockers

Drugs that increase seizure length and may enhance, but also overly prolong, a seizure include

- Theophylline
- Caffeine
- Lithium

- Bupropion
- Clozapine
- Fluoxetine and perhaps other SSRIs
- HCAs (e.g., maprotiline, amoxapine)
- Neuroleptics, especially low-potency phenothiazines
- Possibly trazodone

Anesthesia agents effect seizure duration and extent of spread in the brain.

- Ketamine
  - √ Prolongs seizure.
  - √ Prolongs full recovery time ~ 1 h longer.
- Etomidate
  - √ May slightly prolong seizure.
  - √ Reports of adrenal shutdown with prolonged (hours to days) use.
- Methohexital
  - √ Somewhat shortens seizure, depending on dose.
    - □ 1.2 mg/kg definitely shortens seizure and increases number of seizures needed.
    - □ 0.67 mg/kg reasonable dose for most, except those with tolerance to hypnoanxiolytics (alcohol, benzodiazepines, barbiturates).
- Thiopental, thiamylal
  - √ Definitely shortens seizure length.

Choice of sleeping medication is more limited prior to ECT.

- Avoid agents that shorten seizures (e.g., benzodiazepines, barbiturates)
- Consider agents that have no or positive effects on seizures.
  - √ Trazodone
  - √ Chloral hydrate
  - √ Zolpidem
  - √ Sedative antihistamines

Drugs that minimize cardiac and aspiration risks include β-blockers and anticholinergics.

β-Blockers

- Short-acting β-blockers decrease hypertension and tachycardia.
  - √ Labetolol: 4-minute serum half-life
  - √ Esmolol: 9-minute serum half-life
- Decrease heart rate more than blood pressure.
- Shorten seizures in doses
  - √ > 20 mg labetolol.
  - √ > 200 mg esmolol.

ANTIDEPRESSANTS

- No data to support routine use, but recommended with cardiac risk.
  - ✓ Has risk of bradycardia and hypotension.
    - ▫ May increase effects of post stimulus vagal hyperactivity and cause profound bradycardia or asystole.
- If hypertension more significant risk than tachycardia, then
  - ✓ IV nitroglycerine more effective than β-blocker.
- Avoid mixing potent hypotensive agents (e.g., nitroglycerine with β-blocker).

Anticholinergics

- Brain stimulation results in vagal hyperactivity which can cause
  - ✓ Arrhythmias
  - ✓ Bradycardia
  - ✓ Asystole
  - ✓ Excessive saliva from other pathways
- Without atropine, "vagal" arrhythmias, bradycardia or asystole occurred in 30–70% of ECT treatments.
- Anticholinergic agents (i.e., atropine and glycopyrrolate) can reverse all of these effects.
  - ✓ Glycopyrrolate superior for excessive saliva
  - ✓ Atropine superior for reducing cardiac vagal effects but no significant effect on saliva.

High-risk groups in which atropine should be considered include

- High seizure threshold
  - ✓ Vagal hyperactivity proportional to electrical stimulus
- Failed seizure
  - ✓ Absence of seizure's catecholamine flood increases vagal effects.
- β-blockers used
  - ✓ Will accentuate cardiac vagal effects.
- Cardiovascular risk in patient
  - ✓ Reserpine can lead to cardiovascular collapse or respiratory depression during ECT.

Excessive salivation/secretions not a serious problem but when it is

- Glycopyrrolate recommended

Atropine side effects include

- Tachycardia
- Relaxed lower esophageal sphincter
  - ✓ Increases risk of gastroesophageal reflux/aspiration
- Confusion
  - ✓ Atropine but not glycopyrrolate crosses blood-brain barrier.

Administering anticholinergics

- IV route preferred.
  - ✓ More reliable and faster
  - ✓ Should always have IV established in case of emergency.
- Doses given 2–3 minutes before treatment.
  - ✓ Atropine 0.4–1.0 mg IV
  - ✓ Glycopyrrolate 0.2–0.4 mg IV

Minimizing motor component of seizure

- Musculoskeletal injury common prior to use of muscle paralytic agents.
- Succinylcholine, a depolarizing agent, generally preferred agent and is dosed
  - ✓ 0.4–0.7 mg/kg.
  - ✓ Doses of 1 mg/kg may be used to
    - □ Avoid any muscle movement in patients with significant musculoskeletal problems.
    - □ Possibly reduce post-anesthesia agitation.
  - ✓ Use low end dose for high % adipose tissue and high end for high % muscle mass.
  - ✓ There is no medical need to routinely get spine films prior to ECT because succinylcholine prevents damage.
    - □ However, some still get spine films for medico-legal reasons.
    - □ Advisable if back had significant injury in which any abrupt movement is dangerous or if patient has h/o significant back pain and no films were obtained.
  - ✓ To ablate motor component of seizure give ECT 1–2 minutes after succinylcholine.
    - □ Use absence of fasciculations as guide and expect longer wait in geriatrics and those with compromised circulation.
  - ✓ Inflating BP cuff or tournequet on lower calf of one leg or arm prior to succinylcholine administration allows observation of motor seizure.
    - □ EEG more accurate and usually longer than motor seizure.
- Avoid succinylcholine if patient
  - ✓ Has recent large mass of damaged muscle tissue (e.g., stroke, burns, muscle injury).
    - □ Risks hyperkalemia.
    - □ Use mivacurium, a short-acting, non-depolarizing agent instead.
  - ✓ Is hypocalemic or hyperkalemic.
    - □ Diuretics increase this risk factor.

Augmenting ECT

- For short or failed seizures, use agents that lower seizure threshold.
  - ✓ Caffeine IV 500–2000 mg
    - ◻ Decreases seizure threshold but probably does not increase duration.
  - ✓ Sustained-release theophylline 200 mg given night before ECT
    - ◻ Longer seizures and fewer ECTs needed.
    - ◻ Less immediate confusion and fewer long-term memory deficits
    - ◻ Only one study available.
  - ✓ Hyperventilation
    - ◻ Patient is hyperventilated for 2–3 minutes before ECT.
    - ◻ Modest decrease in seizure threshold and increase in duration
    - ◻ Still see "tolerance" to stimulus requiring increased energy for later treatments.

Psychotropic agents

- Neuroleptics may augment ECT for manic and schizophrenic psychosis.
  - ✓ High potency may be safer.
- TCAs, SSRIs, and MAOIs have questionable positive effects with possible increased complications.
  - ✓ TCAs risk cardiac and other risks.
  - ✓ MAOIs have unproven hypertension risks.
  - ✓ To speed getting started with ECT, antidepressants probably don't need to be completely withdrawn and can be tapered during ECT.
- Lithium risks increased cognitive side effects.
  - ✓ More confusion, disorientation, encephalopathy reported.

Maintaining Therapy

Major depressive episodes usually persist for 6–12 months.

- If drug stopped earlier than 6 months, > 50% relapse rate.

After 1 to 3 months of treating acute depression, maintenance therapy can begin.

- Lowest relapse rate if acute dosage is maintained.
  - ✓ If the patient is symptom-free, continue the same dose.
- If the patient has annoying side effects, slowly lower the dose.
  - ✓ Beware of higher relapse rate.

√ To lower side effects, benign substitutions could be desipramine for imipramine and nortriptyline for amitriptyline.

After the initial 6 months, if there have been at least 4 consecutive symptom-free months, may taper TCA dose no faster than 25 mg q2–3 days. Both TCAs and SSRIs (except fluoxetine) have withdrawal symptoms to be avoided. It is safest to taper antidepressants by about 25% q3–4 weeks. This avoids most withdrawal symptoms and provides opportunity to catch a relapse early while it is still mild.

- If symptoms flicker (with or without stress), maintain acute dose.

Can adjust above schedules as follows:

- If this is the patient's first depression *and* the family's first depression, slowly discontinue TCA at 3–4 months after maximum improvement.
- If the patient has had repeated depressions, or the family has a h/o depression, do not lower TCAs for 9–12 months.
  - √ If frequency of depression is more often than once a year, patient may need to stay on antidepressant indefinitely.
    - □ Unless seasonal and then may only need treatment annually.
  - √ Interpersonal or cognitive-behavioral therapy is highly recommended in frequent relapse to optimize response and as potential prophylactic measures.
- Patients with full recovery are much less likely to relapse upon withdrawal than patients who have had only partial recovery.
- Patients who remain nonsuppressors on the dexamethasone cortisol suppression test are likely to relapse when antidepressants are withdrawn.
- Approximately 10–15% of patients with depression will have chronic depressions and will need to stay on antidepressants for years and perhaps for life.

Seasonal Affective Disorder (Mood Disorder With Seasonal Pattern)

- Treatments superior to placebo include
  - √ 2,500 LUX light 0.5–2 h in early A.M. (5–8 A.M.).
    - □ 60–75% response
  - √ 10,000 LUX light 0.5–2 h in early A.M. (5–8 A.M.).
    - □ > 70% response
    - □ 0.5 h usually enough.
    - □ Always use non-UV light to avoid eye damage.
  - √ Light treatment most effective in depression with hypersomnia or phase-delayed sleep (sleeping in later).
  - √ 20–60 mg propranolol at 5:30–6 A.M. qd

□ Shuts down nocturnal melatonin and resynchronizes body clock.

- Treatments with positive outcomes (> 60% response) but not yet proven superior to placebo include
  √ Fluoxetine 20–40 mg qd
  √ Visor lights
  √ Melatonin 0.5-2 mg qhs
    □ Starts nocturnal melatonin cycle.
  √ High placebo rates seen in some, but not most, trials may be caused by temporary increases in winter sunny days.

Bereavement

- Mild to moderate uncomplicated bereavement responds well to social support.
- Severe acute (< 4 months) or moderate to severe chronic bereavement may benefit from ADs.
  √ TCAs and SSRIs reported to be effective in uncontrolled studies.
    □ Usual AD doses
  √ Vegetative symptoms most responsive.
    □ "Normal" fluctuation of intense depressed mood characteristic of grief is usually less responsive.

Chronic Pain Disorders

ADs may alleviate chronic but not acute pain.

- TCAs are effective by themselves and also augment narcotic efficacy.
  √ No evidence that one TCA more effective than another.
  √ In patients with chronic pains, expect 50% or more improvement in pain 50% of the time.
  √ Equal efficacy in depressed and nondepressed patients.
  √ In patients with neuropathy and migraine, improvement rate often >60%.
  √ Presence of physical findings does not decrease response rate.
- If patients depressed, use the same TCA dose as in treating depression. If not depressed, can use lower (25–75 mg) TCA dose.
- Most studied TCAs are amitriptyline, desipramine, and doxepin.
- SSRIs may help but are less researched.
  √ Fluoxetine
    □ Not effective in diabetic neuropathy (1 controlled study).
    □ Effective in headache (1 controlled study).
  √ Paroxetine
    □ Effective in diabetic neuropathy (1 controlled study).
    □ Not effective in headache (1 controlled study).

- Trazodone marginally effective.
- Bupropion uncertain in pain.

TCAs have also been shown to augment opiate analgesics by

- Slowing development of tolerance.
- Increasing analgesic effect.
  - √ Low doses usually effective.

Premature Ejaculation

SSRIs often delay orgasm.

- This "problem" side effect can help many males with premature ejaculation.
- In males averaging less than 60 sec intravaginally to ejaculation, paroxetine 40 mg increased this to 15 minutes.
  - √ Full effect seen within 3 weeks (too "good" a response?).

Anorexia Nervosa

No single drug has been proven effective by itself or as an adjunct for treating anorexia nervosa. Nevertheless,

- Cyproheptadine, an antihistamine and serotonin antagonist, may help patients gain weight.
  - √ Dose 12–32 mg qd.
  - √ Free of TCAs' cardiovascular effects.
  - √ Do not use in anorectics with bulimic characteristics.
    - ▫ Can increase binge-purge cycle.
- Amitriptyline and doxepin may help anorectics gain weight, but the drugs have significant side-effect risks in this population (e.g., orthostatic BP and severe constipation).
- If severely obsessional, high dose SSRI (e.g., fluoxetine 60 mg qd), might help with
  - √ Weight gain
  - √ Decreased eating and exercise rituals
  - √ Less distorted body image
- If patient is depressed, SSRI safer in this group.

Bulimia

Recommendations for treating bulimics include:

- Fluoxetine (60 mg qd superior to 20 mg qd) or other SSRI.
  - √ Vomiting decreased 56% at 60 mg, 29% at 20 mg, and 5% on placebo.
  - √ Failure on one AD does not predict failure on another.

- Imipramine or desipramine 25 mg qhs.
  - √ Escalate dose by 25 mg q2d up to 200 mg qd for normal-weight bulimics.
- ADs may jump-start treatment with faster initial results, but when used alone are no better than, and often worse than, psychotherapy at 6 months.
- If these trials do not work, consider
  - √ Lithium, or
  - √ MAOI (preferably phenelzine), or
  - √ Opiate antagonist (e.g., naltrexone)
- Avoid amitriptyline and doxepin, since they may stimulate appetite.
- Avoid bupropion because of seizure risk.
  - √ Higher risk in vomiters with electrolyte abnormalities.

Cyproheptadine does *not* help bulimics.

Premenstrual Syndrome (Premenstrual Phase Dysphoric Disorder)

Serotonergic antidepressants reduce behavioral and physical symptoms.

- Fluoxetine 20 mg qd—first choice—> 80% response.
  - √ Responders might use only for 5–10 days premenstrually, but studies usually prescribe throughout the month.
- Other SSRI (less proven) or clomipramine (more side effects)—2nd choice.
- Lithium may augment response and, used alone, has modest positive effects, particularly on mood.
- Women on ADs who are euthymic except premenstrually can have lower blood levels premenstrually.
  - √ Check pre- and postmenstrual levels and, if needed, increase antidepressant dose premenstrually.

"Pseudodementia"

A depression in the elderly that mimics dementia.

- Treat as regular depression. Choose ADs with very low anticholinergic activity.

Pseudobulbar Affect

- Usually caused by subcortical brain damage.
- Patient bursts out crying or laughing without cause.
- Low-dose AD can effectively treat in a few days.

Other Adult Physical Disorders

These ADs have been recommended for treating major depression co-existing with the following physical disorders.

Treatment of Depression with Comorbid Conditions

Disorder[1]	Preferred	Avoid
Allergies (MH)	Doxepin* Trimipramine*	
Cardiac conduction problem (WH)[2]	Buproprion Fluoxetine Fluvoxamine Paroxetine Sertraline	TCAs[2]
Cataplexy (MH)	Desipramine* Fluoxetine Imipramine Protriptyline* Tranylcypromine*	
Congestive heart failure (WH)	SSRIs Bupropion	Nefazodone[3] Trazodone TCAs or venlafaxine?
Constipation (chronic) (MH)	Fluoxetine Fluvoxamine Sertraline Trazodone Venlafaxine	Amitriptyline Doxepin Protriptyline Trimipramine
Diarrhea (chronic) (MH)	Amitriptyline Doxepin Protriptyline Trimipramine	Bupropion SSRI Venlafaxine (except paraxetine)
Diabetes, Type II	Fluoxetine	Amitriptyline Doxepin
Epilepsy (WH)	Desipramine Doxepin Phenelzine SSRIs	Amoxapine Buproprion Maprotiline Trimipramine
Partial impotence (organic) (WH)	Bupropion (MH) Trazodone	Fluoxetine Fluvoxamine Paroxetine Sertraline Phenelzine
Dementia, delirium, cognitive disorder (MH)	Buproprion Fluoxetine Fluvoxamine Nefazodone Paroxetine Sertraline Trazodone Venlafaxine	Amitriptyline Clomipramine Doxepin Imipramine Protriptyline Trimipramine
Irritable bowel syndrome (MH)	Amitriptyline Desipramine Doxepin Nortriptyline	

Treatment of Depression with Comorbid Conditions (Cont.)

Disorder[1]	Preferred	Avoid
	Phenelzine	
	Trazodone	
Migraine headache (MH)	Amitriptyline*	
	Doxepin*	
	Fluoxetine	
	Imipramine*	
	Paroxetine	
	Phenelzine*	
	Sertraline	
	Tranlcypromine	
	Trimipramine	
Narrow-angle glaucoma (WH)	Bupropion	Amitriptyline
	Fluoxetine	Clomipramine
	Fluvoxamine	Doxepin
	Nefazodone	Imipramine
	Sertraline	Paroxetine
	Trazodone	Trimipramine
	Venlafaxine	
Neurogenic bladder (WH)	Bupropion	
	Fluoxetine	
	Sertraline	
	Venlafaxine	
Parkinson's disease (MH)	Amitriptyline	Amoxapine
	Bupropion	SSRIs?
	Doxepin	
	Imipramine	
	Protriptyline	
	Trimipramine	
Peptic ulcers (MH)	Doxepin*	
	Trimipramine*	
Sleep apnea (MH)	Protriptyline*	
	Tranylcypromine*	
Tardive dyskinesia (WH)	Desipramine	Amoxapine
	Imipramine	
	Nefazodone	
	Trazodone	
	Trimipramine	
	Venlafaxine	

[1] MH = might help; WH = won't hurt.
[2] Athough TCAs have quinidine-like, Type 1-A anti-arrhythmic effects, new studies suggest that in MI patients Type 1-A has increased mortality.
[3] Beware of rare bradycardias.
* Efficacy established.

Childhood Stage-4 Sleep Disorders

In children, common difficulties in stage-4 sleep include

- Enuresis
- Sleepwalking
- Night terrors

For childhood enuresis, the following TCAs seem equally effective

- Imipramine
- Desipramine
- Amitriptyline
- Nortriptyline

Often require smaller doses than in treating depression in childhood. For instance,

- Start imipramine at 10–25 mg at hs.
  - √ Increase each week by increments of 10–25 mg if without response,
  - √ Until reaching 50–75 mg/day.
- If necessary, maximum dose is 2.5 mg/kg/day.

Eighty percent of children will reduce bedwetting in less than one week with TCAs.

- Yet total remission is < 50%.

Wetting often returns when drug is stopped.

TCAs are especially useful for short-term treatment, as during summer camp.

TCAs might assist in children with

- Sleepwalking.
- Severe night terrors.
  - √ Adults with night terrors might also be helped by diazepam 5–20 mg or other shorter-acting benzodiazepines.

SIDE EFFECTS

Anticholinergic Effects

Clinicians should select an AD considering its anticholinergic side effects (see page 81 for comparison of ADs).

TCAs are generally much more anticholinergic than neuroleptics.

- Enormous anticholinergic differences among ADs themselves, such as amitriptyline being > 18,000 times more anticholinergic than trazodone.

Anticholinergic actions occur frequently, especially in the elderly.

Most anticholinergic symptoms taper off in 1–2 weeks.

Anticholinergic actions arise in many systems and include symptoms of

- Poor memory, confusion
- Hypotension

- Dry mouth
- Constipation
- Paralytic ileus
- Urinary hesitancy or retention
- Blurred near vision
- Dry eyes
- Narrow-angle glaucoma
- Photophobia
- Nasal congestion

These anticholinergic effects are discussed with their respective organ systems.

Cardiovascular Effects

Patients should be carefully checked for TCA-cardiac interactions.

Cardiac problems with ADs are of 4 general types:

- Blood pressure
- Heart rate
- Cardiac conduction
- Heart failure

Blood Pressure

- *Hypotension* with *dizziness*
  - √ Most common form is orthostatic hypotension.
  - √ MAOIs cause the most hypotension.
  - √ TCAs generate considerable hypotension (with nortriptyline least).
  - √ SSRIs cause almost no hypotension.
  - √ Hypotension more common in
    - □ Cardiac patients (14–24%) than in medically well patients (0–7%).
    - □ The elderly report a 4% injury rate (e.g., fractures, lacerations).
  - √ Measure BPs reclining, sitting, and standing, before and during the first few days of TCA, trazodone ornefazodone treatment.
  - √ Tell patient to deal with hypotension by
    - □ Sitting a full 60 seconds—or longer—if at all lightheaded.
    - □ Standing slowly while holding onto stable object (e.g., bed).
    - □ Waiting at least 30 seconds before walking.
    - □ Consider support stockings or corsets even at night.
    - □ Highest risk time is getting out of bed in middle of night.
  - √ Other management
    - □ Check if patient is on low-sodium diet, antihypertensives. If so, increase sodium or reduce antihypertensive dose.

- □ Increase dose more slowly, even though hypotension may not be dose-dependent.
- □ Try less hypotensive AD.
- □ If BP problems threaten continued use in patients without a cardiac illness or edema, may add sodium chloride (500–650 mg bid-tid) or yohimbine (5 mg tid).
- □ Hydrate with about 8 glasses of fluid a day. Patient must also have adequate sodium intake for this to work.
- □ Add methylphenidate or D-amphetamine.
- □ Greater BP drops may be treated with fludrocortisone (0.1 mg qd-bid), but this should be considered only if AD is only acceptable alternative.
- *Hypertension*
  - √ Venlafaxine only AD with significant hypertensive risk.
    - □ Treatment-emergent hypertension:
      375 mg, 4.5%
      225 mg, 2.2%
      75 mg, 1.1%
      Placebo, 1.1%
    - □ Sustained (3 consecutive visits) hypertension (supine diastolic BP: > 90mm and ≥ 10mm above baseline):
      300 mg, 13%
      201–300 mg qd, 7%
      101–200 mg qd, 5%
      < 100 mg qd, 3%
      Placebo, 2%

Heart Rate Fluctuations

- *Tachycardia*
  - √ Seen with TCAs and venlafaxine.
  - √ Patients may be frightened (unduly) or distracted by tachycardia and benefit from reassurance.
  - √ More common with more anticholinergic TCAs.
  - √ Occasionally seen with noradrenergic TCAs (e.g., desipramine, protriptyline).
- *Arrhythmias*
  - √ After several weeks of TCAs (especially imipramine), a quinidine-like action may ensue, which can cut down premature beats but may increase mortality in MI patients.
  - √ TCAs at toxic plasma levels (e.g., > 500 mg/ml imipramine and desipramine) can induce new arrhythmias.
  - √ At therapeutic doses, trazodone in cardiac patients can induce new arrythmias.
    - □ Of most concern is ventricular fibrillation.
- *Bradycardia*
  - √ Nefazodone has 1.5% risk of bradycardia.

√ Occasional reports of significant bradycardia with fluoxetine.
◻ May occur with other SSRIs.

Cardiac Conduction

- *ECG changes* with TCAs include
  √ Nonspecific ST and T wave changes
  √ Prolongation of PR interval
  √ Widening QRS complex
- TCA doses, and not cardiac disease, incite these ECG alterations.
- TCAs can increase cardiac risk with certain types of heart block.
  √ Some risk with bundle-branch or bifasicular block.
    ◻ Mild risk in first-degree bundle-branch block.
  √ Little risk in first-degree atrioventricular or hemiblock.
  √ Can produce fatalities in patients with second- and third-degree heart block.
- Avoid giving TCAs to patients with pre-existing bundle-branch block, especially with left- and right-sided bundle-branch block.
  √ If patient has a mild, first-degree bundle-branch block, TCAs might help.
  √ TCAs can produce fatalities in patients with second-degree and third-degree heart block.
- If TCA is used in patient with cardiac conduction disease
  √ Monitor serial ECGs.
  √ Monitor TCA level.
- Causing fewer cardiac-conduction problems are probably
  √ Bupropion
  √ Fluoxetine
  √ Fluvoxamine
  √ Nefazodone
  √ Paroxetine
  √ Sertraline
  √ Trazodone (but may create ventricular arrhythmias)
  √ Venlafaxine

Heart Failure

- *Myocardial depression, decreased cardiac output, congestive heart failure*
- *Pedal edema* frequently induced by
  √ Amitriptyline
  √ Trazodone

Sudden death occurs unexpectedly; supposedly due to cardiac arrhythmias.

- About 0.4%, more common after TCA overdose.
  √ Desipramine may be most likely to cause this fatality in O.D.

Gastrointestinal Effects

Constipation and paralytic ileus

- Generally correlated with ACA blockade (see page 23).
- Lowest with fluoxetine, fluvoxamine, sertraline, and desipramine.

Paralytic ileus

- Rare, but potentially fatal.
- Stop TCAs.

Dry mouth (see pages 22–23).

Anorexia, nausea, vomiting, dyspepsia

- Common (21–35%) with SSRIs, bupropion, and venlafaxine.
- Tolerance usually develops over 10–14 days.
- If 2° to TCA, reduce dose.
- If SSRI or atypical, take on full stomach.
  - √ Might add bismuth salicylate (Pepto-Bismol)
  - √ Antacid
    - □ Calcium versions offer least drug interaction problems
  - √ Antireflux agent (e.g., cisapride 5 mg bid)

Diarrhea

- Common (11–16%) with SSRIs.
  - √ Tolerance may develop.
  - √ If without tolerance, loperamide (Immodium) usually works

Peculiar taste, "black tongue" glossitis

Weight gain, appetite, stimulation, carbohydrate craving

- Not usually seen with SSRIs, venlafaxine, bupropion, desipramine, or trazodone.
- TCAs increase appetite and food intake. Correlated with H_1 blockade (see page 81).
- Most common with
  - √ Amitriptyline
  - √ Clomipramine
  - √ Doxepin
  - √ Trimipramine
- Doxepin is one of the most powerful H_1 blockers available.
  - √ Many times stronger than diphenhydramine (Benadryl) or hydroxyzine (Vistaril)
  - √ 25–50 mg provides nearly complete blockade.

Weight loss

- Sometimes seen with
  - √ Bupropion
  - √ Desipramine
  - √ Fluoxetine
  - √ Fluvoxamine
  - √ Paroxetine
  - √ Sertraline
  - √ Venlafaxine
- Is usually minimal.
- In geriatrics on fluoxetine, can be problematic in about 25%.

Renal Effects

Urinary hesitancy or retention (see page 24).

Correlated with ACH blockade (see page 81).

Endocrine and Sexual Effects

Distinguish effects caused by

- Depression
- Medication
- Other causes

Decreased libido, impotence, diminished sexual arousal, impaired orgasms

- Probably highest with SSRIs, clomipramine, and high doses of venlafaxine.
  - √ Postmarketing data suggest at least 15% ↓ libido, ↓ arousal or ↓ orgasm in males and females.
- Impotence seen more with TCAs.
  - √ Often secondary to ACH effects.
  - √ May respond to urecholine.
- Bupropion only AD with reported increases in libido and sexual activity.
- Management
  - √ Lower dose may bring marked improvement.
  - √ For decreased sexual arousal or anorgasmia try
    - □ Cyproheptodine 2–6 mg prn 2 h before intercourse or tid (beware of sedation).
    - □ Yohimbine 2.7–7.1 mg prn 2 h before intercourse or tid (beware of anxiety and insomnia).
    - □ Amantadine 100–400 mg qd (not used prn).
    - □ Bupropion 75–225 mg a day, in divided doses.

√ Yohimbine (5 mg tid) or bethanechol (10 mg tid) may reduce impotence.
√ Cyproheptadine can occasionally interfere with SSRI antidepressant effect.

Priapism

- Related to ∝-adrenergic effects.
  √ Highest when not opposed by anticholinergic effects (e.g., with trazodone, clonidine, risperidone[?]).
- A rare condition of persistent, painful erection.
  √ Most common with trazodone (about 1 in 2,000), and may occur at any dose.
  √ Occurs primarily during 1st month of treatment, but can erupt anywhere from 3 days to 18 months after drug initiated.
  √ Chlorpromazine, thioridazine, and other alpha-adrenergic antihypertensives cause other cases.
- If sexual ability is to be retained, intervention within 4–6 h is mandatory. If treated too late, condition will be irreversible, resulting in permanent impotence.
- All males on trazodone must be warned in advance about priapism.
- Management
  √ Medications and ice packs provide inconsistent results.
  √ Medications include alpha-adrenergic stimulants.
    □ Neosynephrine (10 mg/30cc) injected intracorporally 6cc (2 mg) every 10–15 minutes until response is seen or maximum of 3 doses (total 6 mg) is reached.
    □ Metaraminol 10 mg intracavernosal injection into penis.
    □ Epinephrine if pharmacologic treatment not obtained within 6 h.
  √ May require surgery.
  √ In emergencies, clinicians can call Bristol-Myers Squibb at 800/321-1335.
- *Clitoral priapism* has been reported.
  √ No apparent long-term risk related to this side effect.

Testicular swelling (rare)

- Reported from desipramine.
  √ Stop drug.

Breast engorgement (males and females)

Increased libido

- Sometimes reported with bupropion.

Spontaneous orgasm

- Rare; usually associated with yawning.
- Reported with clomipramine and SSRIs.

- More reports in females.
- Seldom spontaneously reported; usually elicited by MD when patient insists on staying on drug but having minimal antidepressant effect.

Eyes, Ears, Nose, and Throat

All side effects (except nasal congestion) due to ACH blockade (see page 81).

- All rare with fluoxetine and sertraline.

Blurred near vision (see page 27)

Photophobia

- From dilated pupils.

Dry eyes (see page 28)

Narrow-angle glaucoma

- Virtually all TCAs, but especially the most anticholinergic, can precipitate a painful narrow-angle glaucoma.
- If patient might have this type of glaucoma, postpone all anticholinergic agents, including TCAs, until diagnosis is clear (see page 28).

Nasal congestion

- Seen most with trazodone.
  √ May be alpha-adrenergic effect.

Dry bronchial secretions and strained breathing for patients with respiratory difficulty.

Skin, Allergies, and Temperature

Increased, and occasionally *decreased*, *sweating*

SSRIs, venlafaxine, and bupropion increase sweating (7–12%).

- Management
  √ Daily showering
  √ Talcum powder

Skin flushing

Allergies rare, and display

- *Rashes*
  √ Most often reported with desipramine.
  √ Also seen more often when tartrazine is used as a yellow coloring.
- *Jaundice, hepatitis*
- *Urticaria, pruritus*
- *Photosensitivity*

In all cases, medication should be stopped and an unrelated antidepressant tried.

Central Nervous System Effects

Sedation, drowsiness

Except for trazodone (quite sedating) and paroxetine (low-medium sedation), sedation is directly related to H_1 blockade (see page 81 for comparison of ADs).

Most Sedative	Medium Sedative	Least (or not) Sedative
Amitriptyline	Amoxapine	Bupropion (not)
Clomipramine	Imipramine	Desipramine
Doxepin	Maprotiline	Fluoxetine (not)
Trazodone	Nefazodone	Fluvoxamine
Trimipramine	Nortriptyline	Protriptyline
	Paroxetine	Sertraline
	Venlafaxine	

- Sedation, especially fatigue, during first 2 weeks of therapy.
  - √ Infrequently seen at lower doses of fluoxetine and venlaflaxine, but more often seen at higher doses (fluoxetine > 45 mg; venlaflaxine > 250 mg).
- Management
  - √ Give all ADs in single hs dose except those requiring divided dosing, including
    - □ Bupropion
    - □ Nefazodone
    - □ Venlafaxine.
  - √ Switch to less sedating AD, in particular fluoxetine, sertraline, bupropion, trazodone, or nefazodone.

Confusion, disturbed concentration, disorientation, delirium, memory impairment (see page 40)

Effect of Increasing Age on Risk of Confusional States with TCAs	
Age (years)	**Risk Rate (%)**
10–29	0
30–39	4
40–49	25
50–59	33
60–69	43
70–79	50
Overall risk	13

- Switch to a less or non-anticholinergic AD, in particularly fluoxetine, sertraline, bupropion, trazodone, or nefazodone.
  - √ Start with these if > 40 y.o.
  - √ If TCA needed, consider desipramine or nortriptyline.
- *Delirium*
  - √ Dose dependent; in 6% of tertiary TCA-treated patients.
  - √ Occurs with plasma levels of > 450 ng/ml.
  - √ May begin with greater depression or psychosis.
    - □ Increased TCAs or adding neuroleptics may worsen toxicity.
- *Memory impaired*
  - √ Especially in the elderly.
  - √ Determine cause carefully. May be
    - □ Depression
    - □ CNS impairment
    - □ Endocrine or other medical problem (e.g., pneumonia)
    - □ Medication-induced toxicity.
- If patient tries to remember something and can't, the culprit is more organically based; if the person doesn't try at all, depression is more likely.
- Difficulties in word finding and name recall have been reported on all antidepressants, including lithium and MAOIs.
  - √ Frequency and mechanism of this side effect is unknown.

Weakness, lethargy, fatigue
Muscle tremors, twitches, jitters (occasional)
Speech blockage, stuttering
Seizures

- Overall incidence of first seizure without drug is 0.08%.
- Afflicts 0.1% of SSRI patients.
- Afflicts 0.2% of patients on TCA or venlafaxine.
  - √ 2–3% for clomipramine, bupropion (2.3% risk at 600 mg), maprotiline, and amoxapine in high doses.
- More recent reports of seizures with
  - √ Maprotiline when
    - □ Given in high doses (200–400 mg qd),
    - □ Rapidly escalated to 150 mg/day in 7 days, and
    - □ Patients have pre-existing seizures.
  - √ Bupropion given > 450 mg/day or > 150 mg single doses.
    - □ Patients with seizure history or risks, including family h/o seizures, sedative withdrawal, bulimia, multiple concomitant medications, head injury, abnormal EEG, are higher risk.
    - □ Patients with liver disease and resulting increased bupropion levels are higher risk.
- With HCAs, seizures erupt with
  - √ Overdose

- 8.4% rate
- Most with blood level > 1000 mg/ml
- QRS lengthening not a good predictor of seizure.
- √ Pre-existing seizures (including alcohol withdrawal).
- √ Pre-existing neurologic disorder.
- Higher TCA plasma levels (> 450 ng/ml) increase risk of, but are insufficient to cause, seizures.
  - √ Weeks of high TCA plasma levels may occur before seizures.
  - √ High chronic levels typically have no prodromal phase; they generate a single, tonic-clonic, sometimes fatal, grand mal seizure.
- Acute HCA overdose triggers multiple seizures and status epilepticus.

"Spaciness," depersonalization

- Mainly seen with HCA and trazodone.
- Management
  - √ Escalate dose more slowly.
  - √ If side effect persists, switch to another AD.

Yawning without sedation

- Occasionally seen with serotonergic drugs (SSRIs and clomipramine).

Suicidal ideation (S.I.)

- New S.I. rate in first week on HCA about same as placebo (3–3.5%).
- New S.I. rate in first week on fluoxetine, and possibly other SSRIs, slightly lower than placebo (2.5–3.0%).
  - √ In majority of reports of sudden, severe increase in S.I. while on fluoxetine, akathisia/agitation may have contributed.
    - Tell patient to call immediately if akathisia/agitation develops with SSRI.
    - Discontinue SSRI or attempt to treat with benzodiazepine, propranolol, or clonidine.

Paresthesias (infrequent)
Ataxia
Extrapyramidal side effects

- Most often seen with amoxapine.
  - √ Parkinsonian reactions
  - √ Dyskinesia
    - Uncommon.
    - Arises with reduced dose.
    - Disappears quickly.
  - √ Tardive dyskinesia

- Rarely seen with other HCAs.
- Sometimes seen with SSRIs.
- *Agitation/akathisia*
  - √ Extremely difficult to separate agitation from akathisia—physical components strong in both.
  - √ Most common with bupropion and SSRIs, especially fluoxetine.
  - √ Occasionally with protriptyline and desipramine.
  - √ May respond to benzodiazepines, propranolol, or clonidine.
  - √ Preliminary studies indicate most patients have a remission of agitation in 2–4 weeks.
- *Neuroleptic malignant syndrome* (see pages 33–36).
  - √ Amoxapine is the only antidepressant to cause this syndrome.

Tremors

- High-frequency tremors commonly seen, especially with noradrenergic TCAs, lithium (> 300 mg), and venlafaxine.
- Occasionally seen with SSRIs.
- Management of persistent tremor can involve
  - √ Lower TCA doses,
  - √ Propranolol 10–20 mg bid-qid, or
  - √ Low doses of benzodiazepines (e.g., alprazolam 0.25 mg bid).

Insomnia

- Most common with SSRIs, bupropion, venlafaxine, and protriptyline.
  - √ Then with desipramine and amoxapine.
- Use A.M. dosing.
- Add trazodone 25–100 mg qhs or standard hypnotic.

Weird dreams, such as *nightmares, hynagogic hallucinations,* and *vivid dreams*

- Can occur on any AD.
- Usually emerge when AD consumed all at hs.
- May reduce by
  - √ Changing AD.
  - √ Moving part of dose to dinner time.
  - √ Spreading dose throughout day.

Excitement, restlessness, or precipitation of

- *Hypomania, mania*
  - √ With no h/o bipolar disorder
    - □ 2% with TCA
    - □ 1% with SSRIs, bupropion, venlafaxine, and nefazodone.

- With h/o of bipolar disorder
  - □ ≥ 12% with TCA
  - □ ~ 2% with paroxetine, nefazodone, or sertraline
  - □ Reported low with other SSRIs and bupropion.
  - √ In a known bipolar disorder, use full dose anticycling agent first before antidepressant.

Panic attacks or anxiety

- If h/o of panic disorder, start with very low dose.
  - √ Imipramine 10 mg or fluoxetine 5 mg.
- Without h/o of panic disorder, try another antidepressant.
  - √ Reaction may have been idiosyncratic to drug used.
  - √ Less activating drug should be considered (e.g., stop fluoxetine and try paroxetine).

Emotional instability

Delusions, visual or auditory hallucinations, "serotonin syndrome" (see MAOIs, page 155, for more details)

- With SSRIs and clomipramine.
  - √ Usually doesn't occur with sole use of drug in normal doses.
  - √ Occasionally seen in mild forms with very high doses.
    - □ "Mild forms" is to see color trails behind moving objects (sometimes called "tracers" by LSD users).
- Occurs with dangerous combinations:
  - √ SSRI or clomipramine with MAOI (not with selegiline)
  - √ Tryptophan, dextromethorphan, or mepreridine with MAOIs (and possibly SSRIs).
- Must wait 5 weeks after 20 mg fluoxetine stopped, 6–9 weeks after fluoxetine 40 mg stopped, and 2 weeks after sertraline and paroxetine stopped before starting MAOI.
- Patients may experience one, several, or all of these symptoms.
  - √ Restlessness
  - √ Diaphoresis
  - √ Hyperreflexia
  - √ Myoclonus
  - √ Nausea, abdominal cramps
  - √ Diarrhea
  - √ Insomnia
- Management
  - √ Serotonin antagonist cyproheptadine 4–12 mg can alleviate the serotonin syndrome.
  - √ Hospitalize; can be fatal.
  - √ Select less serotonergic antidepressant.

Headache

- Frequently occurs spontaneously in depression; "tension" headache most common.
- In SSRI trials, significant headache reported on placebo in 16–19%.
  √ Same or slightly less than on active drug.
- Determine headache frequency in patient before starting medication; otherwise it may be reported as a "side effect."

PERCENTAGES OF SIDE EFFECTS

Part I

Side Effects	Amitrip-tyline	Amoxa-pine	Bupro-pion*	Clomi-pramine	Desipra-mine
CARDIOVASCULAR EFFECTS					
Hypotension (postural)	32 (10–44)	36 (32–42)	4.3 (2.5–10)	13 (6–30)	6
Hypertension	—	—	1.6	—	—
Dizziness, lightheaded-ness	42.5 (10–65)	> 30	22.3	37 (10–54)	6
Fainting, syncope	—	—	1.2	0.0	—
Tachycardia	20	20	10.8	14.7 (4–30)	6
Palpitations	5	—	3.7	4	—
ECG abnormalities	20	< 2	< 2	20	6
Cardiac arrhythmias	6	< 2	3.7	6	6
Edema	1	—	< 2	—	2
GASTROINTESTINAL EFFECTS					
Dry mouth and throat	58.5 (30–90)	29 (14–30)	27 (10–44)	43 (>30–84)	20
Anorexia, lower appetite	0.0	—	18.3**	12	—
Increased appetite	5	—	3.7	11	—
Nausea, vomiting	5.5	—	22.9	19.5 (2–33)	6
Taste changes	—	—	3.1	—	—
Dyspepsia, upset stomach	5	—	3.1	16 6–14	—
Diarrhea	—	—	6.8**	13	—
Constipation	29.4 (10–38.2)	27 (12–>30)	20.7 (20–30)	33.5 (10–47)	6
Weight gain	> 30	< 2	13.6**	19 (10–30)	6
Weight loss	—	—	23.2**	—	—
RENAL EFFECTS					
Urinary hesitancy or retention	10.5 (2–15)	20	3.9 (1.9–10)	11 (2–30)	—

Side Effects	Amitrip- tyline	Amoxa- pine	Bupro- pion*	Clomi- pramine	Desipra- mine
ENDOCRINE AND SEXUAL EFFECTS					
Menstrual changes	——	——	4.7	12	——
Breast swelling	——	——	——	2	——
Lactation	——	——	——	4	——
Priapism	0.0	0.0	0.0	0.0	0.0
Disturbed sexual function	4.3 (0–10)	——	3.2	16.3 (8–30)	7 (2–10)
EYES, EARS, NOSE, AND THROAT EFFECTS					
Blurred vision	35.2 (10–55.7)	6.5 (2–10)	14.6	20	6
Tinnitus	10	——	——	——	——
Sore throat, flu	——	——	5	10	——
SKIN, ALLERGIES, AND TEMPERATURE					
Rashes	6	11.5 (3–30)	8 ——	7 (2–10)	12
Abnormal skin pigment	——	——	2.2	4	——
Fever, hyperthermia	——	0.5	1.6	4	——
Sweating	22.5 (10–30)	6	22.3	21 (10–30)	——
CENTRAL NERVOUS SYSTEM EFFECTS					
Weakness, fatigue	20	5.5 (2–10)	5**	30 (2–54)	6
Muscle cramps	5	——	1.9**	13	——
Seizures	0.2	0.2	0.36 (0.3–2.2)	2.1 (0.5–3)	< 0.2
Headache	10.5 (2–15)	6	25.7	6	0.2
Slurred speech	——	——	——	3	——
Tremor	25 (5–40)	9 (2–12)	21.1	16.3 (6–33)	6
Drowsiness, sedation	39.6 (30–58.8)	16 (14–30)	19.8	30 (2–54)	6
Insomnia	10.5 (2–15)	20	18.6	8.5 (1.5–30)	6
Confusion, disorientation	11.3 (0–30)	6	8.4	4.5 (2–10)	——
Anxiety, nervousness (mental)	——	——	3.1	15.5 (9–18)	——
Agitation, restlessness, akathisia (motoric)	——	——	31.9	3	——
Excitement, hypomania	5.7 (< 2–15)	6	1.2	< 2	6

* Bupropion side effects based on 300–600 mg dose range no longer used. Might expect lower side effects than indicated here with 300–450 mg dose range. Seizure risk with > 450 mg is > 2%.
**See p. 131.

Part II

Side Effects	Doxepin	Fluox-etine	Fluvox-amine	Impira-mine	Mapro-tiline	Nefa-zodone
CARDIOVASCULAR EFFECTS						
Hypotension (postural)	20	< 1	**	37 (>30–40)	6	4
Hypertension	—	< 1	—	—	—	< 1
Dizziness, lightheaded-ness	20	5.7	11	26.3 (15–30)	7 (2–10)	17
Tachycardia	20	1.2	—	20	6	< 1
Palpitations	—	1.3	3	5	—	< 1
ECG abnormalities	6	< 2	—	20	< 2	< 1
Cardiac arrhythmias	6	1.5	—	6	< 2	< 1
Edema	—	< 1	—	—	—	3
GASTROINTESTINAL EFFECTS						
Dry mouth and throat	43 (>30–56)	9.5	14	30	26 (22–>30)	25
Anorexia, lower appetite	—	9.0	18	—	—	
Increased appetite	—	1	**	—	—	5
Nausea, vomiting	< 2	20.7	40	5	4	2
Taste changes	—	2.2 (1.8–3)	3	—	—	2
Dyspepsia, upset stomach	—	6.2	10	—	—	9
Diarrhea	—	12.2	11	—	—	8
Constipation	31.5 (10–43)	5	10	20	13 (6–30)	4
Jaundice	—	< 1	—	—	—	< 0.1
Weight gain	26	< 1	1	20	20	—
Weight loss	—	13	—	—	—	< 1
RENAL EFFECTS						
Urinary hesitancy or retention	4.5 (<2–10)	1.5	1	20	6	2
ENDOCRINE AND SEXUAL EFFECTS						
Menstrual changes	—	1.7	—	—	—	< 0.1
Breast swelling	—	< 1	—	—	—	< 0.1
Priapism	0.0	0.0	0.0	0.0	0.0	—
Disturbed sexual function	6	15*	8	2.5	—	1
Hypothyroidism	—	< 1	—	—	—	0
HEMATOLOGIC EFFECTS						
Blood dyscrasias	—	< 1	—	—	—	< 0.1
EYES, EARS, NOSE, AND THROAT EFFECTS						
Blurred vision	20	2.8 (2–10)	3	16.7 (10–30)	12 (4–30)	—

Side Effects	Doxepin	Fluo-xetine	Fluvo-xamine	Imipra-mine	Mapro-tiline	Nefa-zodone
Nasal stuffiness	—	2.3	**	—	—	< 1
Sore throat, flu	—	7.8	9	—	—	6
SKIN, ALLERGIES, AND TEMPERATURE						
Allergies	—	1.1	—	—	—	< 1
Rashes	< 2	2.7	**	6	20	< 1
Abnormal skin pigment	—	2	—	—	—	< 0.1
Sweating	20	7.5 (2–8.4)	0.7	20	6	0.0
Fever, hyperthermia	—	< 0.1	3	—	—	< 0.1
CENTRAL NERVOUS SYSTEM EFFECTS						
Weakness, fatigue	6	4.2	5.1	20	4	8
Muscle cramps	—	1.4	**	—	—	< 1
Rigidity	—	< 1	**	—	—	1
Seizures	< 0.2	0.2 (0.2–<2)	0.005	> 3 (0.6–>3)	> 3 (0.2–>3)	< 0.1
Headache	< 2	20.1 (10–30)	4.8	20	3	36
Slurred speech	—	—	—	6	—	—
Tremor	6	13.9	5		(3–30)	2
Drowsiness, sedation	34.5 (30–39)	11.8 (10–30)	22	26 (20–32)	18 (10–30)	25
Insomnia	6	16.9 (10–30)	21	20	2	11
Disorientation, confusion	< 2	1.5	—	4.3	6	7
Restlessness, agitation, akathisia	—	15	2	—	2	< 1
Anxiety, nervousness (mental)	—	10.9 (9.4–15)	12	—	4.5	< 1
Excitement, hypomania	< 2	7.3 (1–30)	2	15 (5–30)	6	1

Part III

Side Effects	Nortrip-tyline	Paroxe-tine	Proptrip-tyline	Sertra-line	Trazo-done	Trimipra-mine	Venla-faxine
CARDIOVASCULAR EFFECTS							
Hypotension (postural)	6	1.2	20	<1	10.1 (3.8–30)	20	1
Hypertension	—	>1	—	<1	1.7	—	2
Dizziness, light-headedness	5.5	13	20	11.7	21.9 (10–30)	20	21
Fainting, syn-cope	—	>1	—	<1	3.7 (2.8–4.5)	—	<1

Side Effects	Nortriptyline	Paroxetine	Proptriptyline	Sertraline	Trazodone	Trimipramine	Venlafaxine
Tachycardia	6	>1	6	<1	3.2 (0.0–10)	6	2
Palpitations	—	2.9	—	3.5	0.0–0.7	—	—
Shortness of breath	—	<1	—	<1	1.2	—	>1
ECG abnormalities	6	<1	20	—	<2	20	<0.1
Cardiac arrhythmias	6	<1	6	—	<2	6	<0.1
Edema	—	<1	—	<1	4.9	—	<1
GASTROINTESTINAL EFFECTS							
Dry mouth and throat	20	18.1	2	16.3	17.7 (2–33.8)	20	22
Anorexia, lower appetite	—	6.4	—	2.8	1.7 (0.0–3.5)	—	11
Nausea, vomiting	2.3	25.7	—	26.1	15.7 (9.9–30)	<2	37
Taste changes	—	2.4	—	1.2	0.7	—	2
Dyspepsia, indigestion	—	1.9	—	6	4.6	—	5
Diarrhea	—	11.6	—	17.7	2.2 (0.0–4.5)	—	8
Constipation	8.6	13.8	20	8.4	13.6 (7–30)	20	15
Weight gain	6	>1	—	<1	4.5 (1.4–10)	20	0.0
Weight loss	—	>1	—	<1	3.4 (1–5.7)	—	<1
RENAL EFFECTS							
Urinary hesitancy or retention	<2	>1	<2	<0.1 (<2–10)	4.8	<2	2
ENDOCRINE AND SEXUAL EFFECTS							
Priapism	0.0	0.0	0.0	0.0	0.05	0.0	<0.1
Disturbed sexual function	<2	15*	<2	15*	1.4	—	1–15*
EYES, EARS, NOSE, AND THROAT EFFECTS							
Blurred vision	5.5	3.6	20	>1	8.3 (2–14.7)	6	6
Nasal stuffiness	—	>1	—	2	4.3 (2.8–5.7)	—	—
SKIN, ALLERGIES, AND TEMPERATURE							
Rashes	<2	1.7	<2	2.1	<2	<2	3
Sweating	2.5	11.2	20	8.4	1.2	6	12

Side Effects	Nortrip- tyline	Paroxe- tine	Proptrip- tyline	Sertra- line	Trazo- done	Trimipra- mine	Venla- faxine
			CENTRAL NERVOUS SYSTEM EFFECTS				
Weakness, fatigue	20	15	20	8.1	6.6	6	12
Muscle cramps	—	1.7	—	1.7	5.4	—	<1
Seizures	0.2	—	0.2	0.1	0.2	0.2	0.26
Headache	<2	17.6	—	20.3	10.4 (2–19.8)	6	25
Incoordination	—	<0.1	—	<1	3.4 (1.9–4.9)	—	<1
Tremor	11.3 (0.0–30)	8	6	10.7	4.9 (2–10)	20	5
Drowsiness, sedation	6.8 (0.0–15)	23.3 (10–30)	<2	13.4	29.1 (20–50)	>30	23
Insomnia	<2	13	20	16.4 (<2–9.9)	5.1	6	18
Disorientation, confusion	11.3 (0.0–30)	1.2	—	>1	3.7 (<20–5.7))	20	2
Agitation	—	2.1	—	5.6	—	—	2
Anxiety, nervousness (mental)	—	5	—	5.6	10.6 (6.4–14.8)	—	13
Excitement, hypomania	8 (2–15)	1	20	0.4	3.3 (1.4–5.1)	<2	0.5

* Postmarket estimates: M = F, ↓ libido ↓ arousal ↓ orgasm. Males primarily ejaculatory delays in SSRIs. Dose-dependent with venlafaxine, significantly increases at 300 + mg.
** Less than or equal to placebo.

PREGNANCY AND LACTATION

Teratogenicity (1st trimester)
- Little evidence of teratogenicity for TCAs.
- New data so far does not show teratogenicity with fluoxetine.
- Fluoxetine and TCA associated with 2-fold higher miscarriage rate.
  √ 13–14% for TCA and SSRI
    □ Unclear if this risk is secondary to mood disorder or drug.
  √ 7% for controls
- Secondary TCAs recommended if AD needed.

Direct Effect on Newborn (3rd trimester)
- Tachycardia, autonomic lability, respiratory distress, muscle spasm, or congestive heart failure has occurred in infants if large TCA doses taken prior to delivery.

- Clomipramine in 3 women caused 3 toxic newborns, with lethargy, acidosis, hypotonia, cyanosis, jitteriness, irregular breathing, respiratory distress, and hypothermia.
- Anticholinergic effect can cause tachyarrhythmia in fetus.
- No human data on sertraline, paroxetine, or venlafaxine, nefazodone, bupropion.
- Non-TCAs presumed safer secondary to decreased side effects.
- Imipramine and desipramine have produced neonatal withdrawal, with colic, diaphoresis, weight loss, cyanosis, rapid breathing, and irritability in newborn.
- Infants of mothers on nortriptyline developed urinary retention.

Lactation
- Present in breast milk.

Drug Dosage in Mother's Milk

Generic Names	Milk/ Plasma Ratio	Time of Peak Concentration in Milk (hours)	Infant Dose (μg/kg/day)	Maternal Dose (%)	Safety Rating*
Amitriptyline	?	?	16	0.90	A
Amoxapine	?	?	< 3 mg	< 0.07	A
Desipramine	?	?	18–40.2	0.5–1.0	B
Doxepin	?	?	0.25	0.01	A
Imipramine	?	1	4.4	0.13	A
Maprotiline	?	?	39.0	1.60	B
Nortriptyline	?	?	8.3–27.0	0.53–1.30	B
Trazodone	0.14	2	9	1.10	B

* A: Safe throughout infancy; B: Reasonably unsafe before 34 weeks, but safe after 34 weeks.

DRUG-DRUG INTERACTIONS

Drugs (X) Interact with:	Antidepressants (A)[1]	Comments
Acetaminophen	X ↓ A ↑	May overuse acetaminophen; increase HCA levels.
Acetazolamide	X ↑	Reduces HCAs' renal excretion; clinical importance unclear; hypotension increased.
*Alcohol	X ↑ A ↑	CNS depression with HCA and trazodone; not seen with SSRIs, bupropion, venlafaxine.

Drugs (X) Interact with:	Antidepres-sants (A)[1]	Comments
Aminopyrine	A ↑ ?	Possible increase in HCA secondary to displaced protein-bound HCA.
Ammonium chloride	A ↓	May increase HCAs' excretion; clinical importance unclear.
Anticholinergics	X ↑	Increased anticholinergic actions with HCAs and paroxetine but not other SSRIs.
Antihistamines	X ↑	Increased drowsiness; use nonsedating antihistamine, such as terfenadine.
*Antipsychotics (see also phenothiazines)	X ↑ A ↑	Potentiate each other; toxicity; more anticholinergic HCAs may diminish EPS; SSRIs may increase EPS and levels of thioridazine, perphenazine, clozapine, and risperidone.
Aspirin	A ↑ ?	Possible increase in HCA secondary to displaced protein-bound HCA.
*Barbituates	X ↑ A ↑	CNS depression; may decrease antidepressant plasma levels.
Benzodiazepines	X ↑ A ↑	CNS depression.
Bethanidine	A ↓	Decreases HCA effect.
Carbamazepine	X ↓ A ↓	Decreases HCA levels and effect; may lower seizure control; increased quinidine-like effect (see quinidine below). Monitor serum levels. SSRIs might decrease carbamazepine levels.
Chloramphenicol	A ↑	Increases HCA level, effect, toxicity.
Chlordiazepoxide (see benzodiazepines)		
Chlorothiazide	A ↑	Thiazide diuretics increase HCA actions.
Cholestyramine	A ↓	Decreased absorption; decreased blood levels.
*Cimetidine	A ↑	Increased blood levels trigger toxicity; give patient less AD or substitute ranitidine or famotidine for cimetidine.
*Clonidine	X ↓	HCAs and probably venlafaxine inhibit clonidine's antihypertensive actions; trazodone, nefazodone (?), bupropion, SSRIs safer.
Cocaine	X ↑	Cardiac arrhythmias and increased BP with HCAs.
Cyclobenzaprine	A ↑	Cyclobenzaprine, which is chemically similar to HCAs, may produce cardiac problems, increased quinidine-like effects.
Debrisoquin	X ↓	Hypotension.
*Dextroamphetamine	X ↑ A ↑	Increase each other's effects.
Dicumarol	X ↓	Increased bleeding time.
Disopyramide (see quindine)		
Disulfiram	A ↑	May increase HCA level.
Doxycycline	A ↓	Decreased HCA level, effect.
†Ephedrine	X ↓	HCAs and direct-acting sympathomimetics (e.g., epinephrine)
†Epinephrine	X ↑	Increased arrhythmias, hypertension, and tachycardia. HCAs inhibit pressor effects of indirect-acting sympathomimetics (e.g., ephedrine). Because HCAs block the reup-

ANTIDEPRESSANTS

Drugs (X) Interact with:	Antidepres- sants (A)[1]	Comments
		take of direct-acting sympathomimetics, their concentration increases at receptor sites. Since indirect-acting sympathomimet- ics require uptake into the adrenergic neu- ron to induce their effects, HCAs block them. The cardiovascular result from the mixed-acting sympathomimetics depends on the % of each group. Avoid HCAs with di- rect-acting sympatomimetics.
Estrogen (see oral contraceptives)		
Fenfluramine	A↑	Raises HCA effects. Could increase risk of serotonin syndrome with MAOI, SSRI, clomipramine.
Fiber, psyllium	A↓	Decreases absorption.
Fluconazole (see imidazole antifun- gals)		
*Fluoxetine	A↑	Increases HCA levels (300% avg.) and tox- icity.
Griseofulvin	A↓	Decreased HCA level, effect.
†Guanethidine	X↓	Lose antihypertensive effect with NE uptake blockers; all HCAs and venlaflaxine; SSRIs, nefazodone, trazodone, bupropion safer.
Haloperidol	X↑ A↑	Increases HCA plasma level; EPS increases with fluoxetine and possibly sertraline and paroxetine.
Halothane	A↑	Increases tachyarrythmias with anticholinergic antidepressants; (HCAs and possibly parox- etine); enflurane with d-tubocurarine safer.
Imidazole antifungals	A↑	Increases nortriptyline and probably other TCA levels and possibly sertraline.
Insulin	X↑	HCA enhances hypoglycemia in diabetics.
Itraconazole (see imidazole antifun- gals)		
Isoniazid	A↑	Increases HCA level, effect, toxicity.
Ketoconazole (see imidazole antifun- gals)		
Levodopa	X↓ A↓	Decreases absorption of HCAs; decreases ef- fect of levodopa.
Lidocaine (see quin- idine)		
Liothyronine (T₃)	A↑	Liothyronine potentiates antidepressant and arrhythmic effects.
Lithium	A↑	Augments antidepressant effects.
Meperidine	X↑ A↑	Potentiate each other; use lower doses of meperidine or another narcotic.
Methyldopa	X↓	Hypotension; amitriptyline biggest problem.
Methylphenidate (see dextroamphetamine)		
Miconazole (see imidazole anti- fungals)		

Drugs (X) Interact with:	Antidepressants (A)[1]	Comments
Molindone	X ↑	Greater molindone effect.
†MAOIs[1]	X ↑ A ↑	Avoid adding HCAs to MAOIs: Risks hypertensive crisis, mania, muscular rigidity, convulsions, high fever, coma, and death. If HCAs are to be used, first taper MAOI, keep patient off MAOI for 10–14 days, maintain MAOI diet during this interval, and then slowly begin HCA. If combine HCAs and MAOIs, start both drugs together or stop HCAs for 2–3 days before adding MAOI. Best to *not* give (1) large doses, (2) IM/IV drugs, (3) imipramine with tranylcypromine, and (4) an MAOI to patients recently on SSRI or clomipramine. Trazodone only antidepressant consistently safe with MAOI but may increase hypotension.
Morphine	X ↑ A ↓	CNS depression; may decrease HCA levels; common with amitriptyline and desipramine; HCA may augment opiate analgesia.
Oral contraceptives (estrogen)	A ↑	Increased HCA level, effect, toxicity; inhibits HCA metabolism; higher estrogen doses may decrease HCA effect.
Pancuronium	A ↑	Increased tachyarrythmias with anticholinergic antidepressant; all HCAs; enflurane with d-tubocurine safer.
*Paroxetine	X ↑ A ↑	Increases HCA level (avg. 200%) and effects of paroxetine and HCA.
Phenothiazines (*see also* antipsychotics)	X ↑ A?	May increase neuroleptic and HCA plasma levels; increased cardiac arrythmias with thioridazine, clozapine, pimozide; increased anticholinergic and hypertensive effects but decreased EPS.
Phenylbutazone	X ↓ A ↑	HCAs may delay absorption of phenylbutazone; increases HCA 2° to displaced protein-bound HCA.
*Phenytoin	X ↓ A ↑ ?	Lower seizure control; may decrease antidepressant plasma levels 2° to induce metabolism; may increase antidepressant plasma level 2° to displaced protein-bound HCA and with SSRI; venlafaxine may be safest alternative. Paroxetine levels decrease.
Prazosin	X ↓	Hypertension; safer to use bupropion, fluoxetine, desipramine, protriptyline.
Procainamide (*see* quinidine)		
Propranolol	X ↓ ↑ A ↓	Patients may become more depressed on β-blockers; venlafaxine may reverse β-blocker effects; HCAs may exaggerate hypotension.
Quinidine	X ↑ A ↑	Because of HCA's quinidine-like effects, possible myocardial depression, diminished contractility, and dysrhythmias, which can lead to congestive heart failure and heart block. Quinidine and HCAs may yield irregular heartbeat early on.
Reserpine	X ↑ A ↑	Patients may develop increased hypotension.

ANTIDEPRESSANTS

Drugs (X) Interact with:	Antidepressants (A)[1]	Comments
Scopolamine	A ↑ ?	Possible increased antidepressant levels secondary to displaced protein-bound antidepressant.
*Sertraline	X ↑ A ↑	Increases HCA level (~ 30%) and effects of sertraline and HCA.
Sulfonylureas	X ↑	HCA enhances hypoglycemia in diabetics.
Thiazide diuretics	X ↑ A ↑	Increased hypotension with HCAs.
Thioridazine	A ↑	Increased HCA arrythmias.
Tobacco smoking	A ↓	Smoking may lower HCA plasma levels; importance unclear.

[1] For extensive list of *potential* interactions with antidepressants, see Appendix P4502D6 and 3A3/4 lists.

Drugs (X) Interact with:	Amitriptyline (A)	Comments
Disulfiram	X ↑	Two cases of organic brain syndrome; cleared when both drugs stopped.
Ethchlorvynol	X ↑	Transient delirium.
Valproic acid	X ↑ A ↑	Increased plasma levels of both drugs.

Drugs (X) Interact with:	Desipramine (D)	Comments
Methadone	D ↑	Desipramine reported to increase by 108%; use together carefully.

Drugs (X) Interact with:	Doxepin (D)	Comments
Propoxyphene	D ↑	Propoxyphene doubles doxepin levels, inducing lethargy; five days after stopping propoxyphene, patient's mental status returns to normal.

Drugs (X) Interact with:	Fluoxetine (F)	Comments
Alprazolam	X ↑	Increased plasma level, confusion. Not seen with clonazepam or triazolam.
Diazepam	X ↑	Confusion. Not seen with clonazepam or triazolam.
Trazodone	X ↑	Increased plasma level.

Drugs (X) Interact with:	Fluvoxamine (F)[1]	Comments
Methadone	X ↑	Increased plasma level.
Theophylline	X ↑	Toxic plasma levels. P4501A2 inhibited by fluvoxamine but not other SSRIs.
Tacrine	X ↑	Fluvoxamine but not other SSRIs.

[1] P4501A2 and 3A4 inhibitor (see Appendix, pages 390–391).

Drugs (X) Interact with:	SSRIs (S)[1]: Fluoxetine Fluvoxamine[2] Paroxetine Sertraline[3]	Comments
β-blockers (see metoprolol)		
Buspirone	S ↑	May augment antidepressant effect.
Calcium channel-blockers Nifedipine Verapamil	X ↑	Enhanced effect.
Dextromethorphan	X ↑ S ↑	Hallucinogen-type reaction reported with fluoxetine—bright colors, distorted shapes; similar serotonergic effects possible with all SSRIs.
Carbamazepine (see P4502D6)		
Cyproheptadine	S ↓	Occasionally acutely reverses antidepressant effect.
Digitoxin, digoxin	X ↑	Two cases of organic brain syndrome; cleared when both drugs stopped. SSRIs can free protein-bound digitoxin; no effect seen in healthy people. Increased plasma levels.
Furosemide	X ↑ S ↑	Rarely SSRIs cause SIADH; additive hyponatremia result.
Lithium	X ↑ ↓	Lithium neurotoxicity may occur at normal levels.
L-tryptophan	X ↑	Serotonin syndrome.
*MAOI	X ↑ S ↑	Prompt serotonin syndrome.[1]
Metoprolol, propanolol	X ↑	Bradycardia and heart block seen; other 2D6 metabolized include timolol and bufarol; consider atenolol as alternative. Probably increased levels of metoprolol and propanolol.
P4502D6 enzyme metabolized drugs: narrow therapeutic index—HCAs, carbamazepine, vinblastine, encainide, flecainide, dextromethorphan.	X ↑	All SSRIs inhibit 2D6 enzyme system; but fluvoxamine only 5%, and sertraline only 15–30% at starting dose. Fluvoxamine does increases imipramine, amitriptyline, and clomipramine by 1A2 path.
Neuroleptics	X ↑	Increased risk for EPS. Increased level for P4502D6 neuroleptics, haloperidol, perphenazine, thioridazine. Fluvoxamine least risk.
Serotonin antagonists (cyproheptadine, risperidone, clozapine)	S ↓	Potentially reverses antidepressant effect.
Tryptophan	S ↑	Prompts agitation, restlessness, and GI distress.
Venlafaxine	X ↑	SSRIs potentially inhibit metabolism of venlafaxine.
Warfarin	X ↑	Increased bleeding time possibly 2° to anticoagulant effects of SSRIs. Displacement of protein-bound warfarin may sometimes occur.

[1] See Appendix 2D6 interactions.
[2] Fluvoxamine's effects on P4502D6 are usually negligible.
[3] Sertraline's effects by 2D6 path, or P4502D6, are small at 50 mg but increase with dose.

ANTIDEPRESSANTS

Drugs (X) Interact with:	Maprotiline (M)	Comments
Propranolol	M ↑	Maprotiline toxicity.

Drugs (X) Interact with:	Paroxetine (P)	Comments
Procyclidine	X ↑	Increased levels (avg. ~ 35%); may occur with other SSRIs.

Drugs (X) Interact with:	Trazodone (T)	Comments
*Barbiturates	T ↑	BP drops; avoid.
Digitalis	X ↑	Increases digitalis.
Clonidine, other antihypertensives	X ↑	May exaggerate hypotensive effects. Alpha drugs may increase priapism risk.

* Moderately important reaction; † Extremely important interaction; ↑ Increases; ↓ Decreases; ↑↓ Increases and decreases; ? Unsure.
1 Interaction not reported with selegeline (Eldepryl).

EFFECTS ON LABORATORY TESTS

Generic Names	Blood/Serum Tests**	Results*	Urine Tests	Results*
Amoxapine	WBC, LFT	↓ ↑	None	
Desipramine	Glucose	↑ ↓	None	
Doxepin	Glucose	↑ ↓	None	
Fluoxetine	ESR, Bleeding time	↑ ↑	Albuminuria	↑
	Glucose	↓		
	Cholesterol, Lipids	↑ ↑		
	Potassium, Sodium	↓ ↓		
	Iron	↓		
	LFT	↑ ↓		
HCAs	Glucose	↑ ↓	None	
Imipramine	Glucose	↑ ↓	None	
Maprotiline	Glucose	↑ ↓	None	
Nefazodone	Hematocrit (hemodilution)	↓		
Nortriptyline	Glucose	↑ ↓	None	
Paroxetine	Sodium	↓		
Sertraline	Bleeding time			
	ALT	↑		
	Cholesterol	↑		
	Triglycerides	↑		
	Uric acid	↓		
Trazodone	WBC, LFT	↓ ↑	None	
Venlafaxine	Cholesterol	↑		

* ↑ Increases; ↓ Decreases; ↑↓ Increases and decreases.
** LFT are liver function tests; AST (SGOT), ALT (SGPT), LDH, bilirubin, alkaline phosphatase.

WITHDRAWAL

Antidepressants do not provoke

- Dependence
- Tolerance
- Addiction, but
- HCAs and SSRIs have a withdrawal syndrome.

Probably because of cholinergic rebound (same symptoms as excessive dose of bethanechol, a cholinergic agonist; will often remit with pure anticholinergic drug), abruptly stopping HCAs can result in

- Flu-like syndrome without fever:
  - √ Anorexia, nausea, vomiting, diarrhea, queasy stomach, cramps
  - √ Increased salivation
  - √ Anxiety, agitation, irritability
  - √ Cold sweat
  - √ Tachycardia
  - √ Tension headache, neck pains
  - √ Chills, coryza, malaise, rhinorrhea, and dizziness
- Sleep disturbances:
  - √ Insomnia
  - √ Hypersomnia
  - √ "Excessive" dreaming
  - √ Nightmares (2° to REM rebound)
- Hypomanic or manic symptoms.

These withdrawal-like symptoms

- Begin 2–4 (and up to 7) days after suddenly stopping HCAs.
- Occasionally are seen as an interdose phenomenon while patient is still on TCA.
  - √ More likely on qd dosing.
  - √ Withdrawal symptoms seen few hours before next dose.
    - □ Treated with bid dosing.
- May persist 1–2 weeks.
- Are not life-threatening.
- Can be treated or prevented by gradually withdrawing HCAs (e.g., imipramine) 25 mg q 2–3 days). Patient can titrate speed faster or slower, based on symptoms.

Studies have shown

- Somatic, GI symptoms occurred in 21–55% of adults acutely withdrawn from imipramine.

- 80% of adults developed symptoms within 2 weeks of being acutely withdrawn from amitriptyline.
- Children are more susceptible than adults.

Sudden withdrawal of SSRIs, except fluoxetine (too long a half-life), can result in withdrawal syndrome with same features as HCA withdrawal plus:

- Serotonergic "pre-migraine" features
  - √ Vertigo, often with emesis
  - √ Visual distortions
  - √ Headache, often migraine-like

Amoxapine, if stopped after 6 months or prescribed in low doses for a long time, can cause tardive dyskinesia (see pages 36–39).

OVERDOSE: TOXICITY, SUICIDE, AND TREATMENT

SSRIs, trazodone, venlafaxine, and bupropion have extremely low lethality when taken alone.

- One fatal overdose with fluoxetine alone.
- No fatal overdoses with others used alone.
- No predictable dose toxicity relationship established.
- Nausea and vomiting most common with SSRI overdose.
  - √ If without aspiration, may reduce risk of death.
- Seizures most common with bupropion maprotiline, clomipramine and seen occasionally with fluoxetine (see page 122).

General management of non-HCA antidepressant overdose:

- Establish and maintain airway, ensure adequate oxygenation and ventilation.
- Activated charcoal, which may be used with sorbitol, may be equally or more effective than emesis or lavage.
- Monitor cardiac vital signs.
- Consider IM or IV diazepam if seizures occur.

HCAs are prone to cause death by suicide; they are about 5–10 times more dangerous than low-potency antipsychotic agents.

- 10–20 mg/kg of HCAs result in moderate to severe toxicity.
- 30–40 mg/kg of HCAs are often fatal for adults.
  - √ Often only 10–15 times daily therapeutic dose.
- Children have died from 20 mg/kg of imipramine.

There may be a latent period of 1–12 h between drug taking and toxicity.

Attempted and completed suicides seem to *decline* with *increased* HCA doses (and presumably, increased antidepressant effect).

Daily Dose (mg)	Prevalence of Suicidal Behavior (%)
0–74	30.4
75–149	10.1
150–249	5.1
> 250	0.5

General management of HCA overdoses is on pages 53–54.

In addition

- For cardiorespiratory problems:
  - √ Hypotension, dizziness (see pages 114–115).
  - √ Cardiac arrhythmias
    - □ When QRS interval is < 0.10, ventricular arrhythmias are less frequent.
    - □ Treat ventricular arrhythmias with phenytoin, lidocaine, or propranolol.
    - □ Phenytoin often preferred because it also treats seizures.
  - √ Supraventricular arrhythmias and
  - √ Cardiac conduction problems
    - □ Give IV sodium bicarbonate to achieve pH of 7.4–7.5.
    - □ Quinidine, procainamide, and disopyramide should be avoided in managing conduction problems and arrhythmia, since they further depress cardiac function.
  - √ Cardiac failure: Use digitalis.
- For severe urinary retention:
  - √ Acid-base problems are quite severe for TCA overdoses.
  - √ Acidosis is usually most severe.
  - √ Dialysis is reasonably useless because of low drug concentrations.
  - √ Void patient by catheter if no recent voiding.

Toxicity and Suicide Data

Generic Names	Toxicity Doses Average (Highest) (g)	Mortality Doses Average (Lowest) (g)	Toxic Levels (μg/ml)	Lethal Supplies (days)
Amitriptyline	1.343 (2)	2.166 (0.50)	≥1	10
Desipramine	——	——	≥1	12
Imipramine	3.1 (5.375)	3.619 (0.50)	≥1	10
Nortriptyline	——	——	≥1	15
Fluoxetine	3	1.8*	2461 ng/ml	90 +

* Mixed overdose with maprotiline.

PRECAUTIONS

HCAs are contraindicated in patients with h/o

- Cardiovascular problems, hypertension, and acute myocardial infarction.
  - √ Hyperthyroidism might foster cardiovascular toxicity, including arrhythmias.
- Using MAOIs, or having consumed them, within past 14 days.
- Hypersensitivity to TCAs.
- Narrow-angle glaucoma.
- Increased intraocular pressure.
- Seizures
  - √ Consider agent other than bupropion, maprotiline, or clomipramine in patients prone to develop seizures due to head injury, neurologic disease, active alcohol or drug abuse, h/o, anorexia nervosa, and bulimia.
  - √ Avoid clomipramine > 250 mg qd in adults and 3 mg/kg (or 200 mg) in children and adolescents.

HCAs can precipitate mania in 12–50% of bipolar patients and increase the chance of rapid cycling.

- It is common for patients recovering from depression to undergo a "switch phase" into a "high" *before* returning to normality.
  - √ This "high" might last only a day and is not worth "overtreating," yet if a true switch has uncovered a manic process, it is best to treat by
    - □ Reducing or stopping TCA dose or
    - □ Adding or pretreating with lithium.
- Although HCA abuse is rare, amitriptyline abuse, with doses up to 2000 mg/day, causes intoxication, followed by prolonged sleep and retrograde amnesia. Halting amitriptyline can be difficult; active treatment is required.

Fluoxetine and paroxetine can significantly (100–1,000%) increase plasma levels of other HCAs and cause toxicity.

- Occasionally fluoxetine is abused for its usually transient stimulating effects.

Venlafaxine can cause hypertension (see Side Effects).

- Monitor BP regularly.

Sertraline increases HCA plasma levels about 30% and occasionally much higher.

Nefazodone can cause bradycardia.

- Monitor heart rate.

NURSES' DATA

Depressed patients are suicidal, and therefore

- Monitor for "cheeking," hoarding, or suicidal indications.
- A sudden disappearance of a side effect (e.g., dry mouth) suggests hiding medication.

Remind patient (and family) that there is a 7–28 day lag on a full therapeutic dose before ADs fully work.

- Remind patient frequently (1–3 times a day), since depressed patients have trouble remembering or believing and need ongoing reassurance.

For constipation, have patient (especially the elderly) ingest fluids and foods with fiber.

Reassure patient on HCA that drowsiness, dizziness, and hypotension usually subside after first few weeks.

- Hypotension is more common among cardiac patients.
  √ Hypotensives often injure themselves.
- For dizzy patients, review hypotension instructions (see pages 114–115).

Reassure patient on SSRIs that nausea often disappears in 7–14 days. Ask about anxiety, agitation, and overarousal. Too often patients do not report these symptoms, assuming it's their illness.

Avoid extreme heat and humidity, as HCAs alter temperature regulation.

Tell male patients about trazodone's rare (1:2,000), but dangerous side effect of priapism, a painful, persistent erection that requires *immediate* treatment.

Help patient find right time of day to take SSRI (activated or sedated?).

- Fluoxetine is usually best in the A.M.
- Paroxetine sedation is not necessarily related to time of ingestion.

PATIENT AND FAMILY NOTES

Tell patients that antidepressants are neither "uppers" nor are they addicting; indeed, they take 1–4 weeks to take antidepressant effect. The most common side effects for HCAs are dry mouth, constipation, urinary hesitancy, and a lightheaded, dizzy feeling on standing. Most HCAs can also be sedating and should be taken at night to help sleep and reduce daytime sedation. Desipramine and protriptyline can be activating and first should be tried in the morning.

SSRIs (fluoxetine, fluvoxamine, paroxetine, sertraline) have different side effects; the most common are nausea, diarrhea, overactivation, insomnia, dizziness, dry mouth, tremor, and drowsiness.

The majority of patients do not get any of these side effects. In a mild form the activating side effect can help increase energy in the morning. If drowsiness occurs, sleep might be enhanced.

In a few patients on venlafaxine, blood pressure goes up; this doesn't usually happen, but just in case, blood pressure should be monitored.

Once the AD takes full effect, patient will need to stay on it another 4–6 months.

- Depression is somewhat like a broken leg: The patient may feel better, but this doesn't mean the healing process is over.
  √ The healing process for depression is usually 6 or more months.
    □ If antidepressants are stopped sooner than this, there is a > 50% chance of relapse.
    □ If there is a major emotional crisis at the planned time of stopping, delay stopping until the crisis has passed.

When starting HCAs or trazodone, patients should be careful driving cars, working around machines, and crossing streets. When first on HCAs, drive briefly in a safe place, since reflexes might be a tad off. This is less likely with other ADs, but same precaution should be followed.

TCAs potentiate alcohol: "One drink feels like 2 drinks."

- Although SSRIs, bupropion, and venlafaxine don't potentiate alcohol, recommend against drinking while depressed.

Patients can take most ADs at any time; food affects only trazodone and sertraline.

- Trazodone's absorption is increased by 20% with food over an empty stomach.
  √ More is absorbed, but peak plasma levels are lowered and delayed.
  √ Take trazodone with meals or all at bedtime.
  √ Sertraline absorption is increased about 25% when taken after a meal.
    □ May try this before increasing, and paying, for a higher dose.

Keep ADs away from bedside or any readily accessible place, where they might be secured by "accident." Store safely away from eager children.

If possible, ingest full dose of HCAs at bedtime to reduce experience of side effects. If patient forgets at bedtime (or once-a-day dose), consume it within 3 h; otherwise

- Wait for next dose.
- Do not double the dose.

For SSRIs, patient may prefer taking once-a-day dose earlier in day. If forgotten, patient can take it within 8 h, unless side effect of insomnia prevents this.

Suddenly stopping ADs can trigger a flu-like syndrome with symptoms of nausea, bad dreams, fast heart beat, aches and chills without a fever in 2–4 days.

- If this happens, call doctor.
- If cannot reach doctor, have patient swallow one AD tablet until a physician is contacted.

4. Monoamine-Oxidase Inhibitors

This chapter discusses monoamine-oxidase inhibitors (MAOI) treatment of

- Major depression (page 150)
- Atypical depression (page 153)
- Dysthymic disorder (pages 153–154)
- Borderline personality disorder (page 154)
- Treatment-resistant depression (page 150)

Other chapters examine the MAOI treatment of

- Anorexia nervosa (Antidepressants, page 109)
- Bipolar depression (Lithium, pages 194–197)
- Borderline personality disorder (Lithium, pages 199–200)
- Bulimia (Antidepressants, pages 109–110)
- Cataplexy (Antidepressants, page 111)
- Irritable bowel syndrome (Antidepressants, page 111)
- Migraines (Antidepressants, page 112)
- Obsessive-compulsive disorder (Anti-anxiety, page 279)
- Narcolepsy (Stimulants, page 361)
- Panic disorders (Anti-anxiety, page 272)
- Social phobia (Anti-anxiety, pages 276–277)
- Treatment-resistant depression (Antidepressants, pages 96–109)

NAMES, COST, CLASSES, MANUFACTURERS, DOSE FORMS, COLORS

Generic Name (Dollars/Dose: 100 pills in mg)*	Brand Names (Dollars/Dose: 100 pills in mg)*	Manufacturers	Dose Forms (mg)**	Colors
		HYDRAZINES		
Isocarboxazid[1]	Marplan	Roche	t: 10	t: peach
Phenelzine	Nardil 37/15	Parke-Davis	t: 15	t: orange
		NONHYDRAZINE		
Tranylcypromine	Parnate 41/10	SmithKline Beecham	t: 10	t: rose-red
		OTHERS		
Selegiline[†]	Eldepryl 128/5	Somerset	t: 5	t: white

* 1994 average wholesale price for 100 pills at this dose (e.g., 78/50 means 100 pills 50 mg cost $78). If depot form, cost is of single dose.
** t = tablets
† Selegiline (formerly called deprenyl) primarily for Parkinson's disease.
[1] Discontinued in spring 1994, but attempts being made to bring it back; therefore, left in this chapter. Company will supply free renewable 3-month prescriptions until spring, 1996. M.D. must contact them at (201) 235-5000.

PHARMACOLOGY

MAOIs best treat depression when at least 80% of brain MAO levels are inhibited.

- MAO-A
  - ✓ Preferentially oxidizes norepinephrine and serotonin.
  - ✓ Also capable of oxidizing tyramine and dopamine, but this is a minor pathway.
  - ✓ Found mainly in the brain.
  - ✓ Generally responsible for antidepressant effect.
- MAO-B
  - ✓ Preferentially oxidizes tyramine, dopamine, and phenylethylamine.
  - ✓ Found mainly in body.
  - ✓ Generally responsible for tyramine's hypertensive effect.
- Platelets and neurons are similar partly because both have
  - ✓ Membrane pump that concentrates serotonin.
  - ✓ Vesicles containing excessive serotonin and MAO.

√ However, low to no correlation between platelet MAO-B and brain MAO-A inhibition.
  ▫ Phenelzine yields slightly better association than tranylcypromine.
- Tranylcypromine and some of its metabolites resemble amphetamine.
  √ Can have direct stimulating effect.
- Eighty percent of platelet MAOI levels are usually inhibited by 60 mg/day of phenelzine or 1 mg/kg.

MAO is found mainly in nerve tissue, the liver, and the lungs.

- MAOIs interfere with hepatic metabolism of many drugs (e.g., barbiturates, atropine).

MAOIs are hydrazines or nonhydrazines.

- Hydrazines (e.g., phenelzine, isocarboxazid) irreversibly inhibit MAO.
  √ Their actions persist after stopping the drug and stop when enzyme resynthesis occurs (about 10–20 days).
- Nonhydrazines (e.g., tranylcypromine) more reversibly inhibit MAO.
  √ Their effects begin sooner (within 10 days) and end faster (within 3–5 days).
- Selegiline is relatively selective for MAO-B up to 10 mg qd and nonselective at 50 mg qd.
  √ Hypertensive risk and antidepressant effect increase with dose.

Plasma half-lives in h (tissue half-lives far longer):

- Phenelzine: 2.8 (1.5–4)
- Isocarboxazid: similar to phenelzine
- Tranylcypromine: 2.4 (1.54–3.15)

DOSES

Generic Names	Equivalent Doses (mg)	Usual Doses (mg/day)	Dosage Range (mg/day)	Starting Doses (mg/day)	Geriatric Doses (mg/day)
Isocarboxazid	10	10–30	10–50	30	5–15
Phenelzine	15	45–60	45–90	15	15–45
Tranylcypromine	10	20–40	10–60	10	10–30

CLINICAL INDICATIONS AND USE

Studies indicate that

- Overall, HCAs, SSRIs, and MAOIs yield the same improvement rates.
- HCAs and SSRIs are equal to MAOIs in treating the non-psychotic depressions (i.e., major depression, dysthymic disorder).
- TCAs with antipsychotics are superior to MAOIs in treating psychotic depression, although ECT may be better than either drug.
- MAOIs are probably superior to TCAs in treating atypical depression (see page 153), treatment-resistant depression, and depression with panic disorder. SSRIs may be nearly as good as MAOIs for these diagnoses, but limited studies available.

In elderly patients

- MAOIs may help more than TCAs because they are less anticholinergic; however, because the elderly are at greater risk for hypotension, and MAOIs may increase this risk, tranylcypromine may be preferred.
- MAOIs may alleviate depression in demented patients.
  - √ Careful supervision of diet by responsible other is essential.
- MAOIs may prevent depression relapse better than HCAs.
  - √ 13% relapse with MAOI vs. 53% with HCA.

Treatment-Resistant Depression

- MAOIs successfully treat 55–70% of depressions, both typical and atypical, that fail to respond to other antidepressants.
  - √ May need higher than usual MAOI doses.
  - √ Tranylcypromine highly effective in anergic bipolar depression resistant to HCA.
    - □ Does not appear to have high risk for inducing mania.
    - □ Phenelzine may also be as effective.

Phenelzine or Tranylcypromine?

- Sometimes MAOI side effects or differences in efficacy help in choosing an MAOI.

When to choose phenelzine?

- Patient has
  - √ Panic attacks (more proven research).
    - □ Superior to TCAs in depression with panic attacks.
  - √ Social phobia (more proven research).
  - √ Hypertension.
    - □ MAOIs were originally developed as antihypertensives.

□ MAOIs are not contraindicated in hypertension controlled by antihypertensives; hypertensive crisis no more likely.

□ Tranylcypromine occasionally causes acute (1–3 h) transient mild hypertension after ingestion, but phenelzine rarely does.

√ Primary insomnia.

□ Somwhat better sleep with phenelzine.

When to choose tranylcypromine?

- Patient has
  √ Obesity: weight gain common (74%) with phenelzine; weight loss sometimes with tranylcypromine.
  √ Diabetes: phenelzine can decrease glucose and increase weight.
  √ Primary sexual dysfunction: phenelzine can worsen it (22%).
  √ Bipolar anergic depression: more proven research with tranylcypromine.
  □ Most patients had reverse vegetative symptoms.

To start therapy

- Tell patient most common acute side effects are mild hypotension, dizziness, palpitations, dry mouth, and sedation.
- Begin with one tablet on first day.
- Boost by one tablet q 1–2 days,
- Until reach 60 mg of phenelzine, 40 mg of tranylcypromine, or 30 mg of isocarboxazid.
  √ 1 mg/kg may be usual best dose for phenelzine.
- May note some improvement after 2–3 days, particularly with tranylcypromine.
- If patient has insomnia with MAOIs, give the last dose before 6 P.M., or at lunch.
- Tranylcypromine is the most stimulating MAOI and usually needs to be given earlier in day.
- Phenelzine exerts a mild to moderate hypnoanxiolytic effect.
  √ May help with sleep.
  √ Can paradoxically cause insomnia at night and hypersomnia in day.

To hasten MAOI effects, may wish to *add*

- Lithium—plasma level ~ 0.6 mEq./1.
- T_3 50 μgm qd.
  √ T_3 25 mgm does not speed MAOI response.
- Phenylalanine 500–2000 mg qd in divided A.M. doses.
  √ Modest elevation in BP and insomnia are main risks.

MONOAMINE OXIDASE INHIBITORS

General Considerations

- Negative results from early MAOI studies were partly due to low doses.
- Plasma levels are not used with MAOIs, but platelet MAO levels sometimes obtained.
  - √ Platelet MAO levels are not usually recommended.
  - √ Platelet MAOs are still very expensive and not reliable, because there is poor correlation between platelet MAO-B (what is measured) and brain MAO-A inhibition.
- Worthless to only measure platelet MAO after treatment.
  - √ Does not measure % of inhibition.
  - √ Need to have baseline MAO activity as reference.
- MAOIs can completely suppress REM sleep.
  - √ Onset of therapeutic response may be correlated with onset of full REM suppression.
- MAOIs lose their antidepressant effects more often than other antidepressants.
  - √ Frequently this tolerance is specific to the MAOI used.
  - √ If tolerance develops, first try higher doses; if this fails
    - □ Change to another MAOI or
    - □ Add augmentation.
  - √ Later, if tolerance develops to second MAOI, patient may again respond to first MAOI.

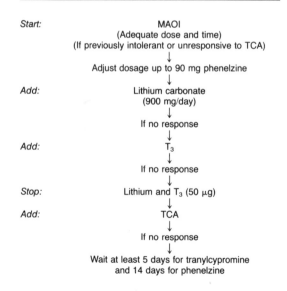

Flow Chart for Treating MAOI-Resistant Patients

Start:	MAOI (Adequate dose and time) (If previously intolerant or unresponsive to TCA) ↓ Adjust dosage up to 90 mg phenelzine ↓
Add:	Lithium carbonate (900 mg/day) ↓ If no response ↓
Add:	T$_3$ ↓ If no response ↓
Stop:	Lithium and T$_3$ (50 μg) ↓
Add:	TCA ↓ If no response ↓ Wait at least 5 days for tranylcypromine and 14 days for phenelzine

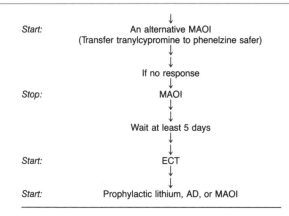

Atypical Depression

MAOIs, particularly phenelzine, are preferred for atypical depression, whose symptoms (as listed below) are often the opposite of melancholia.

- Depressed mood reactive to environmental events and many of the following:
  - √ Overeating, increased appetite, weight gain*
  - √ Carbohydrate or sweet craving
  - √ Hypersomnia, more time in bed, or initial insomnia*
  - √ "Rejection-sensitivity"*
  - √ Profound anergy, "leaden paralysis"*
  - √ Feeling better in the morning and worse as the day proceeds (a reverse diurnal mood variation)
  - √ Phobic-anxiety
  - √ Panic attacks*
  - √ Hypochondriasis/somatization
- Mood reactivity does not predict
  - √ Lowered TCA response.
- MAOIs also superior to placebo and TCAs in
  - √ Mild atypical depression (83% response)
  - √ Chronic atypical depression (70% response).
- MAOIs work equally as well on "atypical" depressions as on "typical" depressions.
- SSRIs and bupropion may also be effective in atypical depressions.

Dysthymic Disorder

Dysthymic disorder is similar to major depression, but dysthymia

- Is less episodic, more constant.

---

* Patients with only one of these symptoms may have < 50% chance of TCA response, but still have ~ 70% chance of MAOI response.

- Has no distinct onset.
- Has rapidly changing or vague neurovegetative signs.

Treatment of dysthymic disorder is controversial.

- If it more closely resembles a major depression, SSRIs or TCAs are the drugs of choice.
  √ Need 6–8 week trial to show full effect over placebo.
  √ At 4 weeks in mild-moderate dysthymics, imipramine and placebo help 50% of patients.
  √ At 6 weeks with imipramine, 70% were improved but placebo was starting to slip back from 50%.
  √ In a fluoxetine vs. placebo study, 63% responded by 8 weeks and only 19% responded to placebo.
    □ Significant improvement compared to placebo didn't occur until 6 to 8 weeks.
- If it more closely resembles an atypical depression, SSRIs or MAOIs are the drugs of choice.

Borderline Personality Disorder

No drug treats borderline personality disorder effectively.
If any agent is prescribed, target specific symptoms.

These agents often include

- Antipsychotics for cognitive problems ("cognitive disorganization under stress"), transient psychosis, and hostilities.
- Lithium for mood swings.
- Benzodiazepines sometimes used for chronic anxiety, but disinhibition and dependency often seen.
- ADs for depression.
  √ SSRIs may be as effective as MAOIs.
  √ TCAs are less effective.
    □ Borderlines usually prefer MAOI over imipramine for mood swings.
- Carbamazepine or valproic acid to decrease behavioral outbursts and mood swings.

Overall, borderlines do better with MAOIs (or possibly SSRIs) and anticonvulsants, carbamazepine, or valproic acid. Neuroleptics best used prn. Neuroleptics over time only decrease hostility and cognitive disorganization under stress.

Always be alert to potential for overdose.

Serotonergic and Noradrenergic Interactions

Combining MAOIs and HCAs or venlafaxine can generate 2 major problems:

- *Serotonergic crisis* (hyperthermic reaction)
- *Noradrenergic crisis* (hypertensive reaction)

Combining MAOI and SSRI generates

- Serotonergic crisis

Serotonergic Crisis Characterized by	Noradrenergic Crisis Characterized by
Elevated temperature, fever	Hypertension (BP increases 30–60 points)
Abnormal muscle movements, such as fasciculations, twitches, myoclonic jerking	Occipital headaches (often radiate frontally and can be violent)
Hyperreflexia	Stiff or sore neck
Generalized seizures (rarely)	Retroorbital pain
	Flushing, sweating, cold and clammy skin
(May see)	Tachycardia > bradycardia
Hypotension	Nausea, vomiting
Anxiety, agitation	
Shivering	*(If severe, may see)*
Enhanced startle response	Sudden unexplained nosebleeds
Insomnia	Dilated pupils, visual disturbances
Confusion, delirium	Photophobia
Seizures, shock	Constricting chest pains
Death	Stroke or coma
	Death

Serotonergic Crisis Caused by Adding to an MAOI	Noradrenergic Crisis Caused by Adding to an MAOI
HCAs, mainly clomipramine	HCA, mainly desipramine
SSRIs	Tyramine-containing foods
Meperidine	Stimulants
Propoxyphene (1 case report)	Ephedrine
Tryptophan	Pseudoephedrine
Dextromethorphan	Phenylephrine
Diphenoxylate?	Phenylpropanolamine
Fenfluramine	Venlafaxine
Venlafarine	
Nefazodone	

TCAs include

- Cyclobenzaprine (Flexeril), a muscle relaxant.
  √ Can potentiate NE, hypertensive crisis.

- Carbamazepine.
  √ Is a very weak NE reuptake blocker and essentially has no serotonin update blocking.
  □ Hypertensive or hyperthermic crisis not reported or likely.

Serotonergic and noradrenergic crises are escalated by

- Dose.
- Sequence of medications.

Adding or Replacing MAOIs, TCAs, and SSRIs

Start With	Add/Substitute	Risks and Instructions
TCA	MAOI	Lower risk of reaction; reduce TCA dose by 50%, slowly add MAOI, taper TCA over 2 weeks.
MAOI	TCA	High risk of reaction; wait 2–4 weeks for phenelzine and 7–10 days for tranylcypromine between stopping MAOI and starting TCA.
MAOI + TCA together		Lower risk of reaction; raise doses slowly.
SSRI/clomipramine	MAOI	High risk; hyperthermic reaction; do not start MAOI until fluoxetine stopped for 5 weeks or negative in serum; and until clomipramine, sertraline, and paroxetine stopped for 2 weeks. Doses of fluoxetine 40 mg or higher probably require stopping 6 or more weeks and serum check advised.
MAOI	SSRI/clomipramine	High risk of hyperthermic reaction; do not overlap; wait at least 2 weeks between stopping MAOI and starting fluoxetine (or clomipramine).
MAOI Hydrazine (Phenelzine)	MAOI Nonhydrazine (Tranylcypromine)	High risk of hypertensive reaction; wait 2–4 weeks before replacing with nonhydrazine.
MAOI Nonhydrazine (Tranylcypromine)	MAOI Hydrazine (Phenelzine)	Moderate-low risk of hypertensive reaction; wait 10–14 days before replacing with hydrazine.
MAOI	Surgery/ECT	Direct-acting pressor agents (e.g., epinephrine and norepinephrine) may cause fewer (or no) hypertensive reactions than indirect-acting pressor agents (including tyramine); if clinically realistic, medically and legally best to stop MAOI 2 weeks before surgery or ECT; regional block is an alternative.
MAOI	Dental work	Local anesthetics with epinephrine may pose a risk; either stop MAOI for 2 weeks, avoid epinephrine, or pretreat 1 h before dental work with nifedipine (10 mg).

- May start MAOI and TCA together, both in low doses initially; or
- Safer to add MAOI to amitriptyline, doxepin, or trimipramine.
- Avoid adding MAOI to imipramine, desipramine, venlafaxine, bupropion, or SSRIs.
- Before starting MAOI, must stop fluoxetine 5–6 weeks and paroxetine or sertraline for 2 weeks.

Trimipramine may cause fewer noradrenergic reactions.
Sleep problems with MAOIs may be relieved by adding

- Trazodone; no dangerous interaction reported, but may potentiate hypotension.
  - √ Occasional reports of subthreshold serotonin syndrome.
    - □ Increased muscle twitches.
- Benzodiazepine hypnotic.
- Sedating TCAs; small potential for hypertension.
  - √ On amitriptyline, 60–80% of patients have no rise BP.
    - □ Limited research suggests that amitriptyline may even protect 50% of patients from hypertensive crisis.

Give patients

- A wallet card describing the MAOI regimen (obtained from Parke-Davis at 800/223-0432).
- MAOI diet and drug information (see below).
- Instructions on how to take their own blood pressure. Sometimes headache is described as feeling like the top of the head was being ripped off. Fire departments will also take BP. (However, not every bad headache is a hypertensive crisis.)
  - √ If diastolic BP > 120 or systolic > 175, treat with nifedipine.
    - □ Risk of kidney damage highest, then
    - □ Cardiac or brain (stroke) damage.
  - √ Nifedipine 10 mg (give patient several for wallet, purse, glove compartment, etc.).
    - □ For fastest actions, bite capsule open and swallow.
    - □ Check BP in 30 minutes; if still elevated, repeat nifedipine and go to ER.
- If any doubts, go to ER immediately.

Emergency room interventions for hypertensive crisis include

- Nifedipine (as above) and
- Phenotolamine 5–10 mg IV slowly.
- If severe reaction, sodium nitroprusside IV slowly.

*Potentially Dangerous Over-the-Counter and Prescription Drug Products**

Ephedrine
Broncholate CS, softgels, syrup
Bronkaid
Bronkolixer
Marax
Mudrane tablets, gel, G elixer
Pazo hemorrhoid ointment
Primatene
Quadrinal tablets
Rynatuss tablets and suspension
Vicks Vatronel nose drops

MONOAMINE OXIDASE INHIBITORS

Potentially Dangerous Over-the-Counter and Prescription Drug Products* (Cont.)

Phenylephrine	Phenylpropanolamine
Atrohist suspension and plus tablets	Atrohist plus tablets
Cerose-DM	Alka-Seltzer plus cold and night-time cold medicine
Codimal	A. R. M. allergy relief
Congespirin for children	Acutrim appetite pills
Comhist LA capsules	Allerest allergy, headache
D.A. chewable tablets	BC cold powder
Dallergy caplets, tablets	Bayer children's cough and cold remedies
Deconsal sprinkle capsules	Cheracol plus head cold/cough formula
Despec liquid	Comtrex multi-symptom cold reliever
Donatussin DC and drops	Contac decongestants
Dimetane decongestant	Coricidin "D" decongestants
Dristan decongestant	Coricidin maximum strength
Dristan nasal spray	Despec caps, liquid
Duo-medihaler	Dexatrim appetite pills
Dura-gest	Dimetane-DC cough syrup
Duratex	Dimetapp
Dura-vent	Duadacin cold and allergy
Endel-HD	Dura-Gest
Entex capsules and liquid	Duratex
Extendryl chewable tablets, Jr. and Sr. T.D. capsules and 4-Way fast-acting nasal spray—new formula Histussin	Dura-Vent
	E.M.T.
Hycomine compound	Entex capsules and liquid
Neo-Synephrine nasal spray and nose drops	Entex LA capsules
Nostril nasal decongestant	Exgest LA tablets
Novahistine elixir and DMX	4-Way cold tablets
Pediacof cough syrup	Gelpirin
Phenergan	Hycomine syrup
Prefrin liquifilm	Naldecon CX, DX, EX
Protid	Nolamine timed-release tablets
R-Tannate tablets and suspension	Nolex LA tablets
Relief eye drops	Ornade spansule caps
Robitussin night relief	Phenylpropanolamine HCL and guaifenssin
Ru-Tuss	Poly-Histine
Rynatan tablets and suspension	Propagest tablets
Rynatus tablets	Robitussin-CF
St. Joseph's nasal congestant	Ru-Tus II caps
Triotann suspension and tablets	Ru-Tuss with hydrocodone
Vanex forte and HD	Sinarest
Vicks sinex decongestant nasal spray and ultra fine mist	Sine-off sinus
	Simulin tablets
	Snaplets-DM, EX
	St. Joseph's cold tablets
	Triaminic
	Triaminicin
	Triamincol
	Tylenol cold medication
	Vanex-forte

Potentially Dangerous Over-the-Counter and Prescription Drug Products* (Cont.)

Pseudoephedrine		Dextromethorphan (also any drug name with *DM* or *Tuss* in it)
Actifed	Ornex	Anatus DM syrup and tablets
AllerAct	P.V. Tussin syrup	Bromarest DM
Allerest no drowsy formula	Pediacare	Bromarest DX
Anatuss LA tablets	Pediacare cold-allergy chewable tablets	Bromfed DM
Anatuss DM		Cerose DM
Atrohist sprinkle capsules	Pediacare cough-cold chewable tablets	Cheracol
Benadryl combinations		Cheracol plus
Bomarest DX cough syrup	Pediacare Infants decongestant drops	Codimal DM
Brexin LA capsules		Comtrex multi-symptom cold reliever
Bromfed capsules (timed release)	Pediacare nightrest	
	Pseudoephedrine hydrochloride tablets	Comtrex day and night
Bromfed DM cough syrup		Comtrex non-drowsy
Bromfed tablets	Robitussin DAC syrup	Dimetane DX cough syrup
Bromfed-PD capsules	Robitussion PE	Dristan cold and flu
CoAdvil	Rondec	Dristan juice mix-in
Codimal LA capsules	Ru-Tuss DE tablets	Humibid DM sprinkle and tablets
Comtrex allergy sinus	Ryna, C, CX	
Comtrex cough formula	Seldane D tablets	Iodur DM
Comtrex multi-symptom	Sinarest no drowsiness	Iotuss DM
Congess Jr. TD capsules	Sine-aid IB caplets	Par-glycerol DM
Congess Sr. TD capsules	Sine-aid maximum strength	Pedia care cough-cold
Contac cold and sinus	Sine-Off, no drowsiness	Pedia care ̀night rest
Dallergy Jr. capsules	Sinutab	Phenergan with dextromethorpan
Deconsal II Tablets	Sudafed	
Dimacol	Toura LA caplets	Poly-histine DM
Dimetane DX cough syrup	Touro A&H capsules	Quelidine poly-histine DM
Dorcol cough and decongestant	Triaminic night light	Rescon DM
	Trinalin tablets	Robitussin DM
Dristan maximum strength	Tuss DA RX	Rondec DM
Dura-Tap/PD capsules	Tussafed drops and syrup	Safe tussin 30
Duratuss HD	Tussar DM	Touro DM
Duratuss tablets	Tussar SF	Tusibron DM
Entex PSE tablets	Tussar-2	Tuss DA
Excedrin sinus	Tylenol allergy sinus medicated gelcaps	Tussafed drops and syrup
Fedahist		Tussar DM
Guaifed capsules	Tylenol allergy sinus nighttime caplets	Tussi-organidin DM
Guaifed PD capsules		Tylenol children's cold plus cough liquid formula
Guaimax D tablets	Tylenol cold	
Isoclor	Tylenol cold and flu	Tylenol cold and flu no drowsiness and hot medicine
Kronofed A Jr.	Tylenol cough	
Lodrane LD capsules	Tylenol flu	
Nasabid capsules	Tylenol med	Tylenol cold medication
Novafed A capsules	Tylenol sinus	Tylenol cough medication
Novafed capsules	Vick's 44-D, 44-M	Tylenol flu maximum
Novahistine DMX	Vick's Daycare daytime cold	
	Vick's NyQuil	

MONOAMINE OXIDASE INHIBITORS

Potentially Dangerous Over-the-Counter and Prescription Drug Products* *(Cont.)*

Pseudoephedrine	Dextromethorphan (also any drug name with *DM* or *Tuss* in it)
Nucofed expectorant	Vick's Pediatric
	Zehrex LA tablets
	Zephrex tablets

*Warning: However complete these lists may appear, there are always new names and new products that might contain drugs that potentiate dangerous MAOI interactions. All cold and cough medicines are forbidden until proven safe (e.g., diphenydramine is safe).

- *Prescription and street drugs* to avoid or be cautious of (see Drug-Drug Interactions for complete list, pages 175–178).
  - √ Sympathomimetics—avoid indirect and mixed-acting agents.
    - □ Less or no effects from direct-acting agents.
  - √ Anti-asthma drugs (bronchodilators)
    - □ Avoid ephedrine.
    - □ Beclomethasone and other nonsystemic steroid inhalers are safer than inhalers containing metaproterenol, albuterol, or other β-adrenergic bronchodilators.
    - □ Asthma patients on MAOIs should have BP and HR measured in office after using their particular bronchodilating drug(s). Most have no problem, but should be carefully monitored.
  - √ Antihypertensive drugs, especially
    - □ Guanethidine
    - □ Reserpine
  - √ Meperidine and dextromethorphan (can be lethal)
  - √ Amphetamines, "pep-pills," appetite suppressants
  - √ Cocaine, crack
  - √ Dopa (dihydroxyphenylalanine), dopamine, levodopa bronchodilating
    - □ L-dopa usually can be used safely at lower doses than usual.
  - √ Buspirone (elevated BPs seen)
- Drugs with lower (or no) risk than previously thought:
  - √ Epinephrine, exogenously administered (or as excreted from adrenals), is not mainly metabolized by MAO (intracellular).
    - □ Patients with severe allergic reactions can safely get epinephrine.
    - □ Some may prefer to do an in-office challenge of epinephrine first to be completely safe.
  - √ Opiates—only meperidine and dextromethorphan proven dangerous.

      □ Morphine and oxycodone presumed safe.

      □ Start at 20–50% of usual dose and monitor 15–60 minutes later.

  √ Anesthetics

      □ May prolong expected sedative or hypotensive effects, but not contraindicated.

      □ Powerful pressor agents may cause hypertension; deamination may be slowed; use low dose or avoid; volume expansion is safer.

      □ If tranylcypromine discontinued, wait only 7 days for normal MAO activity to return.

Foods containing at least 6–8 mg tyramine per serving usually needed to precipitate hypertensive crisis with phenelzine.

  √ For most people ≥ 10 mg tyramine in 4 hours is risky.

  √ For people on tranylcypromine ≥ 5 mg tyramine may be risky.

These foods fall into 4 major groups.

- Aged cheeses
- Air-dried sausages
- Fava pods
    √ Beans are okay, but pod has dopamine.
- Sauerkraut
- Foods to *definitely avoid:*
    √ Aged cheeses (English Stilton, blue cheese, old cheddar, Danish blue, brick, mozzarella, Gruyère, Swiss, etc.) with over 2 mg tyramine per serving.
        □ Because 80% of all hypertensive crises are secondary to consuming aged cheeses, hypertensive crises are called "cheese reactions."
        □ Even some of the more moderate tyramine cheeses (e.g., Brie, Emmentaler, and Gruyère) are included because people eat more than a single slice.
        □ Some cheeses are allowed in any amount: cottage, processed cheese slices, ricotta, and cream cheeses are safe.
        □ Cheeses are particularly risky because the amount of tyramine varies based on location (whether it is the center of a cheese wheel [higher] or on outside), amount of deliberate aging (e.g., soft brie is aged more than firm), amount aging (e.g., time sitting in store or home refrigerator).
    √ Tap and microbrewery beers are suspect because of the increased hops or wort used in the secondary fermentation and the coarseness of filters that may allow baterial contamination and further fermentation.

√ Chianti wine should probably still be avoided, despite questionable findings.

√ Fava (Italian, broad) green beans (because of dopa content in pod).

√ Concentrated yeast extracts (especially Marmite), but
  □ Beware of powdered protein diet supplements containing yeast extracts.
  □ Brewer's yeast is safe.
  □ Yeast used in baking products is safe because of small amount.

√ Pickled herring in brine should be avoided, but other fish are safe.

√ Salami, mortadella, air-dried sausage, chicken liver (by day 5) must be avoided. Bologna, pepperoni, summer sausage, fresh chicken liver, corned beef, and liverwurst are safe.

√ Sauerkraut.

√ Chinese foods, oriental soup stocks (e.g., miso) should be avoided until more evidence becomes available.

√ Phenylalanine in doses ≥ 1 g can occasionally cause modest increase in BP.
  □ Aspartame, the artificial sweetener, contains only 60 mg per average serving.

√ If uncertain, avoid fermented protein food.

• Foods *no longer at risk:*
  √ Chocolate (has phenylethylamine) except in very high amounts
  √ Figs, raisins, overripe fruit, avocados, bananas (don't eat the skins)
  √ Tea, coffee, cola, and other caffeine-containing beverages (some experts limit these to 3 cups/glasses a day)
  √ White and red wine (assuming wine kept under 3 ounces/day), other spirits
  √ Yogurt
    □ Unless unpasteurized or > 5 days old
  √ Caviar, snails, tinned fish
  √ Tinned and packet soup
    □ Unless made from boullion or meat extracts (which can be unsafe in large quantities)
    □ Vegetable protein extracts are okay
  √ Bottled or canned U.S. or Canadian beer (see pages 163–164)
    □ Based on ≤ 4 servings.

Instructions for using the following tables:

• Read all prior cautions first.
• Most people on phenelzine need at least 6–8 mg tyramine consumed within 4 hours to precipitate a hypertensive crisis.

- Tranylcypromine may require less tyramine to cause a hypertensive reaction (~4mg).
- Need to add up all servings ingested at a given time to calculate tyramine ingestion.
- Because each person is different, should initially experiment with totals of 1–2 mg at a sitting.
  √ Then monitor BP before trying higher amounts of tyramine.
- Remember, the cheese contents in the table can be notoriously variable.
- Products are listed from highest tyramine content per serving to lowest.

Tyramine Content of Beers*

Beer	Brewer	Tyramine Concentration μg/ml	Tyramine Content (mg) per Serving**
Beers with Alcohol			
Amstel	Amstel	4.52	1.54
Export Draft	Molson	3.79	1.29
Blue Light	Labatts	3.42	1.16
Guinness Extra Stout	Labatts	3.37	1.15
Old Vienna	Carling	3.32	1.13
Canadian	Molson	3.01	1.03
Miller Light	Carling	2.91	0.99
Export	Molson	2.78	0.95
Heineken	Holland	1.81	0.62
Blue	Labatts	1.80	0.61
Coors Light	Molson	1.45	0.49
Carlsberg Light	Carling	1.15	0.39
Michelob	Anheuser-Busch	0.98	0.33
Genesee Cream	Genesee	0.86	0.29
Stroh's	Stroh's	0.78	0.27
Old Milwaukee	Pacific Western	0.34	0.11
Dealcoholized Beers			
Buckler	Heineken	1.08	0.32
Labatts	Labatt Brewing Co.	1.18	0.36
Molson Exel	Molson Breweries	0.00	0.00
O'doul's Malt Beverage	Anheuser-Busch	2.25	0.68
Sharp's	Miller Brewing Co.	0.37	0.11
Special Light Swan	Special Light Swan Lager	0.97	0.29
Texas Select	San Antonio Beverage Co.	0.82	0.25
Tourtel	Kronenebourg	0.00	0.00
Upper Canada Point Nine	Upper Canada Brewery	0.00	0.00

Tyramine Content of Beers (Cont.)*

Beer	Brewer	Tyramine Concentration μg/ml	Tyramine Content (mg) per Serving**
Particularly Risky Tap Beers			
Kronenbourg	Kronenbourg	37.85	15.94
Rotterdam's Lager	Rotterdam	27.05	9.00
Rotterdam's Pilsner	Rotterdam	29.47	9.82
Upper Canada Lager	Sleeman	112.91	37.62

* Generally U.S. and Canadian canned and bottled beers are safe if ≤ 4 servings consumed; all Canadian beers (Labatt, Molson, Upper Canada, Pacific Western) < 3 μg/ml.
** Based on a 341 ml serving (one bottle).

Tyramine Content of Wines

Wine	Color	Type	Country	Tyramine Concentration (μg/ml)	Tyramine Content (mg) per Serving*
Rioja (Siglo)	Red		Spain	4.41	0.53
Sherry	Red			3.60	0.43
Ruffino	Red	Chianti	Italy	3.04	0.36
Blue Nun	White		Germany	2.70	0.32
Retsina	White		Greece	1.79	0.21
La Colombaia	Red	Chianti	Italy	0.63	0.08
Riesling				0.60	0.07
Brolio	Red	Chianti	Italy	0.44	0.05
Sauterne	White			0.40	0.05
Beau-Rivage	White	Bordeaux	France	0.39	0.05
Beau-Rivage	Red	Bordeaux	France	0.35	0.04
Maria Christina	Red		Canada	0.20	0.20
Port	Red			0.20	0.02
Cinzano	Red	Vermouth	Italy	†	†
LePiazze	Red	Chianti	Italy	†	†

* Based on a 120 ml (4 ounce) serving.
† Nil.

Tyramine Content of Other Alcohol

Type	Tyramine Concentration (μg/ml)	Tyramine Content (mg) per Serving
Ale	8.8	3.0/341 ml
Harvey's Bristol Cream	2.65	0.32 mg/4 ounces
Dubonnet	1.59	0.19 mg/4 ounces
Vermouth	high	high
Bourbon	†	†
London distilled dry gin (Beefeater)	†	†
Gin	†	†

Tyramine Content of Other Alcohol (Cont.)

Type	Tyramine Concentration (μg/ml)	Tyramine Content (mg) per Serving
Vodka	†	†
Rum	†	†
Scotch	†	†

† Nil.

Tyramine Content of Cheeses

Type	Tyramine Concentration (μg/g)	Tyramine Content (mg) per Serving*
Liederkranz	1454.50	21.8
Cheddar (New York State)	1416.00	21.2
English stilton	1156.91	17.3
Cheddar, old center (Canadian)	1013.95	16.4
Blue cheese	997.79	15.0
Swiss	925.00	13.9
White (3-year old)	779.74	11.7
Camembert (Danish)	681.50	10.2
Emmentaler	612.50	9.2
Extra-old	608.19	9.1
Gruyère (British)	597.50	9.0
Brick (Canadian)	524.00	7.9
Gruyère (American)	516.00	7.7
Cheddar (25 samples)	384.00	5.8
Gouda	345.00	5.2
Edam	310.00	4.7
Colby	285.00	4.3
Mozzarella	284.04	4.2
Roquefort (French)	273.50	4.1
Danish blue	256.48	4.1
D'Oka (imported)	234.00	3.5
Limberger	204.00	3.1
Cheddar, center cut (Canadian)	192.00	2.9
Argenti (imported)	168.00	2.5
Romano	159.00	2.4
Cheese spread, Handisnack	133.81	2.0
Gruyère (Swiss)	125.17	1.9
Cheddar, fresh (Canadian)	120.00	1.8
Muenster	101.69	1.5
Provolone	94.00	1.4
Camembert (American)	86.00	1.3
Parmesan, grated (Kraft)	81.08	1.3
Old Coloured, Canadian	77.47	1.2
Feta	75.78	1.1
Parmesan, grated (Italian)	69.79	1.1

MONOAMINE OXIDASE INHIBITORS

Tyramine Content of Cheeses (Cont.)

Type	Tyramine Concentration (μg/g)	Tyramine Content (mg) per Serving*
Gorgonzola	55.94	0.8
Processed (American)	50.00	0.8
Blue cheese dressing	39.20	0.6
Medium (Black Diamond)	34.75	0.5
Processed (Canadian)	26.00	0.4
Swiss Emmentaler	23.99	0.4
Brie (M-C) with rind	21.19	0.3
Cambozola Blue Vein (germ)	18.31	0.3
Brie (d'Oka) without rind	14.65	0.2
Farmers, Canadian plain	11.05	0.2
Cheez Whiz (Kraft)	8.46	0.1
Brie (d'Oka) with rind	5.71	0.1
Cream cheese (plain)	9.04	0.1
Brie (M-C) without rind	2.82	< 0.1
Sour cream (Astro)	1.23	< 0.1
Boursin	0.98	< 0.1
Cottage cheese	< 0.20	†
Cream cheese	< 0.20	†
Havart, (Canadian)	†	†
Ricotta	†	†
Bonbel	†	†

* Based on a 15-gram (single slice) serving.
† Nil.

Tyramine Content in Fish

Type	Tyramine Concentration (μg/g)	Tyramine Content (mg) per Serving*
Pickled herring*	Up to 3030	——
Pickled herring brine	15.1 μg/ml	——
Lump fish roe	4.4	0.2 mg/50 g
Sliced schmaltz herring in oil	4.0	0.2 mg/50 g
Smoked carp	†	†
Smoked salmon	†	†
Smoked white fish	†	†

* Other reports indicate that the tyramine content of pickled herring is nil.
† Nil.

Tyramine Content in Meat and Sausage*

Type	Tyramine Concentration (μg/g)	Tyramine Content (mg) per Serving*
Sausage, Belgian, dry-fermented	803.9	24.1
Liver, beef, spoiled	274	8.2
Sausage, dry-fermented	244	7.3
Salami	188	5.6
Mortadella	184	5.5
Air-dried sausage	125	3.8
Sausage, semi-dried fermented	85.5	2.6
Chicken liver (day 5)	77.25	1.5
Bologna	33	1.0
Aged sausage	29	0.9
Smoked meat	18	0.5
Corned beef	11	0.3
Kolbasa sausage	6	0.2
Liver, beef, fresh	5.4	0.2
Liverwurst	2	0.1
Smoked sausage	1	< 0.1
Sweet Italian sausage	1	< 0.1
Pepperoni sausage	†	†
Chicken liver (day 1)	†	†

* Based on 30 g serving.
† Nil.

Tyramine Content in Paté*

Type	Tyramine Concentration (μg/g)	Tyramine Content (mg) per Serving*
Salmon mousse paté	22	0.7
Country style paté	3	0.1
Peppercorn paté	2	0.1

* Based on 30 g serving.

Tyramine Content in Fruits and Vegetables

Type	Tyramine Concentration (μg/g)	Tyramine Content (mg) per Serving*
Banana peel*	58.35	1.424 mg/peel
Raspberries	54.15	—
Raspberry jam	< 38.0	—
Avocado, fresh‡	23.0	†
Orange	10.0	—
Plum (red)	6.0	—

Tyramine Content in Fruits and Vegetables (Cont.)

Type	Tyramine Concentration (μg/g)	Tyramine Content (mg) per Serving
Tomato	4.0	—
Banana pulp	4.0	1.0
Eggplant	3.0	—
Potato	1.0	—
Spinach	1.0	—
Grapes	†	†
Figs, California-Blue Ribbon	†	†
Raisins (California seedless)	†	†
Fava (Italian) (broad) bean pods**	†	†

* The peel of the banana and the pod of the fava bean contain considerable dopamine; the banana pulp and the actual fava bean carry no risk.
‡ Some claim fresh avocado is nil.
** Dopamine = 700 μg/g.
† Nil.

Tyramine Content in Yeast Extracts

Type	Tyramine Concentration (μg/g)	Tyramine Content (mg) per Serving
Marmite concentrated yeast extract	1184	6.45 mg/10 g
Yeast extracts	2156	—
Brewer's yeast tablets (Drug Trade Co.)	—	191.27 g/400 mg
Brewer's yeast tablets (Jamieson)	—	66.72 g/400 mg
Brewer's yeast flakes (Vegetrates)	—	9.36 g/15 g
Brewer's yeast debittered (Maximum Nutrition)	—	†

† Nil.

Tyramine Content in Other Foods

Type	Tyramine Concentration (μg/g)	Tyramine Content (mg) per Serving
Soy sauce (Japanese)	509.30	—
Soy sauce (Tamari)	466.00	—
Meet extracts (soup, gravy, bases)	199.50	—
Soybean paste	84.85	—
Sauerkraut (Krakus)	56.49	13.87
Beef bouillon mix (Bovril)	—	231.25
Beef bouillon (Oetker)	—	102.00 μg/cube
Soy sauce	18.72 μg/ml	0.2 mg/10 ml
Soy sauce, chemically hydrolized	1.8	—
Cocoa powder	1.45	—
Beef gravy (Franco American)	0.858 μg/ml	< 0.1 mg/30 ml
Chicken gravy (Franco American)	0.46 μg/ml	< 0.1 mg/30 ml

Tyramine Content in Other Foods (Cont.)

Type	Tyramine Concentration (μg/g)	Tyramine Content (mg) per Serving
Chicken bouillon mix (Maggi)	†	†
Vegetable bouillon mix	†	†
Yogurt	< 0.2	†

† Nil.

SIDE EFFECTS

MAOIs are less anticholinergic than TCAs.

- Almost no clinical anticholinergic actions from tranylcypromine.
- Phenelzine can generate anticholinergic episodes over 20% of the time.

Most anticholinergic symptoms taper off in 1–2 weeks (see page 113); they are discussed with their respective organ systems.

Common long term (> 6 months) effects of phenelzine are weight gain (74%), ankle edema (13%), muscle twitching, and decreased sexual function (22%). All but muscle twitching are rare on tranylcypromine.

Cardiovascular Effects

Hypotension

- MAOIs were originally developed as antihypertensives.
- This is their second most important side effect.
- MAOIs produce similar orthostatic hypotension and basal hypotension to HCAs.
  - √ Complaints of dizziness reported by 20–50% of patients on MAOIs.
    - □ About same as for nortriptyline.
  - √ As many as 10% of patients on MAOIs may develop severe injuries (e.g., passing out, fractures).
  - √ Especially frequent in the elderly.
  - √ Common with congestive heart failure.
  - √ Hypotension happens more in people with pre-existing hypertension, although it still afflicts the normotensive.
- Symptoms include
  - √ Dizziness, lightheadedness
  - √ Coldness
  - √ Headaches
  - √ Fainting, especially with salt or fluid restriction.

MONOAMINE OXIDASE INHIBITORS

- Management (see pages 114–115)
- Avoid adding chlorpromazine or thioridazine to MAOIs, because they accelerate hypotension.

Except for BP problems, MAOIs have fewer cardiovascular side effects than HCAs.

- MAOIs cause less myocardial toxicity.
- Exert little effect on heart rate, cardiac conduction, and myocardial function.
  - √ Phenelzine produces a modest decrease in QT interval.
  - √ Still within normal range.
- May be preferable over TCAs for some cardiac patients.

Transient hypertension

This has been reported 1–3 h after MAOI; there are more reports with tranylcypromine.

- √ Subsides 3–4 h after dose.
- √ Occasionally a significant rise seen (e.g., 120/80 → 178/104).

Peripheral edema

- Phenelzine and isocarboxazid produce edema more than tranylcypromine.
  - √ Reported as high as 5–19% with phenelzine.
- Reduce dose; prescribe a diuretic; try support hose.
- Rarely, pericardial edema has been reported.

Gastrointestinal Effects

Dry mouth (see pages 22–23)
Constipation (see page 23)
Hepatotoxicity

- Incidence between 1/3,000–1/10,000.
- Frequency: isocarboxazid > phenelzine > tranylcypromine.
- Tranylcypromine is the preferred MAOI for patients with liver disease.
- Hepatotoxicity displays
  - √ Weakness, malaise
  - √ Rash
  - √ Nausea, anorexia
  - √ Jaundice
  - √ Eosinophilia
  - √ Elevated enzymes.

Flatus (rare)

- Giving oral lactase may help.

Weight gain

- Phenelzine > tranylcypromine.
- Amitriptyline generates more immediate weight gain than phenelzine, but 70% of people eventually gain weight on phenelzine.
- Phenelzine can add > 20 pounds in one year, but typical weight gain is 5–10 pounds.

Renal Effects

Urinary hesitancy or *retention* (see page 24)

Endocrine and Sexual Effects

More common with phenelzine than with HCAs or tranylcypromine, especially

- *Anorgasmia*—22% phenelzine vs. 2% tranylcypromine
- *Impotence*

Also see

- *Decreased libido, difficulties achieving and maintaining erection, slowed or impaired ability to ejaculate*

Management

- See page 118.
- Reduce dose or
- Add cyprohepatidine 2–4 mg qd-bid to alleviate anorgasmia in both sexes.
  - √ Cyprohepatidine may introduce drowsiness, stimulate appetite, or increase carbohydrate craving.
- Methyltestosterone po or by monthly depot injections may improve male sexual dysfunction.
- Bethanechol 10 mg tid may faciliate erectile functioning.

Carbohydrate craving
Falling blood sugar

- More frequent with phenelzine and isocarboxazid.

Eyes, Ears, Nose, and Throat

Narrow-angle glaucoma (see pages 28, 120)
Blurred vision (see page 27)
Dry eyes (see page 28)
Nasal congestion

Meniere's-like syndrome

- Vertigo, tinnitus, nystagmus seen.
  - √ Remits with discontinuation of MAOI.

Skin, Allergies, and Temperature

Decreased sweating
Fever, chills

Central Nervous System Effects

Myoclonic twitches

- MAOIs cause more often than TCAs.
- Most often nocturnal.
- Management
  - √ Reduce or stop MAOIs, or shift doses earlier or spread out doses.
  - √ Change to another MAOI, or
  - √ Add clonazepam, carbamazepine, or valproic acid.
  - √ Sometimes cyproheptadine works.

Speech blockage

- Lower or stop MAOI.

Pyridoxine deficiency

- Isocarboxazid and phenelzine can lead to a pyridoxine (vitamin B_6) deficiency with primarily
  - √ Peripheral neuropathy or
  - √ Muscle spasms, pains, and parathesias.
- Other symptoms include
  - √ Stomatitis
  - √ Anemia
  - √ Hyperacusis (or buzzing in the ear)
  - √ Hyperirritability
  - √ Depression
  - √ Carpal tunnel syndrome
  - √ "Electric shocks" or jumping movements of the extremities
  - √ Ataxia
  - √ Hyperactive deep tendon reflexes, clonus (possibly)
  - √ Convulsions and coma (rarely)
- Treat with pyridoxine 50 mg po bid or 100 mg sustained-release qd.
  - √ Occasionally, higher dose needed.
  - √ Respond in 2–10 weeks.

Seizures

- MAOIs may alter the seizure threshold of patients with epilepsy.

Toxicity

- "Drunk," ataxic, confused
- Reduce dose.

Sedation

- Phenelzine can be directly sedating.
  - √ Can be expected to occur at any time.
- Insomnia often generates daytime sedation.
- Some patients on phenelzine or tranylcypromine experience severe afternoon somnolence and disrupted sleep at night.
  - √ Hypnotics can treat the insomnia, but
  - √ Afternoon somnolence may persist.
    - □ No effective treatment for P.M. somnolence.
    - □ Patient must be warned of risk of accidents, etc., should this occur.

Decreased sleep (sometimes without fatigue), *insomnia*

- If without fatigue, inform patients that they have become more "efficient" sleepers, not insomniacs.
- Tranylcypromine causes initial insomnia most often.
- Switch to phenelzine or
- Move dose(s) to earlier time in day, perhaps before noon.

Nightmares, hypnagogic phenomena, vivid dreams

- Occur more often if MAOIs provided at hs.
- Sleep disturbances more common with MAOIs than with TCAs.
- At higher doses (> 60 mg phenelzine) MAOIs completely suppress REM sleep.
  - √ Patient may report absence of strange dreams (REM) but persistence of mundane dreams (NREM).
    - □ May be useful "side effect" for patients with PTSD.

Psychosis, behavioral problems

- *Stimulation*
  - √ May arise day or night.
  - √ More common with tranylcypromine.
  - √ Management
    - □ Reduce dose or transfer to another drug.
- *Paranoid outbursts, delusions*
  - √ Reduce or stop MAOI.
  - √ May reflect "subclinical" psychosis.
- Manic responses
  - √ Can erupt on MAOIs, with or without TCAs.

□ Hypomania more common (7% phenelzine, 10% on tranylcy-promine)

√ Manic swings may actually be stimulation, which the patient finds unusual and, perhaps, excessive.

√ Management
  □ Reduce, or slow down, MAOI.
  □ Add lithium, carbamazepine, or valproic acid to restrain the "high."

PERCENTAGES OF SIDE EFFECTS

Side Effects	Isocarboxazid	Phenelzine	Tranylcypromine
CARDIOVASCULAR EFFECTS			
Hypotension	15	20	15
Hypertensive crises	3.5	3.4 (0.8–8)	5.8 (2–9.9)
Dizziness, lightheadedness	18.6	17.5	28.3 (5–52.4)
Tachycardia	—	17.5	20
Palpitations	5	5	7.3 (0–10)
Cardiac arrhythmias	4	—	< 2
GASTROINTESTINAL EFFECTS			
Dry mouth and throat	20	30	25.9 (10–47.6)
Anorexia, lower appetite	—	—	4.8
Increased appetite	—	—	0.0
Nausea, vomiting	10	10	6 (0–10)
Dyspepsia, upset stomach	20	20	12.5 (2–19)
Constipation	9.3 (2–20)	9.3 (2–20)	10 (5–19)
Hepatitis	0.02	< 0.01	< 0.001
Weight gain	20	74	6
Edema	7.5	13	—
RENAL EFFECTS			
Urinary hesitancy or retention	6.6	22	2.5
ENDOCRINE AND SEXUAL EFFECTS			
Disturbed sexual function	6.5 (0–10)	22 (0–30)	6
EYES, EARS, NOSE, AND THROAT EFFECTS			
Blurred vision	10.5	17.5	8.5 (2–10)
Tinnitus	—	—	4.8

Side Effects	Isocarboxazid	Phenelzine	Tranylcypromine
SKIN, ALLERGIES, AND TEMPERATURE EFFECTS			
Rashes	6	< 2	6
Sweating	8.5 (2–20)	8 (2–20)	—
CENTRAL NERVOUS SYSTEM EFFECTS			
Weakness, fatigue	6	< 2	< 2
Seizures	—	1	0.0
Parathesias	—	—	4.8
Headache	20	6	14.3
Tremor	5.5	12.5	9.5
Drowsiness, sedation	8 (2–20)	21 (0–30)	12 (0–47.6)
Insomnia	6	17 (15–50)	22 (10–23.8)
Confusion, disorientation	4.3	4.3	6.2 (2–14.3)
Anxiety, nervousness (mental)	—	—	2
Agitation, restlessness (motoric)	4	—	5
Excitement, hypomania	9.3 (2–20)	13.8 (5–30)	17.1 (10–30)
Myoclonic jerks	7	10	7

PREGNANCY AND LACTATION

Teratogenicity (1st trimester)	• Some increased malformations have been found with phenelzine and tranylcypromine; significance unclear.
Direct Effect on Newborn (3rd trimester)	• Most severe risk is hypertensive crisis during pregnancy. √ Probably unacceptable risk to fetus.
Lactation	• In breast milk; safety data is unclear.

DRUG-DRUG INTERACTIONS

Drugs (X) Interacts with:	Monoamine- Oxidase Inhibitors (M)	Comments
Acebutolol (*see also* β-blockers)	X ↑	If an MAOI is stopped, BP of patients on acebutolol may rise.
Albuterol	X ↑	Palpitations, tachycardia, anxiety, increased BP.
* Alcohol	M ↑	May trigger hypertensive crisis (*see* diet-tyramine).
Anesthetics	X ↑	Potentiate CNS depression or excitement, muscle (general) stiffness or hyperpyrexia.

MONOAMINE OXIDASE INHIBITORS

Drugs (X) Interacts with:	Monoamine-Oxidase Inhibitors (M)	Comments
Anticholinergics	X ↑	Increased atropine-like effects.
Antihypertensives	X ↑	Hypotension.
Antipsychotics	X ↑ M ↑	Hypotension; may increase EPS.
* Barbiturates	X ↑	CNS depression.
Benzodiazepines	X ↑	Increased benzodiazepine effect; disinhibition, edema.
β-blockers	X ↑ M ↑	Hypotension, bradycardia, rebound BP increase if stopped.
Bupropion	X ↑	Hypertension; psychosis possible.
Buspirone	X?	Case reports of elevated BP. Wait 10 days after stopping MAOI before starting buspirone.
*Caffeine	X ↑	Irregular heartbeat or high BP; reports of hypertensive crisis; avoid in high quantities.
Carbamazepine	X ↓	Seizures in epileptics; monitor levels.
* Clomipramine	X ↑	Serotonin syndrome: *Do not combine*.
Clonidine	M ↑	May potentiate MAOIs.
* Cocaine	M ↑	Hypertensive crisis (*see* sympathomimetics).
* Cyclobenzaprine	X ↑ M ↑	Fever, seizures, and death reported; cyclobenzaprine is chemically similar to TCAs; *avoid until more data*.
†Dextroamphetamine	M ↑	Hypertensive crisis; tranylcypromine the gravest danger (*see* sympathomimetics).
Dextromethorphan	M ↑	A few reports of serotonergic crisis.
Disulfiram	X ↑	Severe CNS reactions; unclear.
Diuretics (thiazides)	X ↑	BP drop.
Doxapram	X ↑	CNS stimulation, agitation, and hypertension; MAOI may lower doxapram's cardiovascular effect; until more evidence exists, *avoid combination*.
Enflurane	X ↑	*See* anesthetics (general).
†Ephedrine	M ↑	Hypertensive crisis (*see* sympathomimetics).
†Fenfluramine	M ↑	Serotonergic crisis (*see* sympathomimetics).

*Fluoxetine (*see* SSRIs)
 Fluvoxamine (*see* SSRIs)

Drugs (X) Interacts with:	Monoamine-Oxidase Inhibitors (M)	Comments
* Guanadrel	X ↑	Initial hypertension followed by hypotension; wait 10–14 days between drugs.
* Guanethidine	X ↑	Initial hypertension followed by hypotension; wait 10–14 days between drugs.
Halothane	X ↑	See anesthetics (general).
Hydralazine	X ↑	Tachycardia; may increase BP.
* Hypoglycemics (oral)	X ↑	May lower blood sugar.
* Insulin	X ↑	May lower blood sugar.
* Levodopa (L-dopa)	X ↑ M ↑	Hypertensive crisis and CNS stimulation possible. Start with very low doses L-dopa and titrate up very slowly. May also induce akinesia and tremor (see sympathomimetics).
MAOIs	M ↑	Hypertension with phenelzine to tranylcypromine; not reported in other direction.
†Meperidine	M ↑	Serotonergic crisis; other opiates (e.g., morphine, methadone) safer.
†Metaraminol	M ↑	Hypertensive crisis (see sympathomimetics).
Methyldopa	M ↑	Hypertensive reaction may occur in theory.
* Methylphenidate	M ↑	Hypertensive crisis (see sympathomimetics).
Paroxetine (see SSRIs)		
Phenothiazines	X ↑ M ↑	Increased hypotension and anticholingeric effects.
†Phenylephrine	M ↑	Hypertensive crisis (see sympathomimetics).
†Phenylpropanolamine	M ↑	Hypertensive crisis (see sympathomimetics).
†Pseudoephedrine	M ↑	Hypertensive crisis (see sympathomimetics).
* Reserpine	X ↑	Initial hypertension followed by hypotension; wait 10–14 days between drugs.
Sertraline (see SSRIs)		
SSRIs	X ↑	Serotonergic crisis; some deaths; wait at least 2 weeks after stopping MAOI before starting SSRI; wait at least 5 weeks after stopping fluoxetine and 2 weeks after stopping sertraline, paroxetine, or fluvoxamine before starting MAOI.
* Succinylcholine	X ↑	Prolonged muscle relaxation or paralysis only by phenelzine.

MONOAMINE OXIDASE INHIBITORS

Drugs (X) Interacts with:	Monoamine- Oxidase Inhibitors (M)	Comments
Sympathomimetics (indirect): Appetite suppressants †Amphetamines *Cocaine †Cyclopentamine †Ephedrine †Isoproterenol *Levodopa †Metaraminol *Methylphenidate Pemoline †Phentermine †Phenylephrine †Phenylpropanolamine †Pseudoephedrine Sumatriptan †Tyramine	M ↑	Hypertensive crisis generated with indirect-acting sympathomimetics, but not by direct-acting sympathomimetics (e.g., epinephrine does not cause this reaction). Most common with more stimulating tranylcypromine. Sumatriptan may exaggerate serotonin effects. Use decreased dose.
Terfenadine	M ↑	Increased MAOI side effects.
Thiazide diuretics	X ↑ M ↑	Hypotension.
TCAs	M ↑	*Should not add TCAs to MAOIs*; risks noradrenergic or serotonergic crisis. Best to *not* give (1) large doses, (2) IM/IV drugs, (3) imipramine with tranylcypromine, (4) an MAOI to patients recently on SSRIs or clomipramine. Amitriptyline safer: 50–70% of patients have no rise in BP.
Theophylline	X ↑	Palpitations, tachycardia, anxiety.
* Tryptophan	X ↑	*Serotonin syndrome*; tryptophan off American market, but old bottles exist.
Tubocurarine	X ↑	Prolonged muscle relaxation or paralysis.
†Tyramine	M ↑	Hypertensive crisis (*see* sympathomimetics).

* Moderately important interaction; † Extremely important interaction; ↑ Increases; ↓ Decreases.

EFFECTS ON LABORATORY TESTS

Generic Names	Blood/Serum Tests**	Results*	Urine Tests	Results*
Isocarboxazid	LFT	↑	?	
Phenelzine	Glucose	↓	5-HIAA, VMA	—
	LFT	↑		
Tranylcypromine	Glucose	↓	5-HIAA, VMA	—

* ↑ Increases; ↓ Decreases; ? Undetermined.
** LFT = SGOT, SGPT, LDH, alkaline phosphotase, bilirubin.

WITHDRAWAL

MAOIs do not cause

- Dependence
- Tolerance
- Addiction

Abrupt withdrawal from phenelzine, tranylcypromine, and possibly from isocarboxazid, may exhibit

- Agitation
- Nightmares
- Psychosis
- REM rebound can be significant, because MAOIs often completely suppress REM.
    - √ Symptoms decline by re-introducing a low MAOI dose.
    - √ Gradually withdrawing MAOIs one tablet every 3–4 days is safer.
- Tranylcypromine withdrawal may also cause
    - √ Prominent insomnia, disrupted sleep, hypersomnia
    - √ Restlessness, anxiety, depression
    - √ Diarrhea
    - √ Headache
    - √ Tremulousness
    - √ Hot and cold feelings
    - √ Muscle weakness
    - √ Confusion, delirium
    - √ Hallucinations, psychosis
- These patients often have a h/o tranylcypromine abuse.
- Patients on long-term tranylcypromine *may* have greater risk.
- Prevalence of tranylcypromine withdrawal is probably low.

Withdrawal from MAOIs is not life-threatening.

MAOI diet and drug regimen should persist for at least 2 weeks after the last MAOI dose.

OVERDOSE: TOXICITY, SUICIDE, AND TREATMENT

Patients on MAOIs are apt to die from suicide, since a 10-day supply can be lethal.

Overdose symptoms include

- May develop in 4–12 h,
- Maximize at 24–48 h,
- Usually resolve in 3–4 days,
- But may persist for 12–14 days.

MONOAMINE OXIDASE INHIBITORS

Most acute MAOI overdoses exaggerate side effects.

- Early to mild symptoms include
  - ✓ Drowsiness
  - ✓ Dizziness (can be severe)
  - ✓ Headache (can be severe)
  - ✓ Insomnia
  - ✓ Restlessness, anxiety, irritability
  - ✓ Ataxia
- More severe symptoms include
  - ✓ Confusion, incoherence
  - ✓ Tachycardia, rapid and irregular pulse
  - ✓ Hypotension
  - ✓ Seizures
  - ✓ Hallucinations
  - ✓ Hyperreflexia
  - ✓ Fever
  - ✓ Respiratory depression
  - ✓ Increased or decreased temperature
  - ✓ Hyperactivity
  - ✓ Spasm of masticatory muscles
  - ✓ Opisthotonos
  - ✓ Sweating
  - ✓ Rigidity
  - ✓ Coma

The general management of MAOI overdoses include (see pages 53–54).

- Remember that diet and drug interactions may also occur during overdose.

Additional problems include

- Hypotension
  - ✓ May evolve into shock, coma, cardiovascular insufficiency, myocardial infarction, and arrhythmias.
  - ✓ Push fluids.
  - ✓ Pressor amines (e.g., norepinephrine) may help, but the hypertensive effects of these agents may potentiate MAOI effects.
  - ✓ Avoid CNS stimulants and contraindicated drugs.
- Seizures (see pages 122–123).
- For increased temperature, apply external cooling.
- For hepatotoxicity, evaluate liver function tests about 4–6 weeks after MAOI overdose.

Carefully observe patient for at least one week after the overdose.

Toxicity and Suicide Data

Generic Names	Toxicity Doses Average (Highest) (g)	Mortality Doses Average (Lowest) (g)	Lethal Supply of MAOIs (days)
Isocarboxazid	(0.5)		10–12
Phenelzine	(0.750)	1.012 (0.375)	6–10
Tranylcypromine	(0.750)		10–12

PRECAUTIONS

MAOIs *contraindicated* in

- Cerebrovascular disease and congestive heart failure
- Pheochromocytoma
- Food with large amounts of tyramine, dopamine (see pages 161–169)
- Medications listed before (see pages 156–160)
- Recurrent or severe headache unless good home BP monitoring
- Hypersensitivity to MAOIs
- Myelography
  - √ Stop MAOI at least 48 h before myelography.
  - √ Resume MAOI at least 24 h after myelography.
- Liver disease or abnormal liver function
- Children under 16

Tranylcypromine addiction has been reported in a few cases.

- Arises partly from tranylcypromine's stimulating properties.
- A few cases of tolerance without addiction have occurred.
- Maximum doses for each patient ranged from 120–700 mg/day with an average of 267 mg/day.
  - √ Doses of 90–130 mg have been reported to be lower in side effects than lower doses.
- Patients typically presented with delirium and agitation.
- After MAOI is stopped, patients treated best with other class of antidepressant.

MAOIs may suppress anginal pain, which means that patients should be warned about overexertion.

MAOIs may increase symptoms of Parkinson's disease, but more often decrease them, as seen with selegiline.

Use MAOIs *cautiously* in patients with

- Hyperthyroidism

MONOAMINE OXIDASE INHIBITORS

- Diabetes
- Renal impairment
- Epilepsy
- Recurrent or severe headaches (requires good home BP monitoring).
- Hypertension
  - ✓ Monitor for transient BP increase (seen more with tranylcypromine).
  - ✓ Adjust antihypertensives downward if common MAOI hypotensive effect is seen.
- Asthma
  - ✓ Okay if patient managed well with nonsystemic steroids and/or chromalyn.
  - ✓ Acute crisis will require epinephrine, not indirect pressors.
- Severe allergic reactions
  - ✓ Epinephrine probably okay, but test dose with BP monitoring in office advised.

NURSES' DATA

Monitor suicidal patients for "cheeking" or hoarding MAOIs.

Remind patients about a 4–6 week lag on a therapeutic dose before MAOIs fully work.

Tell patients about MAOI diet, stressing its importance without overdoing its seriousness.

- Review the patient's use of
  - ✓ Specific favorite foods, including cooking methods with wine, soy sauce, etc.
  - ✓ Over-the-counter medications (especially nose sprays, cold tablets, diet pills)
  - ✓ Prescription drugs (e.g., TCAs)
  - ✓ Recreational substances (e.g., wine, cocaine)
- Make sure patient knows differences between hypertensive crisis and hypotensive reaction (see pages 114–115, 169–170).
- Make sure patient has nifedipine readily available and knows when to use it.

Tell patients that MAOIs may produce insomnia and overstimulation.

- Excessively caffeinated beverages (e.g., Coke, Mountain Dew) may accelerate anxiety, agitation, and confuse diagnosis.
- If patient experiences insomnia on MAOIs, doctor can change timing and/or dosage of MAOI.

PATIENT AND FAMILY NOTES

Be familiar with MAOI diet and drugs.

Most common side effects include mild hypotension, dizziness, palpitations, dry mouth, sedation, and insomnia.

MAOIs may impair patient's performance of potentially hazardous tasks (e.g., driving a car, working near machinery, crossing streets). When a patient starts MAOIs, he or she should drive briefly in a safe place to check reflexes.

No MAOIs should be left at bedside or at any other easily accessible place.

Keep safely away from children.

For dizzy patients, review hypotension instructions (see pages 114–115).

Carry a Medic Alert card to inform emergency room doctors about MAOIs.

- Inform every physician, surgeon, dentist, and pharmacist about using an MAOI.
- Before buying any over-the-counter drug, check the label, or ask the pharmacist, about the drug's compatibility with MAOIs.

To discourage patients who have h/o suicide or parasuicide attempts from overdosing with MAOIs, inform them that stroke or myocardial infarction is more likely than death.

May take MAOIs with regular meals.

- If forget dose, can consume it within 4 h.
- Otherwise wait for next regular dose.
- Do not double dose.

Buy a BP cuff and learn how to use it in case of suspected hypertension.

Put nifedipine in many accessible places (e.g., wallet, purse, glove compartment, desk at work, etc.).

Must remain on MAOI dietary and drug regimen for 10–14 days after stopping MAOIs.

In restaurants always ask for ingredients of potentially harmful foods.

Do not abruptly halt MAOIs; may develop GI upset and bad dreams 1–3 days after doing so.

- Call physician instead.
- If unable to reach a physician, take one more pill until contacting him or her.

5. Lithium

INTRODUCTION

Lithium salts prevent and treat manic and depressive swings in bipolar disorders.[1] Drugs modulating "highs" and "lows" are called "mood stabilizers."

- Mood stabilizers are lithium and some anticonvulsants.
- This chapter considers lithium, the next, anticonvulsants.

This chapter examines lithium as a treatment for

- Bipolar disorder (pages 190–197)
- Bipolar depression (page 194)
- Cyclothymic disorder (pages 197–198)
  √ Also emotionally unstable character disorder variant
- Unipolar depression (page 198)
- Schizoaffective episode (pages 198–199)
- Borderline personality disorder (pages 199–200)
- Medical disorders (page 200)
  √ On-off syndrome of Parkinsons
  √ Viral syndromes
  √ Cyclic neutropenia

Discussed in other chapters, lithium helps

- Alcoholism (Hypnotics, page 343)
- Aggression (Anticonvulsants, page 234)
- Borderline personality disorder (MAOI, page 154)
- Premenstrual syndrome/LLPD (Antidepressants, pages 110)

---

[1] Clinicians seeking information can call the Lithium Information Center at the Dean Foundation: 608/836-8070 (fax 608/836-8033).

NAMES, COST, MANUFACTURERS, DOSE FORMS, COLORS

Generic Names (Dollars/Dose: 100 pills in mg)*	Brand Names (Dollars/Dose: 100 pills in mg)*	Manufacturers	Dose Forms (mg)**	Colors
Lithium carbonate (4–9/300)	Eskalith (15/300)	SmithKline Beecham	t: 300 c: 300	t: gray c: gray-yellow
	Eskalith CR† (32/450)	SmithKline Beecham	t: 450	t: yellow
	Lithane (13/300)	Miles	t: 300	t: green
Lithium citrate (11–15/480 ml)	Cibalith-S	CIBA	s: 8 mEq./5 ml	s: raspberry
	Lithobid***		t: 300	

* 1994 average wholesale price for 100 pills at this dose (e.g., 78/50 means 100 pills 50 mg cost $78). If depot form, cost is of single dose.
** c = capsules; s = syrup; † = sustained release; t = tablets.
*** At the time of updating this book, lithobid, a slow release preparation, was going to be reintroduced generically.

PHARMACOLOGY

At an intracellular level lithium

- Delays norepinephrine-sensitive adenylate cyclase.
- Reverses or balances calcium-mediated processes.
- Passes through sodium channels.
- At high concentrations, passes through potassium channels.
- Diminishes sensitivity to neurotransmitter receptors.

The GI tract completely absorbs lithium in 6 h.
Lithium's bioavailability is 100%.
Cerebral concentration is 40% of plasma concentration.
Peak plasma levels typically occur in 1½–2 h (range ½–3 h); steady-state plasma levels at 4–5 days.
Lithium's average half-life is 20–24 h and ranges from 8–35 h.

- Lithium clearance is normally 25% of the creatinine.
- Steady state is usually achieved in 4–7 days.

Sustained-release lithium

- Has delayed GI absorption (60–90%), which may slow fluctuations in plasma lithium.
- Peaks at 4–4½ h (range 3½–12 h).
- Releases less lithium in the stomach.
- Delivers more lithium to the small intestine.
- If divided or broken, sustained-release can become fast release.

Lithium citrate is the most rapidly absorbed, usually within ¼–1 h.

- The kidneys excrete 95% of lithium.
- The feces excrete 1%.
  √ Diarrhea usually has only small effect on lithium level.
- Sweat excretes 4–5%.
  √ Hot weather and increases in exercise may lower lithium levels.
- 33–67% of lithium excreted in 6–12 h.
- The rest excreted over 10–14 days.

70–80% of lithium is reabsorbed in the proximal tubules.

- With negative sodium balance there is a compensatory increase.
- Sodium depletion significantly increases lithium retention.

Laboratory Investigations

With lithium treatment, obtain the following tests.

	Before Starting Lithium	Every 6 Months	Every 12 Months
ECG*	Yes	—	Yes
Electrolytes*	Yes	—	—
CBC, differential**	Yes	—	—
BUN, creatinine (creatinine clearance if risk of renal impairment suspected)	Yes	Yes[1]	—
Urinalysis	Yes	—	—
Fasting blood sugar (optional)***	Yes	—	—
T_3RU, T_4RIA T_4I†	Yes	—	—
TSH	Yes	Yes[2]	Yes[2]
Antithyroid antibodies (optional)⊖	Yes	—	—
Calcium ‡	Yes	—	Yes
Pregnancy test (women at risk)	Yes	Optional	Optional
Side-effect checklist	Yes	Yes	—
Physical exam and general medical history****	—	Yes	Yes

* For patients over 40 or with h/o cardiac disease; these patients should also take another ECG one month after obtaining steady-state plasma level.

** Re-obtain new baseline WBC with expected leucocytosis 4–6 weeks after lithium begins; neutrophils most increased.

*** Helps establish baseline to determine later if lithium is significantly altering glucose tolerance. Hypoglycemia greater risk from lithium.

**** Special emphasis on cardiac, renal, thyroid, and dermatologic systems and risk of pregnancy.

† RU = resin uptake; RIA = radio immunoassay; I = free thyroxin index.

‡ Re-obtain serum calcium 2–6 weeks after lithium begins. Futher assays should be done if clinical symptoms of hypercalcemia are seen: neuromuscular signs, ataxia, apathy, dysphoria, depression. Levels approaching 11 mg/dl should be followed closely.

⊖ Can help detect those who are most likely to become hypothyroid.

[1] Check renal function q 2–3 months during frist 6 months of treatment.

[2] Many women who develop hypothyroidism do so within first 2 years. Six-month monitoring recommended. Men and women euthyroid after 2 years can be monitored yearly.

DOSES

Lithium plasma levels determine the most effective dose.
Always base lithium dosage on clinical state and side effects, not solely on plasma level.

Three methods for calculating lithium's initial dose can be informative:

1. One generally can predict the total daily effective lithium dose by giving the patient 600 mg of lithium, checking the lithium level 24 h later, and prescribing the corresponding dose from the table.

24-Hour Lithium Level (mEq/l)	Total Daily Dose (mg)
0.05–0.09	3600
0.10–0.14	2700
0.15–0.19	1800
0.20–0.23	900
0.24–0.30	600
> 0.30	300

2. Another dose predicting method is to obtain a 1.0 mEq/1 plasma level involves taking 900 mg lithium and getting a blood level 12 h later. Then use the equation:

$$d = \frac{2700}{5.61x - 0.21}$$

d = predicted daily dose

x = 12 h lithium plasma level

3. A third, empirically derived, retrospective formula that involves no test doses:

24–h dose = 486.8 + 746.83 × (desired lithium mmol/l) − (10.08 × age in years) + (5.95 × weight in kg) + (92.01 × outpatient or inpatient status) + (147.8 × female or male) − (74.73 × presence or absence of antidepressant)

status: outpatient = 0, inpatient = 1
gender: female = 0, male = 1
cyclic antidepressant: absent = 0, present = 1

- This method cannot be used on patients with impaired kidney function or any medical illness or coprescribed drugs that would alter serum lithium levels.
- Up to 90% of predicted doses are within ± 0.2 mmol/l of desired dose.

Whichever method is used, patients must be carefully monitored for side effects and a lithium plasma level obtained 2–3 days after starting predicted dose to insure against toxicity.

During either the 12- or 24-h test, patients must maintain their normal fluid and salt consumption or the test will be invalid.

Never completely trust any of these tests. Can start at full dose for acute mania to insure rapid onset of effect, but monitor levels and side effects carefully. For hypomanic inpatients and outpatients the urgency to get to the final dose is less and the risks of GI side effects or lithium toxicity unnecessary. Can start very gradually 300 mg qd and get level and then increase 300 mg every 4–5 days until desired level is achieved. Lithium levels can be obtained 5 days after each dosage increase, and when lithium level reaches 1.0 mEq/1, should be checked more frequently.

Condition	Usual Plasma Level (mEq/l)	Extreme Plasma Level Range (mEq/l)	Elderly Plasma Level (mEq/l)
Acute mania	1.0–1.3	0.5–1.5	0.3–1.0
Maintenance	0.60–1.0	0.46–1.2	0.3–0.6

Saliva lithium levels can assist if drawing blood becomes difficult.

- Saliva levels are 1–3 (usually 2) times the plasma level.
- To calculate this ratio for a particular patient, determine several plasma and saliva levels and note their ratio.

Lithium is often given bid, but a single, bedtime dosing usually produces less polyuria and renal structural abnormalities (i.e., sclerotic glomeruli, atrophic tubuli, or interstital fibrosis). With qd dosing

- Increased risk of diarrhea.
- 12-h plasma levels will be about 10–26% higher than on bid dosing.
  - √ In Europe this is usually not recalculated to correspond to plasma levels from bid dosing.
    - ▫ Lower doses generally used.
  - √ Outcomes are no worse with these apparently lower levels, but direct comparisons have not been made.
- Maximum qd dose is usually 1800 mg.

Slow (sustained) release lithium may lower side effects related to peak levels (e.g., tremor, nausea).

- May cause more diarrhea than standard lithium.
- Less blood level fluctuation than standard lithium.

- Twice daily dosing with slow-release lithium may generate 10% higher 12-h serum levels than same dose of standard lithium.
- Does not reduce risk of renal structural abnormalities.

CLINICAL INDICATIONS AND USE

General Information

Lithium carbonate and lithium citrate have no major clinical differences.

- Lithium citrate may have fewer GI and allergic side effects.

Predictors for a good initial lithium response include

- H/o of mania or hypomania associated with grandiosity or elation
- No atypical (schizoaffective) symptoms
- Depressive episodes (past or present) with anergia, hypersomnia, increased appetite
- Less than 4 cycles/year
- Previous compliance with treatment
- Sequence of mania followed by depression
- First-degree relative with bipolar disorder
- Absence of mixed manic/depressive features or neurologic disorder

Other factors that might predict a good initial lithium response are

- H/o "switch" to mania on TCAs or spontaneously
- Augmented TSH response to TRH in depressed bipolar patients
- Any periodic, fully-remitting psychopathology

Most common side effects in beginning of treatment are

- Hand tremor
- Dyspepsia
- Diarrhea
- Polyuria and/or polydipsia
  √ 2° to reduced renal response to ADH

Weight gain, polyuria, thirst, edema, hair loss, acne, benign leucocytosis, and cloudy thinking are more common later in treatment.

Initiating Therapy

Mania

Lithium aborts 60–80% of acute manic and hypomanic episodes in 10–21 days.

Response rates to lithium:

- 70% full initial response
- 20% partial initial response
- 10% no initial response

Lithium is particularly effective in reducing affective and ideational signs of mania, especially

- Elation, grandiosity, expansiveness
- Flight of ideas
- Irritability, manipulative behavior
- Anxiety

To a slightly lesser extent, lithium diminishes

- Pressured speech
- Suspicious feelings
- Insomnia
- Psychomotor agitation
- Threatening or assaultive behavior
- Hypersexuality
- Distractibility

Lithium and neuroleptics or benzodiazepines can all calm acute manic symptoms (e.g., grandiosity, pressured speech). Treatment may begin with

- Lithium by itself.
- Lithium with benzodiazepines if nonpsychotic and agitated or pressured.
- Lithium with antipsychotics, if psychosis is present.
- Lithium with antipsychotics and, if still agitated at full anti-psychotic dose, benzodiazepines.
  - √ Antipsychotics have high risk for TD in bipolar disorder.
    - □ In patients with h/o multiple manic episodes, alternatives to antipsychotics should be considered first.
    - □ Recent evidence suggests that many psychotic manics may respond to clonazepam or lorazepam with lithium without an antipsychotic.
    - □ In patients on first or second episode who do not need anti-psychotics at other times, antipsychotics probably a low risk.

If *lithium alone* is started

- Obtain blood tests (see above).
- Therapeutic and toxic lithium plasma levels are close.
- Treat acutely manic patients with the lowest effective dose, which typically produces lithium levels from 1.0–1.5 mEq/l.
  - √ Lithium has increasing efficacy up to 1.4 mEq/l.
- Start lithium (as predicted by tests) in divided bid or tid doses to reduce initial side effects.
- Most common initial side effect is nausea/dyspepsia.
- This is caused by
  - √ Direct irritation of lithium on gastric mucosa.

□ Lithium citrate or slow-release lithium or full stomach can help.
√ Wide fluctuations in blood levels.
□ Divided dosing or slow-release lithium can prevent this.
- Tremor is also a common initial side effect.
√ Less frequent with slow-release form.
- If not using the earlier formulas, start lithium in a healthy adult with acute mania at 300 mg bid.
√ Increase dose by 300 mg q 3–4 days or tid.
□ This divided dosing can reduce early nausea, but
□ If nausea is posing no problem, qd dosing can be used.
√ Raise dose until
□ Clear therapeutic results, or
□ Plasma level reaches 1.2 mEq/l, or
□ Raise dose further to 1.5 mEq/1 if no therapeutic effect after 10 days and no side effects.
- Measure lithium level around days 4 to 7 to determine plasma level.
√ Draw lithium 12 h after the last dose.
√ Get further lithium levels in 2 weeks or 4–5 days after last lithium increase.
√ Get further lithium levels at the same post-lithium dose time each week or 4–5 days after last lithium increase, to confirm therapeutic plasma level.
√ Obtain levels every month for the next 6 months, and then
□ Every 2–3 months, or
□ If 2 or 3 consecutive lithium levels are stable, can wait 3 months and then 6 months.
- Lithium may work in 7–10 days or may require 3–5 weeks.
- During manic episodes, patients usually need increased lithium.
- Reduce above doses by 50% in patients over 60 or in patients with a renal disorder.
- If lithium does not induce improvement in 3 weeks, add an anticonvulsant (e.g., carbamazepine or valproic acid).

If starting *lithium and antipsychotic jointly*

- Initially, highly manic psychotic patients are best treated with an antipsychotic (e.g., haloperidol, cholorpromazine) *and* lithium.
- Prescribe lithium (as above).
- Initiate a neuroleptic if patient is psychotic and still at low risk for TD.
√ Choose maximum neuroleptic dose in advance to avoid overdosing.
√ Begin with haloperidol 5 mg po or IM bid-qid in patients over 30, since it acts rapidly and sedates minimally, or

L
I
T
H
I
U
M

- ✓ A mildly sedating midpotency neuroleptic (e.g., perphenazine, particularly in young adults at risk for dystonia, can be used 12 mg po or IM bid-qid).
- ✓ Raise neuroleptics qod, such as haloperidol elevated 5 mg qod.
- ✓ If dystonia occurs, add ACA.
- After controlling manic delusions, taper patient off neuroleptic.
- Initiate a benzodiazepine if patient agitated but not psychotic, or still agitated on adequate antipsychotic dose, or if TD risk makes an antipsychotic a poor choice.
  - ✓ Begin with 1–2 mg lorazepam po or IM q 1–4 h prn until agitation is controlled and patient is mildly sedated but not ataxic or stuporous.
  - ✓ Follow with 0.5–2 mg lorazepam po or IM' tid-qid, or for less variation in plasma levels.
  - ✓ Substitute with longer-acting clonazepam 0.25–2 mg po qd-tid.
  - ✓ Higher benzodiazepine dose can be given qhs to ensure sleep (adequate sleep may speed manic recovery).
- When patient switches out of mania, he/she may appear to be overdosed (e.g., somnolent, ataxic) on the same dose that barely controlled the mania.
  - ✓ Hold benzodiazepines until significant side effects disappear.
  - ✓ If neuroleptic dose over 15 mg haloperidol equivalents, attempt to reduce to more usual antipsychotic range (e.g., 5–15 mg).

In treating the elderly

- Start lithium in lower doses (e.g., 300–600 mg/day).
- Consider ½ pill (150 mg) dose additions.
- Monitor lithium q 3–4 days.
- Increase lithium by 150–300 mg until reach an acute therapeutic level between 0.5–0.8 mEq/l.
- Doses over 900 mg/day are often unnecessary and toxic.
- If neurotoxicity develops, may take several days to several weeks to remit, in spite of negligible lithium levels.

If patient develops unresponsive EPS on antipsychotic agents, may replace neuroleptic with clonazepam, carbamazepine, or valproic acid; can also try risperidone or clozapine.

- Pure anticonvulsants do not usually increase depressions.
  - ✓ But clonazepam can, in doses over 1.5 mg qd.
- Act as quickly as antipsychotics and possibly faster, particularly valproic acid (often within 5 days), than lithium.
- Seem especially useful in rapidly-cycling or dysphoric manic patients.
- Clonazepam produces sedation; carbamazepine less so, and valproic acid almost none.
- May magnify CNS toxicity of lithium (e.g., ataxia, confusion).

For lithium-resistant bipolar disorder, see Anticonvulsants (page 227–228)

Bipolar Depression

Lithium is more effective against bipolar than unipolar depressions.

- Lithium alone yields a 75–80% response in bipolar depression.
  - √ May need 6–8 weeks for full response.
  - √ Will also quell subsyndromal depressions.

General indications

- For moderate to severe bipolar depression where faster response is needed, lithium with antidepressants are preferred.
- For mild bipolar depression, first try lithium alone.
  - √ At first, try levels of 0.6–1.0 mEq/ml and increase if no response (e.g., 1.0–1.5 mEq/ml).
  - √ No data for or against using acute manic lithium levels for acute depression (e.g., 1.0–1.5 mEq/ml).
- Antidepressants may decrease cycle length, thereby increasing manic and/or depressive episodes.
  - √ In one study, patients off TCAs had bipolar periods every 150 days, whereas on TCAs, they had one every 50 days.
  - √ TCAs have higher risk than SSRIs, bupropion, or MAOIs.
  - √ If this occurs, reduce antidepressant dosage and pretreat with lithium.
- About 25–35% of patients benefit at some time from adding an AD during a depression.
- Anticonvulsants (*see* Antidepressants for unipolar depression)
  - √ Carbamazepine may relieve bipolar depression.
    - □ Lithium augmentation can also help.
  - √ Valproic acid is not better than placebo in bipolar depression.
    - □ It can prevent or delay its occurrence.
  - √ Valproic acid and carbamazepine probably superior to lithium in blocking antidepressant-induced rapid cycling.
    - □ ADs may be started sooner and used more aggressively.
- Clonazepam may help relieve depression, but in doses of 1.5 mg/qd and more, may cause
  - √ Or exacerbate depression.
  - √ Sedation.
  - √ Disinhibition.

Rapid-cycling patients

- Have more than 3 recurrences in a single year.
- Respond less well to lithium than patients with fewer episodes.
- Often require a full year to respond to lithium.

If rapid cycling occurs

- Check (and treat) for hypothyroidism.
    - √ Occasionally rapid cycling responds to addition of T_4.
        - ▫ Goal is high-normal or slightly hyperthyroid levels.
        - ▫ Has been effective in euthyroid patients.
- Prescribe carbamazepine or valproic acid in addition to lithium if still cycling after 4 months (see pages 227–228).
    - √ If each episode results in hospitilization, may need to start these sooner.
- ADs may trigger rapid cycling.
    - √ Lithium and carbamazepine together more effective than lithium alone for rapid cyling.
- MAOIs, SSRIs, or bupropion preferred over TCAs, but rapid cycling still possible.
- Fluoxetine may not be preferred because of very long half-life.
    - √ However, one study showed that fluoxetine induced mania no longer than with other ADs.
- Bupropion, paroxetine, and nefazodone (1.5–3%) have lowest reported rates of manic induction in known bipolars.

Patients with less severe bipolar illnesses, such as cyclothymia or bipolar II (hypomania and major depression), may improve on lithium.

Maintaining Therapy

Frequency of bipolar relapses in 2 years

- In 20–40% of patients on lithium,
- In 65–90% of patients without lithium.

Although lithium prevents manic and depressive episodes, < 50% achieve complete relief.

- When patients halt lithium, recurrence usually occurs in several weeks to a few months,
    - √ Unless episodes are seasonal or only once or twice a year.

After onset of initial manic episode, maintain bipolar patient on lithium for 9–12 months.

- If manic episode erupts
    - √ Decreased need for sleep is often the first sign.
    - √ Important to interview patient in detail about first signs of mania.
- If possibility of seasonal hypomania in history
    - √ Continue past 1 year anniversary of first episode.

Some experts recommend that all first-episode bipolar patients be treated for life because each new episode may be associated with more rapid cycling. Prospective clinical trials are not yet available to confirm this approach.

- Case reports suggest stopping lithium after even years of stable prophylaxis can result in lithium nonresponsiveness and/or more rapid cycling.

Manage a recurring manic episode by

- Increasing lithium plasma level.
- Adding clonazepam, carbamazepine, or valproic acid.
  √ If still psychotic, add a neuroleptic.

If a depressive episode erupts

- Check lithium level and thyroid function.
  √ Correct, if needed.
- Can raise lithium to acute range 1.0–1.2 mEq/l in 7–10 days.
  √ Some depressions may respond to this higher level.
    □ No controlled research trials available to confirm or disprove this.
- Reluctantly add ADs, because they may aggravate condition (e.g., induce rapid cycling).
- If depression is severe, reluctantly add non-TCA AD (lower risk of inducing mania).
  √ Often augmentation effect is seen with antidepressant in less than 10 days.
  √ Watch out for rapid cycling.
- Some experts suspect that adding an MAOI or bupropion might be safer than a TCA or SSRI, but the only well-controlled trial support paroxetine and nefazone.
- MAOIs, particularly tranylcypromine, are highly effective in treating bipolar anergic depression.
  √ Consider MAOIs if treatment resistance is seen.

If patient is on a combination of lithium and AD, it is probably best to discontinue the AD after 1–2 months of remission to minimize the effect of AD on the mood cycle (unless depression is chronic and/or there are frequent relapses, AD not usually maintained for 6+ months as in unipolar depression).

If patient needs antidepressant but cycles on it, carbamazepine or valproic acid may be preferred maintenance drug to prevent manic episodes and rapid cycling.

"Lifelong" lithium prophylaxis would be favored when

- Patient is male.
- Symptoms showed sudden onset.
- More frequent manic and depressive episodes.
- More than 2 previous (high or low) episodes.
- First episode *not* precipitated by environmental event.
- Poor family and/or social supports.
- Strong family h/o bipolar disorder in first-degree relatives.

In maintenance phase patient should be informed about risks of

- Weight gain
- Edema
- Toxicity
  √ New onset diarrhea, tremors, confused thinking
- Risks in pregnancy

Before stopping lithium

- Discuss pros and cons with patient and family.
- Detail the first signs of mania or depression.
- Instruct everyone about what to do if symptoms emerge.
- Taper lithium gradually rather than abruptly.

If patient stops but then must return to lithium, and if he/she has previously tolerated a particular lithium dose well, restart on this full dose without titrating upwards if no side effects are noted when first starting lithium.

- Have patient report side effects immediately.
- Get lithium level in 3–4 days.

Taper lithium monthly by 300 mg/month.

- This may help "catch" a recurrence before it is out of control.
  √ The recurrence on a lower dose may be milder than on no lithium.
- Suddenly stopping may lead to "rebound" recurrence of mania.

Cyclothymic Disorder/Emotionally Unstable Character Disorder (EUCD)

Cyclothymic disorder shows depression or hypomanic mood swings, which last from a few hours to several days and are usually not environmentally triggered.

- Often responds to lithium or anticonvulsants. A resulting disorder (not in *DSM-IV*), emotionally unstable character disorder, may develop from frequent mood swings, which interfere with emotional and character development.

EUCD patients often have at least one of the following:

- Drug and medication abuse
- Delinquent behavior, problems with authority
- Poor school/work performance
- Sexual promiscuity
- Malingering
- Childhoods with impulsiveness, low frustration tolerance, and hyperactivity

Patients are often women in their late teens to early thirties. These patients have mood shifts like the cyclothymic personality, but whereas cylothymics tend to have responsible adult goals, EUCD patients are immature, young, hedonistic, without goals, confused, "wise-guys." EUCD's mood swings are often missed. Lithium (dosed as in treating acute mania) appears to decrease frequency and severity of

- Depression
- Impulsiveness
- Antisocial behavior

Anticonvulsants (e.g., carbamazepine or valproic acid) may also help.

Unipolar Depression (see pages 84–96)

ADs treat major (unipolar) depression better than lithium.

- However, lithium may be as effective as ADs in preventing relapse.

Patients unresponsive to ADs after 3–6 weeks may benefit from lithium's addition.

- Lithium is favored as a prophylactic agent over ADs in more cyclic (an episode every 6–24 months) unipolar depressions.
- If a depression emerges with "reverse biological signs"—hypersomnia, anergia, overeating—this might be the 1st glimpse of a bipolar disorder possibly helped by lithium.
- If a depression emerges in a patient with a strong family h/o bipolar disorder, lithium might be considered as a prophylactic agent after the second depressive episode.
- Patients who have responded to ECT for chronic depression and who have failed multiple trials of all classes of antidepressants may still get a good prophylactic effect from lithium.

Schizoaffective Disorder

Schizoaffective patients may be diagnosed as "atypical bipolar disorders" with characteristics of

- Chronic psychoses between episodes, or alternatively,
- Reasonably good adjustment between episodes, but with marked, mood incongruent delusions and hallucinations during euphoric or hyperactive periods.

Lithium at 0.8–1.2 mEq/l combined with an antipsychotic reduces affective symptoms in schizoaffective disorders.

- Lithium might help schizoaffective patients who have not responded to other treatments.

Lithium is best for

- Overactivity, excitement
- Posturing, mannerisms
- Confusion
- Insomnia
- Pressured speech
- Irritability
- Episodic timing of symptoms

ADs *and* neuroleptics are best for

- Schizodepressive symptoms.
- Combination is superior to either drug alone.

Anticonvulsants, such as carbamazepine, may treat schizoaffective disorders.

- Valproic acid combined with other agents improved 42–57% of schizoaffective patients.

Borderline Personality Disorder

No drug treats borderline personality disorder effectively.
If any agent is prescribed, target specific symptoms.

These agents often include

- Antipsychotics for cognitive problems ("cognitive disorganization under stress"), transient psychosis, and hostilities.
- Lithium for mood swings.
- Benzodiazepines sometimes used for chronic anxiety (but disinhibition often seen).
- ADs for depression.
  √ MAOIs most effective.
  √ SSRIs may be as effective as MAOIs.
  √ TCAs less effective.
- Carbamazepine or valproic acid to decrease behavioral outbursts and mood swings.

Overall, borderlines do better with MAOIs (or possibly SSRIs) and anticonvulsants (carbamazepine or valproic acid). Neuroleptics best used prn. Neuroleptics over time only decrease hostility and transient psychotic episodes.

Always be alert to potential for overdose.

Medical Conditions

On-off syndrome of Parkinson's

- Reduces off-time compared to placebo.
- Use therapeutic lithium range.

Cyclic neutropenia, leucopenia

- Reduces or eliminates decreased cell cycles.

Viral infections

- Recurrent herpes simplex
  √ Reduced infection rate on lithium.
  √ Probably related to increase in WBC.
- Equivocal effect in reducing viral infections in AIDS.

SIDE EFFECTS

Up to 75% of patients experience some side effect, with 25% having 3 or more side effects.

Lithium's side effects arise from

- Peak blood levels or
- Steady-state levels.

Peak plasma levels

- Occur 1.5–2 h after the dose.
- Most commonly generate lethargy, transient nausea, stomach discomfort, urinary frequency, and fine tremor.
- Can reduce peak plasma level side effects by one of the following:
  √ Substituting sustained-release lithium, or
  √ Giving less lithium in morning and larger dose at hs, or
    □ Hopefully will be asleep during peak.
  √ Starting lithium at lower doses,
  √ Spreading out dosing to tid or qid.

Steady-state levels

- Arise in 4–5 days but sometimes take up to 7 days.
- Reduce by lowering lithium.

Starting patient on salt-restricted diets and thiazide diuretics diminishes sodium, allowing lithium to replace sodium in the cell. However, lithium will be retained along with sodium at the proximal tubule and lithium level will rise so that

- May get toxic lithium plasma level.
- May induce intracellular toxicity with apparently normal plasma level.
- Better to avoid starting thiazide diuretics or salt-restricted diets.
- If they are required, determine the lithium dose based on the patient's clinical state and not on lithium level.
  - √ Lithium should be added slowly with careful monitoring of lithium level.
  - √ Patients already at steady state on thiazide diurectic or salt-restricted diet can have lithium added relatively safely as long as they are maintained.
    - □ Expect lower doses will give adequate plasma leves.
  - √ Potassium- and sodium-sparing diuretics have minimal or no effect on lithium levels.

Hypokalemia can intensify lithium side effects.

Cardiovascular Effects

At therapeutic lithium levels, the most common ECG changes are

- *T-wave flattening or inversion* in 20% of patients (similar to changes seen in hypokalemia.
- *Widening of QRS complex.*

These changes are

- Benign.
- Poorly correlated with serum lithium level.
- Stopped readily by dicontinuing lithium.
- Should not be confused with more serious problems (e.g., hypokalemia).
- May persist or disappear spontaneously during treatment.

At toxic levels ECG changes are

- S-T segment depression.
- Q-T interval prolongation.

Arrhythmias

- Occur usually in patients with pre-existing cardiac diseases.
- Common in sino-atrial node dysfunction with fainting, dizziness, palpitations, or without symptoms.
- Reversed by halting lithium.
- Ventricular arrhythmias rarely reported.

Sudden deaths

- Have occurred on lithium, usually in patients with pre-existing heart disease.
- Consider obtaining a cardiologist's consultation before placing a cardiac patient on lithium.

Gastrointestinal Effects

Initial nausea

- Dose-related, but may arise on normal serum lithium levels.
- Often occurs early in treatment, especially when titrating doses and with fluctuating plasma levels.
- Accompanied by other GI symptoms.

Management

- Do one of the following:
  - √ Ingest lithium with meals, snacks, milk, and if necessary, antacids (avoid sodium bicarbonate, use calcium carbonate).
  - √ Spread out dose or diminish lithium.
  - √ Try sustained-release preparation, which might cause diarrhea.
  - √ Replace with lithium citrate syrup.
  - √ Sometimes lithium carbonate doses can be increased more slowly, without causing GI symptoms.

Chronic nausea, anorexia, vomiting, dehydration, and *fever*

- Vomiting can cause more dehydration, which may elevate plasma lithium.
- Stop lithium until flu-like syndrome ends.

Diarrhea

- More common in toxicity, but can occur with normal serum lithium and with sustained-release or qd dosing.
- Frequency decreases with
  - √ Conventional release lithium.
  - √ Lithium with (highly anticholinergic) TCAs.

Management

- Do one of the following:
  - √ Spread out dosing or reduce lithium dose.
  - √ Add antidiarrheal medication (e.g., loperimides).
  - √ Take lithium during meals.
  - √ Switch to lithium citrate (rapidly absorbed by stomach) or conventional release lithium if patient on sustained-release.

Weight gain, edema

- Common, often causing patients to stop lithium.
  - √ Usually occurs in patients with pre-existing weight problem.
- In those who gain weight on lithium
  - √ 60% gain 15 pounds.
  - √ 20% gain 25 pounds.
- Unclear why some patients gain 40–60 pounds, whereas others add nothing.
- Likely causes:
  - √ Insulin-like effects on carbohydrate metabolism,
  - √ Increased caloric fluid intake, or
  - √ Hypothyroidism.
- Edema may also increase weight.
  - √ Shortly after initiating lithium, patients often accumulate 5–7 pounds of fluid and edema.

Management

- Do one of the following:
  - √ Reduce lithium dose.
  - √ Diminish by starting low-calorie diet, including fluids with normal sodium intake.
  - √ If edema, cautious use of potassium-sparing diuretics.
    - □ Amiloride 5–10 mg qd (don't use if K over 5.5 mEq/1)
    - □ Spironolactone 50 mg qd-bid.
    - □ Furosemide 40 mg bid.
  - √ Substitute carbamazepine for lithium, since carbamazepine does not usually increase weight.

Renal Effects

Polyuria/nephrogenic diabetes insipidus (NDI) (3,000 ml/24h urine and polydipsia lithium)

- Caused by inhibiting renal response to antidiuretic hormone (ADH, also called vasopressin).
- Initial polyuria is associated with
  - √ Higher lithium dose,
  - √ But not usually changes in urine concentration.
- After long-term lithium, polyuria is associated with
  - √ Longer lithium duration and higher serum level.
  - √ Decreases in urine concentration.
- Characteristics include
  - √ Difficulty concentrating urine.
  - √ Urine volume up to 4–8 liters/day.
  - √ Difficulty maintaining serum lithium.

- NDI may exhibit
  - √ Polyuria.
  - √ Nocturia.
  - √ Polydipsia.
    - ▫ Almost always secondary to polyuria.
  - √ Higher sodium.
  - √ Lower potassium.
  - √ Toxicity.
  - √ Dehydration.
- More often occurs with
  - √ Sustained-release lithium.
  - √ Divided dosing of lithium.
- Less often occurs with
  - √ Once daily dosing of regular lithium.
- Rule out diabetes mellitus, kidney disease/damage, metabolic abnormalities, or other drug effects.
- Subclinical polyuria may affect 50–70% of patients on long-term lithium.
  - √ 10% of lithium patients have renal output > 3 liters/day (clinical polyuria/nephrogenic diabetes insipidus).

Management

- Do one of the following:
  - √ Lithium once a day is preferred as initial approach.
    - ▫ Avoid sustained-release lithium.
  - √ Lower or stop lithium.
    - ▫ Benefits seen in 1–3 weeks.
    - ▫ Polyuria may continue in some patients months after stopping lithium.
  - √ Increase non-caloric fluid intake to dilute lithium.
  - √ Add potassium 20 mEq qd.
    - ▫ Often effective for stopping polyuria in open trials.
  - √ Paradoxically, diuretics diminish lithium-induced polyuria.
    - ▫ Sodium- and potassium-sparing diuretics, amiloride, spironolactone, or furosemide are safest because of least effect on lithium level.
  - √ Prescribe amiloride 5–10 mg bid.
    - ▫ Markedly decreases polyuria.
    - ▫ Normal diet and sodium intake.
    - ▫ Less or no effect on lithium level and no effect on serum potassium.
    - ▫ To be safe, still monitor serum lithium and electrolytes.
  - √ Thiazides in *polyuria*
    - ▫ May increase serum sodium.
    - ▫ May decrease serum potassium.
    - ▫ May increase serum lithium by 30–50%.

√ Cautiously treat with hydrochlorothiazide 50 mg/day and by
  ▫ Reducing lithium.
  ▫ Monitoring lithium and electrolyte levels.
√ Combine hydrochlorothiazide with amiloride to prevent hypo-
  kalemia.
√ Carbamazepine added to lithium can halt diabetes insipidus.
  ▫ Probably secondary to antidiuretic effect of carbamazepine.

Tubulo-interstitial nephritis/renal insufficiency

- 10–20% of patients on long-term (≤ 10 yrs) lithium have kidney
  changes.
  √ Interstitial nephrosis
  √ Tubular atrophy
  √ Sometimes glomerular atrophy
- Chronic, serious form with increasing creatinine, usually revers-
  ible.
  √ Frequency unknown.
  ▫ May be > 1% with lithium > 10 years.
- More often seen with long-term lithium therapy.
- Gradual rise in serum creatinine and decline of 24-h creatinine
  clearance.
  √ If creatinine level ≥ 1.6 mg/100 ml, consult with a nephrolo-
    gist.
  ▫ Seriously consider discontinuing lithium while problem is
    potentially reversible.
- Discontinue lithium.

Endocrine Effects

Euthyroid goiter, hypothyroidism

- Mania itself transiently increases TSH to above normal values.
- 20% of lithium patients develop thyroid abnormalities.
- 5–15% have clinical signs or altered hormone levels.
- Lithium inhibits synthesis and release of T_3 (triiodothyronine)
  and T_4 (thyroxine), which stimulates TSH (thyroid-stimulating
  hormone), which stimulate the thyroid gland to re-establish eu-
  thyroidism. During this compensatory process, the gland might
  become large (goiter) or hypothyroid or both.
- Onset typically in 6–18 months.
- Rapid cycling more likely with hypothyroidism and subclinical
  (↑ TSH only) hypothyroidism.
- A euthyroid goiter shows
  √ Normal thyroid function tests.
  √ Increased TSH.
  √ Sometimes anergia.

- Hypothyroidism shows
  - √ A goiter or no goiter.
  - √ Increased TSH (the most sensitive diagnostic test).
  - √ Those who have antithyroid antibodies prior to start of lithium.
- Highest risk groups
  - √ Antithyroid antibodies prior to start of lithium
    - ▫ Uncommon to develop hypothyroidism without antibodies prior to lithium treatment.
  - √ Women
- Timing highly variable.

Management

- Can usually continue lithium with either thyroid disorder.
- Add thyroxine 0.05–0.2 mg/day *or* start thyroxine 0.1 mg qd for 2 weeks and then 0.2 mg qd.
- Monitor TSH.
  - √ If patient is rapid cycler, suppress TSH to low end of normal range.

Hyperparathyroidism

- Serum calcium and parathyroid hormone levels enter high-to-normal range in half of patients in 1st month on lithium.
- Abnormally high levels occur in 5–10% of patients.
- Rarely of clinical significance.
- Symptoms of hyperparathyroidism include
  - √ Mood changes
  - √ Anxiety
  - √ Apathy
  - √ Aggressiveness
  - √ Psychosis
  - √ Sleep disturbance
  - √ Delirium, dementia, confusion
  - √ Convulsions

Glucose tolerance, carbohydrate craving

- Lithium may change glucose tolerance, but it is not diabetogenic.
  - √ Hypoglycemia more common than hyperglycemia on lithium.
- Can accentuate diabetes mellitus.
- No reason to obtain regular glucose tests on most patients.
- Increased sugar in fluids leads to *dental carries*.

Hematologic Effects

Leukocytosis

- Mainly mature neutrophils are increased.
- Reversible, benign, and not indicative of disease.

- WBC around 12,000–15,000/mm^3.
- Rarely need to stop lithium.
- Useful to obtain one baseline WBC while on lithium.
  - √ If patient later gets sick, will be able to determine if "real" leucocytosis occurs.

Skin, Allergies, and Temperature

Usually idiosyncratic rather than dose-related.

Acne and psoriasis are common.

Acne

- May appear or get worse during lithium.
- Try antibiotics and/or retinoic acid.
- May need to lower or halt lithium.

Psoriasis

- Aggravation of pre-existing or dormant psoriasis.
- Dry noninflamed papular eruption is common.
- First try lowering lithium.
  - √ If this fails, begin standard medication for psoriasis; halt lithium treatment if this fails.

Allergic rash

- Patients often develop allergic rashes in hospitals separate from lithium.
  - √ Soaps and detergents are the common culprits, with
    - □ Rash often only on hands, wrist, neck where clothing rubs.
  - √ Hospital foods are other common cause.
- Allergic rash may disappear by changing specific lithium brand/formulation.
  - √ May be caused by binder, additives, dyes in pill and not lithium.
- Test patient with rash with lithium citrate and, if no rash develops, patient not allergic to lithium.

Maculopapular rash

- Occurs with or without psoriasis.
- Is mildly annoying, erythematous rash.
- Relieved with 50:50 zinc ointment.

Alopecia

- May be 2° hypothyroidism.
  - √ Check TSH.
- Occurs in 12% of women; rarely in men.
- Hair disappears anywhere on body.

- Hair can regrow on or off of lithium.
- Sometimes associated with loss of curl or wave.

Management of other skin lesions:

- Antihistamines can best treat urticarial lesions.
- Topical steroids.
- Bacitracin for localized infections.

Central Nervous System Effects

Tremor (fine, hand)

- Dose-related tremor may affect 30–50% patients.
- More likely in those who had a preexisting tremor or a family h/o essential tremor.
- Tremors may disappear after the first 2–3 weeks of constant lithium dose.
- Lithium tremor
  - ✓ Present at rest, but worsens on intentional movement or maintenance of posture.
  - ✓ Worsens with anxiety and performance.
  - ✓ Usually confined to fingers but
    - □ If severe, may involve hands and wrists.
  - ✓ Irregular in amplitude and rhythm.
  - ✓ Jerking fingers with flexion or extension.
  - ✓ Erupting in side thrusts.
  - ✓ Variable in its frequency and intensity throughout the day, and from day to day.
  - ✓ Produces jagged, irregular, hard-to-read handwriting when severe.
- Lithium tremor differs from others in that
  - ✓ In parkinsonism (EPS) tremor, the fingers, hands, and wrist move faster and as a unit; micrographia also appears, but not in lithium tremor.
  - ✓ In Parkinson's disease, the tremor is slow and rhythmic, with prominent rotational and flexing movements (pill-rolling).
  - ✓ In anxiety, the tremor is fine, rapid, and rhythmic with side-to-side movements.
- Lithium tremor may increase with
  - ✓ Greater serum lithium, although it may exist with normal serum levels.
  - ✓ Adding TCAs.
- Tremors may be diminished by one of the following:
  - ✓ More frequent, smaller doses or single qhs dose.
  - ✓ Decreased total lithium dose, especially if serum concentration is > 0.8 mEq/l.

√ Sustained-release lithium preparations.
√ Propranolol 10 mg qid initially.
  □ May escalate dose to 20 mg tid-qid.
  □ Before starting propranolol, r/o congestive heart failure, bronchospasm, or other contraindications to β-blockers.
  □ Alternatives to propranolol are metoprolol (25–50 mg) or nadolol (20–40 mg) bid.
  □ Atenolol debatable alternative because tremor is believed to be a CNS effect and atenolol does not easily get into CNS.
√ *Slowly* increase lithium doses.
√ Stop TCAs.
√ ACAs don't help.

Seizures

- Grand mal (rarely)
  √ Usually in epilepsy patients, if at all.
- Lithium may be appropriate in well-controlled seizures *unless*
  √ Carbamazepine or valproic acid would be more appropriate for the seizures (and also the bipolar disorder).

Memory loss, "dullness of senses," reduced coordination, lethargy, ataxia, inhibited motor skills

- Confirm lithium is the cause.
  √ Compare with baseline function.
  √ The absence of "highs" may account for patients describing these problems.
  √ Hypothyroidism may be the culprit.
  √ Subthreshold depression may be the cause.
- Occur on > 0.8 mEq/l of lithium.
  √ Word recall memory impaired in normal volunteers (i.e., college students).
    □ Also complained of "cognitive blurring."
    □ Younger patients more likely to complain of memory problems.
- Management
  √ Reduce or stop dose.
  √ Suggest remedial memory training.
  √ Thyroid replacement, if necessary.
  √ Assess for antidepressants.

Cogwheeling, mild parkinsonism

- May increase chance of this when patient on AD or neuroleptic.
- Sometimes happens on lithium alone.
- Not very responsive to ACAs but may respond to amantadine.

Pseudotumor cerebri

- Rare.
- Blurred vision often first complaint.
  - ✓ Headache not always present.
- Papilledema seen.
- Elevated lumbar puncture pressure.
- Papilledema usually resolves after a few months off lithium.
- Elevated pressure doesn't always completely resolve.
  - ✓ Shunt sometimes needed.

PERCENTAGES OF SIDE EFFECTS

Side Effects	Lithium
CARDIOVASCULAR EFFECTS	
Dizziness, lightheadedness	20
T-wave changes (benign)	25
ECG abnormalities	20
GASTROINTESTINAL EFFECTS	
Dry mouth and throat	27.5 (10–50)
Anorexia, lower appetite	12.5
Nausea, vomiting	15.2
Dyspepsia, upset stomach	10.3
Diarrhea	14.4
Thirst	26.7
Polydipsia	37.6 (10–55.3)
Weight gain	29.7 (1–60)
Edema	10.2
RENAL EFFECTS	
Kidney defect	15 (< 10–50)
Polyuria	40 (10–60)
ENDOCRINE AND SEXUAL EFFECTS	
Hyperparathyroidism	5
Menstrual changes	5.5
Hypothyroidism (mainly women)	12* (1–20)
Goiter	4.1 (1.7–6.1)
Disturbed sexual function	20

Side Effects	Lithium
EYES, EARS, NOSE, AND THROAT EFFECTS	
Blurred vision	< 1
Vertigo	10
SKIN, ALLERGIES, AND TEMPERATURE	
Acne	18
Rashes	6.3
Abnormal skin pigment	1
Hair loss (mainly women)	12
CENTRAL NERVOUS SYSTEM EFFECTS	
Cogwheeling	8 (5–75)
Weakness, fatigue	10.5 (1–30)
Muscle cramps	5.5
Hypertonia	< 15
Jerking limbs	< 1
Slurred speech	5.5
Rigidity	5.0
Headache	< 40
Resting tremor	37.5 (10–50)
Drowsiness, sedation	22.8 (1– < 40)
Confusion, disorientation	22.8 (1– < 40)
Memory impairment	32.5 (0–45)

PREGNANCY AND LACTATION

Teratogenicity
(1st trimester)

- Lithium clearance increases during pregnancy.
  - √ Monitor lithium levels every 2–4 weeks.
  - √ Need to progressively increase lithium dose.

- Increases in non-cardiovascular abnormalities not well established.

- Higher frequency of congenital cardiac abnormalities, especially a 2.5–400-fold increase of Ebstein's anomaly of the tricuspid valve (i.e., 0.1–0.7% of live births).
  - √ Lower estimate considered more reliable.

- In less severe bipolars with infrequent recurrences, if pregnancy is planned, discontinue lithium before conception; or if menstrual periods are regular, at first missed period.
  - √ Maternal circulation to embryo connects then and not sooner.
- During first trimester, antipsychotics, benzodiazepines, and ECT safest for manic episode.
  - √ Avoid carbamazepine.
    - □ Causes deformities.
  - √ Avoid valproic acid.
    - □ 1–2% neural tube defects.
- In severe bipolar patient stabilized with lithium, continue lithium and follow with ultrasound.
- Goiters observed in newborns; follow mother's thyroid status during pregnancy.

Direct Effect on Newborn (3rd trimester)

- Lithium toxicity may develop in newborn with hypotonia, cyanosis, bradykinesia, depressed thyroid, goiter, atrial flutter, hepatomegaly, ECG changes, cardiomegaly, GI bleeding, diabetes insipidus, or shock.
- Most of these effects reverse in 1–2 weeks, which corresponds to the renal elimination of lithium in the newborn; diabetes insipidus may persist for several months.
- During second and third trimesters, lithium is acceptable. Higher doses are needed to offset higher lithium excretion rate.
- In the last 5 weeks of pregnancy, get weekly lithium levels.
- Discontinue or decrease lithium dose during week before delivery.
  - √ Renal clearance drops rapidly with delivery and mother could become toxic on usual pregnancy dose.
- Discontinue lithium at the onset of labor.

Lactation

- Lithium ranges from 30–100% of maternal level.
- Infant's serum level 10–50% of maternal serum level.
- Average is 40%.

Drug Dosage in Mother's Milk

Generic Name	Milk/ Plasma Ratio	Time of Peak Concentration in Milk (hours)	Infant Dose (mg/kg/day)	Maternal Dose (%)	Safety Rating*
Lithium	0.42	?	0.41	1.8†	B

* B: Unsafe before 34 weeks, but safer after 34 weeks, although some believe it is safe at all times.
† Calculated assuming maternal dose of 20–25 mg/kg/day.

DRUG-DRUG INTERACTIONS

Drugs (X) Interact with:	Lithium (L)	Comments
ACE (Angiotensin-converting enzyme) inhibitors: Benazepril Captopril Enalapril Fosinopril Lisinopril Quinapril Ramipril	L ↑	Increases serum lithium. Lithium toxicity and impaired kidney function may occur; may need to stop lithium or ACE inhibitor.
Acetazolamide	L ↓	Reduces serum lithium and efficacy; sometimes used for detoxification in lithium overdose.
Alcohol	L ↑	Alcohol may increase serum lithium.
Albuterol (*see* bronchodilators)		
Amiloride	L ↑	Potassium-saving diuretic occasionally increases lithium concentration and toxicity.
Aminophylline (*see* bronchodilators)		
Ampicillin	L ↑	Increased lithium effect and toxicity.
Antipsychotics: *Haloperidol *Thioridazine Others	X ↑ L ↑	Occasionally increased neurotoxicity. Rarely not reversible. Lithium plus chlorpromazine may lower both drugs and may generate NMS. Lower lithium levels seen when liquid lithium citrate given with liquid neuroleptic (i.e., chlorpromazine or trifluoperazine), secondary to lithium precipitate being formed.
Antithyroids: Carbimazole Methimazole Radioactive iodine	X ↑	Lithium increases thyroid suppression; may be clinically useful when β-blocker contraindicated for hyperthyroidism.
Baclofen	X ↓	Increases hyperkinetic symptoms when lithium added.
Bronchodilators: Albuterol Aminophylline Theophyilline	L ↓	Theophylline, aminophylline, and possibly albuterol increase lithium clearance and decrease lithium levels; cromolyn and nonsystemic steroids safer.

Drugs (X) Interact with:	Lithium (L)	Comments
Caffeine	L↓ ↑	Increases lithium excretion; heavy coffee drinkers have trouble reaching therapeutic levels on even 2400 mg/day. Increases lithium tremor.
* Calcium Channel-Blockers: *Diltiazem *Nifedipine *Verapamil	L↑ ↓	Lithium-induced neurotoxicity, nausea, weakness, ataxia, and tinnitus. Verapamil may augment anticycling effect of lithium; lithium level may decrease; stop blocker or lower lithium.
Captopril (see ACE inhibitors)		
* Carbamazepine	X↑ L↑	On normal lithium, carbamazepine may induce neurotoxicity; after ceasing one agent for a few days, neurotoxicity vanishes. Also synergistic for anticycling effects.
Corticosteroids: Hydrocortisone Methylprednisolone	L↓	Increases lithium clearance; monitor lithium closely.
Decamethonium	X↑	Prolonged muscle paralysis.
Dextroamphetamine	X↓	Lithium may inhibit dextroamphetamine's euphoria.
Digitalis	X↑ ↓	May cause cardiac arrhythmias, particularly bradyarrhythmias; occasionally lithium reduces effects.
Diuretics (see loop, osmotic, thiazide)		
* Diltiazem (see calcium channel-blockers)		
Enalapril (see ACE inhibitors)		
HCAs (see TCAs)		
Hydroxyzine	L↑	Cardiac conduction disturbances.
Ketamine	L↑	Increased lithium toxicity from sodium depletion.
Loop diuretics: Ethacrynic acid Furosemide	L↑	May increase lithium, but safer than thiazide diuretics. Potassium-sparing diuretics safest (amiloride, spironolatone).
Marijuana	L↑	Increased absorption of lithium; importance unclear.
Mazindol	L↑	A few cases of lithium toxicity after 3 days of mazindol; worse with inadequate salt intake.
* Methyldopa	L↑	Lithium toxicity may develop with a normal lithium level; toxicity ends 1–9 days after stopping methyldopa.
Metronidazole	L↑	Increased lithium level; toxicity.
NSAIDs: *Diclofenac *Ibuprofen *Indomethacin Ketoprofen Mefenamic acid *Piroxicam Phenylbutazone	L↑	Adding many NSAIDs increases plasma lithium 30–61% in 3–10 days. Sulindac and aspirin don't appear to change levels and phenylbutazone averages only 11% increase.

Drugs (X) Interact with:	Lithium (L)	Comments
Osmotic diuretics	L ↓	Decreases lithium level and efficacy.
Pancuronium	X ↑	Prolonged muscle paralysis.
Phenytoin	L ↑	A few cases of lithium toxicity.
Physostigmine	L ↓	May reduce efficacy of lithium.
* Potassium iodide	L ↑	Sometimes Li + KI → hypothyroidism + goiter, which is *no* reason to halt lithium; treat thyroid instead.
* Sodium bicarbonate	L ↓	Decreases lithium level.
* Sodium chloride	L ↓ ↑	High sodium decreases lithium level; low sodium intake may increase serum lithium and toxicity.
Spectinomycin	L ↑	Increased lithium effect and toxicity.
Spironolactone	L ↑	Potassium-saving diuretic may occasionally increase lithium concentration and toxicity.
Succinylcholine	X ↑	Prolonged neuromuscular blockade.
Sympathomimetics: Dobutamine Epinephrine Norepinephrine	X ↓	Lithium usually decreases pressor actions of norepinephrine and other direct-acting sympathomimetics.
* Tetracyclines	L ↑	Lithium plus tetracycline may modestly increase lithium toxicity. Unclear if other tetracyclines (e.g., doxycycline) affect lithium.
Theophylline (*see* bronchodilators)		
† *Thiazide diuretics:* Chlorothiazide Hydrochlorothiazide	L ↑	Any diuretic that promotes sodium and potassium excretion may yield cardiotoxicity and neurotoxicity; potassium-sparing diuretics are safer. Watch for hypercalcemia.
TCAs	L ↑	Increased tremor.
Ticarcillin	X ↑	Hypernatremia.
Triamterene	L ↑	Potassium-saving diuretic may increase lithium concentration and toxicity.
Tryptophan	L ↑	Increases lithium efficacy; tryptophan off American market.
Urea	L ↓	Urea may reduce lithium; scanty clinical evidence.
Valproic acid	L ↑	Increased neurotocity and anticycling effect.
* Verapamil	L ↑ ↓	Lithium-induced neurotoxicity, nausea, weakness, ataxia, and tinnitus.

* Moderately important interaction; †Extremely important interaction; ↑ Increases; ↓ Decreases.

EFFECTS ON LABORATORY TESTS

Generic Names	Blood/Serum Tests	Results*	Urine Tests	Results*
Lithium	^{131}I uptake	↑	Glycosuria	↑
	T_3	↓	Albuminuria	↑
	T_4**	↓	VMA	↑
	Leukocytes	↑	Renal concentrating ability	↓
	Eosinophils	↑	Electrolytes	↑ ↓
	Platelets	↑		
	Lymphocytes	↓		
	Na^+, K^+	↑ ↓		
	Ca^{++}, Mg^{++}	↑ ↑		
	Serum phosphate	↓		
	Parathyroid hormone	↑		
	Glucose tolerance	↑ ↓		
	Creatinine	↑ ^{r}		

* ↑ Increases; ↓ Decreases; ↑ ↓ Increases and decreases; r = rarely.
** = Mania itself may transiently increase TSH and T_4.

WITHDRAWAL

Lithium does not induce

- Dependence
- Tolerance
- Addiction
- Withdrawal

It can be stopped quickly without any apparent physiologic difficulty, but compared to gradual withdrawal, has increased risk of subsequent mania.

OVERDOSE: TOXICITY, SUICIDE, AND TREATMENT

Therapeutic indexes (i.e., toxic dose: effective dose) are

- Antipsychotics = about 100
- TCAs/MAOIs = about 10
- Lithium = about 3

Being a nonmetabolized salt, lithium toxicity results not only from the drug, but also from water and sodium loss based on

- Decreased fluid or food intake (during manic or depressive swings)
- Diuretics

- Fever
- Abnormal GI conditions (e.g., nausea, diarrhea, vomiting)
- Pyelonephritis

Although no clearly defined relationship exists between serum lithium and toxicity, the serum level 12 h after the last dose roughly predicts the acute intoxication's severity. Significant diarrhea in a patient who has not had it before is often the first warning sign of toxicity.

Can occur in patients on stable doses.

- Disorders of water and electrolyte metabolism (e.g., dehydration, vomiting, diarrhea, fever, hypokalema) usually seen at time of intoxication.
  √ Renal insufficiency usually seen at time of intoxication.
    □ Water loss due to impaired renal concentrating ability major predisposing factor.
- Most over 2.0 mEq/1.

Recovery of severe lithium toxicity patients

- 70–80% fully recover.
- 10% display persistent sequelae: dementia, ataxia, polyuria, dysarthria, spasticity, nystagmus, and tremor.
- 10–25% die.

Delirium and other symptoms may continue with lithium plasma level low or none.

- EEG slowing usually accompanies delirium.
- For 4–7 days intracellular lithium may still be high.
  √ Lithium toxicity poisons lithium "pump" in cell membrane.
    □ Takes time to heal.
  √ Wait until side effects stopped before restarting lithium.
- In geriatric and sometimes in others, delirium may continue weeks to months when lithium levels are zero.
  √ Mechanism unknown.

The general management of lithium overdoses includes (see also pages 53–54):

- Induce emesis in the alert patient or use gastric lavage.
- Baseline ECG (to determine arrhythmia, sinus node dysfunction).
- Draw
  √ Blood lithium
    □ Continue to monitor for "secondary peaks" after periods of decline.
  √ Creatinine
  √ Electrolytes

Side Effects by Levels of Lithium Carbonate

Therapeutic Lithium Levels (0.6–1.5 mEq/l)	Mild to Moderate Toxicity (1.5–2.0 mEq/l)	Moderate to Severe Toxicity (2.0–2.5 mEq/l)	Severe Toxicity (Over 2.5 mEq/l)
Central Nervous System Hand tremor Memory impairment *Endocrine* Goiter Hypothyroidism *Gastrointestinal* Diarrhea (mild) Edema Nausea Weight gain *Renal* Polydipsia Polyuria	*Central Nervous System* Dizziness Drowsiness Dysarthria Excitement Hand tremor (course) Lethargy Muscle weakness Sluggishness Vertigo *Eyes, Ears, Nose, Throat* *Gastrointestinal* Abdominal pain Diarrhea Dry mouth Vomiting	*Cardiovascular* Cardiac arrhythmia Pulse irregularities *Central Nervous System* Choreoathetoid movements Clonic limb movements Coma Convulsions Delirium EEG changes Fainting Hyperreflexia Leg tremor Muscle fasciculations Stupor *Eyes, Ears, Nose, Throat* Nystagmus Vision blurred *Gastrointestinal* Anorexia Nausea (chronic) Vomiting (chronic)	*Central Nervous System* Seizures (generalized) *Renal Oliguoria* Renal failure Death

L
I
T
H
I
U
M

√ Urinalysis (look for albuminuria)
√ Serum glucose (before IV fluids used)
- If patient is severely intoxicated
  √ Hemodialysis is first choice for 8–12 h when
    □ Serum lithium betwen 2–3 mEq/l and patient's condition is deteriorating,
    □ Fluid or electrolyte abnormalities are unresponsive to conventional supportive measures,
    □ Creatinine clearance or urine output decreases a lot, or
    □ Serum lithium is not reduced at least 20% in 6 h.
- Serum lithium level often rebounds after hours of hemodialysis; this requires repeated hemodialysis.
- Goal of hemodialysis is to reduce serum lithium less than 1 mEq/l at least 8 h after hemodialysis is completed.
- For less severe intoxication
  √ Restore fluids and electrolyte balance; correct sodium depletion.
  √ Give 0.9% infusion of IV sodium chloride (1–2 liters in first 6 h) when lithium intoxication appears secondary to total body sodium depletion.
  √ Rapid infusion of large volumes of IV potassium diuretic does not seem to help.
- Lithium excretion also fostered by one of the following in IV:
  √ Sodium bicarbonate
  √ Urea
  √ Mannitol
  √ Acetazolamide
  √ Aminophyllline
- Treat convulsions with short-acting barbiturates (e.g., thiopental).

Lithium can be restarted 48 h after the patient is clinically normal. Clinical normality may take days or weeks and does not correlate well with serum lithium levels. This should be done very gradually and not at full therapeutic dose.

- After lithium toxicity, expect interference with cellular sodium-lithium counter transport for 4–5 days.
  √ Intracellular lithium increases and ratio of RBC/plasma lithium goes from average 1:2 to 1:1.
  √ Therefore, serum lithium levels can be low and toxicity still seen.
  √ Restarting lithium too quickly or giving full dose of lithium can poison sodium lithium counter-transport pump. Will need to wait another 4–5 days for it to heal.

√ In geriatric patients delirium and other signs of neurotoxicity can continue for 3–10 weeks.

Toxicity and Suicide Data

Generic Name	Toxicity Dose Average (g)	Mortality Dose Average (g)	Toxic Levels (mEq/l)	Fatal Levels (mEq/l)
Lithium Carbonate	6	10–60	2–4	4–5

PRECAUTIONS

About 33–45% of patients on lithium stop taking the drug during the first year of treatment, because of

- Complaints of memory loss.
- Miss the "highs."
- GI, CNS, thyroid, and less frequently, renal side effects.
- Depressive relapse (13% stopped lithium for this reason in one study).

Close follow-up, especially during the first year, is essential.

Contraindications include

- Vomiting, diarrhea, severe disability, or dehydration.
  - √ Patients should have adequate fluids (2500–3000 ml) at start of treatment.
  - √ Infection, exercising, sweating can increase salt output.
- Hypersensitivity to lithium.
- Cardiovascular disease.
  - √ Patients with sinus node dysfunction ("sick sinus syndrome") should *not* receive lithium.
  - √ Carefully monitor cardiac patients with ECG.
- Renal damage.
- Pregnancy (see pages 211–212).

Cautionary concerns include

- Brain damage.
  - √ Follow mental status closely.
  - √ Can be well tolerated in mentally retarded populations.
- Patients started on lithium who are already on salt-restricted diet or diuretics.
  - √ Patients may need less than expected lithium dose.
  - √ Once stabilized on lithium, there should be no changes in sodium intake or diuretics.

L
I
T
H
I'
U
M

     ✓ If sodium intake or diuretic must be changed, carefully moni-
tor lithium level (q 3 days) and change lithium dose accord-
ingly.
     ✓ If possible, change to sodium and potassium-sparing diuretic
first.
- Patients already on lithium who are started on a diuretic, salt-
restricted diet, or vigorous exercise program.
     ✓ Extensive sweating from running 6 or more miles a day can
reduce lithium level.
     ✓ If diuretic is used, choose sodium- and potassium-sparing.
     ✓ Decrease lithium during sodium restriction.
- Since the ability to excrete lithium dwindles with age, use reduced doses in the elderly.

NURSES' DATA

Remind patients and family about lithium's side effects and the need
to consume stable amounts of salt and sufficient fluids.

- Avoid salt-restricted diets, diuretics, vomiting, diarrhea, excessive
sweating, infection, overexercise, working heavily in hot weather.
- At least initially, patients need 2500–3000 ml/day or 10 8-oz.
glasses of water/day.

Importance of monitoring lithium levels.

- Describe logistics and procedures for monitoring lithium.
     ✓ Draw blood circa 12 h after last dose.
     ✓ Patient should not swallow lithium on morning before blood
test.

Pregnancy warnings.

Be alert to noncompliance.

Remind patients and close relatives that lithium is not an "artificial
chemical," but a naturally-occurring mineral in the water; some find
this reassuring.

PATIENT AND FAMILY NOTES

Have a Medic Alert wallet-card or bracelet indicating lithium's use.

Tell physicians and surgeons, especially cardiologists and GI special-
ists, about taking lithium.

Some of the most common side effects when starting on lithium are
upset stomach, diarrhea, frequent urination.

- These side effects aren't necessarily signs of toxicity. After dose is stabilized, if diarrhea or coarse tremors suddenly start, may be signs of toxicity.
  √ Confused thinking is another sign.
- All of these may subside after dosing and serum levels are stabilized.

To prevent accidents, no lithium should be at bedside or any other quickly accessible place. Keep away from children.

Ingest lithium at regular times each day, as decided with physician.

- Ingest with meals, snack, or milk to diminish GI irritation.

If dose is forgotten, can consume in 8 h.

- Otherwise, wait for next scheduled dose.
- May double dose if done on same day and patient has no side effect from higher single doses.

6. Anticonvulsants

INTRODUCTION

Carbamazepine, valproic acid, and clonazepam are anticonvulsants that prevent and treat bipolar disorders, especially mania. Verapamil (Calan), a calcium channel-blocker, has been shown in preliminary trials (discussed on page 230) to treat acute mania and prevent manic episodes. Gabapentin (Neurontin) is a very low side-effect GABAergic anticonvulsant for partial complex seizures that has not been tested in bipolar disorder.

- Carbamazepine is structurally similar to the TCA imipramine.
- Divalproex is chemically akin to valproic acid; they are discussed together.
- Clonazepam is a benzodiazepine, whose mood-stabilizing operations are examined here, while its other actions are presented in anti-anxiety agents.

This chapter discusses the effects of anticonvulsants and calcium channel-blockers in patients with

- Aggression (pages 233–235)
- Atypical and lithium-resistant bipolar disorder (pages 227–232)
- Bipolar depression and panic disorder (page 232)
- Aggression (pages 233–235)
- Atypical psychosis/partial complex seizure spectrum disorder (pages 235–236)
- Atypical residual hallucinations (flashbacks) in chronic hallucinogen users (page 236)

Other chapters examine the effects of anticonvulsants in patients with

- Alcohol and anxiolytic withdrawal (Hypnotics, pages 341–346)
- Unipolar depression (Antidepressants, pages 84–96, 106–107)
- Schizoaffective disorders (Lithium, pages 198–199)
- Schizophrenia (Antipsychotics, page 12)
- Panic attacks (Anti-anxiety, page 274)

NAMES, COST, MANUFACTURERS, DOSE FORMS, COLORS

Generic Names (Dollars/Dose: 100 pills in mg)*	Brand Names (Dollars/Dose: 100 pills in mg)*	Manu-facturers	Dose Forms (mg)**	Colors
Carbamazepine (60+/200)	Tegretol (146/200)	Geigy	t: 100/200 su:100 mg/5 ml	t: red-speckled/pink su: yellow-orange
Clonazepam	Klonopin† (98/0.5)	Roche	t: 0.5/1/2	t: orange/blue/ white
Divalproex	Depakote (210/250)	Abbott	t: 125/250/500	t: salmon-pink/ peach/lavender
Divalproex so-dium-coated particles	Depakote Sprinkle (185/125)	Abbott	c: 125	c: white-blue
Valproic acid (100+/250)	Depakene (300/250)	Abbott	c: 250 s: 250 mg/5 ml	c: orange s: red

* 1994 average wholesale price for 100 pills at this dose (e.g., 78/50 means 100 pills 50 mg cost $78). If depot form, cost is of single dose.
** c = capsules; s = syrup; su = suspension; t = tablets.
† Was spelled Clonopin.

PHARMACOLOGY

Carbamazepine (CBZ)

- Inhibits kindling, a process that increases behavioral and convulsive responses from a repetition of the same stimulus, and has anticonvulsant properties.
- Absorbed slowly and erratically.
- Average plasma binding is 76%.
- Since carbamazepine induces its own liver metabolism, dose may need increasing after 10 days to five weeks. More induction may occur with each dose increase, so that several more dose increases may be needed to establish a therapeutic level.
- Carbamazepine's half-life diminishes rapidly:
  √ Initially after single dose at 30–65 h.
  √ Three weeks later to 12–20 h.
  √ During chronic therapy about 12 h.
- Carbamazepine produces its chief metabolite in the liver—carbamazepine 10,11-epoxide—with a half-life of 5–8 h.

Valproic acid

- Has anti-kindling, anticonvulsant, and GABAergic effects.
- Quickly and almost completely absorbed.
  √ Divalproex absorption is delayed 3–8 (average 4) h.

√ Absorption more rapid with syrup, with peak levels reached in ¼–2 h.
- Half-life ranges from 6–18 h.
  √ Shorter half-life (~ 9 h) when patients take other anticonvulsants that increase hepatic metabolism.
  √ Increased half-life in children < 18 months (~ 10–67 h) and in patients with cirrhosis or acute hepatitis (up to 25 h).
- Conjugated in liver (~ 70%).
- Excreted as glucuronide, mostly in urine, and to a degree, in feces and air.

Pharmacology of Anticonvulsants

	Carbamazepine	Clonazepam	Valproic Acid
Bioavailability (%)	77	98	100
Plasma-bound (%)	65–80	86 ± ½	90
Volume distribution (liters/kg)	1.4 ± 0.4	3.2 ± 1.1	4 ± 0.9
Peak plasma level (hours)	4–8	1–4	1–4
Half-life (hours)	25–65 acutely 15 ± 5 (after 2–3 weeks)	dival proex 23 ± 5	3–8 13 ± 3
Excretion unchanged (%)	15–25 in feces	< 1 in urine	< 3 in feces and urine

Laboratory Investigations

Before starting on carbamazepine, obtain the following tests.

- A general medical history, especially focus on blood dyscrasias and liver disease.
- CBC with differential and platelet count
  √ ≤ 3500 WBC, consider other drug.
- LFTs, BUN, UA, creatinine
  √ Consider other drug if abnormal.
  √ Use ¼–½ usual dose of CBZ in hepatic disease.
- Serum sodium optional but can be valuable in elderly with high hyponatremia risk.

Before starting on valproic acid, obtain the following tests.

- LFTs
  √ Rule out hepatic dysfunction.
  √ Establish baseline values.
- Platelet counts
- Coagulation tests
  √ Not essential, but if bruising develops, will have a comparison baseline.

DOSES

Valproic acid comes in three clinical forms.

- Divalproex sodium (Depakote), which is an enteric-coated stable compound with equal amounts of valproic acid and sodium valproate (also available as Depakote Sprinkle containing coated particles of divalproex sodium)
- Valproic acid (Depakene capsules)
- Sodium valproate (Depakene capsules and syrup) is valproic acid as the sodium salt.

General Anticonvulsant Doses for Treating Mania

Generic Names	Starting Doses (mg/day)	Days to Reach Steady State Level	Usual Therapeutic Doses (mg/day)	Extreme Dosage Range (mg/day)	Therapeutic Plasma Levels (μg/ml)
Carbamazepine	200–400	4–6	800–1200	200–2000	5–12 (15?)
Clonazepam	1–2	5–8	4–16	0.5–40	?
Valproic acid	500–1500	3–6	1000–1500	750–3000	50–100 (125?)

- Plasma levels should be obtained approximately 12 h after the last dose.
- In acute mania divalproex sodium has been successfully initiated at a dose of 20 mg/kg.
  √ In less urgent situations 15mg/kg is usual.
- Valproic acid therapeutic levels represent total free and bound valproic acid.
  √ Although free valproic acid more accurately determines what gets to the brain, its therapeutic range has not been determined.
  √ Monitoring free valproic acid may be useful when there are changes in medication or clinical conditions that affect protein binding.
- Protein binding of valproic acid decreases with increased therapeutic levels.

CLINICAL INDICATIONS AND USE

General Information

Anticonvulsants

- Clearly control acute mania (with or without lithium).
- Often prevent mania.
- Occasionally treat and prevent unipolar or bipolar depressions.

- Aid more rapid-cycling patients than does lithium.
- Relieve psychotic symptoms secondary to complex partial seizures.
- Infrequently reduce schizophrenia.
- Dampen affective swings in schizoaffective patients.
- Diminish impulsive and aggressive behavior in some nonpsychotic patients.
- Facilitate alcohol and benzodiazepine withdrawal.
- Carbamazepine *starts* its clinical benefits in this sequence:
  - √ < 1 day: seizures
  - √ 6–10 days: mania
  - √ Aggression relief occurs over time and does not fit into this sequence.
- Carbamazepine's *full effect* is
  - √ Within h for epilepsy.
  - √ 2 weeks for mania.
  - √ 2–3 weeks for depression.
- Valproic acid
  - √ Starts to relieve mania in 3–5 days, especially if full initial dose (20 mg/kg) is used.
  - √ Full effect on mania in 5–12 days.
  - √ May not be effective for depression.
- Verapamil (see page 230)

Atypical and Lithium-Resistant Mania

Between 20–30% of bipolar patients do not respond to or tolerate lithium.

Carbamazepine's and valproic acid's efficacy for mania is 55–76%.

- May help up to 60% of rapid cyclers; lithium assists 10–35%.
- Valproic acid equal to lithium and superior to placebo in mania.

Clinical Profiles: Lithium and Carbamazepine or Valproic Acid

Clinical Profile	Lithium	Carbamazepine (CBZ) or Valproic Acid
Mania	+ +	+
Typical		
Dysphoric (mixed)	+	+ +
Rapid cycling	+	+ +
Continuous cycling	+	+ +
Neurological history or findings (head trauma or non-paroxysmal EEG abnormalities)	+	+ +
Depression	+	+ (CBZ)
Prophylaxis of mania and depression	+ +	- (Valproic Acid)

+ = effective; + + = very effective.

If patient has one of the above varieties of atypical mania, start with an anticonvulsant. If lithium fails with acute mania, can add or substitute carbamazepine or valproic acid.

- The chief problem with carbamazepine plus lithium is triggering acute confusion.
  - √ Repeat mental status testing.
  - √ If possible, lower neuroleptic doses and stop ACAs and benzodiazepines.
- Valproic acid with lithium less likely to cause confusion.
- On lithium and carbamazepine or valproic acid, some patients improve whereas others worsen.
- Once carbamazepine or valproic acid is stabilized, can taper off lithium.
- Some patients will worsen as lithium is tapered and will need to stay on both carbamazepine or valproic acid and lithium.
- The elderly are safer on carbamazepine and valproic acid without lithium.
  - √ Valproic acid may often be first choice in elderly because
    - □ Lower CNS side effects.
    - □ Wide therapeutic window.

Initiating Therapy

In treating or preventing mania, start *carbamazepine* at 200 mg qd or 100 mg bid. If mania is severe, begin at 200 mg bid or tid.

Carbamazepine

- For inpatients, increase dose every other day by 100 mg/day, or if mania is severe, 200 mg/day until the patient
  - √ Reaches 800–1000 mg/day,
    - □ Then slow dosage increases.
  - √ Improves sufficiently and
  - √ Is free of significant side effects.
    - □ If dose raised too quickly, common side effects are nausea, vomiting, ataxia, drowsiness, dizziness, diplopia, and clumsiness.
    - □ If side effects occur, lower carbamazepine dose and later raise it more slowly.
  - √ In outpatients, increase dose by 100 mg *every other day.*
- Serum levels should not exclusively determine dosage.
  - √ Draw blood levels no sooner than 4–5 days after changing dose.
- Common initial side effects are diplopia, blurred vision, fatigue, nausea, ataxia, and skin rashes (slightly less common).

Valproic acid

Because of synergistic effect with lithium, it seems safe to combine lithium with *valproic acid*.

* 54–71% of manic patients improve when valproic acid is added to other treatments.
* Valproic acid's efficacy is greater for mania than for depression.
* Patients improve at 4–14 days after obtaining a therapeutic plasma level.
* Dose
  √ Unlike carbamazepine, valproic acid can usually be started at target dose.
  √ If severe acute mania, start at 20 mg/kg with meal.
  √ If rapid treatment not needed, start at 10–15 mg/kg.
    □ To minimize GI and neurologic toxicity, start at 250 mg tid.
    □ Can increase 250–500 mg *every 3 days*, depending on response and side effects.
    □ Start lower and go slower with euthymic, hypomanic, depressed, or elderly patients.
    □ Give tid doses.
  √ Check serum levels in 5 days.
    □ Goal is 50–100 (possibly 125) μg/ml.
* Common early side effects include
  √ GI symptoms (e.g., nausea, diarrhea)
  √ Sedation
  √ Tremor
  √ Benign hepatic transaminase elevations.

Combined treatments (lithium-anticonvulsant, carbamazepine, valproic acid, adding verapamil)

* Synergistic therapeutic and toxic effects are often seen.
  √ Toxic effects can be seen when each drug is in the "normal" serum level range.
* Often low-normal plasma levels of both agents (e.g., lithium 0.8–0.9 mEq/1, carbamazepine 6–8 μg/ml, valproic acid 50–70 μg/ml) are preferred to maximize synergistic therapeutic effects and minimize toxicity.
* Valproic acid can increase carbamazepine plasma levels and carbamazepine can reduce valproic acid plasma levels.
* Verapamil (see below), when used to treat mania, can also have significant toxic interactions.
  √ Increases lithium toxicity without necessarily increasing lithium levels.
  √ Increases carbamazepine levels and toxicity.

Clonazepam may reduce mania but

- Need high doses (> 4 mg qd).
- Risks sedation or disinhibition.
- Rarely used as monotherapy but can facilitate other antimanic treatments.

Verapamil (Calan) appears to stop and prevent mania; other calcium channel-blockers may be effective (e.g., nifedipine and diltiazem), but limited data available.

- Optimum verapamil dosing ~ 80 mg tid or qid
  √ Tied lithium in double-blind study.
- Takes 7–14 days to work.
- Usually well tolerated.
- May increase toxicity of lithium and carbamazepine.
- Contraindicated with recent MI, 2nd and 3rd degree AV blocs, atrial flutter or fibrillation, hypotension, sick sinus syndrome, severe left ventricular dysfunction.
- May overly increase effects of β-blockers and other antihypertensive agents, resulting in bradycardia or hypotension.

When starting a patient on verapamil

- Check BP and heart rate daily both before and after starting.
- Get an ECG before and at 1-week intervals until dose is stabilized.
- Warn patient that dizziness (3.3%), hypotension (2.5%), headache (2.2%), nausea (2.7), and constipation (7.3%) are the most common side effects. Occasionally, extrapyramidal side effects are seen.

Neuroleptics

Clozapine

- Case reports of sustained successful treatment of chronic severe dysphoric mania.
- Other neuroleptics can help.
- Depot haloperidol or fluphenazine may be necessary to control chronic noncompliant bipolar disorder.

ECT is highly effective in acute mania.

- Often only 1–3 treatments needed.
- Consider using it with
  √ Pregnant women
  √ Drug-resistant bipolar disorder
  √ Severe and dangerous manics
  √ Highly suicidal mixed states

Maintaining Therapy

Carbamazepine maintenance considerations include:

- Obtaining a plasma level 5–14 days after establishing the acute dose.
  - √ Carbamazepine induces its own hepatic metabolism.
    - □ Most (~ 90%) autoinduction occurs in the first month of stable dosing.
  - √ Check level 10 days to 3 weeks after maintenance dose established to determine if level is now subtherapeutic.
  - √ Occasionally, some patients' livers continue to autoinduce with each higher dose and a therapeutic level cannot be obtained unless a drug that blocks autoinduction (e.g., valproic acid) is added.
- Monitoring CBC and platelet counts regularly.
  - √ CBC monitoring can detect clinically significant suppressions.
  - √ CBC monitoring is unlikely to pick up serious blood dyscrasias (e.g., aplastic anemia) because they usually develop suddenly, and mild asymptomatic leukopenia is not related to serious idiopathic dyscrasia.
    - □ Serious blood dyscrasias usually present with symptoms such as fever, sore throat, bruising, bleeding, or petechae.
    - □ Instruct patient to report these immediately.
  - √ Consult hematology and consider discontinuing carbamazepine if
    - □ Leukocytes < 3500/mm^3 or
    - □ Neutrophils < 1500/mm^3 or
    - □ Platelets < 100,000/mm^3 or
    - □ Erythrocytes < 3.0 x 10^6/mm^3
  - √ Frequency of CBC monitoring ranges from every two weeks for the first 2–3 months and then, if normal, at 1- to 3-month intervals after that; use the European practice of initially monitoring every 2 weeks for the first 6 weeks; then every 2 months, and after 6 months, every 6 months or year.
    - □ There is no evidence that the European practice results in more problems, but the local "standard of care" and medicolegal considerations perpetuate higher monitoring frequency in the U.S.
    - □ Agranulocytosis is as, or more, common with chlorpromazine, yet CBC on this drug is rarely monitored.
    - □ The reaction is most likely to occur early in treatment and very unlikely after 6 months.
- Monitor LFTs monthly for the first 2–3 months, and then every 4 months or if hepatitis symptoms appear.
  - √ Does not reliably detect liver failure.
  - √ Bilirubin may be best indicator of liver failure.

- Asymptomatic LFTs, leukopenia, or thrombocytopenia can be managed with dose reduction.
  - ✓ They also can spontaneously resolve.
- Hyponatremia occurs
  - ✓ In 6–31% of patients on CBZ.
  - ✓ Most often in elderly.
  - ✓ Occasionally develops months after starting CBZ.

Valproic acid maintenance considerations include:

- Obtaining plasma level 5 days after acute dose is stabilized.
  - ✓ This will serve as a reference for the future.
  - ✓ Further routine plasma levels are not needed unless there is a change in clinical status.
- Obtain repeat LFTs at 3 to 4 month intervals or if symptoms of liver disease appear.
  - ✓ Mild SGOT elevations are not rare but should be monitored for significant changes.
  - ✓ Elevations of bilirubin are clinically more important and warrant a consultation from a specialist and possible discontinuation of valproic acid.
- Some argue that with severe hepatotoxicity rates of less than 1:10,000, LFT monitoring is not regularly needed.
- Patient should report increased bruising or bleeding in case thrombocytopenia develops.
- Disturbing maintenance side effects include
  - ✓ Hair loss
  - ✓ Increased appetite and weight gain.

Depression or Panic Disorder

Bipolar depression

- Carbamazepine and valproic acid have limited evidence for relief of depression.
  - ✓ Both may "augment" antidepressants, as lithium does.
- Clonazepam may help relieve depression, but in doses of 1.5 mg qd and more may cause
  - ✓ Or exacerbate depression
  - ✓ Sedation
  - ✓ Disinhibition

Panic disorder

- Clonazepam stops panic disorder.
- Valproic acid might help.
- Carbamazepine does not prevent panic.

Aggression

Because aggression stems from many sources, no single agent is clearly indicated. Acute aggression differs from chronic aggression, and each requires its own treatment.

Acute aggression is medically managed best by either

- Haloperidol
  - √ Almost always should be limited to psychosis-induced violence.
  - √ Initially, 1–2 mg po or 1 mg IM, q1h until control is achieved.
    - □ Half this dose in the elderly.
  - √ Then haloperidol 2–4 mg or 1 mg IM, q8h.
  - √ Do not use haloperidol for aggression alone for > 6 weeks.
- Lorazepam
  - √ Initially, 1–2 mg po or IM, q1h until calm.
    - □ If IV dose must be given, push slowly and be sure not to inject more than 2 mg IV to prevent respiratory depression and largyngospasm.
    - □ May repeat in ½ h.
  - √ Maintain dose in nonagitated person at 2 mg po or IM tid.
  - √ Taper at 10% a day from the highest dose to avoid withdrawal unless on drug less than a week.
  - √ Do not keep patient on drug for aggression alone for 6 weeks.
  - √ Can risk disinhibition (at lower doses), ataxia, or severe lethargy.
- Trazodone
  - √ Acutely lowers aggression and agitation in demented or mentally retarded patients without impairing cognition.
    - □ Doses up to 500 mg qd have been successfully used.

Chronic aggression, the more common problem, may only diminish *after* a therapeutic dose level exists for 4–8 weeks.

- Should inform patient about this time lag.
- Drug management includes
  - √ Propranolol often used at very high doses 120–240 mg qd (detailed in chapter 7 on anti-anxiety) lowers organically-based violence in patients with
    - □ Alzheimer's disease
    - □ Huntington's disease
    - □ Schizophrenia with agitation or aggression unrelated to psychotic ideas
    - □ Stroke
  - √ Anticonvulsants, especially carbamazepine and valproic acid, can treat aggression and violence in
    - □ Bipolar disorder

ANTICONVULSANTS

        □ Borderline personality disorder
        □ Conduct disorder
        □ Episodic dyscontrol
        □ Other CNS disorders, including mental retardation
        □ Partial complex seizure spectrum disorder (see page 235)
   √ Lithium reduces manic-associated violence and violence in conditions such as PTSD and borderline personality disorder.
   √ Fluoxetine 20 mg for 3+ months may reduce self-injury.
   √ Avoid antipsychotics; aggression is often a chronic problem and patients risk TD, hypotension, and oversedation.
        □ Neuroleptics' only role is to alleviate aggression clearly associated with psychosis.
   √ Avoid benzodiazepines because
        □ They rarely halt chronic violence and
        □ May disinhibit or trigger paradoxical rage attacks.
   √ Buspirone has the advantage over other anti-anxiety agents in being nonsedative and nonaddicting.
        □ Most often used in cognitively impaired populations (e.g., mentally retarded, demented, and possibly prison).
        □ Dosing often 30–60 mg qd.

Psychotropic Drug Treatment of Chronic Aggression

Generic Groups	Indications	Appropriate Dose	Special Clinical Considerations
Anti-anxiety agents	Acute relief of violence or agitation from hypno-sedative effects.	Standard doses	Risks paradoxical rage attacks, oversedation, tolerance, and addiction.
Buspirone	Aggression and anxiety.	10–20 mg tid	Takes 4–10 weeks to work; may get worse before better.
Carbamazepine	Aggression from CNS disorders; also in PTSD and borderline personality disorder.	1200–1600 mg/day in divided doses (serum levels at 6–12 μg/ml)	Monitor for bone-marrow suppression and blood abnormalities. In borderline personality disorder, physician's efficacy rating higher than patient ratings.
Lithium	Aggression and irritability related to manic excitement. Uncontrolled rage triggered by "nothing" or by minor stimuli. Lithium's efficacy is low, but danger of rage merits lithium's consideration.	300 mg tid (serum levels at 0.6–1.2 mEq/l)	Effective for violence in prisoners and mentally retarded.

Psychotropic Drug Treatment of Chronic Aggression (Cont.)

Generic Groups	Indications	Appropriate Dose	Special Clinical Considerations
	Lithium might block outbursts from schizophrenic patients without reducing psychosis. May diminish hostile outbursts from neurologic patients. Does not abate premeditated violence.		
Nadolol	Diminished assaultiveness in 5/6 chronic paranoid schizophrenics.	80–160 mg/day; mean of 96 g/day	Few reports.
Neuroleptics	Aggression related to psychotic ideation. Prompt relief of violence or aggression from sedative effects.	Standard doses for schizophrenia	Oversedation and multiple side effects, such as TD, when used chronically.
Propranolol	Recurrent or chronic aggression or irritability in patients with organic brain disorders or in psychotic patients whose aggression is unrelated to psychotic thought.	200–800 mg/day in divided doses; range is 40–1440 mg/day Start at 20 mg tid; raise by 60 mg/day q 3 days until therapeutic effect or 800 mg/day.	Onset may take 4–8 weeks.
Trazodone	Aggression and agitation.	50–175 mg tid	Monitor for orthostatic hypotension; monitor males for priapism. Effective in demented and metally retarded, but don't use in males who can't report priapism.
Valproic acid	*See* carbamazepine.	750–1750 mg/day in divided doses (serum levels 50–100 μg/ml)	Monitor LFTs and platelets.

A N T I C O N V U L S A N T S

Atypical psychosis/partial complex seizure spectrum disorder

- The term *spectrum* is used because all components of "seizure" are often not seen with each episode.
  - √ May have varying symptoms.
- The term *temporal lobe* is avoided because that is not necessarily where the focus is.
- Signs and symptoms include
  - √ Episodic psychosis with normal intervals.

√ Unusual perceptual symptoms, such as olfactory, tactile, proprioceptive hallucinations, or sensory distortions in which objects look bigger or smaller, walls tilt.

√ Loss of memory for time intervals during which patient may have been unresponsive to environment and/or engaged in repetitive, purposeless activities, such as buttoning and unbuttoning shirt, smacking lips, walking to door and back.
  □ Complex behaviors (e.g., robbing a bank, beating up a person) are not seen.

√ Spontaneously occurring "out of the blue" intense emotional experiences (e.g., rage, sadness, sexual, mystical).

√ Only 50% with these symptoms have abnormal EEGs.

√ Often history of head trauma, infection, or birth complications.

• Symptoms respond to carbamazepine or valproic acid.
  √ Usually need full anticonvulsant blood levels.
  √ Response often within 2–5 days of achieving therapeutic level.
  √ "Typical" psychotic symptoms (e.g., auditory or visual hallucinations) are less likely to respond to an anticonvulsant alone.
    □ May need antipsychotic.

Atypical residual hallucinations (flashbacks) in chronic hallucinogen users

• If impairing normal function, anecdotal evidence suggests that anticonvulsants (carbamazepine or valproic acid) are effective.
• Antipsychotics are not usually effective.

SIDE EFFECTS

General Information

Side effects discussed here are for carbamazepine and valproic acid. Carbamazepine is a tricyclic compound and shares many tricyclic antidepressant side effects, except those involving norepinephrine and serotonin uptake. Clonazepam's side effects are outlined in the antianxiety chapter.

40–50% of patients on carbamazepine have side effects. Side effects for carbamazepine can be minimized by

• Gradually building up dose
  √ Not as necessary for valproic acid
• Using more frequent, smaller doses

So far, side effects appear similar when anticonvulsants are used for

• Psychiatric and neurologic disorders
• Adults and children
  √ Except young children, < 2 y.o., prone to hepatotoxicity.

Most common acute side effects are

- For carbamazepine:
  - √ Symptoms of being "drunk"—ataxia, incoordination, dizziness, lightheadedness, blurred vision, weakness, and fatigue
  - √ Rashes
- For valproic acid:
  - √ G.I. side effects—nausea, dyspepsia, diarrhea
  - √ Sedation
  - √ Tremor

Cardiovascular Effects

Usually benign; carbamazepine only.

Dizziness from orthostatic hypotension.

Decreased atrioventricular conduction times and nodal rhythms; quinidine-like effect.

- AV conduction delay and bradyarrhythmias can occur at therapeutic doses.
  - √ More common in older women.
- Get ECG in patients over 50 y.o.
- Use extreme caution when combining with TCA or other quinidine-like drugs.
- Avoid carbamazepine in patients
  - √ With heart block or at high risk for cardiac conduction abnormalities (e.g., myotonic dystrophy).
  - √ Consider valproic acid as better alternative with this condition.

Gastrointestinal Effects

Dry mouth (see page 22)

Nausea, vomiting, anorexia, indigestion

- Usually transient, these GI symptoms typically occur on empty stomach or if dose is started or increased too rapidly.
  - √ More common with valproic acid.
- Valproic acid (Depakene) affects 15–20% of patients but divalproex sodium (Depakote) under 10%.
- Management
  - √ Switch to divalproex sodium if started on valproic acid.
  - √ If this fails, try divalproex sodium-coated particles ("Sprinkle")
    - □ May give more protection to stomach.
  - √ Move dosage up more slowly.
  - √ Give with meals.
  - √ Try histamine-2 antagonist.
  - √ Often subsides in 1–4 weeks.

Hepatitis, hepatotoxicity

Carbamazepine, and especially valproic acid (15–30%), temporarily raise LFTs slightly during first 3 months of therapy.

- Valproic acid may induce hyperammonemia, often with confusion and lethargy.
- Transient LFT elevations in first month of treatment.
  √ Lower dose if increased LFTs continue.
- High LFTs do not predict liver disease.
  √ Bilirubin may be better indicator.

Carbamazepine causes a rare, occasionally fatal, hypersensitivity reaction with fever and rash during the first month.

Valproic acid generates potentially fatal hepatotoxicity, especially in patients

- Under 2 years old,
- Taking other anticonvulsants, and
- Having severe neurological disease, mental retardation, or inborn error of metabolism.
- With polytherapy
  √ Fatal hepatoxicity occurs
    □ 1:17,000 in 2–21 y.o. (1:500 in < 2 y.o.)
    □ 1:37 in 21–40 y.o.
    □ 1:38,000 in > 40 y.o.

This hepatotoxicity has not been seen in adults with anticonvulsant monotherapy; it is preceded by malaise, weakness, lethargy, anorexia, vomiting, and seizures.

- Valproic acid contraindicated in patients with liver disease.

Weight gain, increased appetite from valproic acid but not carbamazepine.

Constipation (see page 23)

Pancreatitis

- Rare side effect of carbamazepine.

Renal Effects

Few effects, and mainly with carbamazepine (i.e., urinary frequency or urinary retention).

Endocrine Effects

Polydipsia (water intoxication) occurs with hyponatremia and confusion for patients on carbamazepine.

- About 5–25% of patients develop hyponatremia.

- Demeclocycline 300 mg bid and then increased to 600 mg bid often effectively reverses hyponatremia.

Polycystic ovaries/hyperandrogenism

- Seen in up to 80% of women started in long-term treatment on valproic acid before age 20.
  √ Uncontrolled study, true incidence unknown.

Hematologic Effects

Do not start carbamazepine in patients with bone-marrow suppression or who already are leukopenic.

Leukopenia

- Carbamazepine may mildly lower WBC by as much as 25% initially, but this decrease is usually transitory and without adverse effects.
  √ Occurs in about 7–10% of patients.
  √ Women at higher risk than men.
- In 2% of patients carbamazepine induces a persistent leukopenia (moderate: 3000–4000 WBC/mm^3, or severe: < 3000 WBC/mm^3) or a thrombocytopenia (< 100,000/mm^3 platelets).
  √ This compares with a 0.3–0.4% rate for TCAs.
  √ With carbamazepine-induced leukopenia 76% is moderate and 24% severe.
    □ 50% develop the leukopenia within 16 days.
    □ Recovery usually occurs within about 6 days of stopping CBZ.
- If WBC count drops to 4000 mm^3 during carbamazepine therapy
  √ Obtain another WBC count in 2 weeks.
  √ If WBC count does not return to normal in 2 weeks, reduce carbamazepine.
- Consider stopping carbamazepine immediately with any of these symptoms:
  √ WBC count below 3500–4000/mm^3
  √ Neutrophil count below 1500
  √ LFTs increased 3-fold or bilirubin elevated
  √ Fever
  √ Infection, sore throat
  √ Petechiae, bruising
  √ Weakness
  √ Pallor
- Captopril 12.5 mg qd effective in reversing leukopenia (case report).
- Lithium at usual therapeutic levels may protect from leukopenia.
- Valproic acid rarely induces leucopenia (0.4%).
  √ About same rate as TCAs 0.3–0.4%.

Aplastic anemia, agranulocytosis

- Severe and potentially fatal.
- Carbamazepine produces aplastic anemia in < 0.002% of patients.
  - √ This is 5–8 times more than the spontaneous rate (6 per million for agranulocytosis; 2 per million for aplastic anemia) in the general population.
  - √ Frequency probably comparable to other psychotropic drugs.

Mild anemia happens in < 5% of patients on carbamazepine.

Bone-marrow suppression afflicts 3% of carbamazepine users.

May also see
- *Pancytopenia*
- *Eosinophilia*
- *Purpura*

Thrombocytopenia

- *Petechiae, bruising, hemorrhage, nose bleeds, and anemia* occur occasionally on valproic acid.
- More likely with > 2 mg/qd valproic acid.
  - √ If mild thrombocytopenia, reduce valproic acid dose.

Eyes, Ears, Nose, and Throat

Blurred vision (see page 27)

Nasal congestion

Skin, Allergies, and Temperature

Rash

- Allergic rash is the most common carbamazepine side effect.
- Seen in 3–15% of psychiatric patients.
  - √ Usually arises between 9 and 23 days after carbamazepine begun.
  - √ Stop carbamazepine if
    - □ *Exfoliative reaction*
    - □ *Urticaria reaction*
    - □ *Stevens-Johnson syndrome* (acute inflammatory skin disorder with "iris" target lesions).
- Management
  - √ Avoid sunlight; may be a photosensitivity reaction.
  - √ Treat minor rashes with antihistamines.
    - □ Some patients may desensitize over 1–3 weeks.

√ May be allergic to binder in pill, not carbamazepine.
  □ Try different form (e.g., 100 mg chewable, different brand).

Alopecia stems from valproic acid more than from carbamazepine.

- Tends to be transient.
- Case reports tout zinc and/or selenium as effective treatment.

Fever, chills, sweating, lymphadenopathy, muscle cramps, and *joint aches* may arise from carbamazepine.

Pulmonary hypersensitivity arises from carbamazepine with symptoms of hay fever, dyspnea, pneumonitis, or pneumonia.

Central Nervous System Effects

Drowsiness, sedation

- Sedation appears to be dose-related.
- Management
  √ Gradually increase dose from beginning.
    □ Start carbamazepine dose as low as 100 mg/day.
    □ Then increase 100 mg every 3 days up to 400 mg/day.
    □ If patient accommodates to sedation at 400 mg/day, dosage can be increased 200 mg every 3 days.
    □ Can minimize sedation by administering greater proportion of carbamazepine at bedtime.
- Valproic acid is less sedating than carbamazepine, but it can cause substantial *lethargy.*
  √ This usually happens only when combined with other anticonvulsants or sedating drugs.

Tremor is common side effect of valproic acid.

- Reduce dose.
- Add β-blocker.

Confusion from carbamazepine

- May be secondary to
  √ Being on lithium and neuroleptics,
  √ Older age,
  √ CNS disease,
  √ *Hyponatremia,* or
  √ *Water intoxication,* on rare occasions.

Severe skin reactions suggest impending blood dyscrasia.

PERCENTAGES OF SIDE EFFECTS

Side Effects	Carbamazepine	Valproic acid
CARDIOVASCULAR EFFECTS		
Dizziness, lightheadedness, hypotension	11.4 (5.9–40)	< 1
Fainting, syncope	< 1	—
Palpitations	< 1	—
Bradycardia	< 1	—
Chest pain	< 1	—
Decreased cardiac conduction/nodal rhythms	< 1	—
Congestive heart failure	< 0.1	—
Hypertension	< 0.1	—
GASTROINTESTINAL EFFECTS		
Anorexia, lower appetite	—	13 (1–20)
Nausea, vomiting	> 5	13 (1–20)
Dyspepsia, upset stomach	—	8.5*
Diarrhea	3	3
Dry mouth	< 1	< 1
Constipation	—	5
Hepatitis	< 0.001	0.00665 (< 0.010–0.00333)
Salivation	—	3.5
Mouth sores	5.5	—
Weight gain	0.0	5
Weight loss	—	< 1
Edema	0.0	< 1
ENDOCRINE AND SEXUAL EFFECTS		
Menstrual changes	—	20
Inappropriate ADH	5	—
HEMATOLOGIC EFFECTS		
Aplastic anemia	0.00103 (0.0005–0.0020)	< 0.001
Anemia (mild)	5	< 1
Agranulocytosis	0.0017 (0.0001–0.0048)	< 0.001
Blood dyscrasias (all types)	3	—
Bone-marrow suppression	3	< 1
Leukopenia (transient)	8 (7–10)	0.0
Leukopenia (permanent)	2.5	0.0
Petechiae	(2–3.2)	5.5
Bruising easily	5.5	5.5
Thrombocytopenia	2	< 1

Side Effects	Carbamazepine	Valproic acid
EYES, EARS, NOSE, AND THROAT EFFECTS		
Blurred vision	12.5 (> 5–30)	< 1
Double vision	1	< 1
Nystagmus	1	< 1
Sore throat, flu	5.5	—
SKIN, ALLERGIES, AND TEMPERATURE		
Rashes	6.6 (1–15)	5.5
Abnormal skin pigment	5.5	0.0
Hair loss	0.0	5.5
CENTRAL NERVOUS SYSTEM EFFECTS		
Weakness, fatigue	5.5	5.5
Body jerks	< 1	—
Numbness	< 1	—
Headache	5.5	5.5
Ataxia, incoordination	26.8 (10.4–≤ 50)	1.5
Slurred speech	5.3	—
Tremor	0.0	< 1
Drowsiness, sedation	35.4 (10–50)	5.5
Confusion, disorientation	5.5	—
Hallucinations	5.5	—
Depression	5.5	5.5
Switch into mania	11.8	—
Excitement, hyperactive	—	0–11**

* Valproic acid (Depakene) > 15%; divalproex (Depakote) < 8%.
** Only seen in 1 study of hyperactive children, not replicated.

PREGNANCY AND LACTATION

Teratogenicity
(1st trimester)

• Anticonvulsants have an overall 4–5% teratogenic rate when taken during the first trimester.

• Among carbamazepine's teratogenic population, 20% had developmental delay, 26% had fingernail hypoplasia, and 11% had craniofacial defects.

• Valproic acid produces a few malformations akin to fetal hyantoin syndrome—e.g., lumbosacral meningocele, microcephaly, prolonged clotting abnormalities, cleft lip, prenatal growth deficiency.

- Valproic acid poses a 1–2% chance of spina bifida.

- If a woman taking antiepileptics becomes pregnant, stopping the anticonvulsants risks status epilepticus and the child's life; whether to remove antiepileptics depends on nature of the seizure, the mother's condition, etc.

- Only add anticonvulsants during pregnancy if absolutely necessary.

- During first trimester, if a mood stabilizer is needed, lithium is probably safer than carbamazepine or valproic acid to control mania.

- Consider ECT as a safer alternative.

Direct Effect on Newborn (3rd trimester)

- During 2nd and 3rd trimesters, lithium and carbamazepine seem equally safe.

- Valproic acid known to cause hepatotoxicity when serum levels exceed 60 µg/ml; keep serum concentrations < 60 µg/ml.

Lactation

- Carbamazepine present in milk at about 60% of maternal plasma concentration.

- Valproic acid excreted in small amounts into breast milk.

- Clonazepam enters breast milk. Although it does not accumulate, its long half-life may produce apnea. Infants exposed *in utero* or during breastfeeding should have clonazepam serum levels monitored and the CNS depression observed.

Drug Dosage in Mother's Milk

Generic Names	Milk/ Plasma Ratio	Time of Peak Concentration in Milk (hours)	Infant Dose (mg/kg/day)	Maternal Dose (%)	Safety Rating*
Carbamazepine	0.36	?	0.38	2.8	C
Clonazepam	?	?	2 µg†	1.3–3.0‡	C
Valproic acid	0.01–0.07	?	0.27**	1.8	B

* B: Reasonably unsafe before 34 weeks, but safer after 34 weeks; C: Reasonably unsafe before week 44, but safer after 44 weeks.
** Therapeutic dose for neonates 20–40 mg/kg/day.
† Infant therapeutic dose 20–200 µg/kg/day.
‡ Maternal dose not specified, but assumed to be 20–200 mg/kg/day.

DRUG-DRUG INTERACTIONS

Drugs (X) Interact with:	Carbamazepine (C)	Comments
Acetazolamide	C ↑	Increases levels/toxicity.
Alprazolam (see benzodiazepines)		
Antipsychotics	X ↓ C ↓	Decreases neuroleptic and carbamazepine effects (see haloperidol).
Azithromycin (see macrolide antibiotics)		
Barbiturates	C ↓	Phenobarbital raises carbamazepine's metabolism to epoxide; can lower serum level in 5 days, but without causing major clinical effects. Other barbiturates probably act similarly.
Benzodiazepines	X ↓	Diminishes alprazolam and clonazepam plasma levels (20–50%). Other benzodiazepines potentially affected.
* Birth control pills	X ↓	Diminished oral contraceptives levels, loss of effect, pregnancy.
* Cimetidine	C ↑	Increases acutely administered carbamazepine by 30% to produce toxicity in 2 days; chronically taking both drugs poses no particular risk. When cimetidine stopped, carbamazepine toxicity dissipates in about 1 week. Ranitidine can substitute for cimetidine.
Clarithromycin (see macrolide antibiotics)		
Clobazam	X ↓	Reduces plasma levels.
Clonazepam	X ↓	Diminishes clonazepam level.
Clozapine	X ↑ C ↑	Possible synergistic bone-marrow suppression.
* Corticosteroids: Dexamethasone Methylprednisone Prednisolone	X ↓	Carbamazepine may chronically reduce actions and levels of most corticosteroids. May need to increase steroid dose.
Cyclosporine	X ↓	Lowers blood level.
* Danazol	C ↑	Danazol greatly raises carbamazepine levels, at times to toxicity. Other androgen derivatives (e.g., methyltestosterone) may act similarly. If used together, closely monitor carbamazepine level and adjust dose of one or both drugs.
Dexamethasone (see corticosteroids)		
Dextropropoxyphene	C ↑	Increases levels/toxicity.
Digitalis, digoxin	X ↑	May worsen or cause bradycardia.
* Diltiazem	C ↑	On adding diltiazem, toxicity may occur in 1–4 days; halting diltiazem can ignite seizures because carbamazepine declines. Nifedipine, which does not affect

Drugs (X) Interact with:	Carbamazepine (C)	Comments
		carbamazepine clearance, is a safer calcium channel-blocker. Nimodipine may also be safer.
Diuretics	X ↓	Symptomatic hyponatremia; may need periodic electrolytes.
* Doxycycline	X ↓	Carbamazepine may reduce doxycycline's level; it may occur with other tetracyclines.
†Erythromycin (see macrolide antibiotics)		
Ethosuximide	X ↓	Diminishes ethosuximide.
Fentanyl	X ↓	Reduces plasma level and analgesia.
Fluoxetine (see SSRIs)		
Fluphenazine (see haloperidol)		
Flurithromycin (see macrolide antibiotics)		
Gemfibrozil (see lipid lowering agents)		
* Haloperidol	X ↓	Carbamazepine reduces haloperidol by 50–60%, which may, or may not, induce symptoms in 24 h (in rapid-cyclers) to 3 weeks. Serum levels of both drugs may be normal or low; monitor serum levels of both drugs closely.
†Isoniazid (INH)	C ↑	Carbamazepine may increase to toxicity usually in 1–2 days of INH; frequently happens on INH doses > 200 mg/day. Symptoms stop 2 days after INH is halted. INH often reduces therapeutic dose of carbamazepine; when INH is reduced or stopped, serum carbamazepine decreases.
Josamycin (see macrolide antibiotics)		
Lipid lowering agents: Gemfibrozil Isonicotinic acid Niacinamide Nicotinamide	C ↑	Increases carbamazepine levels and high density lipoprotein (HDL).
* Lithium	X ↑ C ↑	Lithium and carbamazepine may increase each other's neurotoxicity and therapeutic effects. Additive effect to decrease thyroid. Lower levels of each may still be therapeutic. Lithium leucocytosis may cancel carbamazepine leucopenia.
Macrolide antibiotics: Azithromycin Clarithromycin Erythromycin Flurithromycin Josamycin Ponsinomycin Troleandomycin	C ↑	Significantly (1–2 times) increases carbamazepine levels/toxicity; may subside in 2–3 days after antiobiotics stopped. Spiramycin probably safe alternative.

Drugs (X) Interact with:	Carbamazepine (C)	Comments
* Mebendazole	X↓	Carbamazepine may impair mebendazole's therapeutic effect at high doses; no special precautions needed. Valproic acid may be safer than carbamazepine.
* Methadone	X↓	Carbamazepine may lower serum methadone and increase withdrawal symptoms; patients may need more methadone or should be switched to valproic acid.
Methylprednisone (see cortiocosteroids)		
Neuromuscular blocking agents (see pancuronium, vecuronium)	X↓	Shortens duration of action.
Niacinamide (see lipid lowering agents)		
Oral contraceptives (see birth control pills)		
Nefazodone	C↑	Potentially increases carbamazepine levels.
Pancuronium	X↓	Shortened neuromuscular blockade.
Paroxetine (see SSRIs)		
Phenytoin	X↑↓C↓	Monitor both serum levels: Unpredictable effects on phenytonin; lower carbamazepine levels.
* Phenobarbatal	X↓C↓	Monitor both serum levels.
Ponsinomycin (see macrolide antibiotics)		
Prednisone (see corticosteroids)		
Prednisolone (see corticosteroids)		
* Primidone	X↓C↑↓	Speeds conversion of primidone to phenobarbital.
* Propoxyphene	C↑	Consistently raises carbamazepine, at times to toxicity.
Propranolol (& other β-blockers are extensively metabolized)	X↓	Theoretically, carbamazepine could speed metabolism of propranolol and other β-blockers. Propranolol may increase anticonvulsant effects of carbamazepine.
Sertraline (see SSRIs)		
SSRIs	C↑	Plasma level increases.
* Tetracycline	X↓	See doxycycline.
Theophylline	X↓	Decreased theophylline half-life and levels.
* Thyroid hormones	X↓	Accelerates elimination of thyroid hormones and may induce hypothyroidism; add thyroid.
TCAs	X↓↑ C↓↑	Carbamazepine may lower imipramine serum levels and probably other HCAs; monitor serum levels and increase HCA

Drugs (X) Interact with:	Carbamazepine (C)	Comments
		doses. Increases shared side effects (e.g., orthostatic hypotension, decreased heart conduction).
Troleandomycin (see macrolide antibiotics)		
Valproic acid	X↓C↑	Diminished valproic acid levels; can increase carbamazepine levels.
Vecuronium	X↓	Reduced level.
* Verapamil	C↑	On adding verapamil, toxicity may occur in 1–4 days. Increases carbamazepine levels, monitor. Halting verapamil can ignite seizures because carbamazepine declines; nifedipine may be safer.
Viloxazine	C↑	Increases levels/toxicity.
* Warfarin	X↓	Impaired hypoprothrombinemic response in several days to a week; adjust anticoagulants when carbamazepine changed.

Drugs (X) Interact with:	Valproic Acid (V)	Comments
Amitriptyline (see TCAs)		
Antacids	V↑	Increases valproic acid absorption; give 1 h apart.
Aspirin (see salicylates)		
Benzodiazepines	X↑	Valproic acid may elevate diazepam; with clonazepam, may cause absence seizures; importance unclear.
Carbamazepine	X↑V↓	Decreases valproic acid; increases carbamazepine (in epoxide form).
Cimetidine	V↑	Increases valproic acid levels; monitor levels or switch to ranitidine.
Chlorpromazine	V↑	Monitor valproic acid levels or switch to alternative neuroleptic (e.g., haloperidol).
Ethosuximide	X↑	Decrease ethosuximide or use alternative.
* Erythromycin	V↑	Increases level/toxicity. May occur with other macrolide antibiotics.
* Felbamate	V↑	Increases level/toxicity; monitor levels; start and withdraw felbamate slowly.
Lithium	X↑V↑	Increases risk of additive neurotoxicity; consider lowering levels of each.
Macrolide antibiotics (see erythromycin)		
Nortriptyline (see TCAs)		
* Phenobarbital	X↑	Increases serum phenobarbital; may prompt toxicity. Cut phenobarbital dose by 30–75% and monitor for decreased valproic acid.
Phenothiazines	V↑	May increase valproic acid levels; monitor.

Drugs (X) Interact with:	Valproic Acid (V)	Comments
*Phenytoin	X↑↓ V↓	Valproic acid initially lowers serum phenytoin by 30%, but in several weeks, phenytoin may exceed pre-valproic acid levels with ataxia, nystagmus, mental impairment, involuntary muscular movements, and seizures. Can also increase phenytoin toxicity by displacement from binding protein. Do not increase phenytoin unless seizures occur. Phenytoin may decrease serum valproic acid, but clinical importance remains unclear.
*Primidone	X↑	Valproic acid escalates serum phenobarbital, which primidone substantially produces. Valproic acid also inhibits phenobarbital metabolism, increasing risk of phenobarbital intoxication.
Propoxyphene	C↑	Increases levels/toxicity.
*Salicylates	X↑ V↑	Salicylates may increase unbound serum valproic acid concentrations to prompt valproic acid toxicity. Symptoms resolve when salicylate stopped. Bleeding time may be prolonged; decreased thrombocytes plus salicylates may yield bleeding, bruising, and petechiae.
TCAs	X↑	Increases levels of nortriptyline and amitriptyline and possibly other TCAs.
Thiopentone	X↑	Lower anesthesia dose of thiopentone.
Warfarin	X↑	Increases unbound warfarin.

*Moderately important interaction; †Extremely important interaction; ↑ Increases; ↓ Decreases; ↑↓ Increases or decreases.

A N T I C O N V U L S A N T S

EFFECTS ON LABORATORY TESTS

Generic Names	Blood/Serum Tests	Results*	Urine Tests	Results*
Carbamazepine	Calcium	↓		
	BUN	↑	Albuminuria	↑
	Thyroid function	↓	Glycosuria	↑
	**LFT	↑		
	WBC, platelets	↓ ↓		
	RBC	↓		
	Sodium	↓		
Clonazepam	**LFT	↑		
Valproic acid	*LFT (mainly AST [SGOT], ALT [SGPT], LDH)	↑	Ketone tests	False ↑
	WBC, platelets	↓		
	Thyroid function	↓		
	Lymphocytes, macrocytes	↑		
	Ammonia	↑		

* ↑ Increases; ↓ Decreases.
** LFT tests are AST/SGOT, ALT/SGPT, alkaline phosphatase, LDH, and bilirubin. Increases in transaminases (SGOT, SGPT, and LDH) are usually benign; increases in bilirubin and other tests suggest hepatotoxity.

WITHDRAWAL

In nonepileptics carbamazepine and valproic acid do not produce
* Psychological dependence
* Tolerance
* Addiction

When suddenly withdrawing a psychiatric patient from carbamazepine or valproic acid, no symptoms emerge. Yet it is safest to withdraw these drugs by 10% qod.

Clonazepam, a benzodiazepine, readily causes withdrawal.

* Hard to get patients off it.
* Withdrawal over months (see pages 335–346)

OVERDOSE: TOXICITY, SUICIDE, AND TREATMENT

Carbamazepine

Acute carbamazepine overdoses produce

* Difficulties in 1–3 h, neuromuscular disturbances most common and prominent.
* In lower overdoses, AV block is common, cardiac monitoring is useful.
* In higher overdoses, respiratory depression, stupor, and coma are more frequent.

Other problems include

* Nausea, vomiting, dry mouth, diarrhea, constipation, glossitis, stomach pain
* Agitation, restlessness, irritability
* Irregular breathing
* Vertigo
* Mydriasis, nystagmus, blurred vision, transient diplopia
* Anuria, oliguria, urinary retention
* Inability to perform rapidly alternating movements
* Hypotension, dizziness, hypertension, tachycardia
* Flushing, cyanosis
* Tremor, twitching, involuntary movements, opisthotonos, athetoid movements, ataxia
* Visual hallucinations
* Speech disturbances
* Hypoactive or hyperactive reflexes
* Seizures (especially in children)

The general management of carbamazepine overdoses is supportive (see pages 53–54).

- To speed elimination, try forced diuresis.
- Dialysis is used only in renal failure.
- Hemoperfusion of questionable help.
- Treat seizures with diazepam or barbiturate, but beware of aggravating respiratory depression.

Valproic Acid

Valproic acid usually causes less toxicity.

- Most serious action is hepatotoxicity in children under 2 y.o. (see page 238).

Symptoms include

- Anorexia and vomiting
- Somnolence, ataxia, and tremor (all respond to reduced dose)
- Rash, alopecia, stimulated appetite
- Heart block
- Coma

Management

- Supportive therapy (see pages 53–54).
- Because valproic acid is rapidly absorbed, gastric lavage is of little value; divalproex sodium delayed-release tablets are absorbed more slowly; gastric lavage or emesis may help if started early enough.
- Hemodialysis and hemoperfusion have reduced valproic acid levels.
- Naloxone may reverse a coma, but it may also trigger a seizure in epileptics by reversing anticonvulsant effects.

Toxicity and Suicide Data

Generic Names	Toxicity Doses Average (Largest) (g)	Mortality Doses Average (Lowest) (g)	Toxic Levels Average (Largest) (μg/ml)	Lethal Levels (mg/l)
Carbamazepine	(> 30)*	(> 60)	> 14	—
Clonazepam	0.01 (0.060)	—	> 80 (ng/ml)	—
Valproic acid	—	—	> 100 (2000)	1970

* Largest surviving dose in child was 10 grams (6-year-old boy); largest surviving dose in small child was 5 grams (3-year-old girl).

PRECAUTIONS

Carbamazepine levels vary since its hepatic metabolism changes between the 2nd and 8th week on the same dose. Follow carbamazepine maintenance considerations on pages 231–232.

Avoid or monitor anticonvulsants closely in patients with

- Cardiovascular disease
  √ Carbamazepine significant risk, but valproic acid is not.
- Renal disease affecting clearance
- Bone-marrow depression, leukopenia, thrombocytopenia
- Hepatic disease, especially if taking valproic acid or drinking excessive alcohol.
- Hypersensitivity to drug
- Carbamazepine's manufacturer advises stopping MAOIs 14 days before starting carbamazepine, but the reason is theoretical (e.g., carbamazepine is a tricyclic), not practical. Many patients do well on carbamazepine and a MAOI; carbamazepine does not significantly block serotonin or norepinephrine uptake.

Because of carbamazepine's moderate anticholinergic properties, cautiously prescribe for patients with increased

- Intraocular pressure
- Urinary retention
- Cognitive difficulties and advancing age

NURSES' DATA

Ensure patients on carbamazepine and valproic acid are aware of early toxicity, especially

- GI distress with valproic acid
- Liver function changes on valproic acid
- Hematologic reactions, weakness, fever, sore throat rarely on carbamazepine; bleeding on valproic acid
- Rashes, especially on carbamazepine
- Renal impairment and urinary retention with carbamazepine but rare with valproic acid
- CNS depression and sedation with carbamazepine but much less frequently with valproic acid
- Neurotoxicity (even on normal levels) with carbamazepine

Because of valproic acid's hepatotoxicity, patients should inform doctors if they are using, or about to use

- Anticonvulsants
  √ Phenobarbital

√ Phenytoin
√ Ethosuximide
- Alcohol, or
- High doses of acetaminophen regularly.

Because of valproic acid's thrombocytopenia risk, patients should inform doctors about regular aspirin risk.

PATIENT AND FAMILY NOTES

Most common side effects with carbamazepine include

- Mild drunk-like symptoms (e.g., ataxia, incoordination, dizziness, lightheadedness, blurred vision, weakness, and fatigue)
- Rashes

Most common side effects with valproic acid include

- GI side effects (e.g., nausea, dyspepsia, diarrhea)

Note that with

- Depakene
  √ If capsules are chewed, they irritate the mouth and throat.
  √ Swallow capsules whole.
  √ Further reduce GI irritation by taking capsules and syrup with food or by slowly raising the dose.
- Divalproex (Depakote)
  √ Sprinkle capsules may be swallowed whole.
  √ They may also be opened carefully and sprinkled on a small teaspoon of soft food, such as applesauce or pudding. The drug-food mixture should be eaten immediately (avoid chewing) and *not* stored for future use.

When starting on carbamazepine, patients should exercise care when driving cars, working around machines, and crossing streets. To test reflexes, drive briefly in a safe place.

Patients may be mildly to considerably disorganized on carbamazepine until the proper dose is found. Carbamazepine's metabolism may require 3–8 weeks to stabilize, prompting several dosage increases during treatment.

If on valproic acid, avoid aspirin unless approved by physician.

- Bleeding, bruises, and petechiae may arise.

Avoid during pregnancy, but at the first sign of pregnancy

- Do *not* immediately stop drug.
- Consult with doctor.

Take valproic acid with meals.

- Food slightly delays absorption of valproic acid, but does not change its bioavailability.

Place anticonvulsants away from bedside or any readily accessible area, where they might be taken by "accident." Keep safely from hungry children.

Have a Medic Alert wallet-card or bracelet signifying anticonvulsant use. Also indicate that the patient is taking the agent for a psychiatric, not an epileptic, disorder.

Take anticonvulsants when doctor prescribes them.

- If forget dose, can consume in 4 h.
- Otherwise wait for next regular dose.
- Do *not* double dose.

Do not suddenly cease anticonvulsants until first discussing with physician; sudden withdrawal of drug can cause a seizure.

7. Antianxiety Agents

INTRODUCTION

Anti-anxiety agents and hypnotics share many characteristics and are known collectively as sedative-hypnotics and, perhaps, more accurately as "hypnoanxiolytics." Because anti-anxiety medications primarily treat daytime tension (and are not necessarily sedating), whereas hypnotics relieve insomnia, and because some newer agent's effectiveness are limited solely to anxiety or insomnia, they are discussed separately.

This chapter presents

- Benzodiazepines
- Buspirone
- Clomipramine
- Clonidine
- Hydroxyzine
- Meprobamate (and other β-blockers)
- Propranolol

Barbiturates are presented in the next chapter.

This chapter focuses on

- Adjustment disorder with anxious mood (page 269)
- Agoraphobia (page 275)
- Anger attacks (page 275)
- Catatonia (pages 283–284)
- Elective mutism (page 277)
- Generalized anxiety disorder (pages 270–271)
- Hypochondriasis (page 281)
- Migraine (page 283)
- Nicotine abuse (page 283)
- Obsessive-compulsive disorder (pages 278–280)

[1] Clinicians seeking information on obsessive-compulsive disorder can call the OCD Information Line at the Dean Foundation 608/836-8070, Fax 608/836-8033.

- Obsessive-compulsive spectrum disorders (pages 280–281)
  - √ Anorexia nervosa
  - √ Body dysmorphic disorder
  - √ Bulimia
  - √ Hypochondriasis
  - √ Paraphilias
  - √ Pathological gambling
  - √ Pathological jealousy
  - √ Sexual obsession
  - √ Trichotillomania
- Panic disorders (pages 271–274)
- Performance anxiety (pages 275–276)
- Post-traumatic stress disorder (pages 281–283)
- School phobia (page 277)
- Separation anxiety (page 278)
- Social phobia (pages 276–277)

Antianxiety agents for disorders explored in other chapters include

- Aggression (Anticonvulsants, pages 233–235)
- Akathesia and dystonia (Extrapyramidal drugs, pages 62–63)
- Alcohol and antianxiety withdrawal (Hypnotics, pages 337–338, 341–343)
- Delirium (Antipsychotics, page 16)
- Dementia (Antipsychotics, page 20)
- Depression (Antidepressants, page 89)
- Nocturnal myodonus (Hypnotics, page 256)
- Mania (Lithium, pages 191, 193)
- Schizophrenia (Antipsychotics, page 11)

NAMES, COST, CLASSES, MANUFACTURERS, DOSE FORMS, COLORS

Generic Names (Dollars/Dose: 100 pills in mg)*	Brand Names (Dollars/Dose: 100 pills in mg)*	Manu-facturer	Dose Forms (mg)**	Colors
BENZODIAZEPINES				
Alprazolam 39-67/0.5	Xanax 68/0.5	Upjohn	t: 0.25/0.5/1/1	t: white (oval)/peach/ blue/white (oblong)
Chlordiazepoxide 3-11/10	Librium 48/10	Roche	c: 5/10/25 p: 20 mg/ml	c: green-yellow/green-black/green-white
Clonazepam	Klonopin 64/0.5	Roche	t: 0.5/1/2	t: orange/blue/blue
Clorazepate 8-39/7.5	Tranxene 134/7.5	Abbott	t: 3.75/7.5/15	t: blue/peach/laven-der
	Tranxene-SD 284/11.25	Abbott	t: 11.25/22.5	t: blue/tan
Diazepam 3-35/5	Valium 57/5	Roche	t: 2/5/10 p: 5 mg/ml	t: white/yellow/blue

Generic Names (Dollars/Dose: 100 pills in mg)*	Brand Names (Dollars/Dose: 100 pills in mg)*	Manufacturer	Dose Forms (mg)**	Colors
Halazepam 42/20	Paxipam	Schering	t: 20/40	t: orange/white
Lorazepam 4-36/1	Ativan 77/1	Wyeth-Ayerst	t: 0.5/1/2 p: 2/4 mg/ml	t: all white
Oxazepam 14–21/15	Serax 75/15	Wyeth-Ayerst	t: 15 c: 10/15/30	t: yellow c: white-pink/ white-red/ white-maroon
Prazepam 33-41/10	Discontinued	All generic	c: 5/10	c: ivory-white/ green-white
Azaspirodecane-dione Buspirone	BuSpar 95/10	Mead Johnson	t: 5/10	t: all white
β-Blocker Propranolol 4-18/40	Inderal 41/40	Wyeth-Ayerst	t: 10/20/40/60/80	t: orange/blue green/pink/yellow
α2-adrenergic agonist Clonidine 3-11/0.1	Catapres 54/0.1	Boehringer Ingel-heim	t: 0.1/0.2/0.3	t: tan/orange/peach
Antihistamines Hydroxyzine 3-25/25	Atarax 80/25	Roerig	t:10/25/50/100 s: 10 mg/5 ml	t: orange/green/ yellow/red
	Vistaril 80/25	Plizer	c: 25/50/100 su: 25 mg/ml	c: green/green-white green-gray
Meprobamate 2-24/200	Equinil 20/200	Wyeth-Ayerst	t: 200/400	t: all white
	Miltown 95/200	Wallace	t: 200/400/600	t: all white

* 1994 average wholesale price for 100 pills at this dose (e.g., 78/50 means 100 pills 50 mg cost $78). If depot form, cost is of single dose.
** c = capsules; p = parenteral; s = syrup; SD = single dose; su = suspension; t = tables.

PHARMACOLOGY

Benzodiazepines mediate the actions of GABA, the brain's major inhibitory neurotransmitter.

- GABA inhibits the firing of neurons by opening the chloride channels on the neuronal membrane.
- This causes a hyperpolarization that requires a greater depolarization to trigger an action potential.

Benzodiazepines are of 4 chemical types:

- 2-keto compounds (clorazepate, chlordiazepoxide, diazepam, halazepam, prazepam, flurazepam)
  - √ Are prodrugs, which means they can be inactive themselves (i.e., prazepam, clorazepate) but have active metabolites (all go to desmethyldiazepam).

□ Clorazepate is rapidly hydrolyzed in the stomach and absorbed; fast onset of action.
√ Are slowly oxidized in the liver.
√ Have very long half-lives.
□ Desmethyldiazepam, a shared metabolite, has 30–200 h half-life.
- 3-hydroxy compounds (lorazepam, oxazepam, temazepam)
√ Are active compounds,
√ Have shorter half-lives,
√ Are metabolized rapidly via direct conjugation with a glucuronide radical, and
√ Do not generate active metabolites.
- Triazolo compounds (alprazolam, triazolam, estazolam)
√ Are active,
√ Have active metabolites,
√ Have short half-lives, and
√ Are oxidized.
- 7-nitro compounds (clonazepam)
√ Are active,
√ Have long half-lives,
√ Have no active metabolites, and
√ Are metabolized by nitroreduction (some by oxidation).

Any agent or disease that interferes with live enzymes (e.g., cimetidine) can block the oxidative metabolism of 2-keto and triazolo compounds.

Pathways of Most Benzodiazepine Anxiolytics

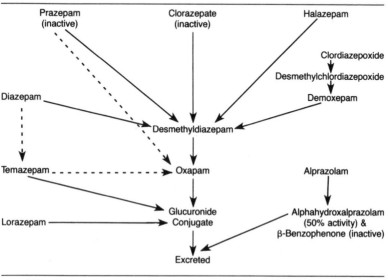

──── Major pathway
------ Minor pathway

Half-lives

- The longer the antianxiety agent's half-life, the more it adversely affects daytime functioning (e.g., hangover) and the more delayed and attenuated its withdrawal symptoms.
- The shorter the half-life, the greater and sooner its withdrawal and anxiety between doses (rebound).
- For the elderly and the hepatically impaired, shorter half-lives are safer.

Lipophilic and Hydrophilic Properties

- Single doses of more lipophilic drugs (e.g., diazepam, clorazepate)
  - √ Enter the brain rapidly,
  - √ Ignite effects promptly,
  - √ Extinguish effects quickly, and
  - √ Vanish into body fat where stored.
- Single doses of less lipophilic drugs (e.g., lorazepam)
  - √ Produce clinical effects more slowly, but
  - √ Provide more sustained relief.

Duration of Effects

- With acute doses, rates of absorption and distribution half-life are critical.
- With repeated doses, distribution is complete; the elimination half-life, which determines the drug's steady-state levels, becomes critical.
- Single doses of highly lipophilic drugs with long half-lives (e.g., diazepam) afford rapid relief but for shorter periods than would be expected by their half-life alone. Multiple doses of these drugs saturate body fat and then provide lasting relief. On the other hand, the less lipophilic lorazepam has a short half-life, but sustains a longer action than diazepam when each are given as single doses, and has a shorter duration of action than diazepam with multiple dosing.

Potency

- High-potency benzodiazepines (e.g., alprazolam) with a relatively high receptor affinity have more withdrawal symptoms than would be expected by just half-life alone.

ANTIANXIETY AGENTS

Pharmacology of Oral Antianxiety Agents

Generic Names	Speed of Onset (Peak Plasma Levels in Hours)	Speed of Distribution (Lipophilicity: Diazepam = 1.0)	Active Metabolites (Half-Life, Hours)	Mean Elimination Half-Life (Hours)*
2-Keto				
Clorazepate	Rapid (1–2)	Rapid (0.79)	Desmethyldiazepam (30–200) Oxazepam (3–21)	30–200
Chlordiazepoxide	Intermediate (0.5–4)	Slow	Desmethylchlor diazepoxide (18) Demoxepam (14–95) Desmethyldiazepam (30–200) Oxazepam (3–21)	50–100
Diazepam	Very rapid (0.5–2)	Rapid (1.00)	Desmethyldiazepam (30–200) Oxazepam (3–21) 3-Hydroxydiazepam (5–20)	30–100
Halazepam	Slow-intermediate (1–4)	Intermediate	Desmethylchlordiazepoxide Oxazepam (3–21)	30–200
Prazepam	Slowest (2.3–6)	Intermediate	Desmethyldiazepam (30–100) Oxazepam (3–21)	30–200
7-Nitro				
Clonazepam	Intermediate (1–2)	Intermediate (0.28)	None	18–50

Pharmacology of Oral Antianxiety Agents *(cont.)*

Generic Names	Speed of Onset (Peak Plasma Levels in Hours)	Speed of Distribution (Lipophilicity; Diazepam = 1.0)	Active Metabolites (Half-Life, Hours)	Mean Elimination Half-Life (Hours)*
3-Hydroxy-				
Lorazepam	Slow-intermediate (1–6)	Intermediate (0.48)	None	10–20
Oxazepam	Slow-Intermediate (1–4)	Intermediate (0.45)	None	3–21
Triazolo-				
Alprazolam	Intermediate (1–2)	Intermediate (0.54)	α-Hydroxy-alprazolam (6–10)**	12–15
Other				
Buspirone	Rapid peak (0.6–15), very slow onset (> 7 days)	Rapid	l-Pyrimidinyl piperazine (16)	2–11
Clonidine	Rapid (3–5)	Slow-intermediate	None	12–16
Hydroxyzine	Rapid (2–4)	Intermediate	None	< 4
Meprobamate	Rapid (1–3)	Intermediate	None	6–16
Propranolol	Rapid (2–4)	Intermediate	None significant	3–5

* Includes all active metabolites; longer in elderly; more important in chronic administration.
** Metabolite half as active as parent.

DOSES

General Antianxiety Doses

Generic Names	Benzodia-zepine Dose Equivalents	Usual Dose for Anxiety (mg/day)	Extreme Dose Range for Anxiety (mg/day)	Therapeutic Plasma Level (μg/ml)	Geriatric Dose (mg/day)
Alprazolam	0.5	1.0–2.0	0.5–8	> 48 ng/ml	0.25–0.5
Buspirone		15–30	15–60	1–6	15–30
Chlordiaze-poxide	10.0	15–75	10–100	> 0.7	5–30*
Clonazepam	0.25	0.5–1.5	0.25–20	5–70 ng/ml	0.25–1.0*
Clonidine		0.2–0.6	0.1–2.0	500	0.2–0.4
Clorazepate	7.5	15–67.5	7.5–90	——	15–60*
Diazepam	5.0	4–30	2–40	300–400 ng/ml	1–10*
Halazepam	20.0	40–80	20–100	——	20–40*
Hydroxyzine	100.0**	200–400	100–600	——	10–50
Lorazepam	1.0	2–6	1–10	——	0.5–1.5
Meprobamate	800.0	400–1200	400–1600	5–20	200–600
Oxazepam	15.0	30–60	30–120		10–30
Prazepam	15.0	30–60	10–60	——	10–15*
Propranolol		30–80	30–240	20 ng/ml	30–60

* Because of exceedingly long half-lives, not generally recommended for use longer than 1 week in elderly or those with impaired hepatic function. Use lorazepam or oxazepam instead.
** Represents sedative equivalent.

CLINICAL INDICATIONS AND USE*

Antianxiety Drug Indications

Generic Names	Anxiolytic	Panic Attacks	Obsessive-Compulsive Disorder	Hypnotic	Muscle Relaxant	Alcohol Withdrawal	Depression	EPS
Alprazolam	+	+	±	+	+	+	±	−
Buspirone	+	−	±	−	−	−	−	−
Chlordiazepoxide	+	−	−	+	+	+	−	−
Clomipramine	−	−	+	−	−	−	+	−
Clonazepam	+	+	±	+	+	+	−	±
Clonidine	±	±	−	±	−	−	−	−
Clorazepate	+	−	−	+	+	+	−	−
Diazepam	+	+	−	+	+	+	−	+
Halazepam	+	−	−	±	+	+	−	−
Hydroxyzine	+	−	−	+	+	−	−	+
Lorazepam	+	+	−	+	+	+	−	+
Meprobamate	+	−	−	+	+	−	−	−
Oxazepam	+	−	−	+	+	+	−	−
Prazepam	+	−	−	−	+	+	−	−
Propranolol	+	±	−	−	?	−	−	+

* This does not reflect FDA sanctioned indications but, rather, where it has been or can be reasonably used. This is even limited, e.g., all benzodiazepines have muscle relaxant properties and ability to prevent alcohol withdrawal.

ANTIANXIETY AGENTS

General Information

Benzodiazepines

Tolerance and physiologic and/or psychological dependence can occur with benzodiazepines. Therefore, they should be

- Ideally, aimed at anxiety from particular stressors.
- Time limited: 1–2 weeks.
- Chronically used for specific, identifiable, symptoms.

In general, risk of dependency is correlated with both dose and duration of use.

- Benzodiazepine dependency may occur on
  - √ 3–4 times the normal daily dose over several weeks.
  - √ Smaller, therapeutic doses over a month.
- Tolerance to daytime benzodiazepine sedative side effects often develops in
  - √ 5–10 days, while tolerance to anxiolytic effect usually doesn't occur.
- Psychological dependency is also most likely if
  - √ A fast onset agent is used (i.e., has a "buzz").
  - √ It is prescribed in dosage intervals that are further apart than duration of action.
    - □ Prn only when "you feel really anxious."
    - □ Tid in benzodiazepine that lasts only 5 h.
    - □ May have interdose withdrawals several times a day that, combined with rapid relief and a "buzz," increases psychological dependency.

Psychological dependency

- Can best be avoided by using a slower onset agent with a long duration of action (e.g., clonazepam).
- If a shorter acting agent is used, make sure it is given at appropriately short intervals.
- Consider prn only when the need is truly intermittent (e.g., 5 times a week and not twice a day).

Avoid meprobamate and barbiturates because they

- Have a higher risk of addiction and are more dangerous in withdrawal than benzodiazepines.
- Have a very low toxicity-to-therapeutic-effect ratio.
- Are more likely lethal as overdoses.
- Induce hepatic enzymes, causing a need for increased doses.

Antidepressants

- May often be the first choice of treatment for many anxiety disorders.
- HCAs, MAOIs, and SSRIs are helpful for a variety of anxiety disorders.
  - √ All are effective for panic disorder.
- Because of low side effects and, in certain conditions, better efficacy, SSRIs are often preferred.
- SSRIs are also effective for
  - √ Obsessive-compulsive disorder and OC spectrum disorders.
  - √ Social phobia.
- MAOs are also effective for
  - √ Social phobia.
- TCAs are also effective for
  - √ School phobia and
  - √ Separation anxiety
- All may also be effective for generalized anxiety disorder (GAD).
  - √ This effect appears to be independent of nonspecific sedating effects.

β-Blockers

- Most often used for performance anxiety or as adjuncts to other drugs.

Propranolol

- Non-selectively blocks β_1 (cardiac) and β_2 (pulmonary) receptors.
  - √ Increases pulmonary resistance.
    - ◻ Contraindicated in asthma.
- Complicates carbohydrate and fat metabolism.
  - √ Risks hypoglycemia in diabetes.
  - √ Relative contraindication in diabetes.
- Most useful against the "flight-or-fight" response—that is, the physical signs of anxiety:
  - √ Palpitations
  - √ Tachycardia
  - √ GI upset
  - √ Tremors
  - √ Sweating
- Only mild improvement of psychological symptoms.
- Before using propranolol, examine and interview patient for
  - √ Cardiovascular problems—r/o bradyarrhythmias, congestive heart failure, Reynaud's disease
  - √ Pulmonary difficulties—r/o asthma

√ Endocrine abnormalities—r/o diabetes
√ Do not give propranolol if above specific conditions are seen.
- Start at 10 mg bid and increase to 80–160 mg/day.
  √ Most patients require small doses of propranolol (e.g., 10–20 mg tid-qid).
  √ Minimal doses minimally drop BP.
  √ Can use heart rate (HR) as guide to dosing.
    □ Decrease HR at least 5–10 beats/min.
    □ Can go down to 60 beats/min if needed.
    □ Make sure patient able to increase HR to > 110 beat/min with exercise.
- Unlike benzodiazepines, propranolol does not dim consciousness, cause drowsiness, or produce drug dependency.
- Taper slowly in patients with pre-existing hypertension, angina, or other coronary artery diseases to avoid rebound hypertension.

β-*blocker alternatives to propranolol* for:

Mainly peripheral sympathetic control

- Propranolol has very high lipid solubility, so easily goes to the brain.
  √ May be associated with fatigue, depression.
  √ May exert some CNS anxiolytic effects.
- Atenolol and nadolol have very low lipid solubility and usually are low in CNS effects.

Pulmonary conditions

- Acetabutolol, atenolol, metoprolol, and betazolol are all cardioselective, mainly block β_1 (cardiac) not β_2 (pulmonary) receptors, and pose a smaller risk of bronchospasm.

High dosage for aggression/agitation

- Propranolol most effectively gets to brain, but also can cause significant hypotension or bradycardia.
- Acetabutolol and pindolol are relatively lipophilic, so in high doses can affect brain but
  √ Also have intrinsic sympathomimetic activity.
    □ May decrease hypotension or bardycardia risk.

Long duration of action
- Propranolol has 4 h half-life.
- Propranolol LA has 10 h half-life.
- Betaxolol has 10 h half-life.
- Nadolol has 22 h half-life.

- Atenolol has 7 h half-life.
- Propranolol LA, nadolol, betazolol, and sometimes atenolol can be given only qd.

Liver impairment

- Kidney excreted β-blockers (atenolol, careolol, and nadolol) are preferred.
- Also consider these in geriatric patients.

Kidney impairment

- Liver excreted β-blockers (propranolol, metoprolol, labetolol, and penbutolol) are preferred.

Clonidine

- May be useful, but many side effects.
- Evaluate for medical complications (e.g., cardiac disorders, moderate/severe hypertension, metabolic or renal disease).
- For anxiety, start at 0.1 mg bid.
  √ Increase by 0.1 mg every 1–2 days.
  √ Reach a final dose of 0.4–0.6 mg/day.
  √ Tolerance may quickly develop.
    □ Consider only for short-term trials.
  √ Taper slowly to avoid rebound hypertension.

Neuroleptics

- Not generally recommended unless neuroleptic is appropriate for other symptoms.
- Low neuroleptic doses (e.g., haloperidol 0.5 mg, chlorpromazine 50 mg, perphenazine 4 mg) tid quell anxiety.
  √ May help near-psychotic anxiety (e.g., in borderline or schizotypal personality disorder or in hypomania/mania.)
    □ May manifest as cognitive disorganization or overvalued ideas.
  √ Neuroleptics do not generate drug dependency.
  √ But they provoke EPS, especially akathisia, which mimics anxiety.
  √ They may be quite sedating.
- Thus, usually better to give benzodiazepines than neuroleptics.
- If neuroleptics used, prescribe high or medium sedating ones, such as chlorpromazine or thioridazine, 25–50 mg qd-qid, or perphenazine 4–8 mg qd-qid.
  √ Use only short trials to avoid EPS or TD.

ANTIANXIETY AGENTS

Antihistamines

- Sedating antihistamines reduce anxiety.
  - √ Their anticholinergic effects may be dangerous to the elderly or the cognitively impaired.
  - √ Their negative sedative effect may outweigh their therapeutic anxiolytic effect.
- Consider hydroxyzine for anxiety in some physical conditions.
  - √ Pruritis due to allergic conditions.
- Examples
  - √ Hydroxyzine 10–50 mg qd-qid.
  - √ Diphenhydramine 10–25 mg bid-qid for daytime sedation.

Trazodone

- Unlike other ADs, can be used acutely in low doses 25–50 mg qd-qid.
- Sedation, hypotension, and priapism (rarely) complicate use.
- Does not usually interfere with cogntive function.
- Doses into the antidepressant range are acceptable.
- Minimal tolerance develops.
- Best given on full stomach to avoid severe peak levels.

Buspirone

- A nonbenzodiazepine antianxiety agent that differs from benzodiazepines.
- Although it has similar efficacy in treating anxiety, it is usually not preferred by those who have tried benzodiazepines.
- Its effect can best be described as "taking the edge off anxiety" rather than ablating it, as with benzodiazepines.
- More recent research suggests that, for a variety of anxiety-related conditions, the 45–60 mg per day dosage range may be optimally effective.
- Although former benzodiazepine users prefer benzodiazepines over buspirone, buspirone is still superior to placebo.
- Effective in GAD, social phobia.
- May be good adjunct in OCD, PTSD.
- Not effective in panic disorder or acute anxiety.

Areas	Buspirone	Benzodiazepines
Effect of single dose	No	Yes
Full therapeutic effect	2 weeks	Days
Sedating	No	Yes
Impairs performance and motor coordination	No	Yes
Interacts with other hypnosedatives	No	Yes
Potentiates alcohol	No	Yes

Areas	Buspirone	Benzodiazepines
Develops tolerance	No	Yes
Produces drug dependency	No	Yes
Suppresses hypnosedative withdrawal	No	Yes

Adjustment Disorder with Anxious Mood

Acute situational anxiety-outcomes

- Mild to moderate severity
  - √ Benzodiazepines, placebo, or supportive counseling all have same good result: 70–80%.
- Marked severity
  - √ Benzodiazepines superior to placebo.
- If it is a single identfiable stressor, e.g., wedding, licensure exam, etc.
  - √ Use time-limited trial.
    - □ May try prn first.
    - □ Many find such great reassurance in knowing they can take something that will help, that they rarely or never use it.
  - √ If it is only for the event itself, it is performance anxiety.
    - □ Consider β-blocker.

Time-limited (less than one month) pervasive stressor with severe or moderate/severe anxiety.

- Goal: To continuously prevent anxiety that interferes with functioning.
  - √ Schedule benzodiazepines continuously to avoid breakthroughs and withdrawals:
  - √ Consider longer-acting benzodiazepines (e.g., clonazepam, clorazepate) for more even blood levels.
  - √ For elderly, employ 50% of the dose provided younger patients; use intermediate half-life benzodiazepines without active metabolites (e.g., lorazepam, oxazepam) to prevent drug build-up.

Time-limited intermittent stressor (if performance anxiety or social phobia, see page 276).

- Prescribe benzodiazepine prn.
- If stressor onset is predictable, take 1–2 h before.
- If stressor duration is predictable, pick benzodiazepine with matching duration of action (e.g., 6 h stressor, try lorazapam).

Indefinite pervasive stressor

- Consider nonbenzodiazepine, which does not induce drug dependency (e.g., buspirone, TCA, trazodone, SSRI).

Generalized Anxiety Disorder (GAD)

Benzodiazepines

- Because short-acting, high-potency benzodiazepines (e.g., alprazolam) prompt more interdose rebound and dependency, long-acting, low-potency benzodiazepines (e.g., clonazepam 0.5–2 mg/day, chlordiazepoxide 25–75 mg/day) are preferred for GAD. Use approach described under adjustment disorder with anxious mood, time-limited pervasive stressor (page 269).
  - √ High placebo rate can be expected (~ 50–60%).
    - □ Consider low initial dosing.
- Many with GAD have intermittent flares of anxiety.
- Try to limit benzodiazepine use for exacerbations of GAD rather than continuous usage.
  - √ Limit trials to 1–4 weeks.
- Withdrawal syndromes when stopping are 5–10%.
  - √ May be secondary to lower doses used than in panic disorder.
- Relapse rate in first year after stopping medication is about 50–70%.
  - √ Decreases to 38% after 40 months.

Buspirone

Since buspirone does not cause drug dependency, and since GAD is a long-term disorder, buspirone appears safer than benzodiazepines.

- Buspirone is *not* effective for prn anxiety.
  - √ Initial effects occur in 1–2 weeks.
  - √ Full effect often requires 4–6 weeks.
- Buspirone must be taken regularly.
- GAD patients improve most if free of benzodiazepines for 1 month.
- Buspirone does *not* prevent benzodiazepine withdrawal.
- Dose for moderate anxiety:
  - √ Start at 5 mg bid-tid for first week.
  - √ Dose ranges from 15–30 mg/day, but may increase to 60 mg/day.
  - √ Move dose up by 2.5–5 mg every 2–4 days until achieving desired dose.
    - □ Assess at 2 weeks if this dose range is effective.
    - □ If not, try 40–60 mg range.
- Dose for severe anxiety:
  - √ If tolerated, go quickly to 40–60 mg range.
  - √ If patient well stabilized on high dose, can very gradually decrease dose (5–10 mg q 10 days) to see if lower dose is equally effective.
    - □ May cause less side effects and is definitely cheaper.

Antidepressants

- Sedating and nonsedating antidepressants (e.g., TCAs, SSRIs, and trazodone) have been used successfully in GAD without depression.
- Prescribe as for depression.
- Expect possible first week activation effects.
- Onset in 2–3 weeks.
- Tolerance does not usually develop.

Propranolol (and other β-blockers)

- Helps in GAD if there are predominant physiologic symptoms (e.g., palpitations, tremor).

Panic Disorders

Choices for treating panic disorders are

- ADs, including TCAs, SSRIs, and MAOIs, but not bupropion and probably not trazodone.
- Benzodiazepines.

TCAs and SSRIs

- ADs are preferred for treating panic attacks.
    - √ Unlike benzodiazepines, ADs are not addicting.
    - √ ADs decrease panic attacks, and to some extent, the anxiety and phobias associated with panic attacks.
    - √ Reduced frequency is more likely than reduced severity of panic attacks.
- Patient does not need a depressed mood for ADs to prevent panic attacks.
    - √ Fluvoxamine shown to be more effective than placebo.
- Because of greater safety and lower side effects, SSRIs are preferred.
- Of TCAs, imipramine has most evidence of antipanic effectiveness.
    - √ Other TCAs (e.g., nortriptyline) have also been reported to be effective.
- Use same doses as in treating depression.
- Beneficial effect requires 1–3 weeks of TCA treatment.
- When patients with panic attacks are started on TCAs or SSRIs, they may initially experience "speediness," insomnia, jitters, or even an increase in panic attacks. Therefore important to
    - √ Start patient on a low dose (for imipramine, around 10 mg; fluoxetine, around 5–25 mg).
    - √ Increase dose by 10 mg qod for imipramine or 5 mg q 3–7 days for fluoxetine.

√ Only if seen as essential, consider adding alprazolam 0.25 mg when beginning AD and then gradually taper the alprazolam when the AD begins to work in 2–3 weeks.

▫ Full effect often takes 6 weeks.

▫ Patients usually are very reluctant to stop benzodiazepines.

√ Final acute AD dose often the same as the doses used for depression.

√ Counsel around this introductory period.

• Patient should initially remain on AD for at least 6 months.

√ Taper drug only when patient is comfortable doing so.

√ Unlike with depressive episode, patient probably needs to continue much longer.

▫ 83% relapse rate if discontinued in 6 months.

▫ 25% relapse rate if discontinued in 18 months.

√ The effective maintenance dose may be lower than the acute dose.

Augmenting TCAs/SSRIs

• TCAs and SSRIs can augment each other in panic disorder.

√ Consider if only partial response seen to one.

√ Monitor TCA plasma level carefully.

• T_3 at 25 μg/day dose not effective and may worsen.

√ Combination risks increasing symptoms (e.g., sweating, tremulousness).

Monoamine-oxidase inhibitors

When depression is associated with panic attacks or severe anxiety

• MAOIs may be the drug of second choice (assuming patient follows diet).

√ When depression is associated with panic attacks or severe anxiety,

• MAOIs (and possibly SSRIs) may be more effective than TCAs, benzodiazepines.

• MAOIs require 1–6 weeks for improvement.

• All MAOIs thwart panic attacks, but

√ Phenelzine is preferred often up to 90 mg/day.

√ May be the best drug for *severe* panic or phobic disorders.

√ Unlike other ADs, they do not increase panic attacks and anxiety when started and may more rapidly reduce symptoms.

Benzodiazepines

• Response often seen in 1–2 weeks.

√ May also be superior to TCAs for phobic avoidance and anticipatory anxiety.

- Low-potency benzodiazepines can be effective (e.g., diazepam) but may induce too much sedation, so high-potency benzodiazepines are recommended. These may be
  - √ Short-acting (e.g., alprazolam) or
  - √ Long-acting (e.g., clonazepam).
- In panic disorder 25% of patients may get depressed on high doses of benzodiazepines (e.g., > 3 mg alprazolam; > 1.5 mg clonazepam; 4–6 mg lorazepam).
- Clonazepam may be superior to alprazolam because clonazepam
  - √ Exhibits little interdose rebound,
  - √ Produces less severe withdrawal than alprazolam, and
  - √ Can be taken bid, whereas alprazolam requires tid-qid dosage.
- For the above reasons, one study showed that 86% of panic patients preferred clonazepam over alprazolam.
- Alprazolam
  - √ Start around 0.25 mg tid or qid, and increase 0.25 mg every 1–3 days.
    - □ Can try 0.5 mg in evening and, if no excess sedation, can begin with 0.5 mg tid or qid.
  - √ Usually effective at 3–5 mg/day.
  - √ Therapeutic dose may require 10 mg/day.
  - √ Range is from 1–10 mg/day.
  - √ Can cause manic symptoms.
  - √ Withdrawal of alprazolam may trigger panic attacks and severe withdrawal symptoms.
    - □ Some patients only get 5 to 6 h duration of action, may have "mini withdrawals" before each dose, and need more than tid dosing.
  - √ Patients withdrawing from alprazolam often have more clinical symptoms than when they first started.
    - □ They have both the original panic symptoms along with new withdrawal symptoms.
    - □ Adding AD for 6–12 weeks to prevent panic attacks may aid subsequent benzodiazepine withdrawal.
  - √ Some patients describe the frequent alprazolam doses as inducing a sense of "impending panic" after just 1–2 h of missing a dose.
    - □ One option is to slowly discontinue alprazolam no faster than 0.25–0.5 mg every 7–10 days for doses above 2 mg/day, and 0.25 every 7–10 days for doses below 2 mg/day.
    - □ Another popular option is to switch from the short-acting alprazolam to the longer-acting clonazepam over a week.
    - □ If clonazepam is chosen, it takes about one week to approach steady state; so can't immediately substitute clonazepam for alprazolam.

ANTIANXIETY AGENTS

□ May need to start clonazepam at full equivalent dose and reduce alprazolam 15–25% a day, with prn alprazolam options available if withdrawal is too fast.

- Clonazepam
  - √ Start at 0.25 mg bid for first 2 days; increase dose by 0.25 mg qd or qod.
  - √ Antipanic effect usually around 1.5–2.5 mg/day.
  - √ Range is from 0.5–4.5 mg/day.
  - √ Because clonazepam sedates, may prefer to dispense most of it at bedtime, with a smaller dose earlier in the day.
  - √ Clonazepam can induce depression in doses over 1.5 mg qd.
  - √ Because of clonazepam's long half-life and tendency to increase LFTs, healthy liver function is essential to avoid toxicity.
    - □ Consider periodic LFTs.
    - □ Clonazepam not associated with liver failure.
  - √ Interdose rebound can occur.
  - √ Some patients can have continuously effective serum levels with qd dosing.
- When stopping alprazolam or clonazepam, titrate very slowly—about 10% per week.
  - √ This is hard to do with clonazepam because its smallest dose form is 0.5 mg.
- Verapamil
  - √ Moderately effective in controlled trial.
    - □ 160 mg qd first week.
    - □ Increase 160 mg qd/week until reach 480 mg.
- Nimodipine (a centrally active calcium channel-blocker)
  - √ 2 successful cases reported.
    - □ Dose 30 mg tid.
    - □ Vascular dilation effect hypothesized as curative.
- Propranolol
  - √ Only one controlled comparison trial found propranolol effective.
    - □ Average dose 183 mg/day.
    - □ 2 weeks until significant effect.
    - □ Bradycardia seen at 1 week but without antipanic effect.
  - √ Although propranolol does not have a proven antipanic effect, when low doses of it (10–20 mg tid-qid) are added as an adjunct, there may be benefits, especially in patients who don't fully improve with TCAs, SSRIs, MAOIs, or benzodiazepines alone.
- Valproic acid
  - √ Possibly effective for panic in usual dose range.
  - √ Carbamazepine is ineffective.
- Bupropion
  - √ Not effective for panic, but may reduce baseline anxiety.

Anger Attacks

- Some may be a variant of panic attacks.
  √ Symptoms are spontaneous and unprovoked.
  √ Same physiologic symptoms as panic attacks.
  √ Anger instead of anxiety experienced.
    □ Experienced as uncharacteristic and inappropriate.
- Case reports of successful use of TCAs and SSRIs.

Phobic Disorders

There are four key drug-responsive types:

- Agoraphobia
  √ Persistent fears of open spaces, leaving home, or any place where it is difficult to escape or gain help.
  √ Arises with, or without, panic attacks.
    □ Some without panic attacks have profound social phobia, PTSD, or OCD.
  √ Often occurs in the elderly.
- Social phobia
  √ Persistent and pervasive fears of being scrutinized by others.
  √ Fear of saying or doing something that will embarrass or humiliate.
  √ Fear of public speaking, public performing, and eating or urinating in public facilities.
  √ Often have physical signs of anxiety.
- Performance anxiety
  √ Significant fear in discrete and limited performing situations (e.g., giving a talk, playing an instrument).
- School phobia and separation anxiety

Medications do not usually treat discrete simple phobias such as fear of bridges, elevators, heights.

Agoraphobia may be treated by

- Alprazolam 3–6 mg/day
- Imipramine 150–300 mg/day
- Other drugs curtailing agoraphobia include
  √ Amitriptyline
  √ Clomipramine
  √ Trazodone
  √ MAOIs
  √ SSRIs
    □ Best tolerated

Discrete (specific) social phobia (performance anxiety)

- β-blockers reduce
  - √ Heart rate
  - √ Tremor
  - √ Dry mouth
  - √ "Butterflies" in stomach
  - √ Anxiety (modestly)
- β-blockers include
  - √ Metoprolol 25–50 mg
  - √ Atenolol 30–100 mg
  - √ Propranolol 10–80 mg
    - □ A trial dose of 10–80 mg propranolol should be given 2 h before anxiety-provoking performance.
    - □ First take a trial dose at home and try to vividly imagine the stressful situation.
    - □ Raise dose if initial dose did not work and side effects are not a problem.
    - □ Then try dose in real-life situation.
    - □ If this works, administer propranolol 2 h before future stressful events.
    - □ If necessary, raise dose by increments of 10 mg.
    - □ Should not be used for an athletic performance—will decrease cardiac output.
  - √ Benzodiazepines will decrease performance anxiety but also decrease performance ability.
  - √ Buspirone up to 60 mg for 6 weeks is ineffective for performance anxiety.
  - √ Maintenance for frequent occurrence of specific social phobias (e.g., walking into a classroom)
    - □ Try long-acting drug (e.g., atenolol or nadolol).
    - □ May be no better than placebo for this purpose.
- If the stressful situation is unpredictable, then chronic β-blocker use or MAOIs are needed.
  - √ MAOIs are superior to β-blockers for discrete social phobia.

Pervasive social phobia (generalized)

- Unlike performance anxiety, social phobia does not usually respond to β-blockers.
- All treatments take 6 to 10 weeks for full effect.
- SSRIs or buspirone might be first choices because of low side-effect risk and lack of physical dependence but
  - √ Less proven than MAOIs.

- MAOIs
  - √ Phenelzine seems more helpful than imipramine, amitriptyline, or atenolol.
    - □ A clear, identifiable, predictable, and specific social phobia did equally well on phenelzine and atenolol, but a more generalized social phobia showed phenelzine superior.
  - √ Phenelzine 45–90 mg/day works well in 6 weeks.
  - √ When patient taken off of phenelzine, symptoms often re-emerge.
  - √ Can reverse the most severe chronic form of social phobia, avoidant personality disorder.
    - □ May take 3–12 months to reverse.
    - □ 70% may no longer be avoidant personality disorder.
- SSRIs
  - √ Initial trials show promise rivaling MAOIs, but more evidence is needed.
    - □ In open trials 67% responded to fluoxetine.
- Buspirone
  - √ Use 45–60 mg; under 45 mg not effective.
  - √ May take 12 weeks.
- Clonazepam in doses 0.5–3 mg (means 2.4 mg/day) effective sooner.
  - √ 70% improved in 6 weeks.
    - □ Significant improvement seen in 1 week.
    - □ When maintained over 6 months, mean effective dose declined to 0.9 mg/day.
- Alprazolam 1–7 mg (2.9 mg/day) improved by 3 weeks.
  - √ No sustained improvement after withdrawal.

Elective mutism

- May be a variant of social phobia.
  - √ Fluoxetine 10–30 mg/day for 12 weeks resulted in substantial improvement.
  - √ Benzodiazepines occasionally helpful.

School phobia and separation anxiety

- Follow TCA precaution procedures for children on pages 94–95.
- SSRIs may be as effective, but as yet less proven.
- For school phobia
  - √ Start children ages 6–8 on 10 mg of imipramine at bedtime.
  - √ Start older children on 25 mg at bedtime.
  - √ Raise dose 30–50 mg/week, depending on child's age.
  - √ Maximum dose is usually around 3.5 mg/kg/day of imipramine.

- For separation anxiety
  - ✓ May benefit from 25–50 mg/day of imipramine, but in conjunction with school avoidance, may need 75 mg/day.
  - ✓ If patient does not respond to imipramine 25 mg/day, unlikely to improve on higher doses.
  - ✓ When children recover completely, it is in 6–8 weeks.
  - ✓ TCAs are rarely continued for longer than 3 months.

Obsessive-Compulsive Disorder (OCD)

Serotonergic drugs are best.

- Drop-out rates are low for OCD patients.
  - ✓ 8–15% usual range.
- 10–15% full remission.
- 70% some response.
- Average response: 40% decrease in symptoms.
- Presence of depression not a prediction of OCD response.
- Presence of tics may predict a lower response with serotonergic agent alone.
  - ✓ Adding pimozide or low-dose haloperidol can significantly increase response.
- Other predictors of poor response include
  - ✓ Fixed belief in necessity of rituals.
  - ✓ Absence of rituals (pure obsessional).
  - ✓ Severe depression.
- Non-serotonergic TCAs and trazodone have limited or no effect.
- Drug treatment best when accompanied by response prevention.
  - ✓ Response prevention alone is slightly superior to drug treatment alone.

Clomipramine is favored by more studies in treating this disorder.

- Obsessions improve more than compulsions.
  - ✓ Response prevention of compulsions is an important co-treatment.
- Dose 200–250 mg/day.
  - ✓ > 250 mg/day risks seizures.
  - ✓ Should wait 10 weeks for a full response.
- Clomipramine may reduce trichotillomania.
- Although drop-out rates are not higher than SSRIs, many patients cannot tolerate clomipramine.
  - ✓ Weight gain,
  - ✓ Excessive tremor,

√ Sweating, and
√ Serotonergic syndrome.

SSRIs

- May be first choice because of much lower side effects.
- Dose often higher than antidepressant dose.
  √ Fluoxetine 20–120 mg/day
    □ Efficacy 20 = 40 = 60 mg
  √ Sertraline 100–200 mg/day
    □ Efficacy 50 = 100 = 200 mg
  √ Paroxetine 20–50 mg/day
    □ Efficacy 20 < 40 mg
  √ Fluvoxamine 200–300 mg/day
- Higher drop-out rates with higher doses.
- Two fixed-dose fluoxetine trials showed 20 mg as good as 60 mg.
- Fluvoxamine has more studies supporting its efficacy than other SSRIs.
  √ Nausea rate is 40% and may be less well tolerated.

Overall, clomipramine and SSRIs give moderate or better improvement in up to 50% of cases.

- In treatment-resistant patients, can be combined with fluoxetine, paroxetine, or sertraline if clomipramine dose is lowered to 25–75 mg.
  √ Clomipramine 100–150 mg with sertraline or fluvoxamine.
  √ Need to carefully monitor clomipramine blood levels and interactive side effects between the 2 drugs before and after adding SSRI.

Monoamine-oxidase inhibitors (phenelzine 45–90 mg/day, tranylcypromine 10–50 mg/day) may help OCD with panic attacks or severe anxiety, social phobia, or intractible depression.

- Open studies suggest equivalent efficacy with clomipramine.
- Recommend trial if clomipramine and fluoxetine fail.

In general, antianxiety agents do not relieve OCD, but fair results from

- Clonazepam (4–10 mg/day).
  √ May be better for augmentation.
  √ In clonazepam trials improvement seen in 3 weeks.
- Buspirone (30 mg/day).
- Both may be better for augmentation.
- Once a successful treatment is found, the OCD patient will need to stay on the medication indefinitely.
  √ 85% relapse rate seen within 2 months of quitting medication.

Possible augmentations for OCD include

- Buspirone (30 mg/day) positive in open trials, but controlled studies have not shown efficacy.
  √ Can try if patient generally anxious.
- Lithium
  √ No better than placebo in controlled study.
  √ Some positive case studies reported.
  √ Try if patient is still depressed.
- The anorectic serotonin releaser fenfluramine (20–60 mg/day)
  √ Neurotoxicity of serotonin neurons reported in animal studies.
  √ Not generally recommended.
- The antipsychotic pimozide (6 mg/day) or haloperidol, especially for patients with tics or schizotypal or psychotic features.
- Stimulants (methylphenidate or dextroamphetamine) may help response.
  √ Dextroamphetamine may be more effective than methyphenidate.

Obsessive-Compulsive Spectrum Disorders

These disorders share many features of OCD.

- Those most closely resembling OCD have unpleasant obsessions.
  √ Hypochondriasis
  √ Pathological jealousy
  √ Body dysmorphic disorder
    □ Open trials successful with clomipramine, fluoxetine, or fluvoxamine
  √ Bulimia
    □ Has some impulsive component
    □ See Antidepressants, pages 109–110
- Those that are like OCD but have a strong pleasure-impulsive component and may better be called impulsive-compulsive disorders are
  √ Trichotillomania
    □ Neuroleptics ineffective
  √ Anorexia nervosa
    □ May respond to fluoxetine 60 mg qd
    □ See Antidepressants, page 109
  √ Gambling
  √ Paraphilias
  √ Sexual "addictions"
- Uncontrolled and a few controlled trials suggest that both types

(predominantly obsessive and predominantly impulsive) initially respond to serotonergic ADs after 8–12 weeks.
√ Preliminary data suggest that the more compulsive types maintain a response while the impulsive types do not.

Hypochondriasis

- May be a variant of OCD.
- Open trial of 14 patients with high-dose fluoxetine (52 mg average) resulted in 10 responders after 12 weeks.
  √ Disease phobia and disease conviction decreased, but not bodily preoccupation.

Paraphilias

- Open trials of fluoxetine suggest that the paraphilic behavior decreases while normal sexual behavior continues.
- Decrease in overall sexual drive as a side effect may contribute to success.
- Controlled trials of antiandrogens (e.g., cyproterone acetate 50–200 mg/day suppresses sexual
  √ Arousal
  √ Fantasy
  √ Activity

Body dysmorphic disorder (BDD)

- SSRIs may help if the belief is an overvalued idea but not fully delusional.
- If delusional, addition of pimozide and perhaps any antipsychotic (e.g., haloperidol) is recommended.
- Patients who consider their body ugly because of its gender, but don't have sexual identity of the other gender, may better be treated as having BDD and not as transexuals needing surgery.

Post-Traumatic Stress Disorder (PTSD)

There is no clear drug treatment for PTSD.

Successful treatment usually associated with 2–6 month (not 4-week) trials. Also, high doses tend to be used.

The positive symptoms of PTSD—re-experiencing the past and increased arousal—respond better than the negative symptoms—avoidance and withdrawal.

More positive findings stem from MAOIs and SSRIs. Both work on intrusion, numbing, and social withdrawal. Amitriptyline may also have similar effects. Specific reported treatments include

- Sertraline (50–150 mg/day)
- Fluoxetine (20–80 mg/day)
  - √ Also diminishes rage reactions.
  - √ Better than imipramine for intrusive symptoms and avoidance.
- Phenelzine (40–90 mg/day)
- Amitriptyline (50–300 mg day)
  - √ Better than placebo for positive distress symptoms as well as for avoidance.
- Imipramine 200–300 mg/day
  - √ Better than placebo for intrusive symptoms but not avoidance.

Try the drug trial for 6–8 weeks.
If it does not work, the next approach depends on the other symptoms.

Drug Treatment of PTSD Symptoms

Symptoms	Drug	Dose
Behaviors		
Irritability, aggression, impulsive-ness, or flashbacks	Carbamazepine	600–1800 mg/day
	Valproic acid	750–1500 mg/day
Startle, hyperarousal, autonomic hyperexcitability	Benzodiazepines	usual dose range
	Propranolol	40–1500 mg/day
	Buspirone	40–80 mg/day
	Clonidine	0.2–0.4 mg/day
	Carbamazepine, Valproic acid	see above
Sleep disturbance, nightmares	Trazodone	50–400 mg qhs
	Zolpidem	10–15 mg qhs
	Phenelzine	30–90 mg/day
	Benzodiazepine, Clonidine, Carbamazepine, Propranolol	see above
Feelings		
Anger, anxiety	Buspirone	40–90 mg
	Lithium*	600–1800 mg
	Trazodone	100–600 mg

* Not anxiety

Clonidine and buprenorphine prn may reduce self-mutilatory behavior.

Benzodiazepines risk dependence/abuse in this population who are frequently alcohol and drug abusers.

- If used, long-acting medium-slow onset drug preferred (e.g., clonazepam 1–5 mg).
- Possible disinhibitory behavior can occur, particularly with initiation of treatment.
- Eventual withdrawal very difficult.

Migraine

- Prophylaxis with propranolol 80 mg bid or tid.
- May take 4–6 weeks for full efficacy.
- SSRIs, TCAs, and MAOIs all reported to be effective.
  √ More than 60% get at least 50% reduction in headache frequency within 4 weeks.

Nicotine Abuse

Hypnosis, nicotine gum, and gradual substitution with lower nicotine-containing cigarettes help only a few smokers.

Nicotine-containing gum and nicotine patches are preferred approaches to withdrawal.

- Nicotine gum not well accepted.
  √ Patient must chew but not swallow saliva.
  √ If saliva is swallowed, more gastric discomfort and less efficacy.

Clonidine 0.2–0.4 mg may substantially decrease anxiety and craving—that is, the mental preoccupation with smoking. However, clonidine may generate sedation and hypotension, which restricts its use to normotensive patients. Rate of nicotine cessation about the same as placebos.

Alprazolam 1.0 mg relieves anxiety, but risks benzodiazepine abuse.

Buspirone (started at 15–30 mg/day and increased to 40–50 mg/day) reduced, but did not stop, smoking in 7/8 subjects.

Bupropion 300 mg in 190 nondepressed treatment failures (e.g., nicotine patch, clonidine, support) yielded

- At 4 weeks 40% abstainers vs. 24% on placebo.
- At 23 weeks, 28% abstainers vs. 21% on placebo.

Treatment-failure nicotine abusers have high rates of prior major depressive episodes and depression relapses when attempting abstinence.

- SSRIs or bupropion recommended in this subgroup, but hard data sparse.
  √ Fluoxetine prevents smoking-cessation-associated carbohydrate cravings, weight gain, and dysphoric mood.

Catatonia

Symptoms include:

- Immobility, mutism, withdrawal/refusal to eat, posturing, grimacing occur in ≥ 75% of cases.

- Staring, rigidity, and negativism in $\geq$ 50% of cases.
- Waxy flexibility, stereotypy, echolalia/echopraxia, and verbigeration in < 50% of cases.

Causes of catatonia

- CNS syndromes are the most common causes.
  - ✓ "CNS" includes medication-induced (neuroleptic-induced).
- Mood disorder most often bipolar or psychotic depression.
- Schizophrenia less common cause.

Acute treatment of catatonia

- Lorazepam 1–2 mg IM prn frequently treats symtoms.
  - ✓ Allows patient to talk, eat, and move.
    - □ Reduces risk of starvation, dehydration, pulmonary emboli.
    - □ Ability to speak increases accuracy of diagnosis—e.g., grandiose thoughts (mania), nihilistic delusions (psychotic depression), confused thinking (delirium), etc.

Maintenance treatment of catatonia

- Benzodiazepine may be continued adjunctively with specific treatment of underlying disorder.
- Lorazepam can be continued orally 1–2 mg q 4–6 h.
- Clonazepam 0.5–1 mg bid can be substituted for lorazepam to provide more sustained effects.

SIDE EFFECTS

Cardiovascular Effects

Hypotension, dizziness, lightheadedness

- Clonidine, propranolol, and sometimes trazodone can induce serious hypotension.
  - ✓ Hypotension milder with benzodiazepines, buspirone, fluoxetine, and venlafaxine than with antipsychotics, TCAs, MAOIs, clonidine, or propranolol.
  - ✓ Hypotension becomes no worse after propranolol > 500 mg/day.
- Management
  - ✓ Measure BPs reclining and standing, before and during, the first few days of clonidine or propranolol.
  - ✓ Increase dose more slowly.
  - ✓ Have patient deal with hypotension by
    - □ Sitting a full 60 seconds—or longer—if at all lightheaded,

        □ Standing slowly while holding onto stable object (e.g., bed), and

        □ Waiting at least 30 seconds before walking.

   √ See pages 22, 114–115, for further management.

Bradycardia

- Propranolol and other β-blockers can cause bradycardia at modest doses.
  - √ Check pulse at rest and after brief exercise.
  - √ Consider decreased dose if resting pulse is under 60/min or exercise pulse is under 110/min.
- If doesn't develop at lower doses, rarely a difficulty after reaching 300–500 mg/day.

Bronchospasm

- Do not give propranolol to asthmatics.
  - √ Stop propranolol if patients start wheezing.
  - √ Consider a more selective agent (e.g., acetabutalol, atenolol, metoprolol, or betazolol) if a β-blocker is necessary.

Raynaud's phenomena

- Cold fingers and toes.
- Do not give β-blocker if patient has history of Raynaud's.

Gastrointestinal Effects

Dry mouth, nasal congestion (see pages 22–23)

- Most common with clonidine, benzodiazepines, and hydroxyzine.
- Nasal congestion alone occurs with trazodone.

Constipation (see page 23)

Renal Effects

Urinary hesitancy or retention (see page 24)

Eyes, Ears, Nose, and Throat

Blurred near vision (see page 27)

- Mild and rare with usual anxiolytics.
  - √ Bethanechol 5–20 mg po tid or qid.

ANTIANXIETY AGENTS

Dry eyes (see page 28)

Narrow-angle glaucoma worsening

- Occurs on several benzodiazepines (e.g., clonazepam, alprazolam).

Central Nervous System Effects

Stuttering

- Mainly with alprazolam.

Incoordination, ataxia

- Occurs with high doses of benzodiazepines.
  - √ Arises in 25% of patients on ≥ 10 mg/day of clonazepam.
- In regular doses, only with meprobamate.

Sedation

- Common for benzodiazepines, clonidine, and propranolol.
  - √ For instance, clonazepam produces drowsiness 50% of the time.
  - √ Buspirone does not normally sedate, although a single 20–40 mg dose can exhaust people.
- Management
  - √ Reduce dose.
  - √ Increase dose slowly.
  - √ With clonidine give ⅔ daily dose q hs and ⅓ q A.M.
  - √ Sedation should be significantly less after 7–14 days on benzodiazepine and after 21 days on clonidine.

Confusion, disorientation, clouded sensorium

- Occurs primarily in the elderly, cognitively impaired, or brain-damaged.
  - √ Caused by small doses of benzodiazepines,
  - √ Often reversible, and
  - √ Misdiagnosed as dementia.
- On propranolol, not dose-related.
  - √ Can be due to chronic, relative hypotension (e.g., severe hypertensive corrected to low "normal").

Amnesia

- Anterograde amnesia especially with IV diazepam and lorazepam.
- Directly related to speed of onset of benzodiazepine.

Rage reactions, anger

- Violent episodes with, or without, a h/o violence.
- Observed with alprazolam and diazepam.

- √ May be more common with fast onset benzodiazepines with a "buzz."
- √ May be secondary to acute disinhibition.
- √ Less with oxazepam.
- Treat instead with haloperidol 5 mg/IM, trazodone 25–200 mg, propranolol, or carbamazepine.

Excitement

- Paradoxical reactions more often occur in children, the elderly, cognitively impaired or brain-damaged.
- Disinhibition (as with alcohol) occurs more often below sedative doses.

Depression

- Occurs most often with
  - √ Propranolol (high doses)—only twice normal rate.
  - √ Symptoms often appear in days.
  - √ Patient usually doesn't report symptoms for weeks.
- Occurs more often with
  - √ Benzodiazepine doses, e.g., > 30 mg diazepam equivalent.
  - √ More common in high-potency benzodiazepines because it is easier to get "high" doses.
    - □ Clonazepam > 1.5 mg
    - □ Alprazolam > 3 mg
    - □ Lorazepam > 4–6 mg
  - √ At these doses there may be 25% rate of new depressions in panic disorder patients within 6 weeks.
  - √ Probably not unique to any particular benzodiazepine.
  - √ Also seen on equivalent quantities of alcohol (i.e., 5–6 drinks/beers a day).
- Can escalate into
  - √ Neurovegetative signs of depression.
  - √ Catatonia.

Manic reactions

- Most often reported with alprazolam.

PERCENTAGES OF SIDE EFFECTS

Side Effects	Benzodiazepines	Buspirone	Clonidine	Propranolol
CARDIOVASCULAR EFFECTS				
Hypotension	4.7	< 1	11.5	9.9
Hypertension	0.0	< 1	0.0	0.0
Dizziness, lightheadedness	13.4 (6.8–30)	13.6 (10–30)	18 (10–30)	10.5 (1.5–30)

Percentages of Side Effects (Cont.)

Side Effects	Benzodiazepines	Buspirone	Clonidine	Propranolol
Fainting, syncope	3.1	< 1	—	5
Tachycardia	7.7	1.3*	0.5	—
Palpitations	7.7	1	0.5	—
Bradycardia	< 1	< 1	0.5	20.7
Raynaud's phenomena	0.0	0.0	+	+
Congestive heart failure	0.0	< 0.1	+	+
Shortness of breath	< 1	< 1	—	5.6
Chest pain	—	1.5	3.3	4
Cold hands and feet	—	—	—	20
Cardiac arrhythmias	0.0	0.0	5.5	0.0
Hyperventilation	—	< 1	—	—
Bronchospasm	0.0	0.0	0.0	+
Edema	—	—	—	9 (2–16)
GASTROINTESTINAL EFFECTS				
Dry mouth and throat	12.6 (10.5–14.7)	5.3* (1–10)	22.8 (1–40)	—
Salivation	4.2	< 1	—	—
Anorexia, lower appetite	+	< 1	5.5	16.6 (1.5–23.5)
Increased appetite	—	< 1	—	—
Nausea, vomiting	7.4 (1–10)	10.8 (6–30)	5.4 (1–10)	14.8 (1.5–23.5)
Gas	—	< 1	—	4
Diarrhea	7 (1–10.1)	2.5	—	12.5
Constipation	7.1 (1–10.4)	1.3* —	7.8 (1–10)	3.8 (1–10)
Incontinence	+	0.0	0.0	0.0
Jaundice	< 1	—	—	—
Hepatitis	0.0	0.0	1	0.0
Weight gain	2.7	+	3.3	—
Weight loss	2.3	—	—	—
RENAL EFFECTS				
Urinary hesitancy or retention	< 1	< 1	0.1	—
Painful urination	< 1	< 1	—	—
Urinary frequency	—	< 1	0.2	1
Nocturia	0.0	< 0.1	1	0.0
ENDOCRINE AND SEXUAL EFFECTS				
Breast swelling	—	—	2.8	—
Disturbed sexual function	11	< 1	4.3	8.7
Menstrual irregularities	0.0	< 1	0.0	0.0
HEMATOLOGIC EFFECTS				
Agranulocytosis	—	—	—	+
Bleeding, bruising easily	—	< 1	—	< 1

Percentages of Side Effects (Cont.)

Side Effects	Benzodiazepines	Buspirone	Clonidine	Propranolol
EYES, EARS, NOSE, AND THROAT EFFECTS				
Burning, itching eyes	+	< 1	6	0.0
Blurred vision	10.6 (1–20.8)	2	5	1.5
Diplopia	+	0.0	0.0	+
Dry eyes	—	—	5.5	+
Vertigo	+	0.0	0.0	0.0
Tinnitus	—	5.5	—	—
Nasal stuffiness	7.3	—	—	—
Painful neck glands	—	—	+	+
SKIN, ALLERGIES, AND TEMPERATURE				
Allergies	3.8	—	+	0.4
Rashes	5.5	1	< 1	1.4
Itch	5.5	< 1	< 1	—
Abnormal skin pigment	—	—	0.2	—
Joint pain	—	—	—	5.5
Fever, hyperthermia	—	< 1	—	< 1
Sweating	—	1	—	—
Laryngospasm/bron-chospasm	0.0	0.0	0.0	+
Angioneurotic edema	0.0	0.0	+	0.0
Edema/facial edema	—	< 1	—	—
Hair loss	—	< 1	+	+
Sore throat	0.0	> 1	0.0	+
CENTRAL NERVOUS SYSTEM EFFECTS				
Weakness, fatigue	17.7 (7.7–42)	7.6 (4–16)	6.3 (4–10)	17 (1.5–29.4)
Muscle cramps	—	1	0.6	2
Uncontrollable limb jerks	—	< 1	—	—
Seizures	—	< 1	—	—
Paresthesias	—	< 1	—	20
Numbness	—	1.4	—	20
Headache	9.1 (5.3–12.9)	10.6 (6–30)	3.3 (1–30)	8.4 (1–17.6)
Ataxia, clumsiness, incoor-dination	17.6 (5–79)	2.5	—	—
Slurred speach	+	< 1	—	—
Tremor	4	1	—	—
Memory loss	+	—	—	11.8
Drowsiness, sedation	35.1 (6.8–77)	12.4 (1–24)	30.8 (10–64)	15 (1.5–30)
Mania, hypomania	+	< 1	—	—
Stuttering	+	—	—	—
Confusion, disorientation	6.9 (1–10)	2.0	+	4.5
Insomnia	6.4	6.7*	3	5.3
Weird dreams	+	5.5	+	4.3 (1–10)
Hallucinations	5.5	< 1	—	5.5

ANTIANXIETY AGENTS

Percentages of Side Effects (Cont.)

Side Effects	Benzodiazepines	Buspirone	Clonidine	Propranolol
Anxiety, nervousness (mental)	4.1	5	3	——
Agitation, restlessness (motoric)	+	20	3	——
Irritable, hostile, angry	5.5	2	——	0.0
Excitement	+	2	——	——
Depression	8.3 (1–13.9)	1.4*	0.8	8.9 (0.1–50)

* Not greater than placebo; + Side effect occurs, but incidence not reported; —— data not available, presumed to be rare.

PREGNANCY AND LACTATION

Teratogenicity
(1st trimester)

- Well-controlled prospective studies with low-potency benzodiazepines (e.g., diazepam, chlordiazepoxide) do *not* show an increased rate of any congenital anomaly, including cleft palate.

- There is no data that other, higher-potency benzodiazepines cause congenital anomalies, but these agents have been insufficiently studied.

- Buspirone does not appear to be teratogenic in animals, but its risk in humans has not been studied.

- The little data on behavioral teratogenicity in humans suggest that there are no long-term behavioral or cognitive effects from *in utero* benzodiazepine exposure.

- When possible, use behavioral techniques, psychotherapy, and caffeine abstinence to manage anxiety.

- Patients should stop benzodiazepines at least 3–4 weeks before attempting to conceive and should remain off them until the first trimester ends.

- Seemingly benign anti-anxiety alternatives (e.g., diphenhydramine) have been associated with increased oral cleft abnormalities and are not recommended.

• If medication is necessary for panic attacks during the first trimester, imipramine may be slightly safer than high-potency benzodiazepines.

Direct Effect on Newborn (3rd trimester)

• Panic disorder typically continues during pregnancy.
√ It is associated with higher rates of pre-eclampsia, preterm labor, prolonged labor, stillbirths, fetal hypoxia, and newborns with lower Apgar scores.

• Hepatically metabolized benzodiazepines (e.g., diazepam) are slowly metabolized by the fetus and neonate and are not recommended.
√ With chronic diazepam administration, cord plasma concentrations are higher than maternal plasma concentrations.
√ The shorter-acting benzodiazpine, lorazepam, develops lower concentrations in cord blood than in maternal blood and may be preferred.

• Benzodiazepines can prolong labor.

• Benzodiazepines, especially in higher doses (e.g., over 25 mg diazepam equivalents), can cause floppy infant syndrome with lethargy, hypotonia, poor sucking, hyporeflexia, apnea, and/or cyanosis.
√ Combining benzodiazepines with narcotics may cause additional floppy infant symptoms.
√ For clonazepam the hypotonia and lethargy typically resolve in 5 days; apnea may persist for 10 days.

• Benzodiazepines may precipitate newborn withdrawal with jitters, tremors, or jerking of extremities, hypertonia, hyperreflexia, vomiting, diarrhea, restlessness, irritability, abnormal sleep patterns, inconsolable crying, chewing movements, bradycardia, and cyanosis.
√ Withdrawal appears within a few days (for lorazepam) to 3 weeks (for chlordiazepoxide, clonazepam) after birth and may continue up to several months.

• To avoid withdrawal, taper and discontinue benzodiazepines before delivery.

ANTIANXIETY AGENTS

- If anxiety risks higher obstetrical complications (e.g., pre-eclampsia), use the best studied benzodiazepines—chlordiazepoxide, diazepam, or lorazepam.
  - √ As easily metabolized and eliminated benzodiazepines, lorazepam and oxazepam have a theoretical but unproven safety advantage for pre-eclampsia.
  - √ Don't use parenteral diazepam with sodium benzoate as a preservative.
    - □ Sodium benzoate can prevent bilirubin binding to serum albumin and cause kernicterus.

- Propranolol (and other β-blockers, e.g., atenolol) may foster intrauterine growth retardation, hypoglycemia, bradycardia, and respiratory depression at birth, and hyperbilirubinemia in neonates.
  - √ If mother already on β-blockers, closely monitor birth for 24–48 h.

- If indicated (e.g., panic attacks), use imipramine or other tricyclic antidepressants instead of benzodiazepines in the last month(s) before delivery.

Lactation

- Benzodiazepines enter breast milk, may addict newborn, and induce withdrawal.

- Benzodiazepines can impair alertness and temperature regulation.

- With longer-acting benzodiazepines, effects persist 2–3 weeks in infants.

- Diazepam accumulates in breast milk, causing sedation, weight loss, respiratory depression, and withdrawal in newborns. Women on diazepam should avoid breast-feeding.

- Clonazepam flows into breast milk. Although it does not accumulate, its half-life is extended, which might encourage apnea. For any infant exposed to clonazepam, useful to monitor serum levels and to check for CNS depression.

- Meprobamate in milk is 2–4 times that of maternal plasma.

- Propranolol is excreted in breast milk; effects unclear.

- Infant oxazepam concentrations are lowest of the benzodiazepines, usually under < 10% of the maternal plasma concentrations.

- For maximum safety, if the mother continues benzodiazepines, assay the baby's plasma level after breast-feeding a week.
  √ Only zero or negligible levels are acceptable.

Drug Dosage in Mother's Milk

Generic Names	Milk/ Plasma Ratio	Time of Peak Concentration in Milk (hours)	Infant Dose (μg/kg/day)	Maternal Dose (%)	Safety Rating*
Clonazepam	?	?	2†	1.3–3.0‡	C
Clonidine	?	?	0.41	7.8	E
Clorazepate	?	?	2.3	?	?
Diazepam	0.16	?	3.3–11.7	2–2.3	B
Hydralazine	?	?	20	0.8	A
Lorazepam	?	?	1.3	2.2	B
Oxazepam	?	1.5	4.5	0.9	A
Prazepam	0.11	22	13.4**	3.2***	B
Propranolol	0.32–0.76	2–5	1.4–11.2	0.2–0.9	A

* A: Safe throughout infancy (probably safe = infant maximum plasma concentration < 10% maternal plasma concentration); B: Reasonably unsafe before 34 weeks, but probably safer after 34 weeks; C: Reasonably unsafe before week 44, but safer after 44 weeks; E: Unsafe up to 34th week because infant plasma concentration approaches and may exceed the mother's, reasonably unsafe from weeks 34–68, and safest after 68th week.
† Infant therapeutic dose 20–200 μg/kg/day.
‡ Maternal dose not specified, but presumed to be 20–200 μg/kg/day.
** Metabolite N-desmethyldiazepam measured.
*** Assuming 100% conversion to metabolite.

DRUG-DRUG INTERACTIONS*°

Drugs (X) Interact with:	Benzo- diazepines (B)	Comments
* Alcohol	X ↑ B ↑	Potentiate each other; with alcohol, shorter-acting benzodiazepines produce less harm than longer-acting ones. Alcohol escalates suicide risk from benzodiazepines.
Aluminum hydroxide (*see* antacids)		
Aminophylline (*see* bronchodilators)		
Amiodarone	B ↑	Increases clonazepam and probably other oxidatively metabolized benzodiazepines.**

Drugs (X) Interact with:	Benzo- diazepines (B)	Comments
Antacids (aluminum hydroxide, magnesium hydroxide)	B ↓	Slows rate but not total amount of GI absorption. Probable clinical effect is to slow onset, perhaps peak magnitude of effect, and prolong duration of effect of single doses. In single but not repeated doses, interfered with transformation of clorazepate to desmethyldiazepam.
Anticholinergics (includes all drugs with anticholinergic properties)	B ↓	Slows time to peak absorption, but not total amount absorbed.
Antifungal imidazoles (see ketoconazole)		
Barbiturates (see also sedatives)	X ↑ B ↓ ↑	Phenobarbital (and probably others) speed benzodiazepine metabolism and lower levels. Potentiate each other's effects.
* Birth control pills	B ↑ ↓	Oral contraceptives may increase 2-keto and triazolo compounds while reducing 3-hydroxy agents.**
Bronchodilators: Aminophylline Theophylline	B ↓	Aminophylline and theophylline rapidly antagonize diazepam, lorazepam, and probably other benzodiazepine effects;.increase benzodiazepine doses.
Caffeine	B ↓	Caffeine (250–500 mg) antagonizes benzodiazepines.
Carbamazepine	B ↓	Decreases alprazolam and clonazepam levels 20–50%.
* Cimetidine	B ↑	Cimetidine may increase most oxidatively metabolized benzodiazepines—(not 3-hydroxy agents**) and raise benzodiazepine's side effects. Ranitidine and famotidine appear less apt to interact with benzodiazepines than cimetidine.
Digitalis	B ↑	Increases benzodiazepines, including diazepam, clonazepam, and alprazolam.
Digoxin	X ↑	Digoxin serum levels increased; monitor levels.
* Disulfiram	B ↑ ↓	Increases oxidatively metabolized benzodiazepine** levels (not 3-hydroxy agents) and sedation. May need to lower benzodiazepines or switch to 3-hydroxy agents.**
Erythromycin (see macrolide antibiotics)		
Estrogen (see birth control pills)		
Fluconazole (see ketoconazole)		
Fluoxetine (and probably paroxetine and sertraline)	B ↑	Increases levels of diazepam and alprazolam and probably other oxidatively metabolized benzodiazepines except clonazepam or triazolam (and probably not lorazepam or oxazepam).

Drugs (X) Interact with:	Benzo-diazepines (B)	Comments
Food	B ↓	Slows absorption; for rapid effect, take on empty stomach.
Isoniazid (INH)	B ↑	INH increases effects of benzodiazepines that require oxidative metabolism**; lower benzo-diazepine dose or switch to 3-hydroxy benzo-diazepines.**
Ketoconazole: Fluconazole Miconazole Trazonazole	B ↑	Increases oxidatively metabolized ben-zodiazepines** but not hydroxy.**
Levodopa (L-dopa)	X ↓	Benzodiazepines may reduce antiparkinson ef-fect; seen with triazolam and temazepam. Oxazepam and flurazepam have not caused this problem. Carbidopa-levodopa agents may help. Monitor, and if parkinsonism wors-ens, stop benzodiazepines.
Magnesium hydroxide (*see* antacids)		
MAOIs	B ↑	Greater intoxication with increased benzodi-azepine levels.
* *Macrolide antibi-otics:* Clarithromycin Erythromycin Flurithromycin Josamycin Ponsinormycin Troleandomycin	B ↑	Decreases clearance of triazolo-benzodi-azepines (alprazolam, triazolam, estazolam); increases benzodiazepine levels and toxicity. Spiramycin okay. Azithromycin possibly okay.
Metoprolol	B ↑	Metoprolol may slightly increase 3-keto com-pounds.** Minimal clinical changes noted; does not occur with atenolol.
Miconazole (*see* ketoconazole)		
Paroxetine (*see* fluoxetine)		
Phenytoin (*see also* sedatives)	B ↑ ↓	Possibly increases benzodiazepine levels, in-cluding diazepam and clonazepam; may in-crease oxazepam clearance with decreased levels.
Physostigmine	B ↓	Reverses benzodiazepine effects; sometimes used after benzodiazepine OD.
Primidone (*see* sedatives)		
Probenecid	B ↑ ↓	Probenecid may increase lorazepam and its side effects. May affect other benzodiaze-pines, but more likely other 3-hydroxy com-pounds.**
Propoxyphene	B ↑	May increase oxidatively metabolized benzodi-azepines (*not* 3-hydroxys).**
Propranolol	B ↑	Propranolol may slightly increase 3-keto com-pounds.** Minimal clinical changes noted; does not occur with atenolol.

ANTIANXIETY AGENTS

Drugs (X) Interact with:	Benzo-diazepines (B)	Comments
Rifampin	B ↓	Reduces diazepam's effects, and probably other oxidatively metabolized benzodiazepines (*not* 3-hydroxy agents).** May need to increase benzodiazepine.
Sedatives (alcohol, antihistamines, sedative-hypnotics, TCAs, low-potency antipsychotics)	X ↑ B ↑	Potentiate each other's sedative effects. Disinhibition increased with alcohol and barbiturates (including primidone).
Sertaline (*see* fluoxetine)		
SSRIs (*see* fluoxetine)		
Theophylline (*see* bronchodilators)		
Tobacco smoking	B ↓	Decreases benzodiazepine levels; increase benzodiazepines or don't smoke.
Traconazole (*see* ketoconazole)		
Valproic acid	B ↑	Valproic acid increases unbound diazepam levels and may inhibit its metabolism while increasing its effects. May also increase levels of other oxidatively metabolized benzodiazepines.**

Drugs (X) Interact with:	Alprazolam (A)	Comments
TCAs	X ↑	Increases TCA levels (20–30%).

Drugs (X) Interact with:	Antihistamines (A) (e.g., diphenhydramine/ hydroxyzine)	Comments
Alcohol	X ↑ A ↑	CNS depression.
Anticholinergics (*see also* pages 61, 69 for list)	X ↑ A ↑	Increased anticholinergic effects.
Antipsychotics	X ↓ A ↑	Hydroxyzine might block antipsychotic actions. Increased CNS depression; increased anticholinergic effects.
Narcotics	X ↑ A ↑	CNS depression.
TCAs	X ↑ A ↑	CNS depression; increased anticholinergic effects.
Sedatives (benzodiazepines, barbiturates)	X ↑ A ↑	CNS depression.

Drugs (X) Interact with:	Buspirone (B)	Comments
Cimetidine	B ↑	May see more minor side effects (e.g., light-headedness).
Food	B ↓ ↑	Decreases absorption speed but increases total amount in body.
Haloperidol	X ↑	Increased haloperidol levels.
MAOI	X ↑	Case reports of elevated BP; do not use together.

Drugs (X) Interact with:	Clonazepam (C)	Comments
Barbiturates	C ↑ ↓	Phenobarbital slightly decreases clonazepam level, but effect is unclear.
Carbamazepine	C ↓	In 5–15 days, carbamazepine may diminish clonazepam by 19–37%. Seizure effect unknown. Unclear if other benzodiazepines react to carbamazepine like clonzepam. Pure 3-hydroxy compounds (lorazepam, oxazepam, temazepam) are less apt to react similarly.** If combine drugs, check carbamazepine levels.
Phenytoin	C ↓	Phenytoin lowers plasma clonazepam, but effect is unclear.
Primidone	C ↓	Primidone may slightly decrease clonazepam level, but effect is unknown.

Drugs (X) Interact with:	Clonidine (C)	Comments
Acebutolol	X ↑ C ↑	Potentiate each other.
Alcohol	X ↑ C ↑	Enhanced sedation and decreased BP.
Antipsychotics	X ↑ C ↑ ↓	Isolated, severe hypotension or delirium, but scanty evidence. More common in patients with impaired cardiac function. May decrease hypotensive effect.
β-blockers (see acebutolol)		
Caffeine	C ↓	Diminished clonidine effect.
Cocaine	X ↑ C ↓	BP rise.
Diuretics	X ↑ C ↑	BP drop.
Enalapril	X ↑	May accelerate potassium loss.
Fenfluramine	C ↑	Possible increased clonidine effect.
Insulin	X ↓	Hyperglycemia; alert patient.
Labetolol	X ↓ C ↓	Precipitous BP drop if both drugs are stopped together.
Levodopa	X ↓	Parkinsonian symptoms may emerge; combine carefully.
Lithium	X ↓	Can decrease hypotensive effect.
Marijuana	X ↑ C ↑	Weakness on standing.
Naloxone	C ↓	May reduce clonidine's antihypertensive action; if so, change clonidine to another antihypertensive or stop the narcotic antagonist.
Nicotinic acid (Niacin)	X ↓	Clonidine may inhibit nicotinic flushing; no special precautions.

ANTIANXIETY AGENTS

Drugs (X) Interact with:	Clonidine (C)	Comments
Nitrates	C ↑	BP drop.
Nitroprusside	C ↑	A few cases of severe hypotensive reactions; be alert to them.
*Propranolol	X ↑	(*See also* propranolol-clonidine below.)
*TCAs	C ↑ ↓	TCAs, especially imipramine and desipramine, may lead to hypotension. TCAs more often may decrease clonidine's effects and may augment the hypertensive response to abrupt clonidine withdrawal. Maprotiline may interfere less with clonidine than might TCAs, although little clinical evidence. Consider alternative antihypertensive. Carefully monitor patients when clonidine is reduced. Gradually tapering clonidine might lower risk.

Drugs (X) Interact with:	Clorazepate (C)	Comments
Primidone	X ↑	Combined use may cause depression, irritability, and aggressive behavior.

Drugs (X) Interact with:	Diazepam (D)	Comments
Ciprofloxacin	D ↑	Increased levels.
Digitalis, digoxin	X ↑	Diazepam may increase digoxin and digitalis.
Gallamine	X ↑	Prolonged neuromuscular blockade.
Isoniazid (INH)	D ↑	INH may increase diazepam; observe combination.
Succinylcholine	X ↓	Reduces neuromuscular blockade and its side effects (i.e., fasciculations, muscle pain, increased potassium, and CPK).

Drugs (X) Interact with:	Lorazepam (L)	Comments
Loxapine	X ↑ L ↑	Isolated respiratory depression, stupor, and hypotension; switch one drug.
Scopolamine	X ↑ L ↑	IM lorazepam may increase sedation, hallucinations, and irrational behavior.

Drugs (X) Interact with:	Meprobamate (M)	Comments
* Alcohol	X ↑ M ↑	Concurrent use induces CNS depression. More than 2 drinks (90–120 ml of 100-proof whiskey) and 200–400 mg of meprobamate usually cause problems. Long-term alcohol ingestion raises tolerance to meprobamate.

Drugs (X) Interact with:	β-Blockers Propranolol (P)	Comments
Acebutolol	X ↑ P ↑	Increased antihypertensive effects of both drugs; adjust doses.

Drugs (X) Interact with:	β-Blockers Propranolol (P)	Comments
Albuterol	X↓ P↓	Decreased albuterol and β-adrenergic blocking effects. Avoid propranolol in bronchospastic disease; cardioselective agents safer.
Alcohol	P↑ ↓	May see variable changes in BP; no special precautions. Slows rate of propranolol absorption.
* Aluminum and magnesium hydroxides	P↓	Aluminum and magnesium hydroxides decrease β-blockers, such as propranolol (60%), atenolol hydroxides (35%), and metoprolol (25%). Clinical results unclear. Avoid combination; otherwise, ingest antacids and propranolol one hour apart. Calcium carbonates may be okay.
Amiodarone	P↑	Bradycardia, arrhythmias.
* Anesthetics	X↑	β-blockers and local anesthetics, particularly those containing epinephrine, can enhance sympathomimetic side effects. Acute discontinuation of blockers prior to local anesthesia may increase anesthetic's side effects. Do not stop chronic β-blockers before using local anesthetics. Avoid local anesthetics containing epinephrine in patients on propranolol.
Anticholinergics	P↓	ACAs can block β-blockers' bradycardia.
†Antidiabetics	X↑ P↓	Blunted recovery from both hypo- and hyperglycemia; decreased tachycardia. Cardioselective β-blockers, such as metoprolol, acebutolol, and atenolol, are preferable in diabetics, especially if prone to hypoglycemia.
Antihistamines	X↓	Decreased antihistaminic effect.
Antihypertensives	X↑	Increased antihypertensive effect.
Anti-inflammatory agents	X↓	Decreased anti-inflammatory effect.
* Antipsychotics (see also anticholinergic)	X↑ P↑	Increased antipsychotic levels with chlorpromazine, thioridazine, thiothixene, resulting in increase of each other's effects, such as hypotension, toxicity, and seizures. Monitor serum levels or decrease dose. Propranolol level not affected.
Antipyrine	X↑	Propranolol, and possibly metoprolol, may increase antipyrine.
* Barbiturates	P↓	Barbiturates may lower propranolol.
β-blockers (see acebutolol) Benzodiazepines (see benzodiazepine-Propranolol above, page 295)		
Calcium channel-blockers: *Bepridil *Dilitiazem *Verapamil	X↑	Bradycardia, heart block, increased left ventricular and diastolic pressure, particularly in those with conduction abnormalities or left ventricular dysfunctioning. Calcium channel-blockers, such as dilitiazem and verapamil, generally potentiate β-blockers. Using nifedipine precludes increase of β-blocker effects on atrioventricular node conduction.

ANTIANXIETY AGENTS

Drugs (X) Interact with:	β-Blockers Propranolol (P)	Comments
		β-blockers not metabolized (e.g., atenolol) should also prevent this pharmacokinetic interaction.
Carbamazepine	P ↓	Might induce β-blocker metabolism and decrease propranolol; combine with caution.
Chlorpromazine	X ↑ P ↑	Levels of both increase.
* Cimetidine (see etinidine)		
* Clonidine	X ↑	β-blockers can aggravate rebound hypertension in patients withdrawn from clonidine within 24–72 h. Symptoms include tremor, insomnia, nausea, flushing, and headaches. Patients receiving propranolol with clonidine should be withdrawn from propranolol *before* the clonidine to reduce danger of rebound hypertension. Noncardioselective β-blockers more likely to cause this reaction than cardioselective β-blockers. Metprolol or another cardioselective β-blocker may be preferable to propranolol.
Cocaine	X ↑	Irregular heartbeat.
Dicumarol	X ↑	Propranolol may produce small increases in dicumarol; effect on prothrombin times is unknown.
Digitalis	X ↑ P ↑	Propranolol can potentiate bradycardia from digitalis; monitor heart rate.
* Diltiazem (see calcium channel- blockers)		
Disopyramide	P ↑	Negative inotropic effects.
†Epinephrine	X ↑	Noncardioselective β-blockers (e.g., propranolol, timolol) substantially raise systolic and diastolic BPs and drop heart rate, sometimes resulting in arrhythmias and stroke. Cardioselective β-blockers (e.g., metoprolol) are safe. Whereas α-agonist sympathomimetics (e.g., epinephrine) are dangerous, pure β-agonist sympathomimetics (e.g., isoproterenol) are safer. Avoid combining noncardioselective β-blockers and α-agonist sympathomimetics; this includes injecting epinephrine as a local anesthetic.
Ergot alkaloids	X ↑	Propranolol may increase vasoconstriction. Using an ergotamine suppository, a patient on 30 mg/day of propranolol developed purple and painful feet. ADRs more common with noncardioselective β-blockers. Employ cardioselective β-blockers.
Etinidine	P ↑	Etinidine may substantially raise concentrations of propranolol and probably other β-blockers that undergo hepatic metabolism (e.g., metoprolol, labetatolol). Ranitidine, famotidine, or nizatidine may be safer than etinidine if an H_2 blocker is required.
Furosemide	P ↑	Furosemide may increase propranolol levels.
Glucagon	X ↓	Propranolol may blunt the hyperglycemic action.

Drugs (X) Interact with:	β-Blockers Propranolol (P)	Comments
* Indomethacin	P ↓	Indomethacin, piroxicam, naproxen, and possibly other nonsteroidal anti-inflammatory drugs (NSAIDs), diminish propranolol's hypotensive effect. Sulindac and salicylates have minimal effect. NSAIDs and other β-blockers can be unpredictable. If BP increases, may need to increase propranolol or decrease or stop indomethacin.
* Isoproterenol	P ↑ ↓	Noncardioselective β-blockers (e.g., propranolol) are risky to combine with isoproterenol to treat asthma. Safer to employ cardioselective β-blockers (e.g., labetalol or metoprolol). No β-blocker is absolutely safe in treating asthma.
* Lidocaine	X ↑	Lidocaine may rise with propranolol, metoprolol, or nadolol.
Marijuana	X ↓	Propranolol delays the increase in heart rate and BP from marijuana. Propranolol may prevent marijuana's impairment of learning tasks and eye reddening effects.
* Methyldopa	X ↓	Patients getting a β-blocker and methyldopa may develop hypertension; monitor. Hypertensive reactions may be helped by IV phentolamine.
MAOIs	X ↓ P ↓	Depression may escalate on β-blockers. Highly anticholinergic MAOIs especially block β-blocker's influence on myocardial tissue.
Naproxen (see indomethacin)		
Nonsteroidal anti-inflammatory drugs (NSAIDs) (see indomethacin)		
Nylidrin	X ↓	Propranolol may reduce nylidrin's greater gastric acid secretion and volume; no special precautions.
* Phenylephrine	X ↑	Phenylephrine added to propranolol may trigger hypertensive episode. A woman on chronic propranolol 160 mg/day developed a fatal intracerebral hemorrhage after dropping 10% phenylephrine in each eye. Phenylephrine 10% eye drops have also produced acute hypertensive episodes without propranolol. Until this reaction is proved, observe patient.
Phenytoin	P ↑	Increased propranolol effect.
Piroxicam (see indomethacin)		
Prazosin	X ↑	β-blockers may increase the "first-dose" hypotensive response to prazosin. Start prazosin cautiously in patients on β-blockers.
Propoxyphene	P ↑	Propoxyphene increases highly metabolized β-blockers (e.g., propranolol, metoprolol), but not β-blockers excreted by kidneys (e.g., atenolol, nadolol).
Quinidine	X ↑ P ↑	Propranolol may inflate quinidine level and foster lightheadedness, hypotension, slower

Drugs (X) Interact with:	β-Blockers Propranolol (P)	Comments
		heart rate, and fainting. Other β-blockers probably act similarly.
*Rifampin	P ↓	Rifampin may decrease propranolol and metoprolol; consider increasing dose or changing to another β-blocker when rifampin is added.
Reserpine	X ↑	Increased reserpine effect with excessive sedation, hypotension, fainting, vertigo, and depression.
Terbutaline	X ↓ ↑	Propranolol may antagonize terbutaline-induced bronchodilation, whereas cardioselective β-adrenergic blockers have little effect on terbutaline and are safer.
*Theophylline	X ↑ ↓	Propranolol raises theophylline but antagonizes bronchodilation; cardioselective agents are safer.
Tobacco smoking	P ↓	Smoking decreases propranolol and may produce irregular heartbeats. If smoking halted, propranolol increases. Smoking patients need higher propranolol doses. Atenolol, and other β-blockers not dependent on liver metabolism, are safer.
Tocainide	X ↓	May worsen congestive heart failure.
TCAs	X ↓ P ↓	Depression may escalate on β-blockers. High anticholinergic TCAs especially block β-blocker's influence on myocardial tissue. Maprotiline toxicity may arise after propranolol added.
Tubocurarine	X ↑	Propranolol may prolong neuromuscular blockade.
Verapamil (see calcium channel-blockers)		
Warfarin	X ↑	Propranolol may produce small increases in warfarin; effect on prothrombin times is unknown.

* Moderately important interaction; † Extremely important interaction; ↑ Increases; ↓ Decreases; ↑ ↓ Increases and decreases.
** *Oxidatively metabolized* includes 2-keto compounds (clorazepate, chlordiazepoxide, diazepam, flurazepam, halazepam, prazepam) and triazolo-compounds (alprazolam, estazolam, triazolam)). *Not oxidatively metabolized* are 3-hydroxy compounds (lorazepam, oxazepam, temazepam, and partially, clonazepam).
° See also Appendix P4503A3/4 for potential interactions (page 390).

EFFECTS ON LABORATORY TESTS

Generic Names	Blood/Serum Tests	Results*	Urine Tests	Results*
Benzodiazepines	WBC, RBC, LFT	↓r↓r ↑	None	
Buspirone	LFT, WBC	↑ ↑ ↓	None	
Clonazepam	LFT	↑	None	
Clonidine	Glucose (transient), Plasma renin activity	↑ ↓	Aldosterone, Catecholamines	↑ ↑

Generic Names	Blood/Serum Tests	Results*	Urine Tests	Results*
Hydroxyzine	None		17-Hydroxycor-ticosteroids	↑ f
Meprobamate	WBC, platelets	↓ r ↓ r	17-Hydroxycor-ticosteroids	↑ f
Propranolol and atenolol	LFT	↑	None	
	T₄, rT₃, T₃	↑ ↑ ↓		
	BUN (with severe heart disease)	↑		
	Antinuclear antibodies (ANA)	↑		

* ↑ Increases; ↓ Decreases; f = falsely; r = rarely; LFT = SGOT, SGPT, LDH, bilirubin, and alkaline phosphotase.

WITHDRAWAL

Antianxiety agents, barbiturates, and nonbarbiturate hypnotics share many withdrawal characteristics, which are discussed together in the next chapter on hypnotics.

Clonidine

- If suddenly withdrawn, serious symptoms of
  - √ Hypertension
  - √ Nervousness
  - √ Headache
  - √ Stomach pain
  - √ Tachycardia
  - √ Sweating
  - √ Other sympathetic overactivity
- Occurs in patients on 0.6 mg/day of clonidine.
  - √ Life-threatening withdrawal from higher doses.
- Starts 18–20 h after the last dose.
- Hypertension may persist 7–10 days.
- Management
  - √ *Do not*
    - □ Halt drug abruptly.
    - □ Use β-blockers; may exaggerate hypertension.
  - √ *Do*
    - □ Taper patient gradually (2–4 days).
    - □ Readminister clonidine.
    - □ If severe, use IV vasodilators.
    - □ Patients on clonidine and propranolol should halt propranolol before stopping clonidine to avoid hypertensive supersensitivity.
    - □ Warn patients about abruptly stopping drug.

Propranolol

* Usually safe to withdraw in psychiatric patients unless there are cardiac problems (e.g., hypertension, angina, or coronary artery disease).

Buspirone

* No withdrawal symptoms from buspirone.
* Because buspirone has no cross-tolerance with benzodiazepines, withdrawal from benzodiazepines is not relieved by buspirone.

OVERDOSE: TOXICITY, SUICIDE, AND TREATMENT

Benzodiazepines

Benzodiazepine overdoses are relatively safe, but if benzodiazepines are consumed with alcohol, barbiturates, or other CNS depressants, they can be fatal. One study showed that only 2 of 1,239 deaths occurred from benzodiazepine overdoses alone.

More rapidly absorbed benzodiazepines (e.g., diazepam, chlorazepate) may generate a "buzz," thereby encouraging abuse.

The effects of a chronic benzodiazepine overdose partly depends on how tolerant the patient has already become on benzodiazepines: The more tolerant, the fewer symptoms.

Chronic benzodiazepine overdoses demonstrate

* Drowsiness
* Ataxia
* Slurred speech
* Vertigo

Acute benzodiazepine overdoses manifest with chronic symptoms *and*

* Somnolence, confusion, lethargy, diminished reflexes
* Hypotension
* Hypotonia
* Coma
* Cardiac arrest (rare)
* Death (rarer)

The general management of benzodiazepine overdoses includes (see also pages 53–54)

* Flumazenil (Mazicon), a specific benzodiazepine receptor antagonist, can reverse the effects of a benzodiazepine overdose

when used IV. Can be used as adjunct to above general management.
- √ Only reverses benzodiazepine (not other sedative-hypnotic) effects.
- √ 75% of overdose patients respond to 1.0–3.0 mg.
- √ Takes 6–10 minutes for dose to have full effect.
- √ Re-sedation from most benzodiazepine overdoses occurs in 20–30 minutes after injection.
- √ Can precipitate benzodiazepine withdrawal.
- √ 1–3% of patients become agitated or anxious after flumazenil.
- 1.1% have seizures.
  - √ Groups at high risk for seizure include OD with HCAs or benzodiazepine dependence.
  - √ Avoid flumazenil in these risk groups or use extreme caution.
- 0.1 mg/minute infusion may reduce risk of withdrawal.
- Monitor for re-sedation and respiratory depression.
- Many benzodiazepines (e.g., alprazolam, lorazepam, temazepam, triazolam) are not reported by urine tests.
  - √ While they are detected, low, possibly therapeutic levels may not be reported by labs that use standardized cut-offs established for drugs of abuse.
  - √ All are detected and reported in overdose situations.
- For hypotension
  - √ Norepinephrine 4–8 mg in 1000 ml 5% D/S or D/W by infusion, or
  - √ Metaraminol 10–20 mg SC/IM.
    - □ 0.5–5 mg by IV or
    - □ 25–100 mg in 500 ml 5% D/W by infusion.
    - □ Stay clear of caffeine and sodium benzoate because they are of questionable benefit.
- Hemodialysis does not alleviate benzodiazepine overdose.
- If normal kidney function, benzodiazepine elimination can be accelerated with forced diuresis, with osmotic diuretics, IV fluids, and electrolytes.

Buspirone

Unlike most antianxiety compounds, buspirone is not a controlled substance and its initial dysphoric effect may discourage overuse.

Acute buspirone overdoses in humans have not been lethal. In animals the LD 50 is 160–550 times therapeutic doses. Overdoses can produce

- Nausea, vomiting, upset stomach
- Dizziness, drowsiness
- Miosis

Management (see also pages 53–54)

* Role of hemodialysis unknown.

Clonidine

Acute clonidine overdoses may arise with

* Hypotension
* Bradycardia
* Lethargy, somnolence
* Irritabiity
* Weakness
* Absent or diminished reflexes
* Miosis
* Vomiting
* Hypoventilation

After large overdoses, may also see

* Reversible cardiac conduction defects or arrhythmias
* Apnea
* Seizures
* Transient hypertension

Management

* As above, plus
* IV fluids, if indicated (e.g., hypotension).
  √ Can add dopamine infusion to treat hypotension.
* IV atropine 0.3–1.2 mg for bradycardia.
* IV furosemide 20–40 mg over 1–2 minutes for hypertension.
  √ If this fails, consider IV tolazoline 10 mg at 30-minute intervals.
* Hemodialysis removes only 5% of clonidine (an alpha blocker); worthless.

Hydroxyzine

Overdoses propagate side effects, especially drowsiness and an occasional hypotension.

Management (see also pages 53–54)

* Hemodialysis of little help.

Meprobamate

Even in low doses, meprobamate can be especially dangerous.

* A 7–10 day supply is often lethal,
* Particularly when mixed with alcohol or other CNS depressants.

Acute meprobamate overdose produces symptoms similar to barbiturate overdose.

- Drowsiness, lethargy, stupor
- Ataxia
- Coma
- Hypotension, shock, respiratory failure
- Death

Meprobamate can be eliminated by peritoneal dialysis, hemodialysis, or with an osmotic diuretic, such as mannitol.

Propranolol

Acute propranolol overdoses present with, and are treated by

- Bradycardia
  - √ IV atropine 0.3–1.2 mg.
  - √ If no response to vagal blockade, cautiously administer isoproterenol 1 mg (maximum 2 mg) in 500 ml 5% D/S or D/W by infusion, generally at a rate of 5 μg/min.
- Cardiac failure
  - √ Provide digitalis and diuretics.
- Hypotension
  - √ Epinephrine—drug of choice in anaphalactic shock,
    - □ 0.5 ml 1:1000 in 10 ml saline IV.
    - □ If no response, give 0.5 ml q 5–15 minutes.
  - √ Levarterenol 4–8 mg in 1000 ml 5% D/S or D/W by infusion.
- Bronchospasm
  - √ Isoproterenol and
  - √ Aminophylline 500 mg IV slowly.

Toxicity and Suicide Data

Generic Names	Toxicity Doses Average (Highest) (g)	Mortality Doses Average (Lowest) (g)	Toxic Levels % (ng/ml)	Fatal Levels % (ng/ml)
Alprazolam	—	—	—	—
Buspirone	—	—	—	—
Clonazepam	—	—	—	—
Clonidine	100	—	(370)	—
Chlordiazepoxide	6.230 (17.00)	0.6–1.0	—	(30)
Clorazepate	0.675	—	—	—
Diazepam	2	0.6–1.0	(900)	(> 50)
Lorazepam	—	—	—	—
Mebrobamate	18.7 (40.0)	20–40 (12)	30–100 μg/ml	100–200 μg/ml (> 200 mg/ml)*

ANTIANXIETY AGENTS

Toxicity and Suicide Data (Cont.)

Generic Names	Toxicity Doses Average (Highest) (g)	Mortality Doses Average (Lowest) (g)	Toxic Levels % (ng/ml)	Fatal Levels % (ng/ml)
Oxazepam	—	—	—	(> 25)
Prazepam	—	—	—	—
Propranolol	2	—	—	—

* More than 50% fatalities.

PRECAUTIONS

Benzodiazepines are contraindicated in hypersensitive patients. Give benzodiazepine medications cautiously to

- Elderly and debilitated people or patients with liver disease. Avoid long or very short half-life benzodiazepines (except oxazepam and lorazepam).
- People who drink alcohol excessively.
- Patients who do not follow the time-limited restrictions on these medications.
- *Avoid* benzodiazepines for patients with
  √ Sleep apnea,
  √ Chronic obstructive pulmonary disease, CO_2 retainers.

Buspirone

- Sometimes triggers restlessness.
- Does not prevent benzodiazepine or barbiturate withdrawal.

Clonidine should be used cautiously for patients with

- Severe coronary insufficiency
- Recent myocardial infarction
- Chronic renal failure
- Generalized rash.

Meprobamate contraindications include patients with

- Allergic reaction to meprobamate or
  √ Carisoprodol
- Epilepsy
  √ Meprobamate may trigger seizures.

Propranolol

- Contraindicated for patients with
  √ Cardiogenic shock (systolic BP < 100mm Hg)

- √ Sinus bradycardia
- √ Greater than first-degree AV block
- √ Congestive heart failure
- √ Bronchial asthma
  - □ Metoprolol, atenolol, and labetolol are less likely to produce bronchospasm.
- √ Hypotension in MI.
- Give cautiously to patients with
  - √ Congestive heart failure, persistent angina, Wolff-Parkinson-White syndrome, and impaired myocardial functioning—all can become worse with propranolol.
    - □ Gradually withdraw propranolol from angina patients over a few weeks.
  - √ Glaucoma screen test.
    - □ Propranolol withdrawal can increase intraocular pressure.
  - √ Hyperthyroidism, thyrotoxicosis.
    - □ May mask (treat?) symptoms.
  - √ Diabetes mellitus.
  - √ Chronic obstructive pulmonary disease.
  - √ Hepatic failure.
    - □ Nadolol and atenolol are kidney excreted.
  - √ Renal failure.
  - √ Depression.
    - □ May feel "washed out" or lethargic.
    - □ May intensify symptoms of depression.
    - □ Others (9%) develop neurovegetative signs of depression.
    - □ Probably less likely with low lipophilic β-blockers atenolol and nadolol.

NURSES' DATA

Most benzodiazepine anti-anxiety actions arise in 15–40 minutes and, thus, efficacy can be determined after 1–2 doses.

Avoid other CNS depressants (e.g., antihistamines, sedating TCAs, anticonvulsants, neuroleptics, or alcohol) without consulting physician.

- Tell patients that they may be unaware of their diminished skills when mixing benzodiazepines and alcohol.
  - √ Avoid alcohol 24–48 h after lorazepam injection. This is probably good advice after any benzodiazepine injection.
- Drinking caffeine counteracts anxiolytics.
  - √ Patients with anxiety disorders tend to be hypersensitive to caffeine.
    - □ Negative effects may occur with "normal" or "usual" amounts of caffeine (e.g., 2–3 cups of coffee).

ANTIANXIETY AGENTS

Tolerance, physical addiction, and withdrawal can occur from benzo-diazepine agents. These symptoms may be hard to distinguish from each other or from anxiety symptoms.

- Inform patients about withdrawal symptoms (see pages 335–337).
- Inform patients about intoxication and overdose symptoms (see page 304).
- Make sure patients realize that a sudden benzodiazepine with-drawal can be fatal and more dangerous than narcotic with-drawal.
- It is generally not recommended to use benzodiazepines in high doses for longer than 3–4 weeks continuously.
- There is no easy way to extinguish a benzodiazepine habit.
  - √ Withdrawal can occur, yet must be done slowly under medical supervision.
  - √ If there is an *acute* question during withdrawal between giv-ing the patient too much or too little benzodiazepines, give too much; it's safer to avoid withdrawal.

Techniques of administration for benzodiazepines include

- IM injections
  - √ Slowly into a single large muscle, especially the upper, outer, and deeper quadrant of the gluteus.
  - √ Rotate sites.
  - √ Insure the injection is for IM, not IV, use.
  - √ Only diazepam, lorazepam, and midazolam are absorbed better IM than po; for the rest, IM is worse than po.
- IV injections
  - √ Differ with different agents, but generally inject slowly, such as IV diazepam 2.5–10 mg for anxiety.
    - □ May repeat in 1–4 h, but
    - □ IV diazepam should not excede 30 mg in 8 h.
- Protect parenteral drugs from light.

PATIENT AND FAMILY NOTES

Patients should be told that the treatment is unlikely to "cure" their problem, but should improve symptoms and overall functioning.

In many cases, particularly with panic disorder, social phobia, obses-sive-compulsive disorder, and PTSD, improvement will take a while and adequate dosing is essential. Thinking that a little dose (other than with benzodiazepines) will help a little bit is inaccurate. Target symptoms should be selected and followed during treatments. Many of the anxiety symptoms may resemble side effects.

Before starting treatment, carefully list anxiety symptoms' frequency, duration, and severity so that this baseline can be compared with the time on medication.

Inform patient that buspirone will not eliminate anxiety, but will take the "edge" off of it and make it more manageable.

Inform patient about side effects. On all anxiolytics, dizziness and lightheadedness may occur.

Possible side effects on benzodiazepines

- Sedation, "fuzzy" thinking, fatigue, clumsiness, and blurred vision may be a problem at first, but tend to wear off a little more each day.
  √ If these do not improve or worsen, call your doctor.
- Decreased mood or sexual interest might occur and some patients get headaches or nausea.

On buspirone

- Side effects don't usually occur, but if they do, the most common are headache, nausea, insomnia, and agitation.

Propranolol can cause

- Fatigue, depression, and decreased sexual interest.

Clonidine risks

- Dry mouth and sedation.

Never stop benzodiazepines, meprobamate, or barbiturates suddenly—induces seizures.

- Suddenly stopping these agents is riskier than suddenly stopping narcotics. Narcotic withdrawal can produce sickness; *benzodiazepine withdrawal can produce death.*

Hypertensive rebound occurs when

- Clonidine is suddenly stopped in any patient.
- Proprandol is suddenly stopped in cardiac patients.

Take antianxiety agent at prescribed time.

- If forget dose, can consume in 2 h.
- Otherwise wait for next regular dose.
- Do not double dose.
- Some long-acting benzodiazepines (e.g., diazepam, clorazepate, clonazepam) can be taken once a day.

When starting benzodiazepines, meprobamate, or barbiturates, patients should drive cars, work around machines, and cross streets carefully. When first on antianxiety agents, drive briefly in a safe place, since reflexes might be a tad off.

Benzodiazepines strongly potentiate alcohol: "One drink feels like 2–3 drinks." Buspirone, propranolol, and clonidine do not potentiate alcohol.

May take benzodiazepines, clonidine, and propranolol at any time; food does not interfere with final effect, but does slow onset of action. Buspirone's absorption is delayed by food, but this does not alter its efficacy.

Keep anxiety medications away from bedside or any readily accessible place, where they might be secured by "accident." Keep safely away from children.

Patients on β-blockers (e.g., propranolol) should inform doctor if they are traveling to high altitudes or engaging in very strenuous exercise.

If doctor prescribes meprobamate or barbiturates, ask him/her if another agent would be superior, since benzodiazepines and other agents have largely superceded them.

8. Hypnotics

INTRODUCTION

Hypnotics induce sleep. There are four main types:

- Benzodiazepines
- Barbiturates
- Barbiturate-like hypnotics
- Selective benzodiazepine receptor agonist (imidazopyridines, i.e., zolpidem)

This chapter focuses on the benzodiazepine hypnotics and zolpidem. It also addresses

- Insomnia (pages 317, 319)
- Sleep movement disorder (page 323)
- Amytal diagnostic interview (pages 324–325)
- Withdrawal from all anxiolytics (pages 335–338)
- Withdrawal from alcohol (pages 341–343)
- Carbamazepine-aided withdrawal of benzodiazepines and alcohol (page 339)
- Pentobarbital-phenobarbital tolerance test (page 340)
- Alcoholism prevention (pages 343–346)

Related topics detailed in other chapters are

- Cataplexy (Antidepressants, page 111)
- Narcolepsy (Stimulants, page 361)
- Night terrors (Antidepressants, page 113)
- Sleep apnea (Antidepressants, page 112)
- Sleepwalking (Antidepressants, page 113)

NAMES, COST, CLASSES, MANUFACTURERS, DOSE FORMS, COLORS

Generic Names (Dollars/Dose: 100 pills in mg)**	Brand Names (Dollars/Dose: 100 pills in mg)**	Manu- facturers	Dose Forms (mg)***	Colors
		BENZODIAZEPINES		
Estazolam	Prosom 84/1	Abbott	t: 1/2	t: white/coral
Flurazepam 11–36/30	Dalmane 56/30	Roche	c: 15/30	c: orange-ivory/ red-ivory
Quazepam	Doral 77/15	Baker Cummins	t: 7.5/15	t: all light orange- white speckled
Temazepam 8–36/30	Restoril 70/30	Sandoz	c: 15/30	c: maroon-pink/ maroon-blue
Triazolam 59–60/0.125	Halcion 69/0.125	Upjohn	t: 0.125/0.25	t: white/blue
		IMIDAZOPYRIDINE (Selective Benzodiazepine Receptor Agent)		
Zolpidem	Ambien 147/10	Searle	c: 5/10	c: pink/white
		BARBITURATES*		
Amobarbital	Amytal	Lilly	p: 50 mg/ml	
Butabarbital	Butisol	Wallace	t: 15/30/50/100	t: lavender/green/ orange/pink
			e: 30 mg/5 ml	e: green
Pentobarbital	Nembutal	Abbott	c: 50/100 su: 30 p: 50 mg/ml	c: orange/yellow
Phenobarbital			Many generic doses	
Secobarbital	Seconal	Lilly	c: 100 p: 50 mg/ml	c: orange
		BARBITURATE-LIKE COMPOUNDS*		
Chloral hydrate 4–9/500			c: 250/500 e: 500 mg/5 ml	c: red/red
Ethchlorvynol	Placidyl 329/500	Abbott	c: 200/500/ 750*	c: red/red/green
Paraldehyde	Paral 197/4 gm	Forrest	e: 30 gm/30 ml	

* Not recommended for general use; cost not included.
** 1994 average wholesale price for 100 pills at this dose (e.g., 78/50 means 100 pills 50 mg cost $78). If depot form, cost is of single dose.
*** c = capsules; e = elixir; p = parenteral; su = suppository; t = tablets.

PHARMACOLOGY

The preceding chapter presented the pharmacology of benzodiazepines.

Benzodiazepine hypnotics exert similar effects on sleep. They

- Extend total sleep time,
- Decrease stage 1,
- Increase stage 2, and
- Reduce stages 3 and 4.
   √ Temazepam prolongs stage 3 in depressed patients.

Specific effects on REM sleep include:

- Decrease REM sleep, except for temazepam and low doses of flurazepam.
- Prolong REM latency—the time to reach REM—except for flurazepam.
- Increase REM cycles, usually in the last part of sleep.

Zolpidem has minimal effect on sleep architecture.

- Stages 3 and 4 ("deep sleep") are preserved.

*Pharmacology of Oral Hypnotic Benzodiazepines**

Generic Names	Speed of Onset (min)	Peak Plasma Level (hours)	Duration of:		
			Half-Life (hours)	Action** (hours)	Active Metabolites***
BENZODIAZEPINES					
2-Keto- Flurazepam	30	0.5–1	67 (47–100)	LA > 40	N-Desalkylflurazepam
3-Hydroxy Temazepam	20–60	2–4	12 (9.5–20)	IA 6–20	None
Triazolo- Estazolam	15–30	2	15 (10–24)	IA 6–8	4-Hydroxyestazolam, 1-Oxoestazolam
Triazolam	20	0.5–1	2–4 (1.5–5.5)	SA < 6	None
Other Quazepam	30	0.5–2	25–40 (2–73)	LA 2–100	2-Oxoquazepam, N-Desalkylflurazepam
IMIDAZOPYRIDINES					
Zolpidem	20–30	1.6	2.5	SA < 6	None

Pharmacology of Oral Hypnotic Benzodiazepines (Cont.)

Generic Names	Speed of Onset (min)	Peak Plasma Level (hours)	Duration of:		
			Half-Life (hours)	Action** (hours)	Active Metabolites***
BARBITURATES					
Amobarbital	45–60	——	25 (16–40)	IA 6–8	——
Aprobarbital	45–60	3	24 (14–34)	IA 6–8	——
Butabarbital	45–60	3–4	34–42 (34–140)	IA 6–8	——
Pentobarbital	15–60	30–60	22–50 (15–50)	SA 3–4	——
Phenobarbital	8–12	10–15	3–4 weeks	LA 80	——
Secobarbital	10–15	15–30	28–30 (15–40)	SA 3–4	——
BARBITURATE-LIKE COMPOUNDS					
Chloral hydrate	30	——	4–14†	——	Trichloroethanol
Ethchlorvynol	15–60	——	10–25‡	5	——
Paraldehyde	10–15	0.5–1	3.4–9.8	IA 8–12	——

*For details on metabolism of benzodiazepine hypnotics, see Antianxiety agents, pages 257–259.
** LA = long-acting; IA = intermediate-acting; SA = short-acting. The figures below represent the duration of action of the compound and its major active metabolites.
*** ——Not available.
† Half-life for trichloroethanol—chloral hydrate's principal metabolite—is 7–10 h.
‡ Half-lives for ethchlorvynol's free and conjugated forms of major metabolite are 10–20 h.

DOSES

Generic Names	Usual Doses (mg)	Dose Ranges (mg)	When to Take Before Bedtime (hours)	Geriatric Dose (mg)
BENZODIAZEPINES				
Estazolam	1	1–2	0.5	0.5
Flurazepam	15–30	15–30	0.5	15
Quazepam	7.5–15	7.5–15	1.5	7.5
Temazepam	15–30	15–30	1–2	15
Triazolam	0.25	0.125–0.5	0.5	0.125
IMIDAZOPYRIDINE				
Zolpidem	10	5–10	0.5	5
BARBITURATES*				
Amobarbital	150–200	65–200	0.5	65
Butabarbital	50–100	50–100	0.5	50
Pentobarbital	100	50–200	0.5	50

Generic Names	Usual Doses (mg)	Dose Ranges (mg)	When to Take Before Bedtime (hours)	Geriatric Dose (mg)
Phenobarbital	100–200	15–600	1	16
Secobarbital	100–200	100–200	0.25	50
BARBITURATE-LIKE HYPNOTICS				
Chloral hydrate	500–1500	500–2000	0.5	500
Ethchlorvynol	500–750	500–1000	0.5	500
Paraldehyde	5000–10,000	2000–15,000	0.5	4000

* Use of these agents for insomnia (or anxiety) is not recommended.

CLINICAL INDICATIONS AND USE

Primary insomnia is defined as a difficulty sleeping that is *not* due to

- Drugs (e.g., prescription, over-the-counter, recreational, alcohol, caffeine)
- Sleep disorders (e.g., narcolepsy, sleep apnea)
- Medical ailments (e.g., pain)
- Mental disorders (e.g., depression, panic attacks, obsessive-compulsive disorder)
- Circadian rhythm difficulties (e.g., jet lag, shift changes)

Recognition and treatment of these other disorders should occur before insomnia is treated as an isolated symptom.

Sometimes the treatment effects. of these primary disorders will be slow and treatment of the secondary insomnia may be needed. For example:

- All antidepressants can help insomnia if it is a symptom of depression, but this may take 3–6 weeks.
- Buspirone can improve anxiety-caused insomnia, but this takes 4–5 weeks.

Insomnia is defined as insufficient sleep that renders the person consistently tired the next day.

- A person sleeping 3 h a night who feels refreshed the next day is a brief sleeper (maybe manic), but not a poor sleeper.
- A person who must sleep 9–10 h a night to feel refreshed the next day is a healthy (albeit inefficient) sleeper.

Barbiturate and barbiturate-like hypnotics are not recommended for the treatment of anxiety or insomnia.

- Brief inpatient use of chloral hydrate for insomnia may be acceptable.
- Amobarbital is indicated for "amytal interviews."

Nonprescription "sleeping pills" are not more effective than placebo and can produce tolerance and rebound insomnia. Most include pyrilamine or methapyriline, both antihistamines; some add an analgesic or anticholinergic agent. Commonly used ones include

- Compoz—methapyrilene (antihistamine), pyrilamine (antihistamine)
- Nytol—methapyrilene, salicylamide (salicylate)
- Sleep-Eze—methapyrilene, scopolamine (anticholinergic)
- Sominex—methapyrilene, scopolamine, salicylamide

Benzodiazepine hypnotics have largely replaced other hypnotics because benzodiazepines

- Are safer as overdoses,
- Cause less respiratory and CNS depression, and
- Induce less drug dependence.

Benzodiazepines marketed as anxiolytics can be as effective as benzodiazepines marketed for anxiety (see below).

Benzodiazepines are effective, but often for as little as 5–14 days.

- No hypnotic has been proven safe for over 6 weeks.

Hypnotics have 2 clear indications: to treat

- Brief (1–7 day) episode of insomnia, and
- Transitory insomnia incited by acute stress or by a marked diurnal rhythm change (e.g., jet lag).

Benzodiazepines most help patients with shorter total sleep time.

Hypnotics create 4 common problems:

- Rapid onset hypnotics (e.g., triazolam) can cause anterograde amnesia.
- If the hypnotic does not induce sleep, it can foster drowsiness, confusion, or agitation the next day.
- Longer-acting hypnotics (e.g., flurazepam, quazepam) may exhaust and impair performance the following day. Can cause
  √ Higher risk of falling in geriatrics.
  √ Increased respiratory depression in those with respiratory problems.
- Hypnotics provoke
  √ Tolerance,
  √ Rebound insomnia, and
  √ Decreased memory function.

Rebound insomnia has several causes:

- Rebound insomnia can be a part of the *general* abstinence syndrome, which arises after the abrupt withdrawal of a *large* dose of any hypnotic taken over a *prolonged* period of time (see Precautions).
- Rebound insomnia can be a *specific* sleep disruption, which occurs after the sudden halting of a *normal* dose of any *briefly* taken and *quickly* eliminated hypnotic. This may be secondary to tolerance developing rapidly and/or rebound of drug-suppressed sleep architecture states. REM suppression may lead to REM rebound and many wake-ups from vivid dreams.
  - √ Hypnotics with rapid (e.g., triazolam) elimination rates generate more rebound insomnia than do hypnotics with longer elimination rates (e.g., flurazepam, quazepam).
  - √ After abruptly stopping hypnotics, shorter-acting drugs produce a more aggravating rebound insomnia the next night, whereas longer-acting hypnotics produce a calmer version in 5–7 nights.
  - √ Rebound insomnia is partly dose-dependent.
  - √ Rebound insomnia from the *greatest and fastest* to the *weakest and slowest:*
    - □ Triazolam
    - □ Temazepam
    - □ Estazolam
    - □ Flurazepam
    - □ Quazepam
  - √ Greater rebound insomnia may increase hypnotic dosage, which
    - □ Aggravates tolerance and
    - □ Fosters drug dependency.
- When rebound insomnia occurs, clinicians should either taper the dose or switch to a different hypnotic.
  - √ Try to remove the patient from all hypnotics.
  - √ If this is not possible,
    - □ May prescribe trazodone 25–100 mg for a few nights.
    - □ May prescribe a sedative antihistamine (e.g., diphenhydramine 50 mg) for a few nights.
    - □ Employ another longer-acting benzodiazepine and gradually taper it.

Short-acting versus long-acting benzodiazepine hypnotics differ according to these criteria:

Characteristic	Short-Acting	Long-Acting
Accumulation with more use	No	Marked
Hangover, sedation next day	Rare	Moderate
Tolerance	Moderate	Mild
Anterograde amnesia	Moderate	Mild
Rebound insomnia risk	Moderate	No
Early morning awakening risk	Mild	No
Daytime anxiety risk	Mild	No
Anxiolytic the next day	No	Moderate
Full benefit on first night	Moderate-marked	Moderate
Full benefit on 7th or 14th night	Low-moderate	Moderate-high

Qualities of Hypnotics

- Estazolam
  - √ Rapid absorption rate
  - √ Intermediate half-life
  - √ Duration of action between triazolam and temazepam
    - ▫ While half-life is slightly longer than temazepam's, it is quickly taken up by adipose tissue.
- Flurazepam
  - √ Rapid absorption rate
  - √ Long half-life
  - √ Sedates during the next day, which may, or may not, diminish with repeated doses.
  - √ In geratric patients, it may accumulate over 1 to 3 weeks and cause confusion and disorientation.
  - √ May work better on second and third nights.
- Quazepam
  - √ Marketed as a "selective" benzodiazepine receptor agent (like zolpidem), but metabolites are nonselective.
  - √ Rapid absorption rate
  - √ Slower onset
  - √ Long half-life
    - ▫ A major metabolite seen with flurazepam, N-desalkyl-flurazepam (also called N-desalkyl-2-oxoquazepam), has a half-life of 73 h and a range of 47–100 h.
  - √ May work better on second and third nights.
    - ▫ Another key metabolite, 2-oxoquazepam, has a half-life of 2–3 h.
    - ▫ Quazepam and 2-oxoquazepam together have a half-life of 39 h.
    - ▫ Accumulation may be a particular risk in geriatric patients.
  - √ Manufacturer claims quazepam does not cause daytime sedation.

- Temazepam
  - √ Slow absorption rate
  - √ Intermediate half-life of 10–20 h
  - √ May take longer to induce sleep.
    - □ Less useful as a prn medication
  - √ Causes little or no daytime sedation.
- Trazodone
  - √ Rapid absorption rate; peaks in 20–30 qhs minutes
  - √ Intermediate half-life
  - √ Large, potentially safe qhs dosage range, 25–250 mg
  - √ No respiratory depression
  - √ Sedates next A.M. or all day in 20% of people.
  - √ Orthostatic BP drop most common side effect
  - √ Tolerance mild to moderate
  - √ Rebound insomnia infrequent
  - √ Priapism ~ 1:2,000 males
  - √ No physical dependence
  - √ Short-term efficacy established in sleep labs.
    - □ Long-term efficacy not studied.
- Triazolam
  - √ Fast absorption rate
  - √ Very short half-life
  - √ No metabolites
  - √ May not treat early A.M. insomnia.
  - √ May provoke early morning awakening and anxiety (e.g., same night rebound may be seen).
  - √ Daytime anxiety more common after 10 consecutive night's use.
  - √ No daytime sedation.
- Zolpidem (20 mg or less)
  - √ Selectively binds to BZ_1 (also called $omega_1$) receptor of GABA complex in doses 20 mg or less.
    - □ Less selective and more like benzodiazepines at higher doses
  - √ No respiratory depression
  - √ Lacks myorelaxant, anticonvulsant effects and ability to block benzodiazepine withdrawal.
  - √ Rapid onset of action
  - √ No or minimal effect on memory
  - √ May not treat early A.M. insomnia.
  - √ No daytime sedation.
  - √ Occasional, mild first-night rebound insomnia
  - √ May be less effective in very anxious patients.
    - □ Has no intrinsic anxiolytic effects.
  - √ No tolerance seen after 5 weeks with 15 mg dose.

Other benzodiazepines marketed for anxiety can also be used for sleep. There are no inherent differences between benzodiazepines for anxiety and those for sleep except how they are marketed.

- If a certain benzodiazepine is already being used for anxiety, it frequently can also be used for sleep.
- Clorazepate and diazepam resemble flurazepam and quazepam in pharmacodynamics and effects.
  - √ Clorazepate and diazepam may have faster onset and, in single doses, may have shorter duration of action.
- Chlordiazepoxide and clonazepam resemble flurazepam and quazepam, but intermediate absorption rate.
- Oxazepam resembles temazepam.
- Alprazolam and lorazepam resemble temazepam and estazolam, but have intermediate absorption rates and, in some patients, longer durations of action (A.M. sedation risk?).

The following nonbenzodiazepines are indicated solely for patients who cannot tolerate the prior hypnotics.

- Chloral hydrate is effective if used for 1–2 weeks.
  - √ Induces modest REM suppression.
  - √ Tolerance quickly develops thereafter.
- Barbiturates are occasionally used for daytime anti-anxiety effects; *better alternatives with greater safety argue against their use.*
- Antihistamines, which do not foster drug dependency, are weak hypnotics and are not generally recommended.
  - √ Commonly prescribed are
    - □ Diphenhydramine 50–100 mg (available over-the-counter in 25 mg capsules) and
    - □ Hydroxyzine 25–100 mg.
  - √ Tolerance develops in 1–3 nights.
  - √ Antihistamines are anticholinergic.
    - □ Increased nocturnal and daytime confusion, which particularly troubles the elderly.
  - √ Cause REM suppression on the night(s) used, followed by nights of significant REM rebound and possible insomnia.
- Tryptophan, which is now off the market, was a fair hypnotic for mild to moderate insomnia in which there are multiple partial awakenings but not full awakening.
  - √ Not addictive.
  - √ Hypnotic dose is 1000–2000 mg.

The choice of the "best" hypnotic for each patient depends on the patient's particular circumstances, in that *some*

- Hypnotics act more quickly (e.g., triazolam faster than temazepam).
- People wake up too early in the morning (e.g., on triazolam more than flurazepam).
- Hypnotics foster more drowsiness the next day (e.g., on flurazepam more than triazolam).
- Shorter-acting hypnotics create more dependence than longer-acting ones (e.g., triazolam more than flurazepam).
- Hypnotics are more lethal or toxic than others (e.g., secobarbital more than triazolam).
- Hynotics cause weird aberrations (e.g., triazolam's traveler's amnesia) and
- Hypnotics promote rebound insomnia more than others (e.g., triazolam more than quazepam).

Historically, other medications have been prescribed for insomnia, but with modern choices, none of these medications holds much value.

Sleep Movement Disorders

- Include nocturnal myoclonus and restless legs syndrome (see page 32).
  - √ Clonazepam 0.5 mg improves sleep, but nothing stops leg movements.

Dubious Hypnotics

Generic Names	Chemical Groups	Hypnotic Ratings	
		Efficacy	Side Effects
Amitriptyline	TCA	Strong	Significant
Chlorpromazine	Antipsychotic	Strong	Significant
Chlorprothixene	Antipsychotic	Strong	Significant
Clomipramine	TCA	Strong	Significant
Diphenhydramine*	Antihistamine	Minimal	Moderate
Doxepin	TCA	Strong	Significant
Hydroxyzine	Antihistamine	Minimal	Moderate
Meprobamate	Anti-anxiety	Moderate	Significant
Mesoridazine	Antipsychotic	Moderate	Significant
Paraldehyde	Hypnotic	Minimal-moderate	Moderate-significant
Thioridazine	Antipsychotic	Strong	Significant
Trimipramine	TCA	Strong	Significant
Tryptophan *‡	Amino acid	Moderate	Minimal

* Can be sold over the counter.
‡ Removed from market in the United States because of toxic batches from Japan. Avoid until legal again.

Sodium Amytal Diagnostic Interview

IV Amylobarbitone is used

- To determine if confusion is neurologically (tends to worsen with amytal) or psychologically (tends to improve with amytal) based.
- To facilitate the diagnosis of a conversion disorder or psychogenically-induced symptoms (e.g., pain).
  - √ Frequently symptoms will remit or improve with amytal and sometimes psychological cause can be determined.
- To facilitate recall of repressed memories for diagnosis and treatment.
  - √ Must carefully avoid any possibility of suggestion (e.g., "Is there another personality in there?").

Amytal interviews are *not* recommended

- To detect malingering or lying.
  - √ Liars and malingerers can easily continue their symptoms and statements during amytal interviews.
- For continuous use as a therapy tool.
  - √ "New" memories may quickly be repressed.

Administering an amytal interview:

- Interview in well-lighted room with patient's head elevated on a bed.
  - √ Prevents sleep.
- Mix 500 mg sodium amytal in 10 cc sterile water (not bacteriostatic).
  - √ Will need more than 500 mg if patient has tolerance to alcohol or sedative hypnotics secondary to abuse.
- Using small butterfly needle, inject 50 mg a minute up to 150 mg and
  - √ Wait 2–4 minutes.
- Attempt to interview, but avoid threatening material.
- After each increment in dose, assess whether there is definite, subtle, or no change.
- Add further increments of 50 mg over 1 minute and then wait 1 minute and reassess before injecting more.
- Increase to point of slurring of speech or lateral nystagmus.
  - √ Test by having patient keep head still and following finger to extreme right and left sides.
- When desired point attained, conduct interview.
- If long interview (> 10 minutes), will need maintenance doses of amytal.

- If patient goes to sleep, try to awaken and interview.
  - √ If fails to awaken or talk coherently, let patient sleep.
  - √ Sometimes can have effective interview later when patient awakens.

SIDE EFFECTS

The side effects caused by benzodiazepine hypnotics are basically the same as those discussed in the previous chapter for benzodiazepine anti-anxiety agents.

Long-acting benzodiazepine CNS effects follow a U-shaped time curve, with the most adverse consequences occurring in the first few days before tolerance develops and then reappearing a week or so later as the drug accumulates.

- This pattern of side effects happens especially in the elderly, who tend to accumulate the long-acting desalkylflurazepam after taking flurazepam or quazepam.
- These side effects are generally based on spontaneous reporting of subjective side effects.
  - √ Memory, attention, and performance tests suggest greater impairment than the table below.
- The degree of CNS side effects varies with drug, dose, and age. To illustrate, the following percentages of CNS side effects arise from oral flurazepam.

Factor	CNS Side Effect (%)
15 mg/night	1.9
30 mg/night	12.3
Patients under 60	1.9
Patients over 80	7.1
Patients over 70, 15 mg doses	2.0
Patients over 70, 30 mg doses	39.0

Note the following side effects:

Respiratory ailments

- Insomniacs with chronic obstructive pulmonary disease, asthma, or other respiratory disorders should *not* receive benzodiazepine or barbiturate-like sleeping pills. They might intensify effects of sleep apnea by increasing central sleep apnea or slowing respiration rate. High risk for peripheral apnea are people who
  - √ Snore
  - √ Have hypertension

    ✓ Are male
    ✓ Are obese
    ✓ Are older (> 55 yrs)
- For central sleep apnea, high risk for people who
    ✓ Are older
    ✓ Have dementia
    ✓ Have other general CNS disorders
- If needed, use trazodone or zolpidem.

Falls, fractures

- Often from *ataxia* and *confusion*
- Can happen during night with any hypnotic.
- Happens more often during day on long-acting hypnotics (e.g., flurazepam).

Hangover

- Common
- Aggravated by
    ✓ Alcohol consumption and
    ✓ Restricted fluid intake.
- Management
    ✓ Reduce, halt, or switch hypnotic.
    ✓ Reduce risk with shorter-acting hypnotic.

Anterograde amnesia

- Particularly common with triazolam.
- Because of its ultra-short half-life, triazolam is often taken for jet lag.
- Symptoms present with
    ✓ A single dose, often just 0.5 mg.
    ✓ Or without alcohol, but are more common with alcohol.
    ✓ Normal behavior; nobody notices any abnormality.
    ✓ On awakening, the patient has no memory of events occurring 6–11 h after ingesting triazolam.
        ◻ Memory loss is longer than sleep duration.
    ✓ May swallow triazolam the following night without difficulty.
- May also be seen with zolpidem, particularly in higher (≥ 20 mg) doses (that effect all benzodiazepine receptors), when it more closely resembles triazolam.
    ✓ Occurs more in 1–3 h range.

Warn patients about this hazard.

PERCENTAGES OF SIDE EFFECTS

Part I

Side Effects	Estazolam	Flurazepam	Quazepam	Temazepam	Triazolam	Zolpidem
CARDIOVASCULAR EFFECTS						
Dizziness, lightheadedness	7	23.9	1.5	13.3	11.4 (4–19.5)	5
Fainting, syncope	< 0.1	—	—	< 1	0.7	—
Tachycardia	< 1	—	—	< 1	—	—
Palpitations	< 1	—	—	< 1	—	2
Shortness of breath	< 1	—	—	< 1	—	1
GASTROINTESTINAL EFFECTS						
Anorexia, lower appetite	< 1	—	—	1.5	—	1*
Nausea, vomiting	4*	0.7	—	5.5	2.8 (1.6–4.6)	6*
Taste changes	—	3.4	—	—	0.6	< 1
Dyspepsia, upset stomach	2*	0.7	1.1	—	1.5 (0.5–2.2)	5*
Diarrhea	—	—	—	3.5	< 0.5	3
Constipation	> 1	0.7	—	5.5	1.4 (< 0.5–2.2)	2
Jaundice	—	—	—	< 1	—	—
RENAL EFFECTS						
Urinary hesitancy or retention	< 1	—	—	5.5	—	< 0.1

Part I (Cont.)

Side Effects	Estazolam	Flurazepam	Quazepam	Temazepam	Triazolam	Zolpidem
EYES, EARS, NOSE, AND THROAT EFFECTS						
Dry mouth and throat	> 1	3.4	1.5	—	0.6	3
Visual changes	< 1	4.6	—	5.5	3 (0.5–4.4)	> 1
Nystagmus	< 0.1	—	—	0.5	—	—
Tinnitus	< 0.1	4.6	—	—	2.9 (< 0.5–4.4)	< 1
Mouth or throat sores	< 0.1	—	—	< 1	—	—
Sinusitis, pharyngitis	1*	—	—	—	—	3–4
SKIN, ALLERGIES, AND TEMPERATURE						
Allergies	< 1	—	—	—	< 0.5	4
Rashes	< 1	0.6	—	5.5	0.2 (0 < 0.5)	2
Itching	1	—	—	5.5	—	< 0.1
CENTRAL NERVOUS SYSTEM EFFECTS						
Weakness, fatigue	11	23.9	1.9	1–2	11.4 (< 0.5–19.5)	1
Lethargy	8	23.9	—	5	11.8 (< 0.5–19.5)	3
Paresthesias	< 1	4.6	—	—	2.9 (< 0.5–4.4)	< 1
Headache	16*	4.6	4.5	—	5.9 (3.8–9.7)	19*

Part I (Cont.)

Side Effects	Estazolam	Flurazepam	Quazepam	Temazepam	Triazolam	Zolpidem
Ataxia, incoordination, clumsiness	4	23.9	—	20	12.8 (4.6–19.5)	>1
Drowsiness, sedation	42	29.5 (23.9–36)	23 (12–34)	18.5 (10–30)	16.1 (14–19.5)	8
Confusion, disorientation	2*	—	—	4 (1–10)	0.7	>1
Decreased concentration	1	—	—	<1	—	<1
Memory loss, amnesia	<1	—	—	0.0	0.7 (0.5–0.9)	1
Insomnia	<1	0.1	—	—	0.3	1
Nightmares, abnormal dreams	2*	0.1	—	—	0.3	1
Hallucinations	<0.1	—	—	3 (<0.5–10)	—	<1
Anxiety, nervousness (i.e., mental)	8*	—	—	—	5.2	1*
Irritability	<1	—	—	5.5	—	<1
Depression, malaise	5*	—	—	5.5	0.7	2
Euphoria	<1	—	—	2.5	0.7	>1
Paradoxical excitement, agitation	<1	2.8	—	0.5	3.8	<1
Drugged feeling/hangovers	3	—	—	—	—	3

—— Data not available.
* Less than or equal to placebo.

HYPNOTICS

Part II

Side Effects	Barbiturates	Chloral Hydrate	Disulfiram
CARDIOVASCULAR EFFECTS			
Hypotension	< 1	—	—
Dizziness, lightheadedness	10.5 (< 1–10)	5.5	—
Fainting, syncope	< 1	—	—
Apnea	< 1	—	—
Hypoventilation	< 1	—	—
Shortness of breath	< 1	—	—
GASTROINTESTINAL EFFECTS			
Nausea, vomiting	3.2	20	—
Bad taste	—	—	5.5
Dyspepsia, upset stomach	—	20	5.5
Diarrhea	5.5	—	—
Constipation	< 1	—	—
Jaundice	< 1	—	< 1
Liver disease	< 1	—	—
ENDOCRINE AND SEXUAL EFFECTS			
Disturbed sexual function	—	—	5.5
HEMATOLOGIC EFFECTS			
Anemia	< 1	—	—
Easy bruising	< 1	—	—
EYES, EARS, NOSE, AND THROAT EFFECTS			
Painful or swollen eyes	5.5	—	5.5
Vision changes	—	—	5.5
Sore throat	5.5	—	—
SKIN, ALLERGIES, AND TEMPERATURE EFFECTS			
Allergies	< 1	—	—
Rashes	3.2	< 1	< 1
Itching	5.5	< 1	—
Fever, hyperthermia	3.2	—	—
CENTRAL NERVOUS SYSTEM EFFECTS			
Hyperkinesia	< 1	—	—
Clumsiness	—	5.5	—
Muscle, cramps	5.5	—	—
Numbness of limbs	—	—	5.5
Headache	< 1	—	5.5
Hangover	20	5.5	—
Ataxia, incoordination	< 1	5.5	—
Slurred speech	5.5	—	—

Part II (Cont.)

Side Effects	Barbiturates	Chloral Hydrate	Disulfiram
Drowsiness, sedation	26.5 (10–33)	5.5	20
Confusion, disorientation	3.2	< 1	—
Insomnia	< 1	—	—
Nightmares	< 1	—	—
Hallucinations	< 1	< 1	—
Anxiety, nervousness (i.e., mental)	< 1	—	—
Agitation, restlessness (i.e., motoric)	< 1	< 1	—
Depression	5.5	—	5.5

PREGNANCY AND LACTATION

Overview
- See discussion of benzodiazepine use during pregnancy in Anti-anxiety chapter (pages 290–293).

- Flurazepam is officially contraindicated during pregnancy.

- With little reason for hypnotics during pregnancy, and given their potential risks, *avoid them.*

Teratogenicity (1st trimester)
- Patients should stop benzodiazepines at least 2–4 weeks before attempting to conceive; they should remain off them until the first trimester ends.
  - √ If menstrual cycle very regular, could take brief trial of short-acting benzodiazepine up to first missed period.
    - □ Maternal-placental circulation not established until then.

- In a study of mothers taking amobarbital, 35% (95/273) of infants had congenital defects.

- Virtually no evidence that pentobarbital, secobarbital, or chloral hydrate are teratogenic.

- Ethchlorvynol may increase malformations.

- Ethchlorvynol (500 mg/day) may also induce infant withdrawal and/or mild hypotonia, poor suck, absent rooting, poor grasp, delayed-onset jitters, and CNS depression.

Direct Effect on Newborn (3rd trimester)

- Flurazepam linked to neonatal depression; mother who received 30 mg of flurazepam 10 days before delivery had sedated, inactive newborn during the first 4 days.

- No apparent harmful effects from secobarbital.

Lactation

- Benzodiazepines enter breast milk; may addict newborn and induce withdrawal.

- Benzodiazepines can impair alertness and temperature regulation.

- With longer-acting benzodiazepines, effects persist 2–3 weeks in infants.

Drug Dosage in Mother's Milk

Generic Names	Milk/ Plasma Ratio	Time of Peak Concentration in Milk (hours)	Infant Dose (µg/kg/day)	Maternal Dose (%)	Safety Rating*
Chloral hydrate	?	?	0.47 mg†	2	B
Phenobarbital‡	?	?	1.56	23–156	D
Quazepam	4.13	3	14.4	5.8	C

*B: Reasonably unsafe before 34 weeks, but safer after 34 weeks; C: Unsafe before week 34, relatively safe from weeks 34–44, and safest after 44th week; D: Unsafe throughout infancy, largely because infant plasma concentrations may appear, and rarely exceed, those of mother.
† Infant therapeutic dose 15–50 µg/kg/day; maternal dose administered as 1.3 g suppository.
‡ Broad range in findings.

DRUG-DRUG INTERACTIONS

After reviewing the benzodiazepine interactions on pages 193–296, examine these other interactions specific to hypnotics. All of these are potentiated by other sedatives and sedating drugs.

Drugs (X) Interact with:	Chloral Hydrate (C)	Comments
* Alcohol	X↑ C↑	This "Mickey Finn" combination yields CNS depression. Patients can have fainting, sedation, flushing, tachycardia, headache, and hypotension. Avoid mixture, especially in cardiovascular problems.

Drugs (X) Interact with:	Chloral Hydrate (C)	Comments
* Dicumarol	X↑	Chloral hydrate may briefly accelerate hypo-prothrombinemic response to dicumarol, but effect quickly disappears. Adverse clinical responses are uncommon, but bleeding may occur. Benzodiazepine hypnotics are preferred. *Don't* give chloral hydrate to patients on anticoagulants.
Furosemide	X↑	Diaphoresis, hot flashes, and hypertension occur with IV furosemide. Give IV furosemide with caution to any patient on chloral hydrate in past 24 h.
Sedatives and sedating drugs	X↑ C↑	Increased sedation, confusion.
TCAs	X↓	Decreased antidepressant effect.
* Warfarin (*see* dicumorol)		

Drugs (X) Interact with:	Disulfiram (D)	Comments
†Alcohol	D↑	(*See* pages 344–346.)
Amitriptyline	X↑	Avoid combination until more information. When amitriptyline was added to disulfiram, 2 cases of a central nervous system cognitive disorder were reported with confusion, hallucinations, and memory loss in 1–4 weeks. Rapid improvement when one or both agents stopped.
Anticonvulsants	X↑	Excessive sedation.
Barbiturates	X↑	Excessive sedation.
* Benzodiazepines	X↑	Disulfiram increases most benzodiazepine levels (not 3-hydroxy compounds, lorazepam, oxazepam, temazepam, and, partially, clonazepam); more sedation. Lower benzodiazepines or switch to 3-hydroxy compounds.
Cephalosporin	D↑	Disulfiram reaction.
Cocaine	D↑	Increased disulfiram effect.
†Dicumarol (*see* warfarin)		
* Isoniazid	D↑	Combination produces ataxia, irritability, disorientation, dizziness, and nausea. Frequency unclear, but combine cautiously. Reduce or stop disulfiram.
* Metronidazole	D↑	Combination produces CNS toxicity, psychosis, and confusion. Avoid combination.
†MAOIs	D↑	*Severe* CNS reactions.
Paraldehyde	X↑	Disulfiram may inhibit paraldehyde's metabolism, leading to toxicity.
* Perphenazine	X↑	Decreases perphenazine's metabolism, risking toxicity.

Drugs (X) Interact with:	Disulfiram (D)	Comments
†Phenytoin	X ↑	Disulfiram consistently increases phenytoin, inducing phenytoin toxicity (e.g., ataxia, mental impairment, nystagmus). Often occurs about 4 h after disulfiram's initial dose. After stopping disulfiram, symptoms may persist for 3 weeks. Avoid combination, but if must use together, observe carefully. Obtain serum phenytoin determinations. Monitor for reduced phenytoin response when disulfiram is stopped.
* Theophylline	X ↑	Disulfiram increases theophylline, which may prompt toxicity. Lower theophylline may be needed. If disulfiram is changed, monitor patient's theophylline level.
†Warfarin	X ↑	Disulfiram increases response to warfarin, which prompts bleeding. If disulfiram is started or stopped in patients taking oral anticoagulants, monitor carefully. Similar interaction with dicumarol likely, but unproven.

Drugs (X) Interact with:	Ethchlorvynol (E)	Comments
Amitriptyline	X ↑ E ↑	Transient delirium noted in patient taking one gram of ethchlorvynol and amitriptyline.
* Anticoagulants	X ↓	Ethchlorvynol may inhibit response to dicumarol and possibly warfarin. May need to adjust oral anticoagulants, or preferably, replace ethchlorvynol with a benzodiazepine.

* Moderately important interaction; † Extremely important interaction; ↑ Increases; ↓ Decreases.

EFFECTS ON LABORATORY TESTS

Generic Names	Blood/Serum Tests	Results*	Urine Tests	Results*
Benzodiazepines	WBC, RBC LFT	↓ r ↓ r ↑	None	
Chloral hydrate	WBC	↓	Ketonuria Glucose** Catecholamines*** 17-hydroxycorticosteroids****	↑ ↑ f ↑ ↓ ↑
Disulfiram	Cholesterol	↑	VMA	↓

* ↑ Increases, ↓ Decreases.
** Use oxidative test instead of copper sulfate.
*** Only flurimetric test.
**** With Reddy, Jenkins, and Thorn procedure.
f = falsely; r = rarely; LFT = AST/SGOT, ALT/SGPT, LDH, bilirubin, and alkaline phosphatase.

WITHDRAWAL

Benzodiazepines, barbiturates, barbiturate-like hypnotics, and alcohol all produce

- Dependency
- Tolerance
- Addiction
- Withdrawal

This withdrawal can be fatal; *never* abruptly withdraw hypnosedatives.

These agents are all cross-reactive, although high-potency benzodiazepines (i.e., alprazolam, triazolam, lorazepam, clonazepam) may not be predictably cross-reactive with lower-potency benzodiazepines such as diazepam and chlordiazepoxide.

In general, likelihood of significant withdrawal symptoms is correlated with dosage and duration of treatment.

- It is possible to have significant withdrawal symptoms in a person taking diazepam 5 mg bid for 2 years.
  - √ Increased risk of significant withdrawal from ordinary anxiolytic dose (not in panic disorder range) is more likely to occur after 6 months of treatment, not before.
- Dependence also is likely to occur if patient takes 3–4 times the normal therapeutic dose for anxiety for 4–6 weeks.
- The higher benzodiazepines doses used to treat panic attacks routinely risk significant withdrawal symptoms if doses are tapered too quickly.
- Patients with a h/o significant withdrawal symptoms, if on the same dose as before, are likely to have
  - √ Significant withdrawal symptoms again.
  - √ Same pattern of withdrawal as before.
- Withdrawal symptoms more common with
  - √ Short half-life benzodiazepins.
  - √ Last half of taper.

Compared to patients who *suddenly* withdraw, patients who *gradually* withdraw have fewer symptoms and no seizures.

Hypnoanxiolytic withdrawal can arise up to 10 days after the last dose. More typical presentations are

- 2–6 days from the last dose of diazepam or clorazepate
- 1–3 days from alprazolam
- 12–16 h from barbiturates

Hypnoanxiolytics with shorter half-lives (e.g., amobarbital, lorazepam, alprazolam) present more severe withdrawal symptoms and earlier peaks (2–3 days). Because of more gradual declines in blood levels, hypnoanxiolytics with longer half-lives (e.g., chlordiazepoxide, diazepam, clorazepate, clonazepam) have less severe withdrawal symptoms and later peaks (5–10 days).

- Benzodiazepine half-lives are longer in older people because they metabolize them more slowly.
  - √ Most likely for benzodiazepines that are converted into active metabolites by the liver (chlordiazepoxide, diazepam, clorazepate, quazepam, flurazepam).
  - √ Least likely for benzodiazepines that are conjugated by the liver and have no active metabolites (oxazepam, lorazepam, temazepam, triazolam, estazolam).

Delayed withdrawal involuntary motor symptoms

- Seen occasionally days or weeks after all other signs and symptoms are gone.
- Usually muscle spasm and/or myoclonus.

Signs and Symptoms of Hypnoanxiolytic Withdrawal*

Stage	Signs and Symptoms	Timing for Alcohol Withdrawal	Untreated Patients (%)
I "SHAKES" (Tremulousness)	Tremor, bad dreams, insomnia, morning sweats, apprehension, blepharospasm, agitation, ataxia, dilated pupils, labile BP, hypertension/hypotension, increased respiration and heart rate, nausea, vomiting, flushed; atypically have transient hallucinations and illusions; seizures—14%.†	5–10 h after last dose; peaks at 24–48 h; usually lasts 3–5 days but may last 2 weeks; may occur on any substance.	80
II HALLUCINATIONS	Auditory hallucinations both vague (e.g., buzzes, hums) and specific (e.g., accusatory voices); visual hallucinations or perceptual disturbances may also occur; clear consciousness; fear, apprehension, panic, tinnitus; other atypical hallucinations and some clouded consciousness may arise; rum fits—3%.	Onset may happen on agent or up to 12–48 h (and infrequently up to 7 days) after last dose; typically persists 1 week, but can extend over 2 months.	5–25
III SEIZURES	Single or multiple grand mal convulsions; occasionally status epilepticus; muscle jerks.	Appears 6–48 h after last dose; peaks at 12–24 h; seizures usually erupt 16 h into withdrawal.	10–25

Signs and Symptoms of Hypnoanxiolytic Withdrawal (Cont.)

Stage	Signs and Symptoms	Timing for Alcohol Withdrawal	Untreated Patients (%)
IV DELIRIUM TREMENS (DTs)	Typical delirium: clouded and fluctuating consciousness, confusion, disorientation, loss of recent memory; illusions and hallucinations (of all types, often scary), autonomic hyperactivity, hyperthermia, agitation, emotional lability, persecutory delusions, severe ataxia, coarse tremor; REM rebound (up to 3–4 months); rum fits—41%; 1–15% of DT patients die.	Appears 48–96 h after last dose; persists 4–7 days without complications; convulsions appear 16 h into withdrawal and psychotic symptoms, 36 h into withdrawal.	15

* This withdrawal pattern applies most to alcohol, barbiturates, and barbiturate-like hypnotics (e.g., ethchlorvynol); happens less often and less severely with benzodiazepines. Stages may evolve gradually or leap ahead. May pass through any stage without going through a previous stage.

† Seizures erupt during any stage. Stage III presents the most intense and frequent seizures. About 20% of patients with DTs have already had a seizure.

Withdrawing Hypnoanxiolytics

Benzodiazepine Taper

Outpatients do not usually require rapid tapers.

- In syndromes that have an effective non-habit-forming alternative treatment (e.g., TCA or SSRI for panic disorder),
  - √ May be better to begin alternative treatment before benzodiazepine taper is started.
    - □ Avoids reemergence of symptoms that can exacerbate and complicate withdrawal.
- Frequently a long-acting drug (e.g., clonazepam) is substituted for a shorter-acting drug (e.g., alprazolam).
- If a slow taper is planned, switching to a long-acting drug is often unnecessary, unless shorter-acting drug is so short that interdose rebound is seen and can't be avoided by very small multiple doses.
- This substitution should not be made abruptly because the short-acting drug will already be at steady state, while the longer-acting drug may take 5 or more days to reach steady state.
- To allow for these different half-lives, the longer-acting drug can be started at the pharmacologically comparable dosage of the short-acting one and, at the same time, the shorter-acting drug can be decreased 25% of the original dose on the first day and 25% of the original dose on each subsequent day.

√ Prn additions of the short-acting drug can be added or
√ For maximum speed, can "load" patient with twice the pharmacological equivalent dose for 2–5 days and then allow the drug to taper itself.
* The speed of the taper depends on the patient's preference.
  √ Reducing doses by a fixed percentage per unit of time rather than by a fixed dose per unit of time provides a more even and gradual taper.
  √ 10% reduction of the last dose every 3 days, or 25% per week, results in a longer but less discomforting result.
  √ 25% reduction of the last dose every 3 days results in a shorter, more uncomfortable result, but without risk of seizures or serious symptoms.
  √ Sometimes patients delay the very end of the taper by halving or quartering the one remaining pill, more for psychological than pharmacologic reasons.

See also alcohol withdrawal (pages 340–343).

Very rapid benzodiazepine withdrawal can be done safely in an inpatient setting, if daily benzodiazepine dose is under 30 mg diazepam equivalents. (See page 362 in Chapter 7 for dose equivalents of benzodiazepines.)

* Patients already on longer-acting benzodiazepines may get no benzodiazepine unless withdrawal symptoms are seen.
  √ Monitor heart rate, BP, temperature, tremulousness.
  √ Give previously used benzodiazepine prn for objective symptoms—not "I feel anxious."
    □ Make prn dose equal to 25% of original daily dose.
* If shorter-acting benzodiazepine has previously been used, switch to a longer-acting one.

Diazepam and Chlordiazepoxide Dose Equivalents of Non-Benzodiazepine Sedatives

	Oral Dose
Diazepam	10 mg
Chlordiazepoxide	25 mg
Alcohol	1.5 oz
Chloral hydrate	1000 mg
Ethclorvynol	750 mg
Meprobamate	400 mg
Pentobarbital	100 mg
Phenobarbital	30 mg
Secobarbital	100 mg

Carbamazepine-Aided Withdrawal

The addition of carbamazepine frequently accomplishes rapid (4–7 days) withdrawal from very high doses of benzodiazepines (or alcohol) with minimal withdrawal symptoms.

- Give 200 mg bid on first day.
- If tolerated, on second day increase to 200 mg qA.M. and 400 mg qhs.
- Beginning on 3rd or 4th day, reduce benzodiazepine dose by 25% of original dose a day.
- Maintain on carbamazepine for 4 or more weeks.
- Monitor vital signs daily.
- Anecdotal evidence suggests that valproic acid can accomplish same result.
  - √ May be preferred option for sedative-hypnotic withdrawal in patients with panic disorder because valproic acid may have antipanic effects and carbamazepine does not.
- Accelerated withdrawal may be risky if there are complicating conditions (e.g., seizure risk) being treated by other medications that might exacerbate withdrawal symptoms (e.g., MAOI).

Attenuating Hypnoanxiolytic Withdrawal

- Neither clonidine nor propranolol have proven to be effective.
  - √ May mask symptoms of severe withdrawal.

Meprobamate Withdrawal

Withdrawal no faster than 10% every 2–3 days.

Immediate withdrawal of 3200 mg/day can induce convulsions, agitation, delirium, or death.

Buspirone

Does not create tolerance, dependence, or withdrawal. It does *not* stop or prevent withdrawal from benzodiazepines.

- Can help alcohol withdrawal.
  - √ Best in highly anxious alcoholics.
  - √ Average dose 45–60 mg daily.
  - √ Longer time to relapse.
  - √ Fewer drinking days.
  - √ Decrease in drinks per day only in highly anxious.

Hydroxyzine

May not produce physical dependence, but tolerance to sedative and anxiolytic effects usually develops.

- REM rebound can cause disturbed sleep on withdrawal.

Preventing Hynoanxiolytic Relapse (Including Alcohol)

- Nonbenzodiazepine treatments for the original panic disorder, anxiety, depression, or insomnia can be instituted before withdrawal is started. These treatments have been discussed previously and may include
  - √ Buspirone for anxiety.
  - √ SSRIs, MAOIs, or TCAs for panic, OCD, depression, or general anxiety.
  - √ Trazodone for insomnia, depression, or general anxiety.

Pentobarbital-Phenobarbital Tolerance Test

This test is seldom used but should be considered for inpatients whose history suggests a high risk for serious withdrawal—e.g., prior history of DTs, high dosages used, extensive mixtures of hypnoaxiolytics (alcohol, barbiturates, and benzodiazepines) or who are very unreliable historians about their drug intake.

To withdraw people from hypnoanxiolytics, the pentobarbital-phenobarbital test can determine the degree of dependence.

Step #1: The patient should not be intoxicated before receiving any pentobarbital.

- If patient has been consuming shorter-acting hypnoanxiolytics, the hypnoanxiolytic test can be delayed 6–8 h.
- If a patient has been using longer-acting hypnoanxiolytics, the hypnoanxiolytic test can be delayed 1–2 days.

Step #2: Give the patient 200 mg of liquid pentobarbital, often the following morning.

Step #3: Examine the patient 50–60 minutes later. Signs of tolerance to a total daily dose of *pentobarbital-equivalents* are shown below.

Possible Findings One Hour After Pentobarbital Challenge

Patient's Condition One Hour After Test Dose	Degree of Tolerance	Estimated 24-Hour Pentobarbital Requirement After Test Dose (mg)
No signs of intoxication	Extreme	Over 850
Fine nystagmus only	Marked	700–850
Slurred speech, mild ataxia, fine nystagmus	Definite	450–700
Coarse nystagmus, positive Romberg, gross ataxia, drowsy	Moderate	300–450
Asleep, but can awaken	None or minimal	< 300

Step #4: The patient's pentobarbital-equivalents can be altered by any of the following circumstances:

- The patient has not ingested the full test dose of pentobarbital or has secretly taken other hypnosedatives.
- Greater anxiety or agitation escalates tolerance.
- A 300 mg test dose is better for patients taking a pentobarbital-equivalent of over 1200 mg/day.
- For elderly patients, the test dose might be 100 mg.
- If the patient shows no intoxication to 200 mg of pentobarbital, the patient's tolerance is over 850 mg/day. If so,
  √ Give patient pentobarbital 100 mg q2h until intoxication is manifested or total dose reaches 500 mg in 6 h (e.g., 200 + 100 + 100 + 100 = 500 mg).
  √ The total dose given in the first 6 h (300–500 mg) is the patient's 6-hour requirement.

Step #5: Figure out the detoxification strategy.
- Establish the patient's phenobarbital-equivalent.
  √ If the patient had nystagmus, mild ataxia, and some slurred speech, might go on 150 mg qid (600 mg/day) of pentobarbital.
- However, it is better to calculate the initial 24-hour pentobarbital-equivalent.
  √ Because phenobarbital has a longer half-life and greater anti-seizure activity than pentobarbital, this 24-hour pentobarbital-equivalent (600 mg/day) is converted to phenobarbital requirements by substituting 30 mg of phenobarbital for 100 mg of pentobarbital. In this example, the phenobarbital-equivalent is 180 mg.

Step #6: Divide the daily phenobarbital dose into thirds (60 mg) and provide each dose every 8 h for the first 48 h.

- After 2 days, phenobarbital dose is diminished by 30 mg/day or by 10%/day (whichever is less) from the original dose. In this case, 10% is less and equals 6 mg.
- If patient is oversedated, reduce the dose slightly.
- If patient displays withdrawal signs, inch the dose up slightly.
- If unsure whether patient has received too much or too little phenobarbital, dispense too much rather than too little, since seizing is a greater risk than sleeping.

Alcohol

Although alcohol withdrawal resembles hypnoanxiolytic withdrawal, a somewhat different procedure might address certain aspects specific to alcohol.

Chlordiazepoxide provides an effective method because it is
- Relatively long-acting,
- Offers less euphoria than diazepam, and
- Affords fewer side effects than other agents.

Chlordiazepoxide risks accumulation in geriatric patients and in those with renal/hepatic disease.
- Lorazepam better alternative in these situations.

Management of alcohol withdrawal involves
- Treating or preventing Wernicke's syndrome with
  - √ Thiamine 100 mg po or IM on admission, and
  - √ Thiamine 50 mg/day po for one month.
- Managing the alcohol withdrawal *per se:*
  - √ If patient not high risk for withdrawal, use symptom-triggered approach: Give chlordiazepoxide 25–50 mg prn based on objective symptoms, i.e., increased autonomic symptoms (BP, HR, temperature), agitation, tremor, disorientation, perceptual (tactile, visual, auditory) disturbances, headache, nausea.
    - □ Check vital signs hourly and repeat as often as needed.
    - □ In many alcoholic patients one or two doses of chlordiazepoxide is enough to accomplish the withdrawal safely.
    - □ This should not be used, or used only very cautiously, in patients who have medications that might mask symptoms (e.g., clonidine, propranolol) or illnesses that might mimic symptoms (e.g., febrile).
- Fixed approach
  - √ Usually used in high-risk patients.
  - √ Chlordiazepoxide 50 mg q6h for total of 4 doses.
  - √ Chlordiazepoxide 25 mg q6h for 8 doses.
- 25–100 mg chlordiazepoxide prn
  - √ Risks over-medication, sedation, and longer hospital stays.
    - □ Particular concern in geriatric patients or those with breathing or hepatic disorders.
  - √ If patient is high risk for withdrawal
    - □ Initiate chlordiazepoxide 200 mg/day for first 2 days.
    - □ Reduce total daily dose of chlordiazepoxide by 25% each day until reaching zero.
    - □ Give extra doses of chlordiazepoxide as needed to prevent withdrawal symptoms.
- If there is adequate social support (or monitoring), low risk for severe withdrawal, and a well-motivated patient, outpatient withdrawal can be implemented.
  - √ Start with chlordiazepoxide 25 mg taken q4h (or less often) for day #1.

H
Y
P
N
O
T
I
C
S

√ Taper by 25% qd until no chlordiazepoxide remains.
√ In very tremulous outpatient, use 100 mg/day of chlordiaz-epoxide.
- Patients with hepatic problems are best withdrawn with ox-azepam or lorazepam, which are not metabolized in the liver.

Alcoholism Prevention and Treatment of Comorbid Conditions

In bipolar alcoholic patients, lithium may reduce alcohol consumption but not depression. However,

- Moderate quantities of alcohol can trigger hypomania and large quantities can cause depression. This can lead to a misdiagnosis of bipolar disorder and unnecessary lithium use.

Some alcoholic patients have a primary mood disorder that should be treated with ADs. Higher chances of primary depression

- If depression during times of sobriety and prior to onset of alco-holism.
- In women alcoholics and those wtih later onset (> 30 y.o.) alchol-ism.
- If depression history in family is independent of substance abuse.

SSRIs are probably preferred antidepressant in alcoholism.

- Lower toxicity.
- May help reduce impulsive drive to drink, even in those who are not depressed.
- Some open studies suggest that SSRIs can help prevent relapse in nondepressed alcoholics.

Buspirone 30–60 mg qd is preferred agent to assist highly anxious alcoholics during recovery.

Treat alcohol-induced *aggression with hallucinosis* with high-potency antipsychotics, such as haloperidol 5 mg.

- Avoid low-potency neuroleptics (e.g., thioridazine) during alcohol withdrawal, since they are more likely to prompt seizures and severe hypotension.
- With aggression alone, consider trazodone 25–150 mg q6h.

The following drugs can be useful in reducing craving and impulse to drink.

Naltrexone (RiVea)

- Usual dose 50 mg po qd
  - √ The serious side effects (e.g., LFT increase, lymphocytosis, GI disturbance) seen at 5-fold higher doses are not seen at this dose.
  - √ Patient must be opiate-free 7–10 days before starting.
  - √ Do not give to patient with hepatitis or liver failure.
- May help reduce
  - √ Alcohol craving
  - √ Number of drinking days
  - √ Percent of patients relapsing
- Side effects in 10% of patients include
  - √ Abdominal pain
  - √ Anxiety
  - √ Fatigue
  - √ Headache
  - √ Insomnia
  - √ Joint and muscle pain
  - √ Nausea
- Side effects in 1–10% of patients
  - √ Anorexia
  - √ Chills
  - √ Constipation
  - √ Decreased potency
  - √ Delayed ejaculation
  - √ Diarrhea
  - √ Dizziness
  - √ Feeling down
  - √ Increased energy
  - √ Increased thirst
  - √ Irritability
  - √ Skin rash
- FDA-approved for alcoholism prevention as well as opiate dependence.

Bromocriptine

- Based on one 6-month placebo-controlled trial, bromocriptine showed decrease in
  - √ Alcohol abuse
  - √ Alcohol craving

Disulfiram

If the goal is to *prevent* the resumption of alcohol consumption, disulfiram might help. All of these treatments work best as part of an overall monitored treatment program and not as the sole treatment. Prior to disulfiram treatment, evaluation should include

- LFTs
- ECG
- Physical exam

If the disulfiram-taking patient drinks alcohol, he or she may experience in 5–10 minutes (usually in this order)

- Flushing
- Sweating
- Throbbing headache and neck pain
- Palpitations
- Dyspnea
- Hyperventilation
- Tachycardia
- Hypotension
- Nausea
- Vomiting

These symptoms should be described in gory detail to the patient new to disulfiram.

More serious reactions generate chest pain, difficulty breathing, more severe hypotension, confusion, and (especially in patients on > 500 mg/day) an occasional death. Reactions occur for 0.5–2 h, often followed by drowsiness and sleep.

- The reaction's dangers increase with higher amounts of disulfiram (> 500 mg/day) or ethanol.
- Reactions can occur up to 14 days after the last drink.

Disulfiram should be avoided in

- Masochistic or suicidal patients.
- Demented or confused patients who forget they ingest disulfiram.
- Patients with severe cardiac disease, moderate-to-severe liver disease, renal failure, peripheral neuropathies, or pregnancy.
- Patients using drugs metabolized by the liver, including TCAs, SSRIs, anticonvulsants, MAOIs, neuroleptics, vasodilators, α- or β-adrenergic blockers, paraldehyde, or metronidazole.
- Patients extremely sensitive to thiuram derivatives in pesticides or rubber vulcanization.
- Patients who refuse to tell any relatives about their use of disulfiram.

- Patients who will not (or cannot) avoid alcohol in aftershave lotions, sauces, cough syrup.

Give disulfiram as follows:

- Wait until at least 12 h after last drink.
- Start on 250 mg qd for 1–2 weeks, and then
  √ 250 mg to patients over 170 pounds and
  √ 125 mg to patients under 170 pounds.
- For faster loading, a patient over 170 pounds, who tolerates the initial 250 mg dose well, can be given 250 mg bid or 500 mg qd for the first 2 days; then return to 250 mg qd.

Side effects include

- Drowsiness, fatigue
- Body odor, halitosis (dose-related), foul taste in mouth
- Headache, tremor, impotence, dizziness
- Rarely hepatoxicity, neuropathy, psychosis

Management

- If there is a severe disulfiram reaction, give diphenhydramine 50 mg IM/IV.
- Treat hypotension, shock, and arrhythmias symptomatically.
- Oxygen is useful for respiratory distress.

Treat alcohol-induced aggression and hallucinosis with high-potency antipsychotics, such as haloperidol 5 mg.

- Avoid low-potency neuroleptics (e.g., thioridazine) during alcohol withdrawal, since they are more likely to prompt seizures and severe hypotension.
- With aggression alone, consider trazodone 25–150 mg q 6 h.

OVERDOSE: TOXICITY, SUICIDE, AND TREATMENT

Benzodiazepines

Benzodiazepine overdoses are discussed in the previous chapter.

Barbiturates and Barbiturate-like Hypnotics

Barbiturates and barbiturate-like hypnotics present high suicide risks.

- About 10 times the daily dose of a barbiturate can be severely toxic.
- Death occurs in 0.5–12% of barbiturate overdoses. These fatalities may happen "on purpose" or from an "autonomous" state in

which the patient falls asleep, awakes in a fog, cannot remember how many pills have already been taken, and overconsumes.

- Autonomous state as a reason for the overdose is usually an alibi and not true.
- The true autonomous state is believed to be quite rare because so many awakenings and ingestions are pharmacologically nearly impossible.
- Patient may truly not remember overdosing secondary to retrograde amnesia.

Barbiturates with shorter half-lives and high lipid solubility are more lethal.

Chloral Hydrate

Chloral hydrate's lethal dose is 5–10 times its hypnotic dose of 1–2 grams. Acute chloral hydrate overdoses display:

Common	Less Common	Infrequent
Stomach distress	Miosis	Esophageal stricture
Hypotension	Vomiting	Gastric necrosis and perforation
Hypothermia	Areflexia	GI hemorrhage
Respiratory depression	Muscle flaccidity	Transient hepatic damage and jaundice
Cardiac arrhythmias		
Coma		

Management of chloral hydrate overdose

- General management as listed in the previous chapter for benzodiazepines.
- Hemodialysis may eliminate the metabolite trichloroethanol.
  √ Peritoneal dialysis may assist.

Ethchlorvynol

Acute ethchlorvynol overdoses generate

- Hypotension
- Bradycardia
- Hypothermia
- Mydriasis
- Areflexia

This may lead to

- Pulmonary edema
- Severe infections
- Peripheral neuropathy

- Severe pancytopenia, hemolysis
- Severe cardiorespiratory depression, apnea
- Deep coma (lasting several weeks)

Management of ethchlorvynol overdoses involve (see also pages 53–54)

- Emphasis on pulmonary care and monitoring blood pressure gases.
- Value of hemodialysis is debated.
- Alkalinization of urine does not increase excretion.

Toxicity and Suicide Data

Generic Names	Toxic Doses Average (g)	Fatal Doses Average Lowest (g)	Toxic Levels* (μg/ml)	Fatal Levels* (μg/ml)
Benzodiazepines				
Estazolam	—	—	—	—
Flurazepam	—	—	—	—
Quazepam	—	—	—	—
Temazepam	—	—	—	—
Triazolam	2	—	—	—
Zolpidem	—	—	—	—
Barbiturates				
Amobarbital	0.4	2–3	30–40	> 50
Butabarbital	—	—	40–60	> 50
Pentobarbital	—	2–3	10–15	> 30
Phenobarbital	—	6–10	50–80 (30–134)	> 80
Secobarbital	—	2–3	10–15	> 30
Miscellaneous				
Chloral hydrate	30	10 (4)	—	—
Ethchlorvynol	50	6	—	—

* *Toxic levels* produce coma, arousal difficulties, significant respiratory depression; *fatal levels* are usually lethal.

PRECAUTIONS

All benzodiazepine, barbiturate, and barbiturate-like hypnotics contraindicated in patients with

- Hypersensitivity to hypnotics or anti-anxiety agents
- Pregnancy
  - √ Benzodiazepines, except for flurazepam, are not contraindicated, but a careful assessment of risk-benefits must be done first.
- Sleep apnea
  - √ Zolpidem and trazodone not contraindicated

Barbiturates and barbiturate-like hypnotics should be avoided in patients with

- Liver impairment
- Alcoholism
- Renal conditions
- Porphyria
- On anticoagulants
- Suicidal ideation

NURSES' DATA

Observe if patients have

- Trouble finding the bed after taking hypnotic
- Trouble walking, falling
- Confusion
- Immediate sleepiness or overstimulation
- Skin rash
- Abdominal pain
- Muscle weakness

Note symptoms of withdrawal, intoxication, or overdose (see pages 304–305, 335–337, 346–348). Withdrawal symptoms may be difficult to distinguish from anxiety, and vice versa.

Ensure that patients do not take hypnotics for pain relief.

Also make sure patients understand the short-term value of hypnotics.

PATIENT AND FAMILY NOTES

If taking a hypnotic, avoid

- Alcohol
  - √ With a hypnotic, one drink feels and acts like 2–3 drinks.
  - √ Worse for barbiturates and barbiturate-like hypnotics.
- Contraceptives, unless doctor concurs.
- Pregnancy
  - √ If become pregnant, do not stop hypnotics until deciding on a withdrawal schedule with doctor.
- Long-term use
- Suddenly stopping hypnotics after long-term use!
  - √ Abrupt hypnotic withdrawal is often more dangerous than abrupt opiate withdrawal—seizures, and worse.

If a doctor prescribes barbiturate or barbiturate-like hypnotic, ask if a benzodiazepine, which is safer, would be better short-term hypnotic.

If the elderly or debilitated are too confused to manage their hypnotics properly, the family may need to dispense them.

Store hypnotics away from the bedside or from any readily accessible location to avert accidental intake. Keep away from youngsters.

Within 6 h of taking a hypnotic, do not work around machines, drive a car, or cross the street.

- The next morning, check if reflexes are a "tad off" by, for example, stepping down on the car break in the driveway.
- There is a 5–10 times higher driving-accident rate in patients on benzodiazepines.
- People on hypnotics are more likely to ignore fire alarms, pain, a full bladder, a crying baby, or telephones.

Triazolam, and zolpidem (to a lesser extent) can cause traveler's amnesia.

The doctor should suggest a specific time period to take a hypnotic (e.g., ½ h, 1 ½ h before bedtime).

If patient forgets a dose

- Can consume it within 6 h of awakening.
  √ Zolpidem often can be taken within 4 h of awakening.
- Otherwise wait for next evening.
- Do not double dose.

May ingest with food, but this may slow onset of sleep.

9. Stimulants

INTRODUCTION

Although abused illegally, stimulants are used clinically to treat

Also discussed is management of

As detailed elsewhere, stimulants treat

NAMES, COST, DEA SCHEDULE NUMBER, MANUFACTURERS, DOSE FORMS, COLORS

Generic Names (DEA Schedule #) (Dollars/Dose: 100 pills in mg)*	Brand Names (Dollars/Dose: 100 pills in mg)*	Manufacturers	Dose Forms (mg)**	Colors
Dextroamphetamine[II] 19/518/5	Dexedrine	SmithKline Beecham	t: 5 e: 5 mg/5 ml	t: orange† e: orange
	Spansule 20/5	SmithKline Beecham	SR-sp: 5/10/15	SR-sp: all brown-clear
Methylphenidate[II] 23–29/5	Ritalin 30/5	CIBA	t: 5/10/20	t: yellow/pale green/pale yellow†
Methylphenidate SR 76/2094/20	Ritalin-SR	CIBA	SR-t: 20	SR-t: white
Pemoline[IV]	Cylert 110/325	Abbott	t: 18.75/ 37.75 ct: 37.5	t: white/ orange/tan ct: orange
Phendimetrazine[IV] 5–9/35	Plegine 59/35	Wyeth-Ayerst	t: 35	t: beige
	Prelu-2 (timed release) 91/105	Boehringer Ingelheim	c: 105	c: celery-green

* 1994 average wholesale price for 100 pills at this dose (e.g., 78/50 means 100 pills 50 mg cost $78). If depot form, cost is of single dose.
** c = capsule; ct = chewable tablet; e = elixir; sp = spansule; SR = sustained release; t = tablets; † = scored.

Similar drugs are marketed for appetite suppression and are occasionally used as alternative stimulants.

- Amphetamines (Schedule II)
  - √ Methamphetamine (Desoxyn)
  - √ Benzphetamine (Didrex)
  - √ Amphetamine plus dextroamphetamine (Obetrol)
- Non-amphetamines (Schedule IV)
  - √ Phentermine (Adipex-P, Fastin, Ionamin)
  - √ Phendimetrazine (Bontrill PDM, Bontril [slow release], Plegine, Pre-lu 2 [timed release])
  - √ Mazindol (Sanorex)
  - √ Diethylpropion (Tenuate, Tenuate Dospan)

PHARMACOLOGY

Stimulants act by

- Directly releasing catecholamines into synaptic clefts and, thus, onto postsynaptic receptor sites.

- Efficiently blocking the reuptake of catecholamines, thereby prolonging their actions.
- Impacting MAO enzymes to slow down metabolism.
- Serve as false neurotransmitters.

Dextroamphetamine

- Rapidly absorbed from GI tract; peak level in 2 h.
- Causes
  √ Increased BP and pulse rate (mean 11/min) especially in African-Americans.
    □ Usually not clinically significant
  √ Decreased appetite.
    □ Reduced weight more than methylphenidate or pemoline
  √ Delayed sleep.

Methylphenidate

- Rapidly absorbed from GI tract.
- Effects persist 2–4 h from a single normal tablet and 3–5 h after extended-release tablets.
  √ Sustained-release tablets are absorbed more slowly and may yield a lower plasma level than regular tablets.
- Has less anorectic and cardiac effects than dextroamphetamine.
  √ Often preferred for children.

Pemoline

- Is rapidly absorbed by GI tract.
- Is chewable and may be better accepted by young children.
- May be smoother and better tolerated.
- Is 50% bound to plasma protein.
- Reaches a steady state in 2–3 days.
- Has less stimulant effect than dextroamphetamine and methylphenidate. Abuse potential possible in animals.
  √ No abuse potential in humans.
- Lower abuse potential makes pemoline first choice in
  √ Kids with potentially drug-abusing parents.
  √ Adult and late adolescent ADHD.
- Reduces appetite and delays sleep in 30% of children.
- Using usual dosing procedure of 18.75 mg qA.M. initially and increasing 18.75 mg q 5–7 days takes 2–4 weeks to establish effective dose.
- If started at 1–2 mg/kg, and if plasma level is > 2 ng/ml (3–4 h later), clinical effect seen in hours.
  √ Takes 2–3 days to achieve steady-state plasma level.

Pharmacology of Stimulants in Children

Generic Names	Peak Serum Levels (hours)	Serum Half-lives (hours)	Onset of Action (hours)	Duration of Action (hours)
Dextroamphetamine	2–4	6–12	0.5–1	4–6
Methylphenidate	1–3	2–4	0.5–1	3–6
Pemoline	2–4 (5–12)	2–12 (acute) 14–34 (chronic)	3–4	12–24

DOSES

Attention-Deficit Hyperactivity Stimulant Doses in Children

Generic Names	Single Usual Starting Dose (mg)	Daily Dose Range (mg/kg/day)	Daily Dose Range (mg/kg/day)	Daily Dose Range (mg/day)
Dextroamphetamine	2.5–5 qd or bid	0.15–0.5	0.3–2.0	5–40
Methylphenidate	2.5–5 qd or bid	0.3–0.7	0.3–2.0	10–60
Pemoline	18.75–37.5 daily	0.5–2.5	0.5–3.0	37.5–112.5

Other Stimulant Doses

Generic Names	Adult Depression (mg/day)	Adult Narcolepsy (mg/day)	Geriatric Patients (mg/day)
Dextroamphetamine*	5–40	20–30	10–15
Methylphenidate*	10–80	10–30	10–30
Pemoline	18.75–150	37.5–75	——

* Usually in bid dosing.

CLINICAL INDICATIONS AND USE

Stimulants

- *Clearly* effective in
  - √ Attention-deficit hyperactivity disorder in children.
  - √ Narcoleptic symptoms of daytime sleepiness and sleep attacks.
- *Probably* effective in
  - √ Treatment-resistant depressions.
  - √ Apathy and withdrawal in medically ill and the elderly.
  - √ Chronic fatigue syndrome.
- *Possibly* effective in
  - √ Residual attention-deficit disorder in adults.
  - √ Mood and motivation symptoms of AIDS and other chronic, debilitating diseases.

Attention-Deficit Hyperactivity Disorder (ADHD)

Children who exhibit symptoms in several settings (the narrower British definition of ADHD) may have more drug responsivity than those who exhibit symptoms in only one or two settings.

Roughly 85–90% of these children respond to stimulants if trials of 2 different stimulants are used.

Short-acting stimulants are the first choice.

- Dextroamphetamine or
- Methylphenidate

If one of these drugs fails, there is a 25% chance the other drug will succeed.

- If a short-acting stimulant lasts only 3–4 h with abrupt return of symptoms, consider sustained-release forms or pemoline.
- Dextroamphetamine spansules can have uneven effects with early intense activity and a significant decline thereafter.
  - √ Anecdotal evidence suggests that sustained-release methamphetamines (Desoxyn Gradument tablets) have a longer and more even effect.

When a stimulant works, it

- Occurs early (often in 2 days),
- Persists, and
- Shows little or no tolerance over months to years.

Single stimulant trials superior to placebo in 70–80% of patients.

- 30% exhibit marked improvement,
- 40% display some benefit, and
- 10–30% are refractory.

Comparison trials of 2 stimulants, dextroamphetamine and methylphenidate, yield superiority of at least one agent over placebo in > 90% of patients.

- If child tolerates drug but with minimal or partial improvement, higher doses are likely to increase improvement.

Stimulants

- Decrease
  - √ Motor activity
  - √ Impulsiveness
  - √ Emotional lability

- Increase
  - ✓ Vigilance and attention
  - ✓ Short-term memory
  - ✓ More "normal" behavior

Stimulants occasionally make some youngsters more active and others more withdrawn and despondent.

- Euphoria is a rare event.
- In "normals," stimulant-induced euphoria appears to begin with puberty and does not occur earlier.

Academic performance and on-task (attention) behavior in classroom is directly related to dosage.

- Continued increases in performance occur up to 20 mg methylphenidate (single dose). Older uncontrolled studies reported doses above 0.6 mg/kg risked decrease in cognitive performance.
- Behavior ratings by teachers suggest maximum improvement at 10 mg (single dose).
- Different problems related to ADHD may respond at different doses.

Dosing

- Dextroamphetamine uses bid-tid and methylphenidate bid-qid dosages.
  - ✓ Typically taken 4 h apart.
  - ✓ Increase individual doses prn every few days by 2.5–5 mg.
- Pemoline can be dispensed once every morning (see page 353).
- Can increase stimulant doses q 2–4 days.
- Scored tablets useful.
- Kids enjoy chewable pemoline.
- If possible, give after meals to reduce appetite-suppressing effects at meal time.
  - ✓ Absorption is not affected by full stomach.

Initiating and Maintaining Therapy

- Methylphenidate may reduce WBC.
  - ✓ Get baseline WBC and monitor every 3 to 6 months.
- Pemoline may increase LFTs.
  - ✓ Get baseline LFT and monitor every 3 to 6 months
- Get baseline HR and BP and monitor for possible increase.
  - ✓ Especially if patient on dextroamphetamine and has African genetics.

- Inform family about most common transient side effects—anorexia, abdominal pain, headaches, irritability and moodiness—and that
  - √ Tolerance to stimulants doesn't usually occur in ADHD.
  - √ No cases of sustained or permanent growth suppression.
  - √ Get baseline height and weight.
  - √ Monitor every 6 months.
  - √ May see rebound growth with "drug" holidays, but
    - □ The social impairment that is frequently experienced on "holidays" and the overall effect on normal emotional maturation argue against holidays.
    - □ Increased nutrition can offset growth problems.
- Inform patient and family of onset insomnia.
  - √ May need to take last dose of day earlier.
- If possible, have assessment include teachers and parents.
  - √ Use Connors or similar scales if possible to rate behavior changes.
  - √ Compare with placebo if possible.
  - √ If without full response, try another stimulant.

Therapeutic responses do not jive directly with serum or saliva levels.

Safe to suddenly stop stimulants.

Safer to use sustained-release forms before TCAs.

Stimulants worsen pre-existing tic disorder and can cause tics in children who have a risk for tic disorder (i.e., personal or family h/o tics).

- Avoid stimulants in children at risk for tics.

TCAs or bupropion may help if

- Stimulants proved ineffective or were not tolerated.
- Single night dosing desirable for compliance.
- Child has a coexisting disorder requiring ADs (e.g., mood disorder).
- Strong family h/o mood disorder.
- Drug-abusing children or parents.

See use of TCAs in children on pages 94–95.

Drawbacks of TCAs are

- Rare but serious cardiovascular side effects (especially in prepubertal children).
- Overdose—high risk or reality.

S
T
I
M
U
L
A
N
T
S

Antidepressants include

- Desipramine, imipramine, nortriptyline, bupropion—first choices.
  - ✓ May work best on impulsivity and attention problems.
  - ✓ May not be as good as stimulants for attention deficit.
- Desipramine has lowest side effects, but concerns about cardiovascular risk have pushed more clinicians to nortriptyline.
- Bupropion well tolerated but divided dosing needed.
  - ✓ And child with seizure risk disqualified.
  - ✓ May work better on attention and hyperactivity and less on impulsivity.
- SSRIs not shown to be effective.

Start imipramine at 10 mg hs and then gradually increase to 75 mg hs.

ADHD improvement with antidepressant often happens in a few days.

- Only occasionally takes weeks as with depression.

Alpha-adrenergic stimulants may help ADHD.

- May have moderate effects alone.
- May be best used to augment other medications.
- Clonidine nonselectively stimulates alpha 2_A, 2_B, and 2_C adrenergic receptors.
- Better than placebo in a few controlled trials.
  - ✓ Can use doses up to 4–5 μg/kg.
    - □ Most common side effect is sleepiness.
    - □ Subsides in 2–4 weeks.
- Guanfacine selectively stimulates alpha 2_A adrenergic receptors, mainly found in brain.
  - ✓ May be better tolerated than clonidine.
- Has lower side effects.
  - ✓ Lower frequency of sedation (21% vs. 35%).
  - ✓ No significant effect on BP.
  - ✓ Rebound hypertension milder and less frequent.
  - ✓ 25% headache, stomachache.
    - □ Usually gone in 2 weeks.
- Guanfacine in 1 open trial
  - ✓ Significantly improved
    - □ Hyperactivity
    - □ Inattention
    - □ Immaturity

√ Did not significantly improve
  □ Mood
  □ Aggression
- Dosing guanfacine
  √ Usual daily final dose 2–4 mg or 0.1 mg/kg given bid or tid.
  √ Start 0.5 mg qA.M.
  √ Add 0.5 mg q 3 days at other dosing times.
    □ Typically noon, 4–5 P.M. qhs.
    □ Because drug has > 12 h half-life, can give largest dose qhs to minimize daytime sedation.

Other drugs suggested for ADHD have important limitations.

- Benzodiazepines and barbiturates can trigger "paradoxical" excitement; *avoid.*
- Diphenhydramine and chloral hydrate promote less agitation but may temporarily induce sleep.
- Neuroleptics (e.g., chlorpromazine 10–50 mg qid) nonspecifically calm but risk many side effects.
- Lithium only assists bipolar patients with impulsiveness, low attention span, and hyperactivity.
  √ Also helps conduct disorders.
  √ May help child with "episodic" ADHD.
- Carbamazepine helps with aggressiveness, impulsivity.
  √ Approved for use in children.

Adult Attention-Deficit Hyperactivity Disorder

Adults with residual attention-deficit disorder (with inattention, impulsiveness, concentration difficulty, anxiety, irritability, and excitability) *plus* a childhood history of ADHD may improve with stimulants.

- Often show poor work or academic performance, temper outburst, antisocial behavior, or alcohol abuse.
- Diagnosis in adults is more difficult than in children.
  √ Many diagnoses may resemble ADHD.
    □ Substance abuse
    □ Bipolar disorder
    □ Personality disorder
    □ Agitated depression
  √ Adults do not tend to have hyperactivity.
  √ There is no neuropsychological or other test that confirms adult ADHD diagnosis.

S
T
I
M
U
L
A
N
T
S

√ Family members and those close to patient can help give corroborating information about diagnosis.
√ A h/o having a paradoxical calming response to stimulants suggests a possible positive response to stimulants.

- Stimulants can help.
  √ Pemoline is probable first choice because of its low abuse potential.
  √ If there is a concern about substance abuse, nonstimulant alternatives discussed above should be considered first, including
    □ Low-sedation TCAs or bupropion
    □ Clonidine or guanfacine

Treatment-Resistant Depression

Stimulants are better than placebo in treatment of resistant depression, geriatric depression, and medically-induced depression.

- Hidden comorbidity of stimulant-responsive syndromes (e.g., sleep apnea, ADHD) might account for some of the response in these groups.

Stimulants are not better than placebo as first treatment of depression.

Stimulants dramatically aid a small, *select* group who

- Have failed on at least 2 other antidepressant classes (e.g., TCAs, SSRIs, MAOIs).
- Have a serious, often life-threatening, ailment (e.g., AIDS, cancer) and who cannot tolerate antidepressants.
- Will soon be booted from a job or school, and who require a stimulant's boost until ADs work.
- Need an adjunct to ADs or need AD augmentation.

Stimulants can generate a true antidepressant effect.

- Effect may begin to outlive duration of action of stimulant.
- Mood on awakening in A.M. may still be improved.

Stimulants develop tolerance more often than conventional antidepressants.

- 20–40% tolerance seen with stimulants.

Childhood and adolescent depressions respond as well to placebo as to ADs.

- Stimulants may be a resonable alternative.

Never add a stimulant to MAOIs: *Hypertensive crisis!*

Treatment-Resistant Obesity

- Positive effects tend to be transient.
  - √ By 6 months no difference between patients who used stimulant and those who did not.
- All appetite suppressants are stimulants except fenfluramine (Pondimin), which is primarily a serotonin releaser.

Narcolepsy

Treatments include

- Methylphenidate and dextroamphetamine for sleep attacks and daytime sleepiness.
  - √ Unlike ADHD, tolerance to stimulants occurs with higher doses.
- Phenelzine or tranylcyromine for sleep attacks.
  - √ Can completely stop REM.
- TCAs (e.g., imipramine) for cataplexy.

Chronic Medically Debilitating Conditions (AIDS, Cancer, Chronic Fatigue Syndrome)

ADs significantly help 50% of those treated, but

- Many could not tolerate side effects, particularly with TCAs.
- Many had no response.

Stimulants should be considered as reasonable alternatives for those who are AD nonresponders or are afflicted with side effects.

Methylphenidate or dextroamphetamine alone reduced mood and organic symptoms in patients with AIDS.

- No common adverse effects except appetite suppression and feeling "hyper."
  - √ More patients actually ate more because they had energy to buy and fix food.
- No tolerance developed.
- Had moderate analgesic effects alone and as augmentation with opiates.

Chronic fatigue syndrome (CFS) has several treatments besides stimulants.

- Amitriptyline in low doses (25–75 mg) superior to placebo.
  - √ Improvement noted in pain (fibromyalgia), sleep, fatigue, and overall functioning.

- Imipramine (25–75 mg) did not show good response in open study.
- Case reports suggest positive results with
  √ Nortriptyline 50 mg.
  √ Clomipramine 75 mg better for pain than depression.
- Cyclobenzaprine (Flexeril), a tricyclic noradrenergic uptake blocker, given 10–40 mg qd better than placebo for
  √ Sleep
  √ Pain severity
  √ Fatigue
  √ Global improvement
- Fluoxetine 20 mg in open studies (N = 50) of CFS without depression improved nearly all patients in areas of
  √ Pain
  √ Fatigue
  √ Functioning
- Bupropion 300 mg qd improved nonresponders to fluoxetine
  √ Mood
  √ Energy
  √ Immune function

SIDE EFFECTS

Stimulant side effects typically arise

- In 2–3 weeks after initiating drug, and
- From dose reduction, causing rebound symptoms.

Elderly develop more side effects.

From the greater to the lesser, stimulants cause:

Subjective Side Effects	Objective Side Effects
Most Common	
Anorexia	Blood pressure changes (up or down)
Insomnia	Tachycardia
Irritability, hyperalertness	Tremor
Weight loss	Dysrhythmias
Nausea	
Headache	
Depression	
Palpitations	
Blurred vision	
Dry mouth	
Constipation	
Dizziness	
Least Common	

Cardiovascular Effects

Blood pressure changes

- Highly variable
  - √ Children with African genetics more often hypertensive.
- Unclear if taking stimulants with meals lowers BP.
- Reduce or stop drug.

Palpitations

Tachycardia

Gastrointestinal Effects

Dry mouth

- Mainly in adolescents

Anorexia

- Reduced appetite occurs in 30% of children given moderately high stimulant doses.

Weight loss

- Usually begins early in treatment and
  - √ May last up to 6 weeks.
  - √ With pemoline, *weight gain* may follow in 3–6 months.

Hepatotoxicity

- Pemoline induces hepatotoxicity in 1–3% of children.
- AST/SGOT and ALT/SGPT gradually increase over first 6 months of treatment.
  - √ Enzymes return to normal after stopping pemoline.

Endocrine and Sex Effects

Suppressed growth

- Some stimulants suppress weight gain in some children; whether stimulants suppress height gain is unlikely.
  - √ Suppressed growth is reported more with dextroamphetamine > methylphenidate > pemoline.
  - √ When methylphenidate is halted, compensatory growth occurs, which eliminates all growth difference between drug and nondrug-treated patients.
- Growth rebound appears during drug-free holidays.

Impotence

Changes in libido

- Both increases and decreases reported.

S
T
I
M
U
L
A
N
T
S

Central Nervous System Effects

Insomnia

- Usually onset insomnia.
- Affects 30% of children on moderately high stimulant doses.
- Often arises early, at times before optimal dose reached.
  - √ May be transient with pemoline.
- Management
  - √ Give more of the stimulant earlier in the day.
  - √ Reduce dose.

Overstimulation

Confusion, "dopey feeling"

- Especially arises with > 1 mg/kg/day of methylphenidate.

Restlessness

- Reduce dose and/or
- Give earlier in day.

Headache

Dizziness

Choreoathetoid movements

- Common with pemoline.

Dysphoria

- Occurs with all stimulants, but especially with methylphenidate patients who display
  - √ Mild dysphoria
  - √ Subtle social withdrawal
  - √ Dulled affect, emotional blunting
  - √ Cognitive "overfocusing"
  - √ Perseveration
- Mild to moderate depression in children.

Euphoria

- Rare in prepubertal children; more common after puberty.

Exacerbation of tics, exacerbation of Tourette's

- Avoid stimulants with these patients.

Psychosis

- Dextroamphetamine doses > 80 mg/day trigger psychosis with
  - √ Agitation
  - √ Tremor

√ Toxicity
√ Hallucinations
√ Paranoid thinking

PERCENTAGES OF SIDE EFFECTS*

Side Effects	Dextroamphetamine	Methylphenidate	Pemoline
CARDIOVASCULAR EFFECTS			
Dizziness, lightheadedness	11.5 (1–23)	7.7 (0–13)	5.5
Lower blood pressure	——	< 1	< 1
Higher blood pressure	> 10	15.8 (1–26)	——
Tachycardia	5.5	15 (1–20)	5.5
Palpitations	5.5	4.4 (1–10)	5.5
Cardiac arrhythmias	< 1	5.5	——
Chest pain	< 1	4.4 (1–10)	——
GASTROINTESTINAL EFFECTS			
Dry mouth and throat	> 10	8.7 (0–17.4)	——
Anorexia, lower appetite	23.1 (1–56)	26.9 (0–72)	14.5 (1–34)
Nausea	5.5	5.1 (1–10)	5.5
Vomiting	5.5	——	——
Bad taste	5.5	——	——
Dyspepsia, upset stomach	5.5	9.7 (1–28)	5.5
Diarrhea	5.5	——	——
Constipation	5.5	6.5	——
Hepatotoxicity	——	——	2
Weight loss	29.5 (1–63)	13.5 (3–27)	5.5
Weight gain	——	4.3	——
RENAL EFFECTS			
Enuresis	——	9 (3–20)	——
ENDOCRINE AND SEXUAL EFFECTS			
Impotence	5.5	——	——
Disturbed sexual function	5.5	——	——
Growth suppression	see text	see text	see text
HEMATOLOGIC EFFECTS			
Easy bruising	——	5.5	——

Side Effects	Dextroamphetamine	Methylphenidate	Pemoline
EYES, EARS, NOSE, AND THROAT EFFECTS			
Blurred vision	5.5	< 1	—
Nystagmus	—	—	5.5
SKIN, ALLERGIES, AND TEMPERATURE			
Unusual sweating	5.5	—	—
Rashes	< 1	5.5	5.5
Hives	< 1	5.5	—
Exfoliative dermatitis	—	5.5	—
Fever, unexplained	—	5.5	—
Joint pain	—	5.5	—
CENTRAL NERVOUS SYSTEM EFFECTS			
Dyskinesias	< 1	3	5.5
Tourette's syndrome	< 1	< 1	< 1
Tics	< 1	—	—
Headache	18.3 (1–31)	9.3 (0–15)	13.8 (1–22)
Drowsiness, less alert	5.5	5.7 (0–17)	5.5
Psychosis (normal dose)	< 1	< 1	< 1
Difficulty arousing	—	15 (11–19)	—
Insomnia	19 (5–43)	16.9 (0–52)	28.7 (< 10–42)
Tremor	5.5	6.5	—
Confused, "dopey"	10.3 (8–12)	3.9 (2–10)	—
Mood changes	< 1	> 10	5.5
Depression	39	8.7 (0–16)	—
Agitation, restlessness (motoric)	> 10	6.7 (3.3–> 10)	—
Irritability, stimulation	25 (17–29)	17.3 (11–19.6)	13.3 (1–21)

* These figures are primarily based on reports of children and adolescents treated for ADHD.

PREGNANCY AND LACTATION

Teratogenicity (1st trimester)

- There is usually no compelling reason that a mother stay on stimulants; therefore they should be discontinued.

- Dextroamphetamine may cause congenital malformations, such as cardiac abnormalities and biliary atresia.

- Methylphenidate not linked with congenital defects.

Direct Effect on Newborn (3rd trimester)	• One case of IV dextroamphetamine use reported in woman to produce withdrawal; experts strongly discourage dextroamphetamine use during pregnancy.
	• Stimulants can increase BP and worsen pre-eclampsia.
	• Stimulants are associated with premature delivery and low birth weight.
Lactation	• One of 3 studies revealed infants of amphetamine-using mothers were more irritable and poor sleepers; no figures given.
	• Methylphenidate: no data.

Drug Dosage in Mother's Milk

Generic Name	Milk/ Plasma Ratio	Time of Peak Concentration in Milk (hours)	Infant Dose (μg/kg/day)	Maternal Dose (%)	Safety Rating*
Amphetamine	2.8–7.5	?	20.7	6.2	C

* C: Unsafe before week 34, relatively safe from weeks 34–44, and safest after 44th week.

DRUG-DRUG INTERACTIONS

Drugs (X) Interact with:	Dextroamphetamines (D)	Comments
Acidifying agents (e.g., ascorbic acid, fruit juice, glutamic acid)	D ↓	Decreases absorption of amphetamines.
* Acetazolamide (and some furosemides)	D ↑	Acetazolamide increases amphetamines. Monitor patients on acetazolamide or on other carbonic anhydrase inhibitors for excessive amphetamine levels.
Alkalinizing agents (*see* sodium bicarbonate)		
Amantadine	X ↑	Increased amantadine effect with stimulation and agitation.
Antihistamines	X ↓	Amphetamines reduce antihistamine's sedation.
Antihypertensives	X ↓	Amphetamines may antagonize antihypertensives.
Antipsychotics: Chlorpromazine Haloperidol	X ↓ D ↓	Amphetamines inhibit antipsychotic actions, while neuroleptics block amphetamines' anorectic and

S
T
I
M
U
L
A
N
T
S

Drugs (X) Interact with:	Dextroamphetamines (D)	Comments
		stimulating effect. Antipsychotics effectively treat amphetamine overdose, but amphetamines should never treat an antipsychotic overdose.
Ethosuximide	X ↓	Amphetamines delay absorption of anticonvulsant ethosuximide.
Fluoxetine (see SSRIs)		
Fluvoxamine (see SSRIs)		
†Furazolidone	D ↑	Amphetamines induce hypertensive crises in patients given furazolidone, especially after 5 days. *Avoid.*
* Guanethidine	X ↓ D ↑	Amphetamines inhibit guanethidine's antihypertensive action. Does hypertensive patient need amphetamines? Use another agent.
Haloperidol (see antipsychotics)		
Lithium	D ↓	Lithium slows weight reduction and stimulatory effects of amphetamines. No special precautions.
Meperidine	X ↑	Amphetamines potentiate analgesic action.
†MAOIs	X ↑	*Hypertensive crisis.* Tranylcypromine is the most dangerous MAOI.
Norepinephrine	X ↑	Amphetamine use may increase pressor response to norepinephrine. Combine with caution.
Phenobarbitol, phenytoin	X ↓	Amphetamines delay absorption. May also decrease seizure threshold.
Propoxyphene	X ↑ D ↑	Can increase CNS symptoms in propoxyphene overdose, causing fatal convulsions.
Opiates	X ↑	Amphetamines potentiate the analgesic and anorectic effect of opiates.
Paroxetine (see SSRIs)		
Sedative-hypnotics	X ↓	Reverses sedative and anxiolytic effects.
Sertraline (see SSRIs)		
* Sodium bicarbonate	D ↑	Hefty sodium bicarbonate can increase amphetamine's effect; preferred by abusers.
SSRIs	X ↑ D ↑	Increased agitation; may augment antidepressant effect.
* TCAs	X ↑ D ↑	Amphetamines may increase TCA effect; can also produce arrhythmias, agitation, and psychosis. TCAs (desipramine, protriptyline) increase amphetamine levels.

Drugs (X) Interact with:	Methylphenidate (M)	Comments
Anticonvulsants: Phenytoin Diphenylhydantoin Primidone	X ↑	Increases plasma levels; isolated cases of intoxication.
* Guanethidine	X ↓ M ↑	Methylphenidate inhibits guanethidine's antihypertensive action. Try another antihypertensive.
* MAOIs	X ↑	Methylphenidate poses less risk than amphetamines for hypertensive crisis, but methylphenidate should still be avoided with MAOIs.
TCAs	X ↑	Methylphenidate may facilitate TCAs' antidepressant and toxic effects and increase TCA levels.
Warfarin	M ↑	Increases levels of methylphenidate; monitor closely.

Drugs (X) Interact with:	Pemoline (P)	Comments
Sedative-hypnotics	X ↓	Pemoline can interfere with anxiolytic and sedative effects.
Anticonvulsants	X ↓	Pemoline may lower seizure threshold.

* Moderately important interactions; † Extremely important interaction; ↑ Increases; ↓ Decreases.

EFFECTS ON LABORATORY TESTS

Generic Names	Blood/Serum Tests	Results*	Urine Tests	Results*
Dextroamphetamine	Corticosteroids Growth hormone Prolactin	↑ ? ?	Steroid determinations	Interferes
Methylphenidate	RBC, WBC Growth hormone Prolactin	↓ r ↓ r ? ?	None	
Pemoline	LFT	↑	None	

* ↑ Increases; ↓ Decreases; ? Inconsistent; r = rarely; LFT are AST/SGOT, ALT/SGPT, LDH, alkaline phosphatase, and bilirubin.

WITHDRAWAL

Stimulants may cause

- Psychological dependence
- Drug misuse

Stimulants less commonly cause

- Physical dependence
- Tolerance (more commonly in narcolepsy)
- Addiction
- Physical withdrawal

From the most to the least abused are

- Dextroamphetamine (Schedule II)
  √ At dosage of > 50 mg/day, can often generate a serious, but not life-threatening, withdrawal.
- Methylphenidate (Schedule II)
  √ Abused orally when mixed with other drugs.
  √ Addicts grind up tablets, inject, and develop emboli.
- Pemoline (Schedule IV)
  √ Is rarely an addiction problem.

Dextroamphetamine and methylphenidate withdrawal symptoms include

- Increased appetite, weight gain
  √ Appetite may be huge for several days.
- Increased sleep
  √ Sleep may be excessive at first and
  √ Often with vivid, disturbing dreams.
- Decreased energy, fatigue, psychomotor retardation
  √ Rapid withdrawal, especially from high doses, can lead to profound inertia, depressed mood ("crashing"), and suicide.
- Paranoid symptoms may persist during withdrawal, but this is uncommon.

Cocaine and Stimulant Withdrawal/Abuse

Management

- Observe patient.
- Prevent suicide.
- Frequently reassure patient.
- Give TCAs.
  √ If patient is depressed.
    □ Since amphetamine and cocaine withdrawal involves noradrenergic activity, TCAs (e.g., desipramine) that increase noradrenergic (over serotonin) function are preferred.
  √ If patient is not depressed.
    □ About half of studies did and half did not show desipramine helps in early abstinence.
    □ Case reports suggest bupropion may help.

□ Case reports suggest SSRIs may lower impulsive craving, but depressed abuser still preferred group for SSRIs.
- Dopamine agonists
  - ✓ Generally have faster onset than desipramine.
  - ✓ Bromocriptine and amantadine in high doses sometimes decrease craving.
    - □ Amantadine better tolerated.
  - ✓ Open trial suggests pergolide decreases sleep and craving. Compared to bromocriptine it has
    - □ Longer duration of action and
    - □ More rapid onset of action.

Chronic amphetamine abuse may be treated best with desipramine.

- Good short-term effect (1–6 weeks).
- Long-term outcome (3–6 months) only modestly improved.

Bupropion may also help, but seizure risk is of concern in ongoing stimulant user.

OVERDOSE: TOXICITY, SUICIDE, AND TREATMENT

Death rarely occurs from overdoses of prescribed stimulants, since there is a large difference between the therapeutic and toxic doses of the drug. Nevertheless, a 10-day supply taken at once can be very toxic, even lethal, especially with children.

Most amphetamine overdoses are from illegal, not clinically obtained, drugs.

Amphetamine overdoses produce

- Agitation (21%)
- Suicidal ideation (12%)
- Chest pain (9%)
- Hallucinations (auditory > visual) (7%)
- Confusion (6%)
- Dysphoria, weakness, lethargy (5%)
- Delusions (5%)

Other symptoms (< 5%) include

- Seizures, hyperreflexia, fever, tremor, rhabdomyolysis, hypertension or hypotension, aggression, headache, palpitations, abdominal pain, rashes, dyspnea, leg pain, and paresthesias.

The general management of stimulant overdoses involves (see pages 53–54).

S
T
I
M
U
L
A
N
T
S

For specific symptoms of stimulant overdoses, other treatments include:

- For seizures
  - √ Short-acting barbiturates (e.g., amobarbital) or
  - √ IV diazepam.
- For agitation
  - √ Haloperidol and diazepam are equally effective.
- For psychosis
  - √ Isolate patient from environmental stimuli, which aggravate psychosis.
  - √ Haloperidol 2.5–5 mg IM prn q2h, or
  - √ Chlorpromazine 25–50 mg IM prn q2h.
- For high blood pressure
  - √ Hasten excretion by acidifying urine with ammonium chloride.
  - √ If hypertension is severe, may employ phentolamine 5 mg IV.
  - √ May employ hypothermic measures if intracranial pressure rises.
  - √ Combat cerebral edema and congestion.

Toxicity and Suicide Data

Generic Names	Toxicity Doses Average (Highest) (mg)	Mortality Doses Average (Lowest) (mg)	Fatal Supplies (days)	Toxic Levels (ng/ml)
Dextroamphetamine	20 (1.5 mg/kg)	400	—	—
Methylphenidate	—	—	—	—
Pemoline	—	—	—	—

PRECAUTIONS

Contraindications include

- Anxiety and agitation
- H/o drug abuse (unless a solid clinical reason)
- Advanced arteriosclerosis, cardiovascular disease, hypertension
- Hyperthyroidism
- Allergy to stimulants
- Glaucoma
- Tics or Tourette's syndrome (in patients or family members)
- MAOIs
  - √ Wait 14 days after MAOI discontinued.

Patients with seizure history or seizure risks are more likely to have seizures with stimulants.

After several months, if patient on pemoline has decreased appetite, fatigue, and stomach fullness, hepatotoxicity should be suspected and liver function tests ordered.

Decrements in predicted growth with pemoline are reported after long-term use of stimulants; observe and chart.

NURSES' DATA

Stress that stimulants have different medical and recreational uses.

- The medical stimulant alleviates specific symptoms, whereas the recreational stimulant triggers a general "buzz."
- Patients given medical stimulants often do not develop a "high" or experience tolerance.

If a question exists about whether an adult or child is illegally trying (or selling) the drug, raise the issue in a reasonable perspective.

Closely monitor the patient's

- Cardiovascular symptoms and vital signs,
- Blood glucose in diabetics (if appetite and food intake are affected),
- Signs of dextroamphetamine or methylphenidate withdrawal, intoxication, or overdose, and
- Slowing of growth.

PATIENT AND FAMILY NOTES

A 10-day supply of stimulants can be lethal for children.

- Patients who take stimulants can sometimes become depressed.
  - √ Patients who suddenly stop taking stimulants also become depressed.
  - √ Monitor a youngster's use of the drug, just as one would any other drug.

Keep stimulants away from bedside or from any readily accessible place to deter accidental intake. For safety, protect other children by keeping pills in a safe place.

Family and patients should not make a "big deal" about taking stimulants: "It's a medication, like any medication."

Tell families that

- Most common temporary effects are anorexia, insomnia, abdominal pain, headaches, irritability, and moodiness.

- Temporary growth suppression may occur, but this usually is not permanent.

Tell families to *avoid*

- Excessive sodium bicarbonate because it alkalinizes the urine, which reduces amphetamine excretion and prolongs its effects.
- Starvation and unprescribed dietary changes (e.g., increased vitamin C, citric acid intake) acidify the urine, which induces ketosis, accelerates amphetamine elimination, and lowers its effect.

Stimulants have no long-term effective role in weight-loss programs. Beware of

- A few weight-loss clinics touting the lifelong use of stimulants alone or with SSRIs in morbidly obese.

If anxiety erupts, excessive caffeine may be the culprit.

If patient neglects a dose

- Can consume the medication up to 3 h later.
- Otherwise, wait for next dose.
- Never double the dose.

If patient forgets a long-acting (sustained-release) pill

- Take it the next morning.

Dosage Times

- Dextroamphetamine
  - √ Give tablet or elixir early—possibly on awakening—or 30–60 minutes before breakfast.
  - √ Offer other doses at 4–6 h intervals.
    - ▫ Do not take within 6 h of bedtime, especially sustained-acting products.
    - ▫ Doses gobbled after breakfast or lunch are less likely to alter sleep or food intake.
  - √ If side effects (e.g., insomnia, anorexia) arise, try the once-a-day dextroamphetamine spansule.
- Methylphenidate
  - √ First dose with breakfast, which might reduce stomachaches.
  - √ Do not take within 6 h of sleep.
  - √ If insomnia or anorexia develop, consider the (8-hour) methylphenidate-SR tablet.
  - √ Avoid the methylphenidate-SR tablet at first; try it later.
- Pemoline
  - √ Give as a single morning tablet and increase the morning strength. For fast loading see page 353.

Appendices

1. DRUG IDENTIFICATION BY GENERIC NAME

Generic	Brand Name	Chief Action
acebutolol	Sectral	β-blocker (CS)
acetaminophen*	Tylenol	Analgesic
acetazolamide	Diamox	Carbonic anhydrase inhibitor
acetophenazine	Tindal	Neuroleptic
albuterol	Proventil	Sympathomimetic (DA) β
alprazolam	Xanax	Anti-anxiety
aluminum hydroxide*	Gelusil	Antacid
amantadine	Symmetrel	Antiparkinsonian, antiviral
ambenonium chloride	Mytelase	Cholinomimetic
amiloride	Midamor	Potassium-sparing diuretic
aminophylline	Mudrane	Bronchodilator
amiodarone	Cordarone	Antiarrhythmic (III)
amitriptyline	Elavil	TCA
amobarbital	Amytal	Hypnotic
amoxapine	Asendin	HCA
ampicillin	Omnipen	Penicillin
anisotropine	Valpin	Anticholinergic
antipyrine	Auralgan	Analgesic(otic)
asternizole	Hismanal	Antihistamine (H1)
atenolol	Tenormin	β-blocker (CS)
atropine	Atropine Sulfate	Anticholinergic
azatadine	Optimine	Antihistamine
azithromycin dihydrate	Zithromax	Antibacterial (macrolide)
baclofen	Lioresal	Skeletal muscle relaxant
beclomethasone	Vanceril	Corticosteroid
benazepril	Lotensin	Antihypertensive (ACE)
benztropine	Cogentin	Antiparkinsonian
bepridil hydrochloride	Vascor	Calcium channel blocker
betaxolol	Kerlone	β-blocker (CS)
bethanechol	Urecholine	Peripheral anticholinesterase

Generic	Brand Name	Chief Action
biperiden	Akineton	Antiparkinsonian anticholinergic
bromocriptine	Parlodel	Prolactin inhibitor, antiparkinsonian, dopamine agonist
bupropion	Wellbutrin	Atypical antidepressant
buspirone	BuSpar	Anti-anxiety
butabarbital	Butisol	Anti-anxiety
caffeine	No Doz	CNS stimulant
calcium carbonate*	Tums	Antacid
captopril	Capoten	Antihypertensive (ACE)
carbamazepine	Tegretol	Anticonvulsant, anticycling
loperimide	Imodium	Antidiarrheal
carbidopa-levodopa	Sinemet	Antiparkinsonian
docusate*	Colace	Stool softener
carisoprodol	Soma	Muscle relaxant
casanthranol*	Peri-Colace	Laxative
cephalosporin	Keflex	Antibiotic
chloral hydrate	Noctec	Hypnotic
chloramphenicol	Chloromycetin	Antibiotic
chlordiazepoxide	Librium	Anti-anxiety
chloroquine	Aralen	Antimalarial
chlorothiazide	Diuril	Thiazide diuretic
chlorpheniramine*	Chlortrimeton	Antihistamine
chlorpromazine	Thorazine	Neuroleptic
cholestyramine	Questran	Hypolipidemic
cimetidine	Tagamet	H_2-receptor antagonist
ciprofloxacin	Cipro	Antibacterial
clarithromycin	Biaxin	Antibacterial (macrolide)
clidinium	Quarzan	Anticholingeric
clomipramine	Anafranil	TCA
clonazepam	Klonopin	Anti-anxiety, anticonvulsant
clonidine	Catapres	Antihypertensive, α_2 agonist
clorazepate	Tranxene	Anti-anxiety
clozapine	Clozaril	Neuroleptic
cotrimoxazole	Bactrim, Septra	Antibiotic
cyclobenzaprine	Flexeril	Muscle relaxant (tricyclic)
cyclosporine	Sandimmune	Immunosuppressant
cyproheptadine	Periactin	Antihistamine, serotonin antagonist
danazol	Danocrine	Androgen derivative, gonadotropin inhibitor
dantrolene	Dantrium	Skeletal muscle relaxant
desipramine	Norpramin	TCA
dexamethasone	Decadron	Corticosteroid
dextroamphetamine	Dexedrine	Stimulant
dextromethorphan*	"DM" products see page 159	Cough suppressor
diazepam	Valium	Anti-anxiety
dichloralphenazone	Midrin	Analgesic-sedative
diclofenac sodium	Voltaren	Anti-inflammatory (NSAID)
dicumarol	Dicumarol	Anticoagulant (oral)
dicyclomine	Bentyl	Anticholinergic

Generic	Brand Name	Chief Action
digoxin	Lanoxin	Cardiac glycoside
diltiazem	Cardizem	Calcium channel-blocker
diphenylhydantoin	Dilantin	Anticonvulsant
diphenhydramine*	Benadryl	Antihistamine
dipyridamole	Persantine	Platelet inhibitor
disopyramide	Norpace	Antiarrhythmic (1)
disulfiram	Antabuse	Antialcohol
divalproex	Depakote	Anticonvulsant, mood stabilizer
dobutamine	Dobutrex	Sympathomimetic (DA) α β
docusate*	Colace	Stool softener
dopamine	Intropin	Sympathomimetic (MA) α β
doxapram	Dopram	Respiratory stimulant
doxepin	Sinequan	TCA
doxycycline	Vibramycin	Tetracycline antibiotic
droperidol	Inapsine	Antiemetic, anti-anxiety, neuroleptic
edrophonium chloride	Tensilon	Cholinomimetic
enalapril	Vasotec	Antihypertensive (ACE)
enflurane	Ethrane	Anesthetic (general)
ephedrine*	Vatronol	Sympathomimetic (IA) α β
epinephrine*	Primatene	Sympathomimetic (DA) α β
ergotamine tartrate	Ergostat	Ergot alkaloid
erythromycin	Pediazole	Antibacterial (macrolide)
estazolam	ProSom	Hypnotic
estrogens, conjugated	Premarin	Estrogen
ethacrynic acid	Edecrin	Loop diuretic
ethchlorvynol	Placidyl	Hypnotic
ethosuximide	Zarontin	Anticonvulsant
famotidine	Pepcid	H_2-Blocker
felbamate	Felbatol	Anticonvulsant
fenfluramine	Pondimin	Serotonergic anorectic
flecainide acetate	Tambocor	Antiarrhythmic (1)
fludrocortisone	Florinef	Mineral corticoid
flumazenil	Mazicon	Benzodiazepine antagonist
fluoxetine	Prozac	SSRI
fluphenazine	Prolixin	Neuroleptic
flurazepam	Dalmane	Hypnotic
fluvoxamine	Luvox	SSRI
fosinopril	Monopril	Antihypertensive (ACE)
furazolidone	Furoxone	Antibiotic
furosemide	Lasix	Loop diuretic
gabapentin	Neurontin	Anticonvulsant
gallium nitrate	Ganite	Hypocalcemic
gemfibrozil	Lopid	Hypolipidemic
glucagon	Glucagon	Antihypoglycemic
glutethimide	Doriden	Hypnotic
glyburide	Micronase	Hypoglycemic
glycopyrrolate	Robinal	Anticholinergic
griseofulvin	Fulvicin	Antibiotic
guanadrel	Hylorel	Antihypertensive

Generic	Brand Name	Chief Action
guanethidine	Ismelin	Antihypertensive
haloperidol	Haldol	Neuroleptic
halothane	Flurothane	Anesthetic
hydralazine	Apresoline	Antihypertensive
hydrochlorthiazide	Aldoril	Thiazide diuretic
hydroxyzine	Atarax, Vistaril	Antihistamine, anti-anxiety
hyoscyamine	Levsin	Anticholinergic, antispasmodic
ibuprofen*	Advil	NSAID
imipramine	Tofranil, Janimine	TCA
indomethacin	Indocin	NSAID
ipratropium bromide	Bronkosol	Bronchodilator
isocarboxazid	Marplan	MAOI
isoniazid	Rifamate	Antibiotic
isoproterenol	Isuprel	Sympathomimetic (DA) β
isosorbide	Isordil	Antianginal
itraconazole	Sporanox	Antifungal
ketamine	Ketalar	Anesthetic (general)
ketoconazole	Nizoral	Antifungal
ketoprofen	Orudis	NSAID
ketorolac tromethamine	Toradol	NSAID
labetalol	Normodyne	β-blocker (CS)
levodopa	Larodopa	Antiparkinsonian
lidocaine*	Xylocaine	Anesthetic (local), antiarrhythmic
liothyronine (T_3)	Cytomel	Thyroid hormone
lisinopril	Prinivil, Zestril	Antihypertensive (ACE)
lithium	Eskalith, Lithane, Lithobid	Mood regulator, anticycling agent
lorazepam	Ativan	Anti-anxiety
loxapine	Loxitane	Neuroleptic
magnesium hydroxide*	Maalox	Antacid
maprotiline	Ludiomil	HCA
mazindol	Sanorex	Anorectic agent
mebendazole	Vermox	Anthelmintic agent
mefenamic acid	Ponstel	NSAID
meperidine	Demerol	Opiate
meprobamate	Miltown, Equanil	Anti-anxiety
mesoridazine	Serentil	Neuroleptic
metaproterenol	Alupent	Sympathomimetic (DA) β
metaraminol	Aramine	Sympathomimetic (MA) α β
methabarbital	Mebaral	Anti-anxiety
methadone	Dolophine	Opiate analgesic
methimazole	Tapazole	Antithyroid drug
methotrimeparazine	Levoprome	Phenothiazine analgesic
methylphenidate	Ritalin	Stimulant
methyltestosterone	Android	Androgen derivative
metoclopramide	Reglan	Dopamine blocking antiemetic
metoprolol	Lopressor	β-blocker (CS)
metronidazole	Flagyl	Antibiotic
molindone	Moban	Neuroleptic
morphine	Roxanol	Narcotic

Generic	Brand Name	Chief Action
nadolol	Corgard	β-blocker (CS)
naloxone	Narcan	Narcotic antagonist
naltrexone	ReVia	Narcotic antagonist
naproxen*	Anaprox, Aleve	NSAID
nefazodone	Serzone	Antidepressant
neostigmine	Prostigmin	Anticholinesterase, cholinomimetic
nicotine	Habitrol	Smoking substitute
nifedipine	Procardia	Calcium channel-blocker
nipodipine	Nimotop	Calcium channel-blocker
nitrofurantoin	Macrodantin	Antibiotic
nitroprusside	Nipride	Antihypertensive
nizatidine	Axid	NSAID
norepinephrine	Levophed	Sympathomimetic (DA) α β
nortriptyline	Aventyl, Pamelor	TCA
omeprazole	Prilosec	Gastric acid pump inhibitor
ondansetron	Zofran	Antiemetic
orphenadrine	Norflex	Anticholinergic
oxazepam	Serax	Anti-anxiety
pancuronium	Pavulon	Neuromuscular blocker
paraldehyde	Paral	Hypnotic
pargyline	Eutonyl	MAOI
paroxetine	Paxil	SSRI
pemoline	Cylert	Stimulant
penbutalol	Levatol	β-blocker (NCS)
pentazocine	Talwin	Opiate agonist-antagonist
pentobarbital	Nembutal	Hypnosedative
pentoxifylline	Trental	Hemorheologic agent
pergolide	Permax	Dopamine agonist
perphenazine	Trilafon	Neuroleptic
phenelzine	Nardil	MAOI
phenmetrazine	Preludin	Anorectic agent
phenobarbital	Luminal	Anticonvulsant, sedative
phentermine	Fastin	Sympathomimetic anorectic
phentolamine	Regitine	Antihypertensive
phenylbutazone	Butazolidin	NSAID
phenylephrine*	Neo-Synephrine	Sympathomimetic (MA) α β
phenylpropanolamine*	Acutrim	Sympathomimetic (IA) α β, anorectic
phenytoin	Dilantin	Anticonvulsant
physostigmine	Antilirium	Anticholinesterase
pimozide	Orap	Neuroleptic
pindolol	Visken	β-blocker (NCS)
piroxicam	Feldene	NSAID
prazepam	Centrax	Anti-anxiety
prazosin	Minipress	Antihypertensive
primidone	Mysoline	Anticonvulsant
probenecid	Benemid	Uricosuric agent, antigout
procainamide	Pronestyl	Antiarrhythmic (1A)
prochlorperazine	Compazine	Antiemetic, dopamine blocker
procyclidine	Kemadrin	Antiparkinsonian, anticholinergic

Generic	Brand Name	Chief Action
promethazine	Phenergan	Antihistamine, antiemetic
propantheline	Pro-Banthine	Anticholinergic
propoxyphene	Darvon	Opioid analgesic
propranolol	Inderal	β-blocker (NCS)
protriptyline	Vivactil	TCA
pseudoephedrine*	Sudafed	Sympathomimetic (IA) α β
psyllium*	Metamucil	Bulk laxative
pyrimethamine	Danaprim	Antimalarial
quazepam	Doral	Hypnotic
quinapril	Accupril	Antihypertensive (ACE)
quinidine	Quinidine	Antiarrhythmic (1-A)
quinine	Quinamm	Skeletal muscle relaxant
ramipril	Altace	Antihypertensive (ACE)
ranitidine	Zantac	H_2 blocker
reserpine	Serpasil	Antihypertensive
rifampin	Rifadin	Antibiotic
risperidone	Risperdal	Antipsychotic
scopolamine	Transderm Scop	Anticholinergic, antiemetic
secobarbital	Seconal	Hypnotic
selegiline	Eldepryl	MAOI B
spectinomycin	Trobicin	Antibiotic (macrolide)
spiramycin		Antibiotic (macrolide)
spironolactone	Aldactone	Potassium-sparing diuretic
succinylcholine	Anectine	Neuromuscular blocker
sulfadoxine	Fansidar	Antimalarial
sulfamethoxazole	Gantanol	Antibacterial
sulindac	Clinoril	NSAID
sumatriptan	Imitrex	Antimigraine agent, $5HT_3$ agent
tacrine	Cognex	Cholinergic, antidementia
temazepam	Restoril	Hypnotic
terbutaline	Brethine	Sympathomimetic (DA) β
terfenadine	Seldane	Antihistamine
tetracycline	Achromycin	Antibiotic
theophylline*	Bronkaid	Bronchodilator
thiopental	Pentothal	Anesthetic (general)
thioridazine	Mellaril	Neuroleptic
thiothixene	Navane	Neuroleptic
ticarcillin disodium	Ticar	Antibacterial
timolol	Blocadren	β-Blocker (NCS)
tocainide	Tonocard	Antiarrhythmic (1)
tranylcypromine	Parnate	MAOI
trazodone	Desyrel	Atypical antidepressant
triamterene	Dyrenium	Potassium-sparing diuretic
triazolam	Halcion	Hypnotic
trifluoperazine	Stelazine	Neuroleptic
trihexyphenidyl	Artane	Antiparkinsonian, anticholinergic
trimethobenzamide	Tigan	Antiemetic dopamine blocker
trimethoprin	Bactrim, Septra	Antibiotic
trimipramine	Surmontil	TCA

Generic	Brand Name	Chief Action
troleandomycin	Tao	Antibacterial (Macrolide)
tubocurarine	Tubocurarine	Neuromuscular blocker
tyramine		Sympathomimetic (IA) α β
urea*	Debrox	Earwax drops
valproic acid	Depakene	Anticonvulsant, mood stabilizer
vecuronium bromide	Norcuron	Neuromuscular blocker
venlafaxine	Effexor	Antidepressant
verapamil	Isoptin	Calcium channel-blocker
vinblastine	Velban	Antineoplastic
warfarin	Coumadin	Anticoagulant (oral)
yohimbine*	Yocon	Presynaptic α_2 antagonist
zidovudine	Retrovir	Antiviral
zolpidem	Ambiem	Hypnotic

Codes:
* Can be sold as nonprescription drug.
NSAID = nonsteroidal anti-inflammatory drug.
β-blockers: (CS) = cardioselective; (NCS) = noncardioselective.
Sympathomimetics: (DA) = direct acting; (IA) = indirect acting; (MA) = mixed acting; α = alpha agonist; β = beta agonist.
ACE = angiotensin converting enzyme inhibitor.

2. DRUG IDENTIFICATION BY BRAND NAME

Brand Name	Generic	Chief Action
Accupril	quinapril	Antihypertensive (ACE)
Achromycin	tetracycline	Antibiotic
Acutrim	phenylpropanolamine*	Sympathomimetic (IA) α β, anorectic
Advil	ibuprofen*	NSAID
Akineton	biperiden	Antiparkinsonian anticholinergic
Aldactone	spironolactone	Potassium-sparing diuretic
Aldoril	hydrochlorthiazide	Thiazide diuretic
Altace	ramipril	Antihypertensive (ACE)
Alupent	metaproterenol	Sympathomimetic (DA) β
Ambiem	zolpidem	Hypnotic
Amytal	amobarbital	Hypnotic
Anafranil	clomipramine	TCA
Anaprox, Aleve	naproxen*	NSAID
Android	methyltestosterone	Androgen derivative
Anectine	succinylcholine	Neuromuscular blocker
Antabuse	disulfiram	Antialcohol
Antilirium	physostigmine	Anticholinesterase
Apresoline	hydralazine	Antihypertensive
Aralen	chloroquine	Antimalarial
Aramine	metaraminol	Sympathomimetic (MA) α β
Artane	trihexyphenidyl	Antiparkinsonian, anticholinergic

Brand Name	Generic	Chief Action
Asendin	amoxapine	HCA
Atarax, Vistaril	hydroxyzine	Antihistamine, anti-anxiety
Ativan	lorazepam	Anti-anxiety
Atropine Sulfate	atropine	Anticholinergic
Auralgan	antipyrine	Analgesic(otic)
Aventyl, Pamelor	nortriptyline	TCA
Axid	nizatidine	NSAID
Bactrim, Septra	trimethoprin	Antibiotic
Benadryl	diphenhydramine*	Antihistamine
Benemid	probenecid	Uricosuric agent, antigout
Bentyl	dicyclomine	Anticholinergic
Biaxin	clarithromycin	Antibacterial (macrolide)
Blocadren	timolol	β-Blocker (NCS)
Brethine	terbutaline	Sympathomimetic (DA) β
Bronkaid	theophylline*	Bronchodilator
Bronkosol	ipratropium bromide	Bronchodilator
BuSpar	buspirone	Anti-anxiety
Butazolidin	phenylbutazone	NSAID
Butisol	butabarbital	Anti-anxiety
Capoten	captopril	Antihypertensive (ACE)
Cardizem	diltiazem	Calcium channel-blocker
Catapres	clonidine	Antihypertensive, α_2 agonist
Centrax	prazepam	Anti-anxiety
Chloromycetin	chloramphenicol	Antibiotic
Chlortrimeton	chlorpheniramine*	Antihistamine
Cipro	ciprofloxacin	Antibacterial
Clinoril	sulindac	NSAID
Clozaril	clozapine	Neuroleptic
Cogentin	benztropine	Antiparkinsonian
Cognex	tacrine	Cholinergic, antidementia
Colace	docusate*	Stool softener
Compazine	prochlorperazine	Antiemetic, dopamine blocker
Cordarone	amiodarone	Antiarrhythmic (III)
Corgard	nadolol	β-blocker (CS)
Coumadin	warfarin	Anticoagulant (oral)
Cylert	pemoline	Stimulant
Cytomel	liothyronine (T_3)	Thyroid hormone
Dalmane	flurazepam	Hypnotic
Danaprim	pyrimethamine	Antimalarial
Danocrine	danazol	Androgen derivative, gonadotropin inhibitor
Dantrium	dantrolene	Skeletal muscle relaxant
Darvon	propoxyphene	Opioid analgesic
Debrox	urea*	Earwax drops
Decadron	dexamethasone	Corticosteroid
Demerol	meperidine	Opiate
Depakene	valproic acid	Anticonvulsant, mood stabilizer

Brand Name	Generic	Chief Action
Depakote	divalproex	Anticonvulsant, mood stabilizer
Desyrel	trazodone	Atypical antidepressant
Dexedrine	dextroamphetamine	Stimulant
Diamox	acetazolamide	Carbonic anhydrase inhibitor
Dicumarol	dicumarol	Anticoagulant (oral)
Dilantin	phenytoin	Anticonvulsant
Diuril	chlorothiazide	Thiazide diuretic
"DM" products see page 159	dextromethorphan*	Cough suppressor
Dobutrex	dobutamine	Sympathomimetic (DA) α β
Dolophine	methadone	Opiate analgesic
Dopram	doxapram	Respiratory stimulant
Doral	quazepam	Hypnotic
Dyrenium	triamterene	Potassium-sparing diuretic
Edecrin	ethacrynic acid	Loop diuretic
Effexor	venlafaxine	Antidepressant
Elavil	amitriptyline	TCA
Eldepryl	selegiline	MAOI B
Ergostat	ergotamine tartrate	Ergot alkaloid
Eskalith, Lithane, Lithobid	lithium	Mood regulator, anticycling agent
Ethrane	enflurane	Anesthetic (general)
Eutonyl	pargyline	MAOI
Fansidar	sulfadoxine	Antimalarial
Fastin	phentermine	Sympathomimetic anorectic
Felbatol	felbamate	Anticonvulsant
Feldene	piroxicam	NSAID
Flagyl	metronidazole	Antibiotic
Flexeril	cyclobenzaprine	Muscle relaxant (tricyclic)
Florinef	fludrocortisone	Mineral corticoid
Flurothane	halothane	Anesthetic
Fulvicin	griseofulvin	Antibiotic
Furoxone	furazolidone	Antibiotic
Ganite	gallium nitrate	Hypocalcemic
Gantanol	sulfamethoxazole	Antibacterial
Gelusil	aluminum hydroxide*	Antacid
Glucagon	glucagon	Antihypoglycemic
Habitrol	nicotine	Smoking substitute
Halcion	triazolam	Hypnotic
Haldol	haloperidol	Neuroleptic
Hismanal	asternizole	Antihistamine (H_1)
Hylorel	guanadrel	Antihypertensive
Imitrex	sumatriptan	Antimigraine agent, $5HT_3$ agent
Imodium	loperimide	Antidiarrheal
Inapsine	droperidol	Antiemetic, anti-anxiety, neuroleptic
Inderal	propranolol	β-blocker (NCS)
Indocin	indomethacin	NSAID

Brand Name	Generic	Chief Action
Intropin	dopamine	Sympathomimetic (MA) α β
Ismelin	guanethidine	Antihypertensive
Isoptin	verapamil	Calcium channel-blocker
Isordil	isosorbide	Antianginal
Isuprel	isoproterenol	Sympathomimetic (DA) β
Keflex	cephalosporin	Antibiotic
Kemadrin	procyclidine	Antiparkinsonian, anticho- linergic
Kerlone	betaxolol	β-blocker (CS)
Ketalar	ketamine	Anesthetic (general)
Klonopin	clonazepam	Anti-anxiety, anticonvulsant
Lanoxin	digoxin	Cardiac glycoside
Larodopa	levodopa	Antiparkinsonian
Lasix	furosemide	Loop diuretic
Levatol	penbutolol	β-blocker (NCS)
Levophed	norepinephrine	Sympathomimetic (DA) α β
Levoprome	methotrimeparazine	Phenothiazine analgesic
Levsin	hyoscyamine	Anticholinergic, antispas- modic
Librium	chlordiazepoxide	Anti-anxiety
Lioresal	baclofen	Skeletal muscle relaxant
Lopid	gemfibrozil	Hypolipidemic
Lopressor	metoprolol	β-blocker (CS)
Lotensin	benazepril	Antihypertensive (ACE)
Loxitane	loxapine	Neuroleptic
Ludiomil	maprotiline	HCA
Luminal	phenobarbital	Anticonvulsant, sedative
Luvox	fluvoxamine	SSRI
Maalox	magnesium hydroxide*	Antacid
Macrodantin	nitrofurantoin	Antibiotic
Marplan	isocarboxazid	MAOI
Mazanor	mazindol	Anorectic agent
Mazicon	flumazenil	Benzodiazepine antagonist
Mebaral	methabarbital	Anti-anxiety
Mellaril	thioridazine	Neuroleptic
Metamucil	psyllium*	Bulk laxative
Micronase	glyburide	Hypoglycemic
Midamor	amiloride	Potassium-sparing diuretic
Midrin	dichloralphenazone	Analgesic-sedative
Miltown, Equanil	meprobamate	Anti-anxiety
Minipress	prazosin	Antihypertensive
Moban	molindone	Neuroleptic
Monopril	fosinopril	Antihypertensive (ACE)
Mudrane	aminophylline	Bronchodilator
Mysoline	primidone	Anticonvulsant
Mytelase	ambenonium chloride	Cholinomimetic
Narcan	naloxone	Narcotic antagonist
Nardil	phenelzine	MAOI
Navane	thiothixene	Neuroleptic
Nembutal	pentobarbital	Hypnosedative

Brand Name	Generic	Chief Action
Neo-Synephrine	phenylephrine*	Sympathomimetic (MA) α β
Neurontin	gabapentin	Anticonvulsant
Nimotop	nipodipine	Calcium channel-blocker
Nipride	nitroprusside	Antihypertensive
Nizoral	ketoconazole	Antifungal agent
No Doz	caffeine	CNS stimulant
Noctec	chloral hydrate	Hypnotic
Norcuron	vecuronium bromide	Neuromuscular blocker
Norflex	orphenadrine	Anticholinergic
Normodyne	labetalol	β-blocker (CS)
Norpace	disopyramide	Antiarrhythmic (1)
Norpramin	desipramine	TCA
Omnipen	ampicillin	Penicillin
Optimine	azatadine	Antihistamine
Orap	pimozide	Neuroleptic
Orudis	ketoprofen	NSAID
Paral	paraldehyde	Hypnotic
Parlodel	bromocriptine	Prolactin inhibitor, antiparkinsonian, dopamine agonist
Parnate	tranylcypromine	MAOI
Pavulon	pancuronium	Neuromuscular blocker
Paxil	paroxetine	SSRI
Pentothal	thiopental	Anesthetic (general)
Pepcid	famotidine	H_2-blocker
Peri-Colace	casanthranol*	Laxative
Periactin	cyproheptadine	Antihistamine, serotonin antagonist
Permax	pergolide	Dopamine agonist
Persantine	dipyridamole	Platelet inhibitor
Phenergan	promethazine	Antihistamine, antiemetic, neuroleptic
Placidyl	ethchlorvynol	Hypnotic
Pondimin	fenfluramine	Serotonergic anorectic
Ponstel	mefenamic acid	NSAID
Preludin	phenmetrazine	Anorectic agent
Premarin	estrogens, conjugated	Estrogen
Prilosec	omeprazole	Gastric acid pump inhibitor
Primatene	epinephrine*	Sympathomimetic (DA) α β
Prinivil, Zestril	lisinopril	Antihypertensive (ACE)
Pro-Banthine	propantheline	Anticholinergic
Procardia	nifedipine	Calcium channel-blocker
Prolixin	fluphenazine	Neuroleptic
Pronestyl	procainamide	Antiarrhythmic (1A)
ProSom	estazolam	Hypnotic
Prostigmin	neostigmine	Anticholinesterase, cholinomimetic
Proventil	albuterol	Sympathomimetic (DA) β
Prozac	fluoxetine	SSRI
Quarzan	clidinium	Anticholingeric
Questran	cholestyramine	Hypolipidemic

Brand Name	Generic	Chief Action
Quinamm	quinine	Skeletal muscle relaxant
Quinidine	quinidine	Antiarrhythmic (1-A)
Regitine	phentolamine	Antihypertensive
Reglan	metoclopramide	Dopamine blocking anti-emetic
Restoril	temazepam	Hypnotic
Retrovir	zidovudine	Antiviral
ReVia	naltrexone	Narcotic antagonist
Rifadin	rifampin	Antibiotic
Rifamate	isoniazid	Antibiotic
Risperdal	risperidone	Antipsychotic
Ritalin	methylphenidate	Stimulant
Robinal	glycopyrrolate	Anticholinergic
Roxanol	morphine	Narcotic
Sandimmune	cyclosporine	Immunosuppressant
Seconal	secobarbital	Hypnotic
Sectral	acebutolol	β-blocker (CS)
Seldane	terfenadine	Antihistamine
Serax	oxazepam	Anti-anxiety
Serentil	mesoridazine	Neuroleptic
Serpasil	reserpine	Antihypertensive
Serzone	nefazodone	Antidepressant
Sinemet	carbidopa-levodopa	Antiparkinsonian
Sinequan	doxepin	TCA
Soma	carisoprodol	Muscle relaxant
Sporanox	itraconazole	Antifungal
Stelazine	trifluoperazine	Neuroleptic
Sudafed	pseudoephedrine*	Sympathomimetic (IA) α β
Surmontil	trimipramine	TCA
Symmetrel	amantadine	Antiparkinsonian, antiviral
Tagamet	cimetidine	H_2-receptor antagonist
Talwin	pentazocine	Opiate agonist-antagonist
Tambocor	flecainide acetate	Antiarrhythmic (1)
Tao	troleandomycin	Antibacterial (macrolide)
Tapazole	methimazole	Antithyroid drug
Tegretol	carbamazepine	Anticonvulsant, anticycling
Tenormin	atenolol	β-blocker (CS)
Tensilon	edrophonium chloride	Cholinomimetic
Thorazine	chlorpromazine	Neuroleptic
Ticar	ticarcillin disodium	Antibacterial
Tigan	trimethobenzamide	Antiemetic dopamine blocker
Tindal	acetophenazine	Neuroleptic
Tofranil, Janimine	imipramine	TCA
Tonocard	tocainide	Antiarrhythmic (1)
Toradol	ketorolac tromethamine	NSAID
Torecan	thiethylperazine	Antiemetic dopamine blocker
Transderm Scop	scopolamine	Anticholinergic, antiemetic
Tranxene	clorazepate	Anti-anxiety
Trental	pentoxifylline	Hemorheologic agent

Brand Name	Generic	Chief Action
Trilafon	perphenazine	Neuroleptic
Trobicin	spectinomycin	Antibiotic (macrolide)
Tubocurarine	tubocurarine	Neuromuscular blocker
Tums	calcium carbonate*	Antacid
Tylenol	acetaminophen*	Analgesic
Urecholine	bethanechol	Peripheral anticholinesterase
Valium	diazepam	Anti-anxiety
Valpin	anisotropine	Anticholinergic
Vanceril	beclomethasone	Corticosteroid
Vascor	bepridil hydrochloride	Calcium channel-blocker
Vasotec	enalapril	Antihypertensive (ACE)
Vatronol	ephedrine*	Sympathomimetic (IA) α β
Velban	vinblastine	Antineoplastic
Vermox	mebendazole	Anthelmintic agent
Vibramycin	doxycycline	Tetracycline antibiotic
Visken	pindolol	β-blocker (NCS)
Vivactil	protriptyline	TCA
Voltaren	diclofenac sodium	Anti-inflammatory (NSAID)
Wellbutrin	bupropion	Atypical antidepressant
Xanax	alprazolam	Anti-anxiety
Xylocaine	lidocaine*	Anesthetic (local), anti-arrhythmic
Yocon	yohimbine*	Presynaptic α_2 antagonist
Zantac	ranitidine	H_2 blocker
Zarontin	ethosuximide	Anticonvulsant
Zithromax	azithromycin dihydrate	Antibacterial (macrolide)
Zofran	ondansetron	Antiemetic

Codes:
* Can be sold as nonprescription drug.
NSAID = nonsteroidal anti-inflammatory drug.
β-blockers: (CS) = cardioselective; (NCS) = noncardioselective.
Sympathomimetics: (DA) = direct acting; (IA) = indirect acting; (MA) = mixed acting; α = alpha agonist; β = beta agonist.
ACE = angiotensin converting enzyme inhibitor.

3. DRUG INTERACTIONS—CYTOCHROME P450 ENZYMES

P450 Enzyme System

Function: Oxidation of substances (drugs) to make them more hydrophilic and easily eliminated.

Coding Subtypes: Each human P450 enzyme is the expression of a unique gene. Most 450 enzymes involved in drug metabolism belong to three distinct gene families (I, II, III). A special coding system is used. For example: P450 IID6 is a very specific subtype where II is first number, D is first letter, and 6 is second number.

- First number—expressed as I, II, III (or 1, 2, 3), represents families with > 40% amino acid sequence homology.
- First letter—represents subfamilies with > 55% amino acid homology.
- Second number—represents the single gene that controls the enzyme's expression.

There are four P450 enzymes (IA2, IID6, IIIA3, and IIIA4) that control a majority of the drug metabolism of psychiatric drugs. IIIA3 and IIIA4 are essentially the same enzymes, each controlled by a different gene, and are often descriptively condensed to IIIA3/4.

Definitions of Substrates, Inhibitors, and Inducers of P450 Enzymes

Substrates: Drugs metabolized by the specific enzyme.

Inhibitors: Drugs that interfere with the enzyme's oxidation of substrates and raise plasma levels of drugs that depend on that enzyme.

Competitive inhibitors are drugs that are substrates of the enzyme but compete with other substrates. All substrate drugs have the potential to be inhibitors if they compete with another substrate drug. *Noncompetitive inhibitors* are not metabolized by the particular enzyme that they inhibit.

Inducers: Drugs that increase a specific enzyme's activity and lower levels of substrates metabolized by that drug.

P450 IID6 (Hydroxylation)

No known inducers.

Populations deficient in this enzyme:

- 5–8% of Caucasians
- < 3% of Asians and Africans
- Nearly 0% of Japanese

Drug Interactions—P450 IID6

Substrates (drugs metabolized by IID6)	Inhibitors (all are also substrates unless indicated)

Antidepressants
TCAs:
   amitriptyline
   clomipramine
   desipramine
   imipramine
   N-desmethyl-clomipramine
   nortriptyline
   trimipramine
Atypical:
   m-cpp (anxiogenic metabolite of
      nefazodone and trazodone)
   venlafaxine
 	
Neuroleptics
Phenothiazines:
   e.g., trifluoperazine
Other:
   clozapine (minor?)
   risperidone
 	
β-Blockers*
bufarol
labetolol
metoprolol
penbutolol
propranolol
timolol
 	
Antiarrhythmics
encainide
flecainide
mexitiline
propafenone
 	
Other
carbamazepine
methamphetamine
Probable:
   captopril
   dextroamphetamine
   papaverine
   phenacetin
   yohimbine
	SSRIs
	demethylsertraline,
	fluoxetine,
	norfluoxetine,
	paroxetine
	sertraline
	
	TCAs
	desipramine
	
	Neuroleptics
	chlorpromazine
	fluphenazine
	haloperidol†
	perphenazine
	thioridazine
	
	Opiates
	codeine (to form morphine)
	dextromethorphan
	ethylmorphine
	
	Other
	cimetidine
	debrisoquine
	diltiazem
	diphenhydramine
	labetolol
	lobeline
	nicardipine
	propafenone
	quinidine†
	quinine
	vincristine

A
P
P
E
N
D
I
C
E
S

† Not metabolized by IID6.
* Not atenolol.

P450 IIIA3/4 (carboxylation, dealkylation, hydroxylation, N-demethylation)

No genetic polymorphism.

Higher activity in women.

Drug Interactions—P450 IIIA3/4

Substrates	Inhibitors	Inducers
ANTIDEPRESSANTS	**ANTIDEPRESSANTS**	carbamazepine
(Demethylation)	fluoxetine (weak)	dexamethasone
amitriptyline	fluvoxamine	estrogen
clomipramine	nefazodone	ethanol
imipramine	sertraline	ethinylestradiol (?)
BENZODIAZEPINES	*Calcium channel-blockers:*	glucocorticoids
Triazolobenzodiazepines:	diltiazem	isoniazid
alprazolam	felodipine	phenylbutazone
estazolam	nifedipine	phenytoin
midazolam	verapamil	rifampicin
triazolam	**ANTIMYCOTIC AZOLES***	sulfinpyrazone
2-keto benzodiazepines:	fluconazole	tamoxifen (?)
clorazepate	itraconazole	
chlordiazepoxide	ketoconazole	
diazepam	miconazole	
flurazepam		
halazepam	**MACROLIDE ANTIBIOTICS***	
prazepam	azithromycin	
Antiarrythmics:	clarithromycin	
lidocaine	erythromycin	
propafenone	troleandomycin	
quinidine	*Probable:*	
Calcium channel-blockers:	flurithromycin	
nifedipine	josamycin	
diltiazem	ponsinomycin	
felodipine	*Other:*	
verapamil	amiodarone	
H–1 blockers:	ciprofaxine (?)	
astemizole	grapefruit juice	
terfenadine		
Other:		
aflatoxin B.		
alfentanil		
cocaine		
cortisol		
cyclosporine		
debrisoquine		
hexobarbital		
lovastatin		
methobarbitol		
tamoxifen		
testosterone		
theophylline		
warfarin		

* Spiramycin has no effect and azithromycin probably none.

P450 1A2 (N-methylation, N-demethylation)

No genetic polymorphism; all have this gene.

Drug Interactions—P450 1A2

Substrates	Inhibitors	Inducers
acetaminophen	cimetidine	aminoglutethimide
caffeine	ciproflaxine	barbiturates
clozapine	disulfiram	carbamazepine
haloperidol	fluvoxamine	omeprazole
propranolol	**MACROLIDE**	phenytoin
tacrine	*Antibiotics:*	primidone
tertiary TCAs (minor	azithromycin?	rifabutin
pathway)	clarithromycin	rifampin
theophylline	erythromycin	*Polyaromatic hydrocarbons:*
	troleandomycin	
	pentoxiphylline	charcoal broiled foods
	theophylline	cigarette smoking
	verapamil	smoked foods

4. SYMPTOM CHECKLIST

When patients gripe about side effects, do their complaints stem from the medication or from another problem, such as a psychiatric or a medical disorder?

The symptom checklist helps answer this question. Patients fill it out *before* they start on a medication so the clinician can detect symptoms unrelated to the medication. Subsequently, patients complete it every week or month to uncover symptoms that occurred only *after* the medication began. (I find that most "side effects" decline on medication.)

For patients and doctors alike, the list saves office time for exploring more personal matters, while insuring that clinicians still know about any key side effects.

APPENDICES

SYMPTOM CHECKLIST

Patient's name _____ Date _____

Do You Have Any of the Following Symptoms?	Yes	No	Does It Make You Uncomfortable? Yes	No
Dizziness/lightheadedness	□	□	◇	◇
Faint	□	□	◇	◇
Rapid or pounding heart	□	□	◇	◇
Dry mouth, throat, or nose	□	□	◇	◇
Always hungry	□	□	◇	◇
Diminished appetite	□	□	◇	◇
Nausea or vomiting	□	□	◇	◇
Upset stomach	□	□	◇	◇
Diarrhea	□	□	◇	◇
Constipation	□	□	◇	◇
Jaundice	□	□	◇	◇
Weight gain	□	□	◇	◇
Edema (swelling ankles or hands)	□	□	◇	◇
Increased thirst	□	□	◇	◇
Different menstruation	□	□	◇	◇
Swollen breasts	□	□	◇	◇
Fluid discharge from breast	□	□	◇	◇
Decreased sexual interest	□	□	◇	◇
Lack of energy	□	□	◇	◇
Bruising easier	□	□	◇	◇
Sores in mouth	□	□	◇	◇
Blurred vision	□	□	◇	◇
Ringing in the ears	□	□	◇	◇
Skin rash	□	□	◇	◇
Increased sweating	□	□	◇	◇
Insomnia	□	□	◇	◇
Excessive sleeping	□	□	◇	◇
Weird dreams/nightmares	□	□	◇	◇
Stiff tongue	□	□	◇	◇
Body stiff or rigid	□	□	◇	◇
Difficulty in swallowing	□	□	◇	◇
Tremors, shakes, jitters	□	□	◇	◇
Unsteady gait	□	□	◇	◇
Slurred speech	□	□	◇	◇
Headache	□	□	◇	◇
Drowsiness	□	□	◇	◇
Poor memory	□	□	◇	◇
Nervousness	□	□	◇	◇

CURRENT MEDICATIONS: DRUG NAME AND DOSE

_____   _____

_____   _____

_____   _____

_____   _____

392

Bibliography

ANTIANXIETY, HYPNOTICS

Adler L, Angrist B, Peselow E, Corwin J and Rotrosen J. Noradrenergic mechanisms in akathisia: Treatment with propranolol and clonidine. *Psychopharmacol Bull* 23:21–25, 1987.

Albeck JH. Withdrawal and detoxification from benzodiazepine dependence: A potential role for clonazepam. *J Clin Psych* 49:43–48 (suppl.), 1987.

Ankier SI and Goa KL. Quazepam: A preliminary review of its pharmacodynamic and pharmacokinetic properties and therapeutic efficacy in insomnia. *Drugs* 35:42–62, 1988.

Black B and Uhde T. Treatment of elective mutism with fluoxetine: A double-blind, placebo-controlled study. *J Am Acad Child and Adolescent Psych* 33:1000–1006, 1994.

Bradford J, et al. Double-blind placebo crossover study of cyproterone acetate in the treatment of the paraphilias. *Arch Sex Behav* 22:383–402, 1993.

Bromberg FG, et al. (Eds.). Clomipramine vs phenelzine in OCD: Controlled trial. *Psychiatry Drug Alerts* 7:18, 1993.

Bruce M, Scott N, Shine P and Lader M. Anxiogenic effects of caffeine in patients with anxiety disorders. *Arch Gen Psych* 49:867–869, 1992.

Cassano GB, Perugi G and McNair DM. Panic disorder: Review of the empirical and rational basis of pharmacological treatment. *Pharmacopsychiatry* 21:157–165, 1988.

Castaneda R and Cushman P. Alcohol withdrawal: A review of clinical management. *J Clin Psych* 50:278–284, 1989.

Chouinard G, et al. Alprazolam in the treatment of generalized anxiety and panic disorders: A double-blind placebo-controlled study. *Psychopharmacology* 77:229–233, 1982.

Conant J, et al. Central nervous system side effects of β-adrenergic blocking agents with high and low lipid solubility. *Cardiovascular Pharm* 13:656–661, 1989.

Cowley D, Roy Byrne P and Greenblatt D *Benzodiazepines: Pharmacokinetics and Pharmacodynamics in Benzodiazepines in Clinical Practice: Risks and Benefits,* Washington DC: APA Press, 1991.

Frishman W, et al. Clinical pharmacology of the new beta-adrenergic blocking drugs: Part 4. Adverse effects. Choosing a β-adrenoreceptor blocker. *Am Heart J* 98:256–262, 1979.

Garner SJ, Eldridge FL, Wagner PG and Dowell RT. Buspirone, an anxiolytic drug that stimulates respiration. *Am Rev Respir Dis* 139:945–950, 1989.

Gawin F, Compton M and Byck R. Buspirone reduces smoking. *Arch Gen Psych* 46:989–990, 1989.

Gillin JC and Byerley WF. The diagnosis and management of insomnia. *N Eng J Med* 322:239–248, 1990.

Greenblatt DJ and Koch-Weser J. Adverse reactions to propranolol in hospitalized medical patients: A report from the Boston Collaborative Drug Surveillance Program. *Am Heart J* 86:478–484, 1973.

Herman JB, Brotman AW and Rosenbaum JF. Rebound anxiety in panic disorder patients treated with shorter-acting benzodiazepines. *J Clin Psych* 48:22–26, 1987.

Hewlett W, et al. Clomipramine, clonazepam, and clonidine treatment of obsessive-compulsive disorder. *J Clin Psychopharmacol* 12:420–430, 1992.

Kales A, et al. Quazepam and temazepam: Effects of short- and intermediate-term use and withdrawal. *Clinical Pharmacology and Therapeutics* 40:376–386, 1986.

Kales A, et al. Rebound insomnia and rebound anxiety: A review. *Pharmacology* 26:121–137, 1983.

Keck PE, Jr, Taylor VE, Tugrul KC, McElroy SL and Bennett JA. Valproate treatment of panic disorder and lactate-induced panic attacks. *Biol Psychiatry* 33:542–546, 1993.

Knapp MJ, et al. A 30-week randomized controlled trial of high-dose tacrine in patients with Alzheimer's disease. *JAMA* 271:985–991, 1994.

Kranzler HR, Burleson JA, Korner P, Del Boca FK, Bohn MJ, et al. Placebo-controlled trial of fluoxetine as an adjunt to relapse prevention in alcoholics. *Am J Psych* 152:391–397, 1995.

Kushner MJ, et al. You don't have to be a neuroscientist to forget everything with triazolam—but it helps. *JAMA* 259:350–352, 1988.

Lion JR. Benzodiazepines in the treatment of aggressive patients. *J Clin Psych* 2:25–26, 1979.

McClusky HY, et al. Efficacy of behavioral versus triazolam treatment in persistent sleep-onset insomnia. *Am J Psych* 148:121–126, 1991.

McDougle CJ, Goodman WK, Leckman JF and Price LH. The psychopharmacology of obsessive compulsive disorder: Implications for treatment and pathogenesis. *Psych Clin N Am* 16:749–765, 1993.

Morris HH and Estes ML. Traveler's amnesia: Transient global amnesia secondary to triazolam. *JAMA* 258:945–946, 1987.

Nagy LM, Morgan CA, Southwick SM and Charney DS. Open prospective trial of fluoxetine for posttraumatic stress disorder. *J Clin Psychopharmacol* 13:107–113, 1993.

Nikaido AM and Elinwood EH. Comparison of the effects of quazepam and triazolam on cognitive-neuromotor performance. *Psychopharmacology* 92:459–464, 1987.

Noyes R, et al. Diazepam and propranolol in panic disorder and agoraphobia. *Arch Gen Psych* 41:287–292, 1984.

Ontiveros A and Fontaine R. Social phobia and clonazepam. *Can J Psych* 35:439–441, 1990.

Perse T. Obsessive-compulsive disorder: A treatment review. *J Clin Psych* 49:48–55, 1988.

Pinder RM, et al. Clonazepam: A review of its pharmacological properties and therapeutic efficacy in epilepsy. *Drugs* 12:321–361, 1976.

Ray WA, Griffin MR and Downey W. Benzodiazepines of long and short elimination half-life and the risk of hip fracture. *JAMA* 262:3303–3307, 1989.

Rickels K, et al. Methylphenidate in mildly depressed outpatients. *Clinical Pharmacology and Therapeutics* 13:595–601, 1972.

Ries R, Roy-Byrne P, Ward NG and Neppe VM. Carbamazepine for benzodiazepine withdrawal. *Am J Psych* 145:536–537, 1989.

Rosebush PI, Hildebrand AM, Furlong BG and Mazurek MF. Catatonic syndrome in a general psychiatric inpatient population: Frequency, clinical presentation, and response to lorazepam. *J Clin Psych* 51:357–362, 1990.

Roy-Byrne P, Ward NG and Donnelly P. Valproate in anxiety and withdrawal syndromes. *J Clin Psych* 50:44–48, 1989.

Scharf M, et al. A multicenter, placebo-controlled study evaluating zolpidem in the treatment of chronic insomnia. *J Clin Psych* 55:192–199, 1994.

Scharf MB, Fletcher ACPK and Graham JP. Comparative amnestic effects of benzodiazepine hypnotic agents. *J Clin Psych* 49:134–137, 1988.

Schneider LS, Syapin PJ and Pawluczyk S. Seizures following triazolam withdrawal despite benzodiazepine treatment. *J Clin Psych* 48:418–419, 1987.

Silver JM, Sandberg DP and Hales RE. New approaches in the pharmacotherapy of posttraumatic stress disorder. *J Clin Psych* 51:33–38, 1990.

Sussman N. Treatment of anxiety with buspirone. *Psych Anls* 17:114–120, 1987.

Teboul E and Chouinard G. Principles of benzodiazepine selection. Part I: Pharmacological aspects. *Can J Psych* 35:700–710, 1990.

Teboul E and Chouinard G. A guide to benzodiazepine selection: Part II: Clinical aspects. *Can J Psych* 36:62–69, 1991.

Teoh SK, Mello NK, Mendelson JH, Kuehnle J, Gastfriend DR, Rhoades E and Sholar W. Buprenorphine effects on morphine- and cocaine-induced subjective responses by drug-dependent men. *J Clin Psychopharmacol* 14:15–27, 1994.

Tesar GE, et al. Clonazepam versus alprazolam in the treatment of panic disorder: Interim analysis of data from a prospective, double-blind, placebo-controlled trial *J Clin Psych* 48:16–19, 1987.

Trimble MR. Worldwide use of clomipramine. *J Clin Psych* 51:51–54, 1990.

Watts VS and Neill JR. Buspirone in obsessive-compulsive disorder (letter). *Am J Psych* 145:1606, 1988.

ANTIPSYCHOTICS AND ANTIDEMENTIA

Alvir J and Lieberman J. A reevaluation of the clinical characteristics of clozapine-induced agranulocytosis in light of the United States experience (editorial). *J Clin Psychpharmacol* 14:87–89, 1994.

Barbee JG, Mancuso DM, Freed CR and Todorov AA. Alprazolam as a neuroleptic adjunct in the emergency treatment of schizophrenia. *Am J Psych* 149:506–510, 1992.

Bauer M and Mackert A. Clozapine treatment after agranulocytosis induced by classic neuroleptics. *J Clin Psychopharmacol* 14:71–73, 1994.

Binder RL and Jonelis F. Seborrheic dermatitis in neuroleptic-induced parkinsonism. *Arch Dermatol* 119:473–475, 1983.

Bitter I, Volavka J and Scheurer J. The concept of neuroleptic threshold: An update. *J Clin Psycopharmacol* 11:28–33, 1991.

Bodkin A, Cannon S, Cohen B, Alpert J, Zornberg G and Cole J. Selegiline treatment of negative symptoms of schizophrenia and schizo-affective disorder. Presented at the annual meeting of the American College of Neuropsychopharmacology, San Juan PR, December 1992.

Breier A, et al. Effects of clozapine on positive and negative symptoms in outpatients with schizophrenia. *Am J Psych* 151:20–26, 1994.

Chengappa KNR, Baker RW and Harty I. Seizures and clozapine dosing schedule (letter). *J Clin Psych.* 55:456, 1994.

Collins PJ, Larkin EP and Shubsachs APW. Lithium carbonate in chronic schizophrenia: A brief trial of lithium carbonate added to neuroleptics for treatment of resistant schizophrenic patients. *Acta Psychiatr Scand* 84:150–154, 1991.

Dabiri LM, Pasta D, Darby JK and Mosbacker D. Effectiveness of Vitamin E for treatment of long-term tardive dyskinesia. *Am J Psych* 151:925–926, 1994.

Davis JM, Matalon L, Watanabe MD and Blake Lesley. Depot antipsychotic drugs: Place in therapy. *Drugs* 47:741–773, 1994.

Devinsky O, et al. Clozapine-related seizures. *Neurology* 41:369–371, 1991.

Douyon R, Angrist B, Peselow E, Cooper T and Rotrosen J. Neuroleptic augmentation with alprazolam: Clinical effects and pharmacokinetic correlates. *Am J Psych* 146:231–234, 1989.

Easton MS and Janicak PG. Benzodiazepines (BZ) for the management of psychosis. *Psych Med* 9:25–36, 1991.

Ereshefsky L, Watanabe MD and Tran-Johnson TL. Clozapine: An atypical antipsychotic agent. *Clin Pharm* 8:691–709, 1989.

Farlow M, Gracon SI, Hershey LA, Lewis KW, Sadowsky CH and Dolan-Ureno J. A controlled trial of tacrine in Alzheimer's disease. *JAMA* 268:2523–2565, 1992.

Feinberg SS, Kay SR, Elijovich LR, Fishbein A and Opler L. Pimozide treatment of the negative schizophrenic syndrome: An open trial. *J Clin Psych* 49:235–238, 1988.

Fenton W, et al. Risk factors for spontaneous dyskinesia in schizophrenia. *Arch Gen Psych* 51:643–650, 1994.

Fleishman SB, Lavin MR, Sattler M and Szarka H. Antiemetic-induced akathisia in cancer patients receiving chemotherapy. *Am J Psych* 151:763–765, 1994.

Freedberg KA, et al. Antischizophrenic drugs: Differential plasma protein binding and therapeutic activity. *Life Sciences* 24:2467–2474, 1979.

Ganzini L, Heintz R, Hoffman WF, Keepers GA and Casey DE. Acute extrapyramidal syndromes in neuroleptic-treated elders: A pilot study. *J Geriatr Psych Neurol* 4:222–225, 1991.

Gardos G and Cole JO. Weight reduction in schizophrenics by molindone. *Am J Psych* 134:302–304, 1977.

Gelenberg AJ, Bellinhausen B, Wojcik JD, Falk WE and Sachs GS. A prospective survey of neuroleptic malignant syndrome in a short-term psychiatric hospital. *Am J Psych* 145:517–518, 1988.

Gelenberg AJ, Bellinghausen B, Wojcik JD, Falk WE and Farhadi AM. Patients with neuroleptic malignant syndrome histories: What happens when they are re-hospitalized? *J Clin Psych* 50:178–180, 1989.

Glazer WM, Morgenstern H and Doucette JT. Predicting the long-term risk of tardive dyskinesia in outpatients maintained on neuroleptic medications. *J Clin Psych* 54:133–139, 1993.

Goff D and Baldessarini RJ. Drug interactions with antipsychotic agents. *J Clin Psychopharmacol* 13:57–67, 1993.

Goff DC, et al. An open trial of buspirone added to neuroleptics in schizophrenic patients. *J Clin Psychopharmacol* 11:193–197, 1991.

Goff DC, Amico E, Dreyfuss D and Ciraulo D. A placebo-controlled trial of trihexyphenidyl in unmedicated patients with schizophrenia. *Am J Psych* 151:429–431, 1994.

Goldman D, Hien DA, Haas GL, Sweeney JA and Frances AJ. Bizarre delusions and DSM-III-R schizophrenia. *Am J Psych* 149:494–499, 1992.

Greenberg WM. Mechanism of neuroleptic-associated priapism (letter). *Am J Psych* 145:393–394, 1988.

Guzé BH and Baxter LR, Jr. Neuroleptic malignant syndrome. *N Eng J Med* 313:163–166, 1985.

Haller E and Binder RL. Clozapine and seizures. *Am J Psych* 147:1069–1071, 1990.

Haring C, et al. Influence of patient-related variables on clozapine plasma levels. *Am J Psych* 50:64–65, 1989.

Heikkinen H, Outakoski J, Meriläinen V, Tuomi A and Huttunen MO. Molindone and weight loss (letter). *J Clin Psych* 54:160–161, 1993.

Hemstrom CA, Evans RL and Lobeck FG. Haloperidol decanoate: A depot antipsychotic. *Drug Intelligence and Clinical Pharmacy* 22:290–295, 1988.

Horiguchi J. Low serum iron in patients with neuroleptic-induced akathisia and dystonia under antipsychotic drug treatment. *Acta Psychiatr Scand* 84:301–303, 1991.

Hymowitz P, Frances A, Jacobsberg LB, Sickles M and Hoyt R. Neuroleptic treatment of schizotypal personality disorders. *Comprehensive Psychiatry* 27:267–271, 1986.

Javitt DC, Zylberman I, Zukin SR, Heresco-Levy U and Lindenmayer JP.

Amelioration of negative symptoms in schizophrenia with glycine. *Am J Psych* 151:1234–1236, 1994.

Kane J, Honigfeld G, Singer J, et al. Clozapine for the treatment-resistant schizophrenic: A double-blind comparison with chlorpromazine. *Arch Gen Psych* 45:780–796, 1988.

Kane JM. The current status of neuroleptic therapy. *J Clin Psych* 50:352–355, 1989.

Keepers GA and Casey DE. Use of neuroleptic-induced extrapyramidal symptoms to predict future vulnerability to side effects. *Am J Psych* 148:85–89, 1991.

Knapp MJ, Knopman DS, Solomon PR, Pendlebury WW, Davis CS, Gracon SI and the Tacrine Study Group. A 30-week randomized controlled trial of high-dose tacrine in patients with Alzheimer's disease. *JAMA* 271:985–991, 1994.

Kotin J, et al. Thioridazine and sexual dysfunction. *Am J Psych* 133:82–85, 1976.

Lederle Laboratories. (1985). *Loxitane.* Pearl River NY: J. Maxmen.

Levenson JL and Fisher JG. Long-term outcome after neuroleptic malignant syndrome. *J Clin Psych* 49:154–156, 1988.

Levi-Minzi S, Bermanzohn PC and Siris SG. Bromocriptine for "negative" schizophrenia. *Compr Psychiatry* 32:210–216, 1991.

Levinson DF and Simpson GM. Neuroleptic-induced extrapyramidal symptoms with fever. *Arch Gen Psych* 43:839–847, 1986.

Lieberman JA, Kane JM and Johns CA. Clozapine: Guidelines for clinical management. *J Clin Psych* 50:329–338, 1989.

Lindenmayer JP, Grochowski S and Mabugat L. Clozapine effects on positive and negative symptoms: A six-month trial in treatment-refractory schizophrenics. *J Clin Psychopharmacol* 14:201–204, 1994.

Marder SR, Van Putten, T, Aravagiri M, Hawes EM, Hubbard JW, et al. Fluphenazine plasma levels and clinical response. *Psychopharmacol Bull* 26:256–259, 1990.

Marder SR and Meibach RC. Risperidone in the treatment of schizophrenia. *Am J Psych* 151:825–835, 1994.

Opler LA and Feinberg SS. The role of pimozide in clinical psychiatry: A review. *J Clin Psych* 52:221–233, 1991.

Owen MW, Pickar D, Doran AR, Breier A, Tarell and Paul SM. Combination alprazolam-neuroleptic treatment of the positive and negative symptoms of schizophrenia. *Am J Psych* 143:85–87, 1986.

Owen RR, Jr and Cole JO. Molindone hydrochloride: A review of laboratory and clinical findings. *J Clin Psychopharmacol* 9:268–276, 1989.

Pope HG, Jr, et al. Frequency and presentation of neuroleptic malignant syndrome in a large psychiatric hospital. *Am J Psych* 143:1227–1233, 1986.

Rajiv T, Greden JF and Silk KR. Treatment of negative schizophrenic symptoms with trihexyphenidyl. *J Clin Psychopharmacol* 8:212–215, 1988.

Remington GJ, et al. Prevalence of neuroleptic-induced dystonia in mania and schizophrenia. *Am J Psych* 147:1231–1233, 1990.

Rosebush PI, Stewart TD and Gelenberg AJ. Twenty neuroleptic re-challenges after neuroleptic malignant syndrome in 15 patients. *J Clin Psych* 50:295–298, 1989.

Rosebush PI, Stewart T and Mazurek MF. The treatment of neuroleptic malignant syndrome: Are dantrolene and bromocriptine useful adjuncts to supportive care? *Br J Psych* 150:709–712, 1991.

Rosebush PI and Stewart T. A prospective analysis of 24 episodes of neuroleptic malignant syndrome. *Am J Psych* 146:717–725, 1989.

Sachdev P and Loneragan C. The present status of akathisia. *J Nerv Ment Dis* 179:381–391, 1991.

Sautter F, McDermott B and Garver D. Familial differences between rapid neuroleptic response psychosis and delayed neuroleptic response psychosis. *Biol Psychiatry* 33:15–21, 1993.

Sethi BB and Dube S. Propranolol in schizophrenia. *Neuropsychopharm Biol Psych* 7:88–89, 1983.

Shalev A, Hermesh H and Munitz H. Mortality from neuroleptic malignant syndrome. *J Clin Psych* 50:18–25, 1989.

Sheehy LM and Maxmen JS. Phenelzine-induced psychosis. *Am J Psych* 135:1422–1423, 1978.

Silver H and Nassar A. Fluvoxamine improves negative symptoms in treated chronic schizophrenia: An add-on double-blind, placebo-controlled study. *Biol Psychiatry* 31:698–704, 1992.

Silverstone T, Smith G and Goodall E. Prevalence of obesity in patients receiving depot antipsychotics. *Br J Psych* 153:214–217, 1988.

Siris SG, et al. The use of antidepressants for negative symptoms in a subset of schizophrenic patients. *Psychopharmacol Bull* 27:331–335, 1991.

Susman VL and Addonizio G. Reinduction of neuroleptic malignant syndrome by lithium. *J Clin Psychopharmacol* 7:339–341, 1987.

Szymanski S, Lieberman JA, Picou D, Masiar S and Cooper T. A case report of cimetidine-induced clozapine toxicity. *J Clin Psych* 52:21–22, 1991.

Tandon R, DeQuardo JR, Goodson J, Mann NA and Greden JF. Effect of anticholinergics on positive and negative symptoms in schizophrenia. *Psychopharmacol Bull* 28:292–295, 1992.

Van Putten T, Marder SR and Mintz J. Serum prolactin as a correlate of clinical response to haloperidol. *J Clin Psychopharmacol* 11:357–361, 1991.

Watkins PB, Zimmerman HJ, Knapp MJ, Gracon SI and Lewis KW. Hepatotoxic effects of tacrine administration in patients with Alzheimer's disease. *JAMA* 271:992–998, 1994.

Wilkins JN, Marder SR, Van Putten T, et al. Circulating prolactin predicts risk of exacerbation in patients on depot fluphenazine. *Psychopharmacol Bull* 23:522–525, 1987.

Wilson WH and Claussen AM. Seizures associated with clozapine treatment in a state hospital. *J Clin Psych* 55:184–188, 1994.

Winker A. Tacrine for Alzheimer's disease: Which patient, what dose? *JAMA* 271:1023–1024, 1994.

BIBLIOGRAPHY

Woerner MG, Saltz BL, Kane JM, Lieberman JA and Alvir MJ. Diabetes and development of tardive dyskinesia. *Am J Psych* 150:966–968, 1993.

Woerner MG, Kane JM, Lieberman JA, et al. The prevalence of tardive dyskinesia. *J Clin Psychopharmacol* 11:34–42, 1991.

Wolf MA, et al. Low dose bromocriptine in neuroleptic-resistant schizophrenia: A pilot study. *Biol Psychiatry* 31:1166–1168, 1992.

Wolk SI and Douglas DJ. Clozapine treatment of psychosis in Parkinson's disease: A report of five consecutive cases. *J Clin Psych* 53:373–376, 1992.

Wolkowitz OM, Turetsky MA, Reus VI and Hargreaves WA. Benzodiazepine augmentation of neuroleptics in treatment-resistant schizophrenia. *Psychopharmacol Bull* 28:291–295, 1992.

Yadalam KG and Simpson GM. Changing from oral to depot fluphenazine. *J Clin Psych* 49:346–348, 1988.

EXTRAPYRAMIDAL DRUGS

Adler LA, Angrist B, Weinreb H and Rotrosen J. Studies on the time course and efficacy of β-blockers in neuroleptic-induced akathisia and the akathisia of idiopathic Parkinson's disease. *Psychopharmacol Bull* 27:107–111, 1991.

Arana GW, Goff DC, Baldessarini RJ and Keepers GA. Efficacy of anticholinergic prophylaxis for neuroleptic-induced acute dystonia. *Am J Psych* 145:993–996, 1988.

Bartels M, et al. Treatment of akathisia with lorazepam: An open clinical trial. *Pharmacopsychiatry* 20:51–53, 1987.

Barton A, Bowie J and Ebmeier K. Low plasma iron status and akathisia. *J Neurol Neurosurg Psychiatry* 53:671–674, 1990.

Braude WM, Barnes TRE and Gore SM. Clinical characteristics of akathisia: A systematic investiation of acute psychiatric inpatient admissions. *Br J Psych* 143:139–150, 1983.

Brown KW, Glen SE and White T. Low serum iron status and akathisia. *Lancet* 1:1234–1236, 1987.

Fisch RZ. Trihexyphenidyl abuse: Therapeutic implications for negative symptoms of schizophrenia? *Acta Psychiatr Scand* 75:91–94, 1987.

Goff DC, et al. The effect of benztropine on haloperidol-induced dystonia, clinical efficacy and pharmacokinetics: A prospective, double-blind trial. *J Clin Psychopharmacol* 11:106–112, 1991.

Lipinski JF, Zubenko GS, Barriera P, et al. Propranolol in the treatment of neuroleptic-induced akathisia. *Lancet* 2:685–686, 1983.

McEvoy JP. A double-blind crossover comparison of antiparkinson drug therapy: Amantadine versus anticholinergics in 90 normal volunteers, with an emphasis on differential effects on memory function. *J Clin Psych* 49:20–23, 1987.

Nemes ZC, Rotrosen J, Angrist B, Peselow E and Schoentag R. Serum iron levels and akathisia. *Biol Psychiatry* 29:411–413, 1991.

Neppe VM and Ward NG. The management of neuroleptic-induced acute extrapyramidal syndromes. In Neppe VM (Ed.), *Innovative Psychopharmacotherapy 152–176*, NY: Raven Press, 1989.

O'Loughlin V, Dickie AC and Ebmeier KP. Serum iron and transferrin in acute neuroleptic-induced akathisia. *J Neurol Neurosurg Psychiatry* 54:363–364, 1991.

Sachdev P and Loneragan C. The present status of akathisia. *J Nerv Ment Dis* 179:381–391, 1991.

Tune L, Carr S, Hoag E and Cooper T. Anticholinergic effects of drugs commonly prescribed for the elderly: Potential means for assessing risk of delirium. *Am J Psych* 149:1393–1394, 1992.

Wells BG, Cold JA, Marken PA, Brown CS, Chu CC, et al. A placebo-controlled trial of nadolol in the treatment of neuroleptic-induced akathisia.. *J Clin Psych* 52:255–260, 1991.

ANTIDEPRESSANTS, MAOIs

Anton RF and Burch EA, Jr. Amoxapine versus amitriptyline combined with perphenazine in the treatment of psychotic depression. *Am J Psych* 147:1203–1208, 1990.

Artigas F, Perez V and Alvarez E. Pindolol induces a rapid improvement of depressed patients treated with serotonin reuptake inhibitors. *Arch Gen Psych* 51:248–251, 1994.

Bouckoms A and Mangini L. Pergolide: An antidepressant adjuvant for mood disorders? *Psychopharmacol Bull* 29:207–211, 1993.

Bresnahan DB, Pandey GN, Janicak PG, et al. MAO inhibition and clinical response in depressed patients treated with phenelzine. *J Clin Psych* 51:47–50, 1990.

Brinkley JR. Pharmacotherapy of borderline states. *Psych Clin N Am* 16:853–884, 1993.

Browne B and Linter S. Monoamine oxidase inhibitors and narcotic analgesics: A critical review of the implications for treatment. *Br J Psych* 151:210–212, 1987.

Charney DS, et al. Drug treatment of panic disorder: The comparative efficacy of imipramine, alprazolam, and trazodone. *J Clin Psych* 47:580–586, 1986.

Cooke RG, Joffe RT and Levitt A. T_3 augmentation of antidepressant treatment in T_4-replaced thyroid patients. *J Clin Psych* 53:16–18, 1992.

Cornelius JR, Soloff PH, George A, Ulrich RF and Perel JM. Haloperidol vs. phenelzine in continuation therapy of borderline disorder. *Psychopharmacol Bull* 29:333–337, 1993.

Cowdry RW and Gardner DL. Pharmacotherapy of borderline personality disorder. *Arch Gen Psych* 45:111–119, 45.

Davidson J. Seizures and bupropion: A review. *J Clin Psych* 50:256–261, 1989.

Davis JM, Janicak PG and Bruninga K. The efficacy of MAO inhibitors in depression: A metaanalysis. *Psych Anls* 17:825–831, 1987.

Dilsaver SC. Antidepressant withdrawal syndromes: Phenomenology and pathophysiology. *Acta Psychiatr Scand* 79:113–117, 1989.

Dunleavy DLF and Oswald I. Phenelzine, mood response, and sleep. *Arch Gen Psych* 28:353–356, 1973.

Gardner DL and Cowdry RW. Pharmacotherapy of borderline personality disorder: A review. *Psychopharmocol Bull* 25:515–522, 1989.

Gelenberg AJ. New perspectives on the use of tricyclic antidepressants. *J Clin Psych* 50:3, 1989.

Georgotas A, McCue RE, Friedman E and Cooper TB. A placebo-controlled comparison of the effect of nortriptyline and phenelzine on orthostatic hypotension in elderly depressed patients. *J Clin Psychopharmacol* 7:413–416, 1987.

Glassman A, et al. The safety of tricyclic antidepressants in cardiac patients (commentary). *JAMA* 269:2673–2675, 1993.

Glassman AH and Roose SP. Cardiovascular effects of tricyclic antidepressants. *Psych Anls* 17:340–342, 1987.

Goodwin FK, et al. Potentiation of antidepressant effects by 1-triiodothyronine in tricyclic nonresponders. *Am J Psych* 139:34–38, 1982.

Greden JF. Introduction: Part III. New agents for the treatment of depression. *J Clin Psych* 55:32–33 (suppl.), 1994.

Gunderson JG. Pharmacotherapy for patients with borderline personality disorder. *Arch Gen Psych* 43:698–700, 1986.

Harrison WH, et al. MAOIs and hypertensive crisis: The role of OTC drugs. *J Clin Psych* 50:64–65, 1989.

Hellerstein DJ, Yanowitch P, Rosenthal J, Wallner-Samstag L, Maurer M, et al. A randomized double-blind study of fluoxetine versus placebo in the treatment of dysthymia. *Am J Psych* 150:1169–1175, 1993.

Himmelhoch JM, Thase ME, Mallinger AG and Houck P. Tranylcypromine verses imipramine in anergic bipolar depression. *Am J Psych* 148:910–916, 1991.

Höschl C. Do calcium antagonists have a place in the treatment of mood disorders? *Drugs* 42:721–729, 1991.

Howland RH. Pharmacotherapy of dysthymia: A review. *J Clin Psychopharmacol* 11:83–92, 1991.

Hudson JI and Pope HG, Jr. Affective spectrum disorder: Does antidepressant response identify a family of disorders with a common pathophysiology? *Am J Psych* 147:552–564, 1990.

Hunt KA and Resnick MP. Clomipramine-induced agranulocytosis and its treatment with G-CSF. *Am J Psych* 150:522–523, 1993.

Jacobson SJ, Jones K, Johnson K, Ceolin L, Kaur P, Sahn D, Donnenfeld AE, Rieder M, Santelli R, Smythe J, Pastuszak A, Einarson T and Koren G. Prospective multicentre study of pregnancy outcome after lithium exposure during the first trimester. *Lancet* 339:530–533, 1992.

Kahn D, Silver JM and Opler LA. The safety of switching rapidly from tricyclic antidepressants to monoamine oxidase inhibitors. *J Clin Psychopharmacol* 9:198–202, 1989.

Katz R and Rosenthal M. Adverse interaction of cyproheptadine with serotonergic antidepressant (letter). *J Clin Psych* 55:314–315, 1994.

Keck PE, et al. Frequency and presentation of neuroleptic malignant syndrome in a state psychiatric hospital. *J Clin Psych* 50:352–355, 1989.

Keck PE, Jr, Vuckovic A, Pope HG, Jr, et al. Acute cardiovascular response to monoamine oxidase inhibitors: A prospective assessment. *J Clin Psychopharmacol* 9:203–206, 1989.

Klaiber EL, Broverman DM, Vogel W and Kobayashi Y. Estrogen therapy for severe persistent depressions in women. *Arch Gen Psychiatry* 36: 550–554, 1979.

Lappin R and Achuincloss E. Treatment of the serotonin syndrome with cyproheptadine (letter). *N Engl J Med* 331:1021–1022, 1994.

Lederle Laboratories. (1987). *Asendin*. Pearl River NY: J. Maxmen.

Levitt AJ, Joffe RT and Kennedy SH. Bright light augmentation in antidepressant nonresponders. *J Clin Psych* 52:336–337, 1991.

Liebowitz MR, et al. Phenelzine vs. imipramine in atypical depression: A preliminary report. *Arch Gen Psych* 41:669–677, 1984.

Liebowitz MR, Schneier F, Campeas R, Hollander E, Hatterer J, Fyer A, Gorman J, Papp L, Davies S, Gully R and Klein DF. Phenelzine vs atenolol in social phobia: A placebo-controlled comparison. *Arch Gen Psych* 49:290–300, 1992.

Lipinsky JF, et al. Fluoxetine-induced akathisia: Clinical and theoretical implications. *J Clin Psych* 50:339–342, 1989.

Maany I, et al. Increase in despiramine serum levels associated with methadone treatment. *Am J of Psych* 146:1611–1613, 1989.

Mann JJ. Loss of antidepressant effect with long-term monoamine oxidase inhibitor treatment without loss of monoamine oxidase inhibition. *J Clin Psychopharmacol* 3:363–366, 1983.

Marin DB, Kocsis JH, Frances AJ and Parides M. Desipramine for the treatment of "Pure" dysthymia versus "Double" depression. *Am J Psych* 151:1079–1080, 1994.

McGrath PJ, et al. A double-blind crossover trial of imipramine and phenelzine for outpatients with treatment-refractory depression. *Am J Psych* 150:118–123, 1993.

Murphy DL. The behavioral toxicity of monoamine oxidase-inhibiting antidepressants. In Garrattini S, et al. (Eds.), *Advances in Pharmacology and Chemotherapy* (vol 14), 71–103, New York: Academic Press, 1977.

Nelson JC, Mazure CM, Bowers MB, Jr and Jatlow PI. A preliminary, open study of the combination of fluoxetine and desipramine for rapid treatment of major depression. *Arch Gen Psych* 48:303–307, 1991.

Palladino A, Jr. Adverse reactions to abrupt dicontinuation of phenelzine (letter). *J Clin Psychopharmacol* 3:206–207, 1983.

Pare CMB, Kline N, Hallstrom C and Cooper TB. Will amitriptyline prevent the "Cheese" reaction of monoamine oxidase inhibitors? *Lancet* July 24:183–186, 1982.

Peet M. Induction of mania with selective serotonin re-uptake inhibitors and tricyclic antidepressants. *Br J Psych* 164:549–550, 1994.

Perry PJ, Zeilmann C and Arndt S. Tricyclic antidepressant concentrations in plasma: An estimate of their sensitivity and specificity as a predictor of response. *J Clin Psychopharmacol* 14:230–240, 1994.

Prien RF and Kupfer DJ. Continuation drug therapy for major depressive episodes: How long should it be maintained. *Am J Psych* 143:18–23, 1986.

Quitkin FM, McGrath PJ, Stewart JW, et al. Phenelzine and imipramine in mood reactive depressives. *Arch Gen Psych* 46:787–793, 1989.

Quitkin FM, Stewart JW, et al. Phenelzine versus imipramine in the treatment of probable atypical depression: Defining syndrome boundaries of selective MAOI responders. *Am J Psych* 145:306–311, 1988.

Razani J, et al. The safety and efficacy of combined amitriptyline and tranylcypromine antidepressant treatment. *Arch Gen Psych* 40:657–661, 1983.

Remick RA, Jewesson P and Ford RWJ. Monoamine oxidase inhibitors in general anesthesia: A reevaluation. *Convulsive Therapy* 3:196–203, 1987.

Richelson E and Nelson A. Antagonism by antidepressants of neurotransmitter receptors of normal human brain in vitro. *J Pharmacol Experimental Therapeutics* 230:94–102, 1984.

Richelson E. The pharmacology of antidepressants at the synapse: Focus on newer compounds. *J Clin Psych* 55:34–39, 1994.

Rickels K, et al. Antidepressants for the treatment of generalized anxiety disorder: A placebo-controlled comparison of imipramine, trazodone, and diazepam. *Arch Gen Psych* 50:884–895, 1993.

Rickels K, Amsterdam JD, Clary C, Puzzuoli G and Schweizer E. Buspirone in major depression: A controlled study. *J Clin Psych* 52:34–38, 1991.

Robinson DS, Lerfald SC, Bennett B, Laux D, Devereaux E, et al. Continuation and maintenance treatment of major depression with the monoamine oxidase inhibitor phenelzine: A double-blind placebo-controlled discontinuation study. Presented at the 30th Annual Meeting of the New Clinical Drug Evaluation Unit (NCDEU), May 29–June 1, 1990, Key Biscayne, Florida.

Roose S, et al. Comparative efficacy of selective serotonin reuptake inhibitors and tricyclics in the treatment of melancholia. *Am J Psych* 151:1735–1739, 1994.

Roose SP, Glassman AH and Dalack GW. Depression, heart disease, and tricyclic antidepressants. *J Clin Psych* 50:12–16, 1989.

Sacchetti E, et al. Are SSRI antidepressants a clinically homogeneous class of compounds? (letter). *Lancet* 344:126–127, 1994.

Schlager D. Early-morning administration of short-acting β-blockers for treatment of winter depression. *Am J Psych* 151:1383–1385, 1994.

Shulman KI, Walker SE, MacKenzie S and Knowles S. Dietary restriction, tyramine, and the use of MAOIs. *J Clin Psychopharmacol* 9:397–402, 1989.

Sternbach H. The serotonin syndrome. *Am J Psych* 148:705–713, 1991.

Stewart JW, McGrath PJ and Quitkin FM. Can mildly depressed outpatients with atypical depression benefit from antidepressants? *Am J Psych* 149:615–619, 1992.

Stewart JW, McGrath PJ, Quitkin FM, et al. Chronic depression: Response to placebo, imipramine, and phenelzine. *J Clin Psychopharmacol* 13:391–396, 1993.

Stewart JW, McGrath PJ, Rabkin JG and Quitkin FM. Atypical depression: A valid clinical entity? *Psych Clin N Am* 16:479–495, 1993.

Sullivan EA and Shulman KI. Diet and monoamine oxidase inhibition: A reexamination. *Can J Psych* 29:707–711, 1984.

Tailor SAN, Shulman KI, Walker SE, Moss J and Gardner D. Hypertensive episode associated with phenelzine and tap beer: A reanalysis of the role of pressor amines in beer. *J Clin Psychopharmacol* 14:5–14, 1994.

Teicher MH, et al. Severe daytime somnolence in patients treated with an MAOI. *Am J Psych* 145:1552–1556, 1988.

Thase ME, Mallinger AG, McKnight D and Himmelhoch JM. Treatment of imipramine-resistant recurrent depression, IV: A double-blind cross-over study of tranylcypromine for anergic bipolar depression. *Am J Psych* 149:195–198, 1992.

Tingelstad J. The cardiotoxicity of the tricyclics. *J Am Acad Child and Adolescent Psych* 30:845–846, 1991.

Walsh BT. Use of antidepressants in bulimia. *Clin Pediatrics* 28:127–128, 1989.

Ward NG. Pain and Depression. In Bonica J (Ed.), *The Management of Pain* 2nd ed (vol 1), 310–319, Philadelphia: Lea & Fibiger, 1990.

Ward NG. Tricyclic antidepressants for chronic low back pain: Mechanisms of action and predictors of response. *Spine* 11:661–665, 1986.

Wesner RB and Noyes R, Jr. Tolerance to the therapeutic effect of phenelzine in patients with panic disorder. *J Clin Psych* 49:450–451, 1988.

Woods SW, et al. Psychostimulant treatment of depressive disorders secondary to medical illness. *J Clin Psych* 47:12–15, 1986.

Young WF, Jr, et al. Human monoamine oxidase. *Arch Gen Psych* 43:604–609, 1986.

LITHIUM, ANTICONVULSANTS, AND MOOD STABILIZERS

Alpert M, Allan ER, Citrome L, Laury G, Sison C and Sudilovsky A. A double-blind, placebo-controlled study of adjunctive nadolol in the management of violent psychiatric patients. *Psychopharm Bulletin* 26:367–371, 1990.

American Psychiatric Association. Practice guideline for the treatment of patients with bipolar disorder (Suppl.). *Am J Psych* 151:1–36, 1994.

Amsterdam JD, Maislin G and Rybakowski J. A possible antiviral action of lithium carbonate in herpes simplex virus infections. *Biol Psychiatry* 27:447–453, 1990.

Ballenger JC. The clinical use of carbamazepine in affective disorders. *J Clin Psych* 49:13–19, 1988.

Bauer MS and Whybrow PC. The effect of changing thyroid function of cyclic affective illness in a human subject. *Am J Psych* 143:633–636, 1986.

Bone S, et al. Incidence of side effects in patients on long-term lithium therapy. *Am J Psych* 137:103–104, 1980.

Bowden C, et al. Efficacy of divalproex vs lithium and placebo in the treatment of mania. *JAMA* 271:918–924, 1994.

Brewerton T and Jackson C. Prophylaxis of carbamazepine-induced hyponatremia by demeclocycline in six patients. *J Clin Psych* 55:249–251, 1994.

Brooks SC and Lessin BE. Treatment of resistant lithium-induced nephrogenic diabetes insipidus and schizoaffective psychosis with carbamazepine. *Am J Psych* 140:1077–1078, 1983.

Brown WT Side effects of lithium therapy and their treatment. *Can Psych Assoc J* 21:13–21, 1976.

Browne TR Clonazepam: A review of a new anticonvulsant drug. *Arch Neurol* 33:326–332, 1976.

Calabrese JR, et al. Predictors of valproate response in bipolar rapid cycling. *J Clin Psychopharmacol* 13:280–283, 1993.

Cohen LS, Friedman JM, Jefferson JW, Johnson EM and Weiner ML. A reevaluation of risk of in utero exposure to lithium. *JAMA* 271: 146–150, 1994.

Cummings MA, Haviland MG, Wareham JG and Fontana LA. A prospective clinical evaluation of an equation to predict daily lithium dose. *J Clin Psych* 54:55–58, 1993.

Dunner DL and Fieve RR. Clinical factors in lithium carbonate prophylaxis failure. *Arch Gen Psych* 30:229–233, 1974.

Faedda GL, et al. Outcome after rapid vs gradual discontinuation of lithium treatment in bipolar disorders. *Arch Gen Psych* 50:448–455, 1993.

Gelenberg AJ and Stone Hopkins H. Report on efficacy of treatments for bipolar disorder. *Psychopharmacol Bull* 29:447–456, 1993.

Gleason RP and Schneider LS. Carbamazepine treatment of agitation in Alzheimer's outpatients refractory to neuroleptics. *J Clin Psych* 51:115–118, 1990.

Goodnick P. Verapamil prophylaxis in pregnant women with bipolar disorder (letter). *Am J Psych* 150:1560, 1993.

Hetmar O, Brun C, Clemmesen L, Ladefoged J, Larsen S and Rafaelsen OJ. Lithium: Long-term effects on the kidney: II. Structural changes. *J Psychiatr Res* 21:279–288, 1987.

Himmelhoch JM, et al. Adjustment of lithium dose during lithium-chlorothiazide therapy. *Clin Pharmacology and Therapeutics* 22:225–227, 1977.

Jefferson JW, et al. Lithium Encyclopedia for Clinical Practice (2nd ed.). Washington DC: American Psychiatric Press, 1987.

Jefferson JW. Cardiovascular effects and toxicity of anxiolytics and antidepressants. *J Clin Psych* 50:368–378, 1989.

Jefferson JW. Mood stabilizers: A review. In: Dunner D (Ed.), *Current Psychiatric Therapy*, 246–250, Philadelphia: WB Saunders, 1993.

Joffe RT and Singer W. A comparison of triiodothyronine and thyroxine in the potentiation of tricyclic antidepressants. *J Psychiatr Res* 32:241–251, 1990.

Kafantaris V, et al. Carbamazepine in hospitalized aggressive conduct disorder children: An open pilot study. *Psychopharmacol Bull* 28:193–199, 1992.

Kane J, et al. Extrapyramidal side effects with lithium treatment. *Am J Psych* 135:322–328, 1989.

Kastner T, Finesmith R and Walsh K. Long-term administration of valproic acid in the treatment of affective symptoms in people with mental retardation. *J Clin Psychopharmacol* 13:448–451, 1993.

Lee H, et al. A trial of lithium citrate for the management of acute agitation of psychiatric inpatients: A pilot study (letter). *J Clin Psychopharmacol* 12:361–362, 1992.

Levy RH and Kerr BM. Clinical pharmacokinetics of carbamazepine. *J Clin Psych* 49:58–61, 1988.

Markoff RA and King M, Jr. Does lithium dose prediction improve treatment efficacy? Prospective evaluation of a mathematical method. *J Clin Psychopharmacol* 12:305–308, 1992.

Mattes J. Valproic acid for nonaffective aggression in the mentally retarded. *J Nerv Ment Dis* 180:601–602, 1992.

Mazure C, et al. Valproate treatment of older psychotic patients with organic mental syndromes and behavioral dyscontrol. *J Am Geriatric Soc* 40:914–916, 1993.

McElroy SL, et al. Valproate in psychiatric disorders: Literature review and clinical guidelines. *J Clin Psych* 50:23–29, 1989.

McElroy SL, Keck PE, Jr., Pope HG, Jr., Hudson JI and Morris D. Correlates of antimanic response to valproate. *Psychopharmacol Bull* 27:127–133, 1991.

McEvoy JP, Hogarty GE and Steingard S. Optimal dose of neuroleptic in acute schizophrenia: A controlled study of the neuroleptic threshold and higher haloperidol dose. *Arch Gen Psych* 48:739–745, 1991.

Nambudiri DE, Meyers BS and Young RC. Delayed recovery from lithium neurotoxicity. *J Geriatr Psych Neurol* 4:40–43, 1991.

Neppe VN, Tucker JG and Wilensky AJ. Introduction: Fundamentals of carbamazepine use in neuropsychiatry. *J Clin Psych* 49:4–6, 1988.

Pellock JM. Carbamazepine side effects in children and adults. *Epilepsia* 28:S64–S70, 1987.

Plenge P, Mellerup ET, Bolwig TG, Brun C, Hetmar O, Ladefoged J, Larsen S and Rafaelsen OJ. Lithium treatment: Does the kidney prefer one daily dose instead of two? *Acta Psychiatr Scand* 66:121–128, 1982.

Post RM, Trimble MR and Pippenger CE. *Clinical Use of Anticonvulsants in Psychiatric Disorders.* New York: Demos, 1989.

Post RM. Time course of clinical effects of carbamazepine: Implications for mechanisms of action. *J Clin Psych* 49:35–46, 1988.

Prien RF and Potter WZ. NIMH workshop report on treatment of bipolar disorder. *Psychopharmacol Bull* 26:409–427, 1990.

Ragheb M. The clinical significance of lithium-nonsteroidal anti-inflammatory drug interactions. *J Clin Psychopharmacol* 10:350–354, 1990.

Ratey JJ, Sorgi P, Gillian A, O'Driscoll MA, Sands S, et al. Nadolol to treat aggression and psychiatric symptomatology in chronic psychiatric inpatients: A double-blind, placebo-controlled study. *J Clin Psych* 53:41–46, 1992.

Ricketts R, et al. Fluoxetine treatment of severe self-injury in young adults with mental retardation. *J Am Acad Child and Adolescent Psych* 32:865–869, 1993.

Ross DR, Coffey E, Ferren EL, Walker JI and Olanow CW. On-off syndrome treated with lithium carbonate: Case report. *Am J Psych* 138:1626–1627, 1981.

Sanborn K and Jefferson JW. Everyman's guide to the fluctuating lithium level: Obvious and obscure reasons why serum lithium levels change. *Anls Clin Psych* 3:251–258, 1991.

Schou M. Lithium treatment during pregnancy, delivery, and lactation: An update. *J Clin Psych* 51:410–413, 1990.

Sernyak MJ and Woods SW. Chronic neuroleptic use in manic-depressive illness. *Psychopharmacol Bull* 29:375–381, 1993.

Souza FGM and Goodwin GM. Lithium treatment and prophylaxis in unipolar depression: A metaanalysis. *Br J Psych* 158:666–675, 1991.

Stanislav S, et al. Buspirone's efficacy in organic-induced aggression. *J Clin Psychopharmacol* 2:126–130, 1994.

Tohen M, et al. Blood dyscrasias with carbamazepine and valproate: A pharmacoepidemiological study of 2,228 patients at risk. *Am J Psych* 152:413–418, 1995.

Tupin JP, et al. Long-term use of lithium in aggressive prisoners. *Compr Psych* 14:311–317, 1973.

Valles V, Guillamat R, Vilaplana C, Duno R, Almenar C and Almenar C. Serum iron and akathisia. *Biol Psychiatry* 31:1172–1183, 1992.

Van Putten T, Marder SR, Mintz J and Poland RE. Haloperidol plasma levels and clinical response: A therapeutic window relationship. *Am J Psych* 149:500–505, 1992.

VanValkenburg C, Kluznik J, Merrill R and Erickson W. Therapeutic levels of valproate for psychosis. *Psychopharmacol Bull* 26:254–255, 1990.

Vestergaard P. Clinically important side effects of long-term lithium treatment: A review. *Acta Psychiatr Scand* 305:11–33, 1983.

Yassa R, et al. Lithium-induced thyroid disorders: A prevalence study. *J Clin Psych* 49:14–16, 1988.

Yudofsky SC, Silver JM and Hales RE. Pharmacologic management of aggression in the elderly. *J Clin Psych* 51:22–28, 1990.

STIMULANTS

Angrist B, D'Hollosy M, Sanfilipo M, Satriano J, Diamond G, Simberkoff M and Weinreb H. Central nervous system stimulants as symptomatic treatments for AIDS-related neuropsychiatric impairment. *J Clin Psychopharmacol* 12:268–272, 1992.

Derlet RW, et al. Amphetamine toxicity: Experience with 127 cases. *J Emerg Med* 7:157–161, 1989.

Elia J, Borcherding BG, Rapoport JL and Keysor CS. Methylphenidate and dextroamphetamine treatments of hyperactivity: Are there true nonresponders? *Psychiatr Res* 36:141–155, 1990.

Fernandez F, et al. Methylphenidate for depressive disorders in cancer patients. *Psychosomatics* 28:455–461, 1987.

Holmes VF, Fernandez F and Levy JK. Psychostimulant response in AIDS-related complex patients. *J Clin Psych* 50:5–8, 1989.

Hunt R, et al. An open trial of guanfacine in the treatment of attention-deficit hyperactivity disorder. *J Am Acad Child and Adolescent Psych* 34:50–54, 1995.

Johnson M, et al. Methylphenidate in stroke patients with depression. *Am J Physical Med Rehab* 71:239–241, 1992.

Klein RG, et al. Methylphenidate and growth in hyperactive children: A controlled withdrawal study. *Arch Gen Psych* 45:1127–1130, 1988.

Klein RG and Mannuzza S. Hyperactive boys almost grown up: III. Methylphenidate effects on ultimate height. *Arch Gen Psych* 45:1131–1134, 1988.

Lazarus A. Neuroleptic malignant syndrome: Detection and management. *Psych Anls* 15:706–711, 1985.

Lazarus LW, Winemiller DR, Lingam VR, Neyman I, Hartman C, Abassian M, Kartan U, Groves L and Fawcett J. Efficacy and side effects of methylphenidate for poststroke depression. *J Clin Psych* 53:447–449, 1992.

Rapport MD, Denney C, DuPaul GJ and Gardner MJ. Attention deficit disoder and methylphenidate: Normalization rates, clinical effectiveness, and response prediction in 76 children. *J Am Acad Child and Adolescent Psych* 33:882–893, 1994.

Rosenberg PB, Ahmed I and Hurwitz S. Methylphenidate in depressed medically ill patients. *J Clin Psych* 52:263–267, 1991.

Satel SL and Nelson JC. Stimulants in the treatment of depression: A critical overview. *J Clin Psych* 50:241–249.

Sylvester C. Psychopharmacology of disorders in children. *Psych Clin N Am* 16:779–791, 1993.

Wilens T, et al. Nortriptyline in the treatment of ADHD: A chart review of 58 cases. *J Am Acad Child and Adolescent Psych* 32:343–349, 1993.

GENERAL

American Psychiatric Association. Treatment of Psychiatric Disorders. Washington DC: A Task Force Report of the American Psychiatric Association, 1989.

American Psychiatric Association. Diagnostic and Statistical Manual of Mental Disorder (4th ed.) Washington DC: Author, 1994.

Arana GW and Hyman SE. *Handbook of Psychiatric Drug Therapy* (2nd ed.). Boston: Little, Brown, 1991.

Baastrup PC, et al. Adverse reactions in treatment with lithium carbonate and haloperidol. *JAMA* 236:2645–2646, 1976.

Bernstein JG. Psychotropic drug induced weight gain: Mechanisms and management. *Clin Neuropharmacol* 11:194–296, 1988.

Bezchlibnyk-Butler KZ and Jeffries JJ (Eds.). *Clinical Handbook of Psychotropic Drugs* (2nd ed.). Lewiston NY: Hogrefe & Huber, 1990.

Brophy JJ. Suicide attempts with psychotherapeutic drugs. *Arch Gen Psych* 17:652–657, 1967.

Cohen LS, Heller VL and Rosenbaum JF. Treatment guidelines for psychotropic drug use in pregnancy. *Psychosomatics* 30:25–33, 1989.

Coplan JE and Gorman JM. Treatment of anxiety disorder in patients with mood disorders. *J Clin Psych* 51:9–13, 1990.

Gelenberg AJ, Bassuk EL and Schoonover SC (Eds.). *The Practitioner's Guide to Psychoactive Drugs* (3rd ed.). New York: Plenum, 1991.

Griffith HW. *Complete Guide to Prescription and Non-prescription Drugs* (5th ed.). Los Angeles: Body Press, 1988.

Hansten PD and Horn JR. *Drug Interactions: Clinical Significance of Drug-Drug Interactions.* Philadelphia: Lea & Febiger, 1994.

Klein DF and Davis JM. *Diagnosis and Drug Treatment of Psychiatric Disorders* (2nd ed.). Baltimore: Williams & Wilkins, 1969.

Kranzler HR and Cardoni A. Sodium chloride treatment of antidepressant-induced orthostatic hypotension. *J Clin Psych* 49:366–368, 1988.

Kunik ME, Yudofsky SC, Silver JM and Hales RE. Pharmacologic approach to management of agitation associated with dementia (2, Suppl). *J Clin Psych* 55:13–17, 1994.

Mammen GJ (Ed.). *Clinical Pharmacokinetics in Drug Data Handbook* (2nd ed.). Auckland, New Zealand: AIDS Press, 1990.

Maxmen JS and Ward NG. *Essential Psychopathology and Its Treatment.* New York: Norton, 1995.

Shinn AF and Hogan MF (Eds.). *Evaluations of Drug Interactions.* New York: Macmillan, 1988.

Shlafer M and Marieb EN (Eds.). *The Nurse, Pharmacology, and Drug Therapy.* Redwood City CA: Addison-Wesley, 1989.

Stoudemire A, Moran MG and Fogel BS. Psychotropic drug use in the medically ill: Part I. *Psychosomatics* 31:377–391, 1990.

Talbott JA, Hales RE and Yudofsky SC (Eds.). *Textbook of Psychiatry.* Washington DC: American Psychiatric Press, 1988.

Thompson JW, Ware MR and Blashfield RK. Psychotropic medication and priapism: A comprehensive review. *J Clin Psych* 51:430–433, 1990.

Wender PH and Klein DF. *Mind, Mood and Medicine: A Guide to the New Biopsychiatry.* New York: Meridian, 1981.

[1]*Drug profile tables* provide names, classes, manufacturers, dose forms, colors,
and costs.

INDEX